Machine Embroidery

Techniques and projects

Machine Embroidery

Techniques and projects

Claire Fell

Crowood

First published in 2020 by
The Crowood Press Ltd
Ramsbury, Marlborough
Wiltshire SN8 2HR

enquiries@crowood.com
www.crowood.com

© Claire Fell 2020

All rights reserved. No part of this publication may be reproduced or transmitted in any form or by any means, electronic or mechanical, including photocopy, recording, or any information storage and retrieval system, without permission in writing from the publishers.

British Library Cataloguing-in-Publication Data
A catalogue record for this book is available from the British Library.

ISBN 978 1 78500 701 9

The book is dedicated to the following people:
Mum and Dad – thank you for putting up with my artistic mood swings;
Nan, who brightened up rainy days with her button tin;
Aunty Rita and Uncle John – I could not have done this without you;
and Felicity, for sharing her skills and enthusiasm.

Graphic design and typesetting by Peggy & Co. Design
Printed and bound in India by Parksons Graphics

CONTENTS

Introduction   7

CHAPTER 1   Equipment, Tools and Materials   9
CHAPTER 2   Setting Up the Machine and Workspace   27
CHAPTER 3   Designing for Machine Embroidery   41
CHAPTER 4   Raising the Teeth – Using Set Stitches for Machine Embroidery   53
CHAPTER 5   Lowering the Teeth – Free Machine Embroidery with an Embroidery Foot   83
CHAPTER 6   Thread-painting   97
CHAPTER 7   Using Water-soluble Film   117
CHAPTER 8   Experimenting with Stitches and Tension   141
CHAPTER 9   All That Glitters   171
CHAPTER 10   Embroidering the Landscape   205
CHAPTER 11   Animals and Birds   231
CHAPTER 12   Finishing Your Work   247

Templates   268
Suppliers   285
Bibliography   286
Index   287

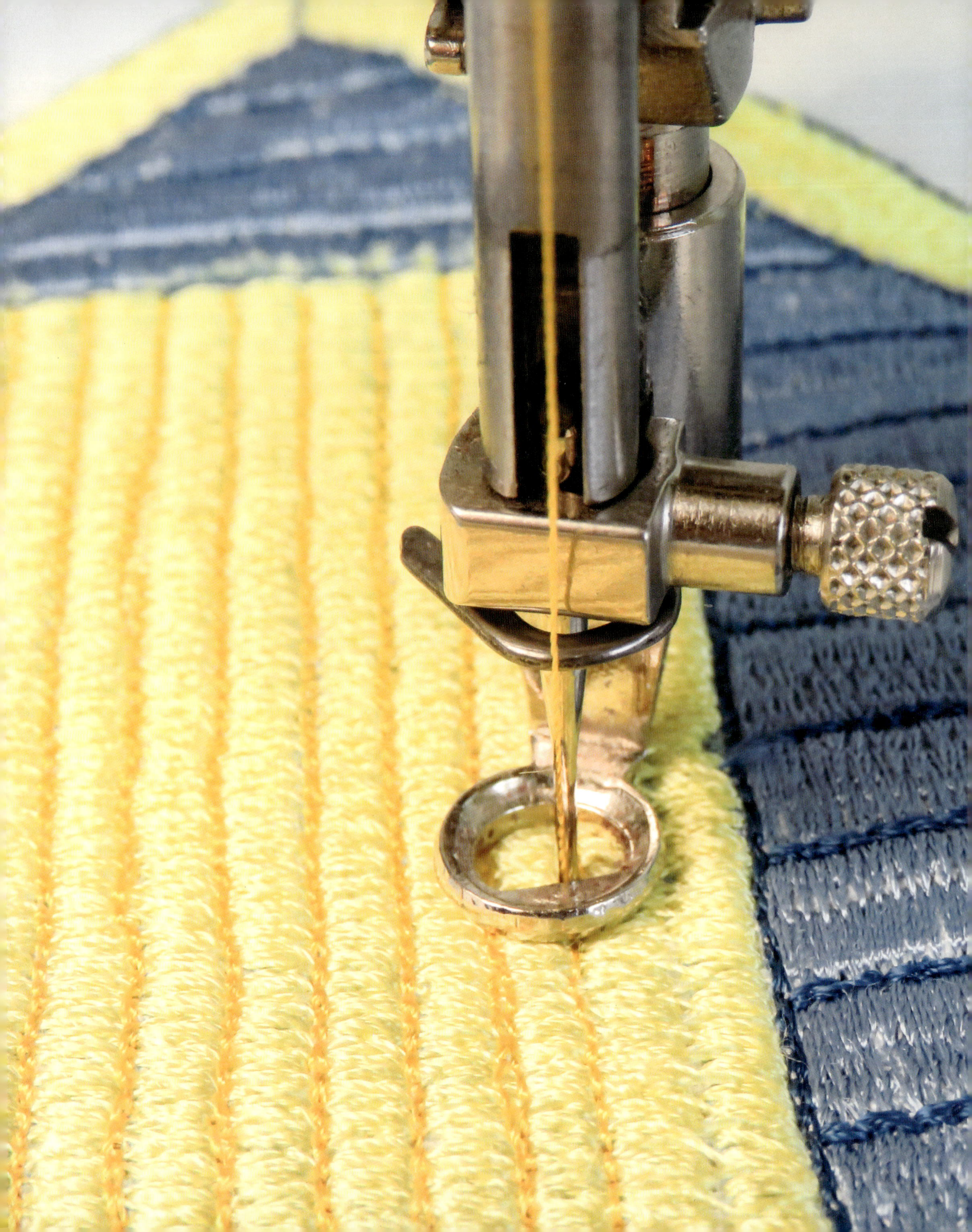

Introduction

What is Machine Embroidery?

The simplest definition of machine embroidery is *to decorate a piece of cloth with stitches using a piece of equipment that has several mechanical moving parts.*

Machine embroidery can be created with the feeder teeth up or down, and this can be achieved on a manual or computerized embroidery machine.

Machine Embroidery with the Feeder Teeth Up

Embroidery with the feeder teeth up and presser foot refers to making patterns with set stitches such as straight, honeycomb, zigzag or satin stitch. This type of embroidery relies on the presser foot and feeder teeth to feed the fabric over the needle plate to create the embroidery stitches.

Machine embroidery with the feeder teeth up can be very effective when used to embellish a background fabric. Rows of set pattern stitching can be very decorative when sewn with threads that are variegated or grouped next to one another. Embroidery with the feeder teeth up may also be very useful if the design requires the stitches to be of the same length or width.

Machine Embroidery with the Feeder Teeth Down

Free machine embroidery is produced with the feeder teeth down and a darning or embroidery foot attached. The feeder teeth have been disengaged so the person doing the embroidery has total control over the movement of the fabric and the placement of the stitches.

The machinist must learn how to control the speed of the machine with the foot pedal whilst moving the hooped fabric to create the stitches. The only thing the machine does is respond to the foot control to make the needle go up and down to form the stitch.

The only stitches used for free machine embroidery are straight and zigzag; this is because the user moves the hoop to direct the fabric and produce their own stitch pattern. It is much easier to produce free machine embroidery because the fabric can be moved in any direction to create patterns or designs that aren't governed by the friction of the foot.

Computer Machine Embroidery

Computer embroidery machines do the stitching for you; the machine, foot and hoop are controlled by a computer program. The user chooses the design, sets up the hoop and threads the machine and tells it to start sewing. Digitizing or programming designs from scratch takes time and skill; most users prefer to buy or download free designs. Embroidery machines do have their merits as designs can easily be resized, reproduced and shared, and it's magical to watch a machine sew by itself.

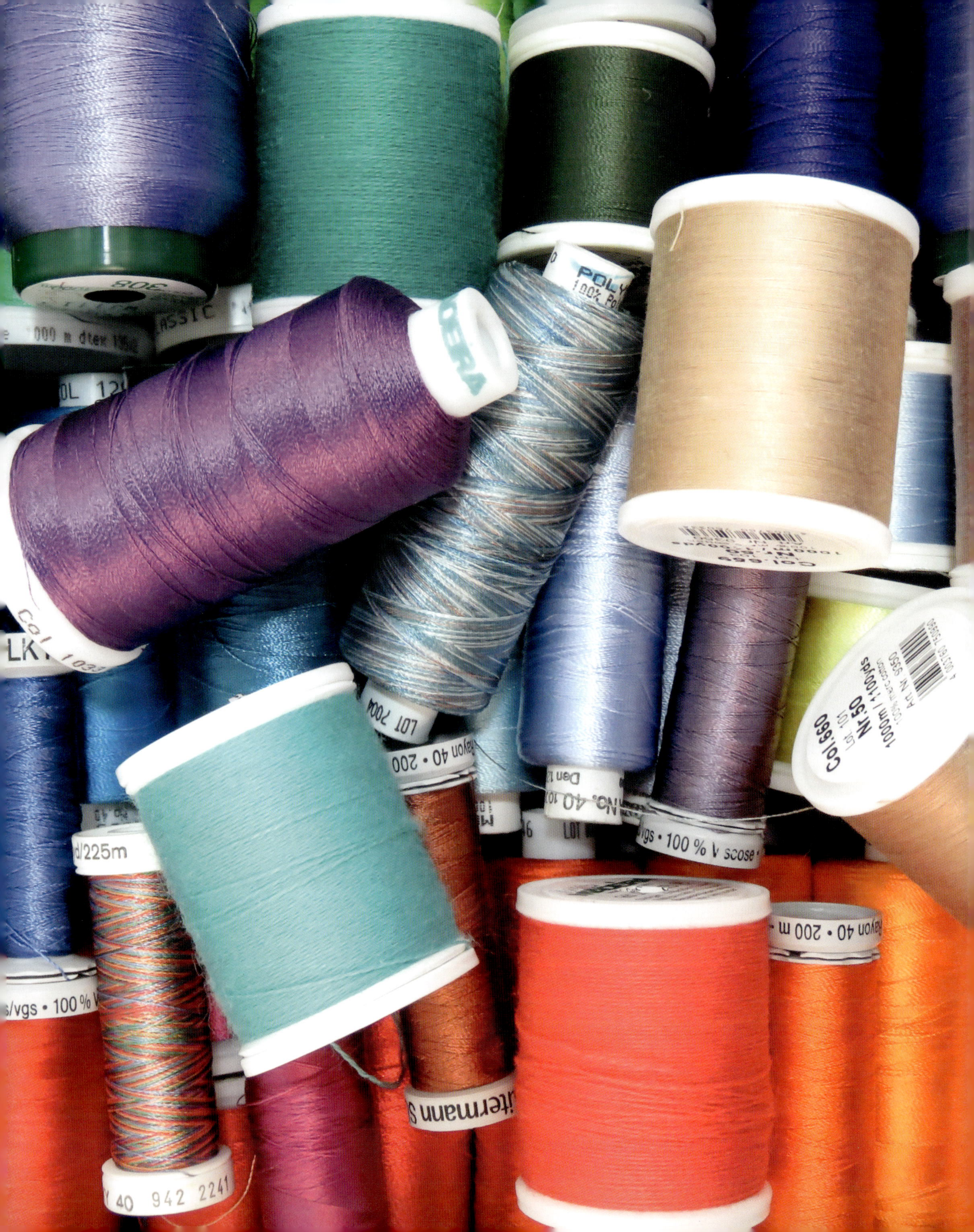

LOT 7004
d/225m
942 2241
Col.660
Nr.50
1000m / 1100yds

CHAPTER 1

EQUIPMENT, TOOLS AND MATERIALS

This chapter is about the tools and materials needed for machine embroidery. To learn the basics you need a sewing machine with feeder teeth that lower, a darning or embroidery foot, size 90/14 universal machine needles, plain cotton fabric, good-quality rayon, viscose, polyester or cotton machine threads, fabric scissors, embroidery scissors, embroidery hoop and pencil.

THE SEWING MACHINE

A good-quality sewing machine is essential for machine embroidery; it must have straight and zigzag stitch, plus the ability to drop or cover the feeder teeth. The machine must be sturdy because lightweight models have a tendency to bounce across the table when sewing at speed. Most machines are called free arm, which means they have a removable flat surface or free arm table which is taken away for sewing cuffs or trouser hems. The free arm table is useful for machine embroidery because it provides a stable surface for the hoop.

Dropping the Feeder Teeth for Free Machine Embroidery

Feeder teeth grip the fabric to move it over the needle plate; by contrast dropping the feeder teeth disengages the mechanism so the fabric remains in the same position. The person operating the machine must now move the fabric because the feeder teeth are not touching it. The foot must also be swapped to a darning or embroidery foot because a presser foot would grip onto the needle plate and stop the fabric moving.

You can still do machine embroidery if the feeder teeth can't be lowered. My beloved Janome JF 1018s does not have drop feed; it came with a plastic clip-on darning plate. I have embroidered many projects with this machine, although it did take a while to get used to using a darning plate because it is slightly raised. I have used lots of other sewing machines and I find that simple machines often give the best results. If you can't drop the teeth or use a darning plate, you could remove the teeth entirely and solely use the machine for free machine embroidery.

Darning Plate

Darning plates clip over the needle plate to stop the feeder teeth coming into contact with the fabric. I stick my darning plate to the needle plate with double-sided tape to stop it coming loose whilst sewing. Darning plates can cause problems as they narrow the gap between the embroidery foot and the fabric, causing loss of movement or friction. The narrow gap between the embroidery foot and needle plate means the embroidery foot may need to be removed each time an embroidery hoop is put in position; this can be annoying if the fabric needs re-positioning to stitch a large embroidery.

Buying a Second-hand Machine

If you want an 'old school'-style machine the second-hand market may be your only option. Be careful! I inherited an old machine but when I began sewing the machine made a funny noise and caught fire. I recently bought a Bernina 801 from an online auction site: vintage Berninas are favoured by many textile artists because they are reliable and sturdy. I discovered

Basic sewing machines will be used throughout this book. Front: my Janome JF 1018s which has a darning plate to cover the feeder teeth. Rear: my second-hand Bernina 801 with a darning (embroidery) foot attached.

my purchase had a few blemishes and was in need of a replacement foot pedal and good service. If you buy second-hand, see if you can test the machine before you buy it, then get it serviced by a professional.

Whether your machine is new or old it needs to be a sturdy workhorse. There is a big difference between sewing the odd seam and doing machine embroidery. When sewing a seam the machine is working slowly so it has a chance to cool down and rest: when doing machine embroidery the foot pedal is pressed down for a long time, which means the motor can get hot because it's working harder.

Sewing Machine Accessories

The instruction booklet is the most important machine accessory. It tells you how to thread the machine and wind bobbins and which dials or buttons change the stitch type and length. It explains how to drop the feeder teeth and alter the top and bottom thread tensions. The most useful part of the instruction book is the problem-solving section; if the machine plays up the answer is usually in the manual.

Sometimes these booklets list optional parts: for example, your machine may not come with a darning foot. It is essential to know the make and model of your machine for ordering extra bobbin cases or feet. If you have lost the instruction book it's easy to download it for free from the internet.

Bobbins

The bottom thread is wound onto a bobbin, which is inserted into a bobbin case and loaded into the machine. Bobbins can be made of metal or plastic; they can be flat, domed or have holes in them. Bobbins should not be wound by hand because this creates uneven tension and stitch problems. A wound bobbin should be neat with no loose threads, lumps or tangles; think of a new reel of thread – this is what a perfectly wound bobbin should look like. Refer to the instruction booklet for more information about winding bobbins for your machine. Bobbins need to be stored carefully because the threads can easily unwind and become knotted; I prefer to use a silicone bobbin ring because the bobbins stay put and do not tangle.

Bobbin Case

The bobbin case holds the bobbin in position and tensions the thread so the machine can make the stitches. The wound bobbin is inserted into the bobbin case so the thread passes through the tension slot and under the tension spring. The tension spring is a curved piece of metal secured by a tiny screw, which is loosened or tightened to alter the distance between the tension spring and the outside of the bobbin case.

Make sure you are using the right bobbin and bobbin case for the machine as the wrong one could damage the machine,

It's a good idea to invest in a spare bobbin case for loose tension bobbin work or cable stitch because having a spare saves setting-up time.

resulting in expensive repairs. I mark my spare bobbin case with a permanent marker or nail polish so I know it's the spare. Accidentally using the loose bobbin case will cause tension problems and make you think something is wrong with the machine.

Sewing Machine Feet

The style of sewing machine feet does vary: some feet are attached directly to the machine and others have a long or short shank for clipping on. Individual machine feet have a specific job to do: for example, there is the straight-stitch foot for straight stitch and utility stitches like zigzag or tricot stitch, the zip foot for attaching zips or the darning foot for embroidery.

Darning Foot or Embroidery Foot

The most important foot for free machine embroidery is the darning or embroidery foot. Such feet can be made of metal or a combination of metal and plastic; some have a spring to allow the foot to bounce over the fabric. Embroidery feet don't come into contact with the needle plate; their function is to stop the fabric lifting up with the needle whilst allowing the fabric to move freely over the needle plate.

Big feet (which may be made of plastic or metal) are available for machine embroidery; these are suitable for those who need accuracy or have vision problems. The foot is bigger to prevent fabric bounce and the large opening in the centre provides clear visibility.

Presser or Straight-stitch Foot

The presser or straight-stitch foot is used for sewing straight and zigzag stitches, plus set utility or patterned stitches. This foot must be used with the feeder teeth up and the stitch length set to a suitable distance because the feeder teeth grip the fabric and move it along. The presser foot can be used for sewing seams when making items up, for tacking (basting) the fabric to show where the edge of a design is, for appliqué with zigzag or satin stitch or for layering patterned utility stitches to make decorative embroidery.

Other Utility Feet

The machine may have other utility feet, perhaps ones for zip or buttonhole insertion, blind hemming or overlocking: these are all used with the teeth up. They are not used for machine embroidery but they may be needed to turn embroideries into finished items like bags or wearable art.

Zip Foot

This foot is used with straight stitch and is essential for sewing zips into garments, bags or cushions. The zip foot has a special shape so that it can be positioned close to the zip without being pushed aside by the zip slider.

Buttonhole Foot

This foot is used with buttonhole stitch, which may be automatic, and it may have a slot to measure the button. Buttonholes can be decorative or functional; I use my buttonhole foot to create tab fastenings for bags and cushions.

Appliqué Foot

This foot has a channel on the base for stitching neat zigzag or satin stitch; the channel helps the foot to glide over the stitches to stop them getting caught on the foot.

Cording Foot

This foot is used for couching or wrapping yarns. It has a metal flap that covers three channels that guide the thread into position as it is stitched with zigzag. This foot can be used to add decoration to abstract machine embroidery.

Machine Needles

Always buy good-quality needles: Schmetz, Madeira, Klasse, Organ and Pym are good brands to choose. Any brand of needle will fit your machine because needle sizes are standardized. There are two things to consider when buying needles: size and type. Size refers to the size of material or thread to be sewn and type refers to the job to be done or material to be sewn. Never use overlocker needles in the sewing machine because they are designed for a different job.

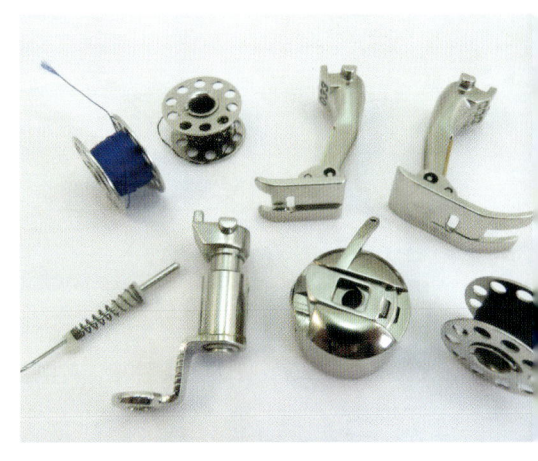

Machine accessories. Top, L to R: wound bobbins, buttonhole foot with a large groove for neater satin stitch, standard presser foot for straight stitch. Bottom, L to R: spring needle, darning (embroidery) foot, bobbin case, bobbin.

Needle Size

Machine needles are numbered by size: the higher the number the larger the needle. Needle size corresponds to the fabric or thread used. No. 60/8 is for fine silks or organza and lightweight threads, 70/10 and 75/11 for lightweight fabrics and threads and 80/12 for mediumweight fabrics and no. 50 thread weight. None of these sizes are suitable for machine embroidery unless using ultra-fine threads. Large sizes such as 110/18 and 120/20 are only suitable for upholstery fabric or very heavy canvas.

The best size for machine embroidery is 90/14 universal needle. This size is suitable for medium to heavy fabrics such as calico or denim, so it's a perfect choice for machine embroidery. If you are still having problems with thread shredding or needle breakage try moving up to size 100/16, which is used on heavy fabrics like canvas.

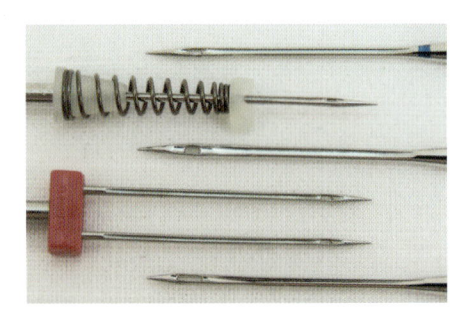

Machine needles. From top: sharp size 90/14 universal needle, spring needle, Madeira Lana needle size 110/18, Schmetz 4/80 twin needle for parallel rows of stitch, 90/14 metallic needle with an elongated eye.

Needle Type

The point of the needle is designed for specific jobs: for example, ball point needles have a rounded tip so they do not ladder knitted fabrics, leather needles have a triangular point for piercing tough leather or PVC and universal needles have a point suitable for most woven fabrics. Ball point and leather needles are not suitable for free machine embroidery.

Universal Needle

This is the best needle type for machine embroidery because it's suitable for all types of woven fabrics including cotton, silk and synthetics. Universal needles are often cheaper than their specialist counterparts.

Jeans Needle

These needles have a sharper point and stronger shaft. They are designed for use with thick materials like denim, canvas or cotton duck. Denim needles can be used for embroidery on thicker materials such as denim or canvas.

Metallic Needle

Metallic threads have a texture that can wear a groove in the eye of the needle, causing the thread to shred or break. Metallic needles have been designed to prevent this: they have a longer eye to help the thread glide through. If you use a lot of metallic threads I recommend investing in some metallic needles because the thread does not break so often.

Quilting Needle

These specialist needles have a point that is designed to pierce multiple layers of fabric without thread breakage. They are suitable for machine embroidery on quilts.

Topstitch Needle

These needles have a large eye to allow thicker decorative threads to be sewn. They can be used to create stitching like the decoration seen on jeans pockets.

Embroidery Needle

The embroidery needle has a larger eye and scarf to help embroidery threads sew without shredding or missing stitches. These needles are suitable for rayon, viscose or cotton. I don't use them as I find that a universal needle works perfectly fine for standard size no. 40 or 30 threads.

Specialist Thread Needle

Thread manufactures sometimes develop needles to help their threads perform better: for example, Madeira Lana thread is made from a blend of acrylic and wool; it doesn't perform well when used with a normal needle but it sews beautifully when used with a needle designed for it.

Twin Needles

These stitch two parallel rows of top thread. They have a single shank and two shafts; the distance between the shafts depends on the size of the needle. Twin needles are used with the feeder teeth up; they are not suitable for free machine embroidery because the needles could twist and break with fast hoop movements. These needles are traditionally used for piping or pin tucking, as they sew two rows of topstitch and one row of bottom stitch. Using different thread colours creates a shadow effect that is very decorative when used with patterned utility stitches.

Spring Needle

This type of needle is designed for machine embroidery without a darning or embroidery foot. It has a metal spring round it which is held by plastic at the top; the plastic at the bottom is loose, allowing the spring to move as the needle goes up and down. The tiny parts act like a darning foot, preventing the fabric being pulled up as the needle pulls out.

TOOLS

Tools are essential for fiddly jobs; you may find yourself raiding the toolbox for tools more suited to DIY than embroidery. Keep a set of tools specifically for use with the machine or embroidery because you do not want to transfer oil, paint or dust onto the fabric.

Tweezers

A pair of reverse-action tweezers with curved tips is indispensable for removing thread caught in the machine's mechanism. Reverse tweezers are easier to use because they are squeezed to open them. Some have grooves near the tips to help them grip better.

Soft Brush

A pastry brush or soft paintbrush is ideal for cleaning fluff from behind the race and from under the feeder teeth. I used to blow the fluff away but I have learnt the hard way that blown lint can navigate around your glasses and end up in your eyes. A brush collects the fluff in its bristles; the bristles can then be cleaned over a bin or washed in soapy water.

Machine Oil

Sewing machine oil keeps the moving parts lubricated and prevents squeaking or grating. Do not use the kind of oil used for oiling bikes or general maintenance. You need to use a light oil formulated for sewing machines; this can be found in haberdashery or sewing machine shops.

Magnet

A telescopic engineer's magnet is useful when picking up spilled pins or a needle that's fallen in a hard-to-reach place. Magnets can be troublesome: if you allow them to magnetize your scissors they will pick up stray pins and magnetize those as well.

Screwdriver

A small slotted screwdriver is essential for altering the tension screw on the bobbin case. You will also need a larger slotted screwdriver for tightening the embroidery hoop or needle clamp and removing screws to carry out simple machine maintenance or repairs.

Pliers

Combination pliers are a useful addition to the toolkit. I sometimes over-tighten the needle clamp and can't undo it. Pliers are great for gripping and pulling needles through tough embroideries or thick fabric. Make sure you pull the needle through at the right angle because you could snap it or break the eye.

Craft Knife

A craft or Stanley knife is essential for cutting the card mount board or paper used in projects. Freestyle hand-held cutters can also be used to cut mount board; they are easier to grip and produce the consistent neat bevel that is required when cutting window apertures in mount board.

Cutting Mat

A self-healing cutting mat will protect your work surface from the blade of your craft knife or rotary cutter. Do not use an iron on your cutting mat because it will melt and warp it.

Metal Ruler

A metal ruler with a raised edge is essential when using a craft knife or rotary cutter. The raised edge prevents the blade slipping and causing unwanted accidents.

A pastry brush is ideal for cleaning fluff from difficult-to-reach areas, angled tweezers are used to remove caught threads, the little bottle holds machine oil vital for lubrication, and screwdrivers are used to alter bobbin tension and for machine maintenance.

Scissors

You need a variety of scissors in your toolbox: each pair has a different job to do. Using scissors for the wrong job can permanently dull the blades, rendering them useless.

Embroidery Scissors

Sharp embroidery scissors are used to trim threads close to the fabric. These scissors can be straight, curved, angled or shaped (traditionally) like a stork. Embroidery scissors must not be used for cutting anything else; cutting fabric with them dulls the blades, making it harder to trim threads neatly.

Large Fabric Scissors

Robust scissors or dressmaking shears are a must because it's easier to follow the blade of large scissors when cutting long straight lines. It's better to cut the fabric with scissors rather than tear it: ripping the fabric causes damage to the warp and weft and distorts the weave. However, torn fabric can be useful in some projects as

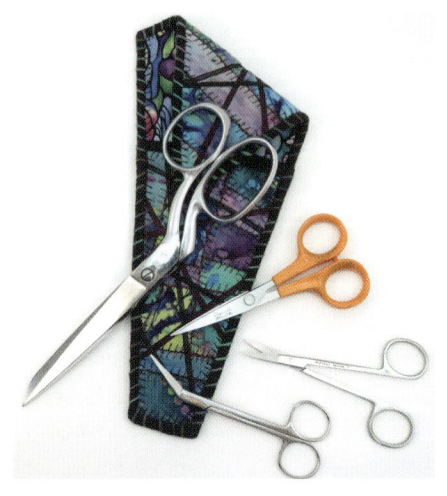

Dressmaking shears rest on their crazy patchwork case; medium-sized scissors are good for cutting yarns and fabrics. The small embroidery scissors have angled blades to make snipping thread close to the embroidery easier.

frayed edges can be decorative additions to aged embroideries or folk art-style work.

Medium-size Fabric Scissors

General scissors for snipping fabric or yarns are also useful. These should be medium in size so they don't cause a sore thumb when used repetitively. Some scissors have gel inserts or soft-touch handles to prevent strain.

Pinking Shears

Pinking shears have serrated blades, and can create a decorative edge to fabric. The zigzag edge may reduce fraying, but will not stop it altogether.

Paper Scissors

These are needed for cutting out patterns or sheets of paper-backed heat-fusible glue, Angelina fibres or metal foils. Paper backings and plastic films dull the blades of fabric scissors and make them blunt: it's

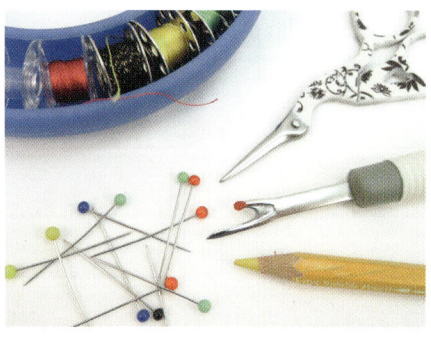

The silicone bobbin ring stores bobbins safely; glass-headed pins are good for visibility when machining; watercolour pencils are very useful for marking dark fabrics; the stork scissors are both pretty and functional.

not pleasurable to cut fabric with blunt scissors so keep them separate from your fabric scissors.

Other Essentials

Rotary Cutter

A rotary cutter is a circular blade housed in an ergonomic handle. Such cutters are great for cutting out projects that need ultra-straight edges. If you struggle cutting straight lines with scissors, use a rotary cutter. The only drawback is that you need to use a cutting mat to prolong the life of the blade and protect the work surface.

Seam Ripper

Quick unpicks or seam rippers make quick work of mistakes. They have a point to pick up the stitch, a sharp blade to cut and a protective plastic tip to prevent rips. Seam rippers can be used on the back of embroideries to remove stray stitches one by one, and can also be used to remove larger areas of stitching. Do be careful

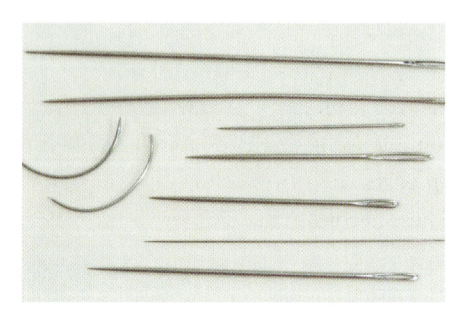

Hand needles. From top: darners (two shown) are ideal for securing buttons or brooch backs; sharps produce very neat slip-stitch seams; chenille or crewel needles have a sharp point and a large eye which makes threading easier; beading needles are fine and flexible; fine curved needles are good for sewing up seams with invisible slip stitch.

when using one because it's easy to be over-enthusiastic and make a hole in the fabric.

Pins

Pins are vital for pinning seams, keeping soluble film in place or securing yarn snips. Glass-headed pins are best because they're more visible. Avoid plastic-headed pins, as the heads can melt under the heat of an iron. My worst habit is sewing over pins! Not only do they go with a bang, they can also break the needle and mark the needle plate. Dispose of any bent pins or ones that have nicks out of them as they can mark the fabric or snag it.

Hand-sewing Needles

You need an assortment of hand-sewing needles for embellishing the surface of embroideries or sewing up finished projects. Buy good-quality needles because you get what you pay for; cheap ones have a tendency to bend or snap.

Sharps

Sharps are fine needles with a sharp point, suitable for general seam sewing, lacing up edges or sewing on small press studs. These needles are available in many sizes.

Darners

Long thick darning needles can have a sharp or slightly round point; both types usually have a long eye. Darners can be used to secure buttons or beads with large holes onto fabrics that are stiffened with dense embroidery. They can also be used for lacing thick embroideries over card ready for mounting and framing.

Embroidery Needles

These are sometimes called chenille needles. They have a large eye and a very sharp point, and are usually used for decorative stitching with thicker fancy threads. Embroidery needles can be used for general sewing if you have difficulty threading needles with small eyes.

Beading Needles

These are very thin, long and flexible. The eye is very small and elongated so it can be difficult to thread one with the naked eye. Beading needles are used to sew tiny beads or sequins onto fabric.

Curved Needles

These are tricky to use because they can twist in your fingers. Once you get used to gripping them they are invaluable for sewing up box sides or tricky seams with invisible slip stitches.

IRONS

A good iron is essential for preparing fabric, finishing projects and experimenting. I use a steam iron without the water for pressing embroideries, setting fabric paint and bonding interfacing and heat-fusible glue and for fusing Angelina fibres. The holes in the iron plate can cause uneven heat distribution; the solution is to move the iron over the surface to ensure an even distribution of heat.

It is important to keep the iron clean: I use a sheet of baking parchment to protect the plate of the iron. A dirty iron can be disastrous for a finished embroidery – you don't want to smear iron gunk over an embroidery during the final press.

I sometimes use a travel iron and baking parchment for bonding Angelina and metallic foil because this iron has lower temperature settings and a Teflon coating for easier cleaning. Other specialist irons are available to the textile artist: the Clover mini-iron looks like a soldering iron; it has a flat triangular head for securing intricate appliqué or ironing hard-to-access places.

Ironing Cloth

Pressing cloths are usually made from cotton muslin or thin white cotton. Using an ironing cloth protects the surface of the fabric from unwanted dirt or shine. A pressing cloth act as a buffer, preventing the embroidery from becoming flattened by the heat and pressure of the ironing process.

It is essential to learn how to use the iron properly since poor ironing skills can cause more wrinkles around an embroidery motif. I prefer dry pressing with a dry cloth to remove handling marks. If the fabric remains creased I use a damp cloth to remove the stubborn wrinkles. Pushing the iron away from the embroidery nudges the wrinkles outwards towards the edge of the fabric.

Stain Removal

When making an embroidery it may become marked or soiled. Vanish soap stain bar can be used to remove stubborn marks left by pen or pencil. Some fabrics or dyes are sensitive to the ingredients of Vanish so test a small area first; do not use varnish on wool or silk.

DRAWING SUPPLIES AND RELATED ITEMS

Office supplies are vital for design work: the crafter's essentials include plain paper, tracing paper, tissue paper, pencils, ruler, tape measure, set square, eraser, gel pens, ballpoint pens, pencil sharpener, coloured pencils or felt tips and fine-tipped permanent pens.

Paper and Card

Choose a good-quality plain paper for drawing or designing. I use smooth A4 paper for some of my design work because it's the correct size for scanning or copying. If you like working with geometry or linear patterns it may be worth investing in some squared, triangular or graph paper. Tracing paper is an important addition because it makes copying a design or reversing it easy, especially if you don't have access to a printer or photocopier. Tissue paper can also be used to trace designs and transfer them onto fabric. Some projects require card, foam or mount board for lacing and framing and mounting work to a professional standard.

Pencils and Crayons

Graphite or coloured pencils can be used for designing or for marking fabric; what you choose is down to personal choice. I prefer to use hard pencils for drawing, designing and marking pale fabric because they don't leave much graphite behind. Soft graphite or pigments can mark the thread as it passes through the drawn line. Water-soluble artist's pencils show up well on dark fabrics; they are a cheap alternative to dressmaker's pencils.

Dressmaker's Chalk Pencil

Chalk pencils are used to mark fabrics for cutting or to make guidelines for dressmaking. Dusty chalk is the ideal medium for marking dark fabric because it can be easily brushed away once work is completed.

Eraser and Pencil Sharpener

A pencil sharpener will be needed to keep the pencils and crayons sharp; they may have one or two holes to accommodate different pencil sizes. I prefer cheap handheld plastic sharpeners. You need a white artist's eraser to remove mistakes; keep the eraser clean as a dirty one will leave indelible smudges on the paper. Erasers can be cleaned by rubbing the dirty bit on a scrap of clean paper or fine sandpaper.

Pens and Markers

Pens used for design and design transfer can be permanent, water-based or vanishing. Black permanent or water-based pens can be used to finalize a design on paper or make it dark enough to be traced through the fabric ready for stitching. Biro or ballpoint pens must never be used on fabric because the oil-based ink smudges and marks the threads. Water-soluble film is tricky to draw on but fine-tipped permanent pens work well because the ink dries instantly. Water-based Stabilo Fineliners also work well because they are available in colours to match the thread or fabric used. Vanishing fabric markers are used to mark cloth; these are designed to fade with water or disappear within two days of use.

Accurate Measuring

Tape measure and ruler are essential for accurate measuring. Use either imperial inches or metric centimetres or millimetres, whichever you prefer. I use both, and find myself using inches for one project and centimetres for another. However, *they must not be mixed within the same project*.

It is easier to take short measurements with a ruler because a ruler is less likely to move or kink like a tape measure. Beware: some imperial tape measures are subdivided into tenths of an inch, others into eighths of an inch; not noticing the slight difference can cause problems with measurements.

Geometry Set

A geometry set will provide the tools for accurate drawing and measuring. A simple set will contain a short ruler, two set squares, a protractor and a pair of compasses. Set squares are used to make sure that squares and rectangles have sides at 90-degree angles. A protractor is marked with measurements up to 180 degrees and is used to measure angles other than those given by the set square. If your designs contain circles or curves a pair of compasses will help you to draw them accurately.

Ruler, metal set square, plastic protractor and a pair of compasses are essential tools for accurate design work and measuring.

Printing and Copying

Having access to a printer and scanner does save a lot of time: designs can be copied, reduced, reversed or enlarged. If you don't have access to a scanner or printer you may be able to find one in your local library or office supplies shop. If you have access to a computer this is even better because you can scan your designs, store them or share them electronically.

Paint and Dye

Choose the correct paint, thinking about the colour, weight and composition of the fabric. Transparent paints are best for white or pale fabrics whilst opaque paints are more suitable for use on dark fabrics. Silk paints are designed to flow into the weave of delicate silk fabrics; some brands can be used on other finely woven fabrics such as cotton or synthetic silk. Thin paints are more suitable for watercolour wash effects or silk painting with gutta outlines or batik.

Thick fabric paints like Dylon or Lumière sit on the surface of the fabric; such paints work best on cotton, calico or canvas. Some fabric paints can be thinned with water but others may need a translucent extender to thin them. All fabric paints need to be fixed with heat when dry to make them permanent. If painting more than one layer the first must be fixed before applying another: some paints are fixed by ironing, others need to be fixed with steam.

Acrylic paints are suitable for use on most natural cotton fabrics. Acrylic colours are waterproof once dry; do test a sample for compatibility and permanence. Such paints don't work well on fabrics like polyester, acrylic or natural wool because the fibres repel the paint.

Top, L to R: Dylon fabric paint, Javana silk paint, Chromacolour acrylic paint. Front: round bristle, soft flat and rigger brushes.

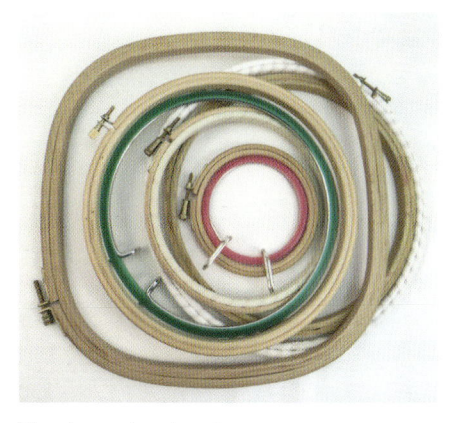

Wooden or bamboo hoops are easy to use because they grip the fabric better. The largest hoop shown is 25.5cm (10in.) square and the smallest is a 7.5cm (3in.) metal hoop.

Brushes

Brushes are numbered according to size: the higher the number the larger the brush head. The brush heads are made of synthetic or natural fibres. Brush shapes for painting details include detail, round and rigger. Small brush sizes are reserved for painting details: use a size 0 or smaller round or detail brush to paint really small details, such as the white of an eye or a pupil.

Mop brushes are suitable for use with silk paints because they are good at picking up large amounts of liquid paint to create watercolour-effect washes. Flat, bright or filbert-shaped brushes have stiffer bristles which are more suitable for use with thicker paints; sizes 10 or 12 are good for painting backgrounds. Stencil brushes are perfect for creating clouds in landscape images or scumbling texture; they can move the paint around in a rough manner without damaging the brush or surface of the fabric.

Hoops

Hoops used for machine embroidery are the same as the ones used for hand embroidery, the only difference being that a hoop used for machine embroidery needs to be narrow enough to slip under the embroidery foot. A hoop is essential for machine embroidery because it keeps the fabric taut. The fabric needs to be drum-tight because the tension of the thread pulls the fabric in; this can cause a problem if the tension is altered or the fabric is densely stitched. The edge of the hoop acts like a handle, providing something firm to hold so the fabric can be moved with more control; trying to move bunched-up fabric is not easy. Hoops can be bound with tape or bias binding to help them grip the fabric better; binding a hoop also prevents it marking the fabric.

The best diameter sizes for machine embroidery are 6, 7 or 8 inches. (Note that imperial inch sizing persists despite metrication. While 6 inches equates with 15cm and 8 inches to 20cm, the equivalent to 7 inches may be sold as 17, 17.5 or 18cm.) These sizes hold the fabric firm and there is enough space for a range of movement without having to re-hoop frequently. Small hoops restrict movement, resulting in smaller stitches, whilst large hoops can hold the fabric loosely, rock on the machine or be difficult to set up.

Wooden or bamboo hoops are the best option for machine embroidery. Wooden hoops are also available in a square format; this style is really handy for realistic embroideries. Avoid plastic hoops because they are rigid and do not grip the fabric well. Metal hoops have a gap so they can't grip the fabric evenly; they have a rim underneath which can catch on the darning plate and also they can spring off when you are sewing if they have not been set up properly.

Embroidery threads containing viscose, rayon or polyester are most popular because of their sheen and strength. Good-quality threads should have the size indicated on the spool alongside the colour, fibre content and lot number.

Metallic threads come in a variety of shades: gold, silver and copper are the most popular; bright colours and Astro shades are also available. Gütermann Sulky and Madeira are good-quality brands to choose.

TOP THREADS

Threads for machine embroidery are available in a variety of fibres and weights. Thread weight or thickness is categorized by numbers: thicker threads have low numbers whilst thin threads have high numbers; for instance, thread no. 12 is very thick and thread no. 60 is very thin. Thread size no. 40 is the most popular for machine embroidery.

Polyester

Polyester is a synthetic fibre made from ethylene, a chemical derived from petroleum. Polyester threads are not as smooth as viscose or rayon, they are spun differently and can feel less flexible; they also have a tendency to loop around themselves. Don't let this put you off, as polyester threads are very usable and available in lots of colours. Madeira have a range called Polyneon in which there are some wonderful variegated colours ideal for set fancy stitches or patterns stitched with free machine embroidery.

Viscose and Rayon

Viscose and rayon are made from regenerated plant cellulose; these threads have a shiny surface and soft texture whilst offering flexibility and strength. Because of their ability to mimic the luxury of silk, viscose and rayon are the most popular choice for machine embroidery. Madeira Classic no. 40 is probably the most widely recognized brand of viscose thread; it is a firm favourite with textile artists and tutors because of the quality and range of colours available.

Cotton

Cotton is a natural fibre spun from the protective casings of cotton seeds. It is often overlooked by machine embroiderers but it has a lovely matt texture ideal for subdued stitching effects. Cotton fibres are naturally long, strong and non-shedding; the process of mercerization alters the structure of the cotton fibre, giving it more strength and lustre.

Silk

Silk threads are made from the cocoon of the silk moth. Silk machine embroidery threads are very expensive to buy and have limited colour options, so I have never used them in my work.

Wool

Wool threads are spun from the fleece of sheep. Wool-mix threads have a matt fluffy texture and are quite thick so they need a special needle for successful sewing. Wool threads can be distressed with Velcro, once sewn, to tease the fibres out and make them fluffier so extra care must be taken whilst sewing to protect the surface of the embroidery.

Metallic

Metallic threads are a composite of fibres, the inner core being wrapped with a polyester filament or thin metal foil. Some metal threads contain silver or aluminium with a clear polyester coating to prevent tarnishing. Metallic threads feel rough when handled; they should not curl or twist when unwound from the spool. When sewing with metallic threads use a needle designed for metallics because it will have a large eye for the thread to pass through without shredding.

Mylar

Mylar is a manmade polyester film that has been rolled flat and cut to form long filaments which resemble tiny ribbons. These types of thread often perform better in the bobbin. Mylar can also be found in composite metallic threads; it can have iridescent, holographic or metallic finishes.

Invisible Threads

These threads are sometimes called mono filaments; they are available in clear and smoke colours. Such thread is used when you want the stitching to be as unobtrusive as possible: for example, when securing yarn and fabric scraps to a base fabric or using thicker threads on the bobbin where you don't want the colour affected. Some invisible threads are made of nylon; these may melt if ironed, so if heat is involved use polyester thread instead. Nearly-invisibles are slightly thicker and are made from twisted polyester. Empress Mills produce a nearly-invisible called HT Poly Backing thread; it is very strong and works well as a top thread for loose bobbin techniques.

Bobbin and Other Threads

Top and bottom thread unite to form the stitch so don't skimp on the quality of the bobbin thread. If the tension is set up right you only need white, neutral or black thread for the bobbin. Good-quality overlocking thread can be used on the bobbin; this thread comes on a big cone and is very economical. It must have a polyester content and be the non-fluffy kind. Special thread can be bought for the bobbin which is thinner than top thread so it does not add bulk to the embroidery: a good example is Madeira Bobbinfil which is available in black or white.

Sew-all Thread

Threads for machine embroidery are not suitable for sewing up seams because they are not strong enough. If you are making your embroidery into a finished item use Gütermann Sew-All thread or an equivalent such as Coats Moon for strong seams. These threads are made from polyester so they are suitable for most fabrics.

Strong Thread

Buttonhole or heavy-duty thread is needed to lace the back of embroideries ready for framing. If you don't have strong thread you can use doubled or quadrupled lengths of Sew-All thread.

HAND EMBROIDERY THREADS

You may need to use decorative threads to hand-finish a machine embroidery. Embellishing the work with hand-sewn embroidery adds more interest, detail or texture. Stranded cotton, silk floss or cotton perle are much thicker than machine embroidery threads: using them ensures that your hand-sewn stitches stand out.

Stranded Cotton

Stranded cotton comes in a skein. It is traditionally used for cross stitch and usually has six strands that can be further divided or colour-mixed to make a finer thread. Stranded cotton is available in plain and variegated shades.

Floss

Floss is a twisted non-divisible thread which is a little thinner than cotton perle; it can be made from a variety of fibres including cotton, silk, rayon or viscose. Cotton embroidery floss is sometimes called pearl cotton.

Cotton Perle

This is a thick twisted cotton with a slightly shiny surface. Available in plain or variegated colours, it works well for hand embroidery and loose tension bobbin work.

Thick Threads for Couching and Use in the Bobbin

Threads used in the bobbin should be smooth and no thicker than double knitting yarn, otherwise they won't pass through the tension spring. Stranded cotton, floss, cotton perle, knitted chain and thin yarns are suitable for use in the bobbin for under-thread work. Any type of fibre or yarn can be used as long as it is not too fluffy or loopy.

Some thick threads won't fit through the tension spring; these can be couched onto an embroidery using a cording foot and zigzag stitch. Some of the threads mentioned above can also be couched onto the surface of an embroidery.

Wrapped Gimp

This has a cotton core covered with another thread, usually shiny viscose or rayon. Gimps work well when couched either by hand or machine and they can be wrapped further by using satin stitch or zigzag on the machine. Once wrapped, gimps can be twisted to make cords for tassels or handles for bags.

Knitted Chain

The knitted structure of the yarn means it is more flexible for following contours of curved designs. This type of yarn is

Thick yarns or threads can be wound onto the bobbin for under-thread bobbin embroidery or couched onto abstract embroideries. Stranded, double- or four-ply cotton can be hand-stitched to add bold texture to abstract or realistic embroideries.

Fashion yarns can be chopped up and included in embroideries topped with water-soluble film; the film helps to secure the yarns whilst they are stitched. Double knit, four-ply and chunky, woven tape, knitted chain, bouclé, roving, eyelash and feather are suitable yarns.

A good selection of natural fabrics is essential for thread-painted machine embroideries. From top: cream silk haboti, natural silk shantung, plain-weave undyed linen, two types of calico (one has more dark slubs, the other has an open weave), untreated cotton canvas and white cotton.

really striking if it has been space-dyed (where multiple colours are applied along the length of each strand) or when it has metal threads running through it.

Yarns for Chopping

Remnants of yarn or wool can be chopped up to make abstract fabrics or landscape images, secured with soluble film and stitched. Most yarn weights are suitable for inclusion in embroideries. Common yarn weights are cobweb, two-ply, four-ply, double knit, sport, Aran and chunky. Fashion yarns are available in many textures and compositions: popular ones are feather, eyelash, tape, bouclé and roving. They may be plain-dyed, space-dyed or tweedy; space-dyed yarns are economical because they have more than one colour on a ball.

Fabrics

The type of fabric chosen depends on the embroidery project. Dense machine embroidery needs something robust so realistic thread-paintings work best on 100 per cent white cotton or neutral calico. The pale colour and smooth surface means the design can easily be transferred to the fabric. Most fabrics need to be stabilized by interfacing or soluble film to provide a suitable support for machine embroidery.

Cotton

The thread count and quality of cotton does vary so choose a cotton that has a fine warp and weft and close weave. 100 per cent white cotton is best for embroidering landscapes because it can be painted with fabric paints. Cotton needs to be washed before use because it can have chemicals left in by the manufacturing process. Washing the fabric also closes the weave, preventing shrinkage whilst stitching. Printed cotton fabrics can have some lovely designs; look for old prints – these are becoming more desirable because of the vintage market. The printed designs can be traced to stitch onto another fabric or they can be embellished with heavy embroidery.

Calico

This is an unbleached cotton available in various weights; the quality does vary. It is essential to wash calico before use because it is full of size; this gluey stiffener can be tricky to remove, and leaving the calico to soak is the best way to remove it. After soaking rinse until the water runs clear.

Canvas and Cotton Duck

Canvas and cotton duck are heavyweight fabrics traditionally used for artists' canvases, backing church altar frontals and many other projects. Plain woven cotton duck is really good for embroidery and it accepts paint really well. The thick weave means that the fabric can be frayed before mounting on another background. Canvas and cotton duck need washing before use; this removes any chemical residues and tightens the weave.

Linen

Linen can be lovely to embroider on but it is prone to creasing and this can be impossible to remove even with damp pressing.

Poly Cotton

Poly cotton is made from a blend of natural cotton and polyester. It can be plain-dyed or printed. I tend to use the plain poly cotton fabrics for lining large bags. Scraps of cotton or poly cotton can be used to test the machine before starting a new project.

Fat Quarters

Printed 100 per cent cotton quilting fabrics are fun to use for crazy patchwork or appliqué. Bold patterned pieces work wonderfully well when used as a backing with yarn or thread snips and water-soluble film. Buying fat quarters is a quick way to build up a stash of patterned fabrics for inspiration and future projects.

Synthetic Lining

Artificial silks are made from rayon, viscose or polyester. Synthetic linings can have a plain, satin or jacquard weave, be plain-dyed, printed or have a shot effect. Artificial dupion or taffeta is thicker than lining material; it may have a slubby texture or jacquard pattern. Synthetic linings can be used for projects that don't require bulk: they can be used for appliqué, for lining bags or chopped or torn into strips

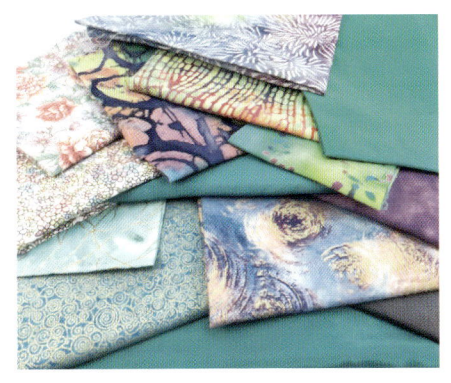

Cotton quilting and synthetic lining fabrics can be used together in projects because they are lightweight and have similar weaves. These fabrics are suitable for use as backgrounds, appliqué with heat-fusible glue and chopping for inclusion in water-soluble machine embroideries.

for use in landscape or abstract images. Artificial silk can be sensitive to heat, melting or bubbling on contact with a very hot iron.

Velvet and Velour

Velvet has a rich, soft surface and can be made of silk, cotton or synthetic fibres. Velvet is woven whilst velour is knitted. Velvet has a definite pile which causes problems when completing projects or pressing embroideries. Velvet 'fidgets' – I have known velvet to move up to 2.5cm (1in.) whilst a pinned seam is being stitched.

Cotton furnishing velvets have a very dense matt texture that takes painted Bondaweb and transfer foils really well. Cotton velvets are suitable for making sturdy bags or cushions.

Synthetic dress velours are designed for use in dance or theatrical costumes and they can stretch one or both ways. It is therefore important to back stretch velours with a stiff iron-on interfacing before using them in projects.

An assortment of synthetic fabrics. Organza is very versatile: it can be chopped up, torn, used to alter the back ground colour or embroidered with the support of a wash-away stabilizer. The luxurious surface of synthetic velvet is ideal for showcasing metallic embroidery designs and crushed velvet is a good choice for evening bags.

Organza and Chiffon

Organza is a translucent fabric woven from polyester, cotton or nylon. It is very versatile; it can be cut into tiny snips to create a new embroidered fabric, used as a backing for embroidering motifs ready to cut out for appliqué or covering a base fabric to change the colour. Organza is heat-sensitive: it melts on contact with a hot iron.

Shot organza has different colour warp and weft threads so the fabric shows different colours depending on the drape. Mirror organza has a shiny smooth surface, whilst crystal organza has a glittery effect to the weave. Tissue organza is often coarser; it can fray or catch on the needle when stitched, and may be woven from metallic or opalescent threads.

Glitzy fabrics are a welcome addition to an embroiderer's stash. From top: foil-printed stretch knit, lilac iridescent tricot, metallic blue net, holographic animal print, green iridescent tricot, printed foil sequin dance fabric, red microdot foil stretch knit, red metallic woven-tissue organza, gold sequin dot knitted lurex and iridescent woven organza.

Chiffon

Chiffon is a transparent plain weave fabric, usually made of nylon. Charity shops are often good places to hunt for chiffon scarves for projects. It can be layered to create subtle colours or shadows in landscape images. It usually has a matt texture whilst organza is shiny and reflective.

Nets and Tulle

Tulle is a transparent net traditionally used for bridal veils; it is finer than net. Nets and tulle can be plain or metallic and can be bought with embroidered or printed patterns. Nets can be layered to change the colour of a background fabric and can also be cut up and used in soluble film embroideries.

Dance Fabric

Foiled or sequinned dance fabrics can be used to add areas of glitz to a bland embroidery. Woven and knitted Lurex appeals to the inner magpie; the sparkly metallic colours work well when used sparingly. Lurex fabrics can be plain metallic, patterned and even hairy.

Tricot Lamé

Tricot is a knitted fabric bonded to a synthetic film. Tricot lamé can be metallic or iridescent; it does not fray when cut. It is used in modern church vestments but is also suitable for metallic or fantasy projects.

Paper Lamé

Paper lamé is a woven metallic which is made from transparent nylon thread and polyester filaments. It frays badly and melts easily so care must be taken when using it.

Devoré

Burnt-out or devoré fabric has chemically etched surface patterns. Such fabrics need to contain cellulose fibres such as cotton, rayon or viscose for the etching process to work; the cellulose areas are eaten away and heat-treated to reveal a translucent weave or knit.

INTERFACING AND BACKINGS

Interfacing is applied to the back of the fabric to stiffen it. It can be woven or non-woven, fusible or tear-away and is available in light, medium or heavy weights. The kind you use depends on the fabric and project. Medium- or lightweight is good for backing soft bags. If you prefer working without a hoop, one or two layers of heavy fusible interfacing or tear-away prevents the fabric shrinking or distorting. Note that tear-away interfacing (or stabilizer) is also known as 'stitch and tear' but there is a specific brand called Stitch 'n' Tear.

Pelmet Vilene

This is a very firm white heavyweight non-woven interfacing. It is traditionally used to stiffen tiebacks for curtains and (obviously) to back pelmets. It can be used to stiffen embroidery projects such as needlecases or evening bags. Pelmet Vilene does not have a heat-fixable glue backing so it needs to be fixed in place with heat-fusible glue or sewn in.

Felt

Felt can be made from synthetic fibres or from wool. I use felt for the pages in needle books. It is very useful for padding embroideries or for covering the back of finished hoop-framed embroideries.

Wadding

Wadding is used to raise the surface of quilted embroideries. I use it to soften box linings. It is often available under the name Dacron. Wadding comes in 4oz or 2oz weights. The remnants can be shredded to pad trapunto embroidery or to stuff pincushions.

HEAT-BONDABLE GLUE

Heat-bondable or heat-fusible glue is a fine web of glue supported by a waxy backing paper. Patterns can be drawn onto the backing paper but the image must be reversed, otherwise the bonded fabric will be the wrong way round. There are many brands on the market: Vilene Bondaweb is

Heat-fusible glue or webbing is used for appliqué or transfer foil techniques. Many kinds are available: black and white Mistyfuse is more delicate than Bondaweb which is backed by waxpaper.

Soluble film is essential for some embroidery techniques. L to R: Aquabond sticky paper-backed soluble fabric, Romeo heavyweight water-soluble film, Aquasol white soluble fabric, Avalon lightweight water-soluble film, Aquatics water-soluble paper, mediumweight extra film and spray glue for securing fabrics.

Fusible film and fibres are ironed between layers of baking parchment to fuse them together. Once fused the film can be cut up and incorporated into embroideries. Top: Angelina and Crystalina fibres; centre: Angelina film; bottom: metallic transfer foil (used with heat-fusible glue to add luxurious accents to embroideries).

very popular in the UK; other brands are called Heat-n-Bond Ultra, Heat-n-Bond Light or Steam-A-Seam 2.

Mistyfuse

This is a heat-fusible glue that has no backing paper; it is available in black or white. The web of glue is more decorative than standard fusible glues. Mistyfuse retains some of the transparency of the fabric so it is suitable for use with organza and it can be used for decorative foiling techniques.

Vilene Hotspots

These are small dots of heat-activated glue printed onto a backing paper. Hotspots are available in a variety of sizes and are used for decorative foiling techniques.

OTHER USEFUL ITEMS

Baking Parchment

This popular kitchen staple is invaluable for use in embroidery projects. Its non-stick properties make it ideal for protecting the iron when using heat-fusible interfacing or glue; if these get onto the iron they can easily mark the fabric. Baking parchment helps the iron to glide over the surface to ensure a smooth clean bond. Baking parchment is essential when using transfer foils or Angelina fibres and film; these would simply melt with direct contact to the iron and make a mess. Designs can be traced onto it to aid the positioning of fabric pieces for complex applique designs.

Dressmaker's Carbon

Designs can be transferred onto fabric using dressmaker's carbon, which is available in white, yellow, red or blue. Note that if you press down too hard when drawing it can mark the fabric in other places.

Water-soluble Film and Fabric

Water-soluble film is an embroidery topping or backing that dissolves on contact with water. Such films are transparent and can look like cling film or have a dimpled matt surface. They are available in different grades: thin, medium and heavy. Water-soluble fabrics are white, can be woven or non-woven, and may have a soft feel like fleece or be rigid like paper.

Water-soluble film is very useful as it can be used to stabilize fabrics, to transfer a design or to top fabrics to stop embroidery stitches disappearing into the pile. This versatile medium can even be used as a basis on which to create fabrics with snips of yarn or fabrics. Heavyweight films can be used on their own to create machine lace or motifs ready for appliqué.

Metallic Transfer Foils

These were originally used in the card-making industry. They have a clear backing which holds the metallic-effect leaf, which is released from the backing by using heat-fusible glues such as Mistyfuse or Bondaweb.

Angelina and Fusible Film

Angelina film is an iridescent hot-fix film – think of oil on water or fairy wings. Sheets of hot-fix film are sandwiched between layers of baking parchment and ironed at a low temperature to fuse them together. Heat-fusible Angelina fibres are thin slivers of hot-fix film and they will bond to

Beads and sequins are used to embellish finished embroideries. Clockwise from top L: cup sequins, amethyst lustre seed beads, gold faceted crystal rondelles, two-hole plastic button, large crystal rondelles, four-hole imitation shell button, frosted bugles, frosted cube and triangle beads, twisted metallic bugles, AB seed beads and crystal bi-cones.

Trimmings can be used to add finishing touches to embroideries; they can also be cut up and used to make a background fabric. Shown here are black daisy lace, red rickrack, pink satin ribbon, black net lace, cream guipure lace and red organza ribbon.

Sequins

Sequins are plastic shapes (usually discs) with a hole punched in the middle for fastening on by sewing. They can be flat or cup-shaped, and the most popular finishes are metallic, holographic, lustre or AB. Sequins must be attached to the embroidery when it is finished because heat from the iron distorts and melts them.

each other to create sheets of iridescent fibres. Crystalina is a crinkly version of Angelina; it has a wavy texture. Once fused, both types can be stitched and incorporated into embroideries.

Beads

More sparkle can be added to an embroidery by adding seed beads and bugles. Popular bead shapes are round, seed, bugle, faceted bi-cone, round and oval. I prefer to use glass, crystal, semi-precious, haematite or good-quality plastic beads. Beads do vary in quality: cheaper ones or seconds might have irregularities in hole size which cause problems when threading. Beads and sequins can also be used to disguise a mistake or marked fabric.

Seed Beads

These round beads are the smallest and the most useful to have in your bead box. Seed beads are made of glass and may be transparent, silver-lined, colour-lined, opaque, frosted matt, lustre or AB (aurora borealis). Seed beads with luxurious finishes such as lustre or AB work really well when teamed with black velvet and metallic embroidery.

Bugle Beads

Bugle beads are long tubes made of glass and they can be faceted, twisted or plain. They can have the same finishes as seed beads; metal lined or opaque AB colours are more popular.

Crystal Beads

These are more decorative than regular seed beads. Made from cut glass or lead crystal, they can be transparent or have silver cores; some have lustre or AB finishes. Crystal beads are often faceted to show the brilliance of the glass; popular shapes are round, oval, bi-cone or rondelle. I use faceted crystal beads to decorate the centre of flower brooches or to add sparkle to box lids.

Trimmings

Decorative trimmings can be used to hide raw edges or add the finishing touch to a project. Cut trimmings fray so remember to tuck the ends under when sewing them to an embroidery. Painting the cut edge with clear fabric glue prevents fraying; this method works well on satin ribbon. Pale trimmings can be darkened with fabric paint but note that the paint needs fixing when dry. Some trimmings melt when ironed so it's advisable to test a small sample.

Ribbons

These can be made from natural or synthetic fibres. Types of ribbon include double satin, organza, velvet and grosgrain. They can be secured to an embroidered background with straight or patterned stitches using a presser foot and raised feeder teeth. They can be used to make decorative closures for boxes, books and bags, to hide seams or to conceal the edge of the fabric.

Guipure Lace

This form of lace is quite bold. It does not have a net background; instead the patterns are connected by bars of lace. White guipure lace can be dyed with fabric paints or dyes.

Bias Binding

This binding works well on projects that are quilted or too thick to turn through. I use it to finish the edges of quilts, sewing wraps and scissor cases. Bias binding can also be used to wrap wooden embroidery hoops because it's easier to manipulate around curved shapes than fabric cut on the straight.

Fastenings and Findings

If you plan to turn your embroideries into wearable or functional items you may need to add fastenings such as zips, buttons or press studs.

With careful planning small embroideries can be turned into wearable art. Brooch backs can be sewn onto small pieces or jewellery findings used to make necklaces or earrings. Little bells can add an element of fun to needlecases, scissor keepers or key rings.

Zips

Zips can be separating, non-separating or invisible, and the teeth can be made from metal, plastic or nylon. A zip may be needed to finish a project so you need to choose the right zip for the job you need it to do. A bag may need a nylon zip to create an inner pocket or close a make-up bag; a cushion may need an invisible zip if you want it to remain hidden in the back panel or side seam.

Press Studs and Magnetic Clasps

Press studs come in many sizes and can be made of metal or clear plastic. The metal variety usually have a black or chrome finish. Small totes or dolly bags can be fastened with sew-on press studs. Larger totes can be secured with bigger press studs sewn to a decorative tab for a secure finish. Clutch or evening bags or totes look more professional with magnetic clasps, which are a bit tricky to fit but worth the effort.

Velcro

Hook-and-loop tape is available in many colours and can be sewn in or have a sticky backing for attachment. Velcro may be too ugly to use in embroidery projects but it does have its uses: for example, it can be used on the back of embroideries to hang them or to fix them to another surface. The rough side of Velcro can be used to tease out the fibres of embroidered wool thread.

Buttons

These come in a huge variety of sizes, materials and finishes, such as plastic, bone, shell, metal, wood or glass. The flat type may be attached through two or four holes. Buttons with a shank can be used to decorate the centre of flower brooches or fasten bags. Flat buttons can be sewn onto abstract embroideries, crazy patchwork, pincushions or needlecases. If the buttons don't quite match the project they can be sanded, painted or used upside down to get the right finish.

Magnetic bag fastenings have four parts; the prongs are pushed through cuts made in the fabric and secured with a slotted metal disc. Sew-on press studs may be an easier option for securing bag closures. Brooch backs can be sewn onto the back of embroideries to create wearable art.

Tape and Adhesive

Masking tape is ideal for temporarily fixing paper or fabrics, or to seal the back of picture frames. Masking tape becomes a permanent fixative if it is left in position. It also doubles up as a handy lint removal tool; gently apply the sticky side to remove unwanted fluff. Double-sided tape is handy for fixing embroideries to greetings cards or sticking card stock together to make it thicker. Sticky foam pads can be used to add dimension to mounted embroideries. Impex Original High-Tack All-Purpose Very Sticky Glue or similar adhesive is essential for box making; it is very sticky and dries clear, and can also be used watered down to stop fabrics or ribbons fraying. Araldite is another useful thing to have in the tool box because some surfaces won't stick with regular glue. Araldite is an epoxy resin, and the chemical reaction ensures suitable surfaces stay bonded together. (Always test glue on a sample before using them in a project.)

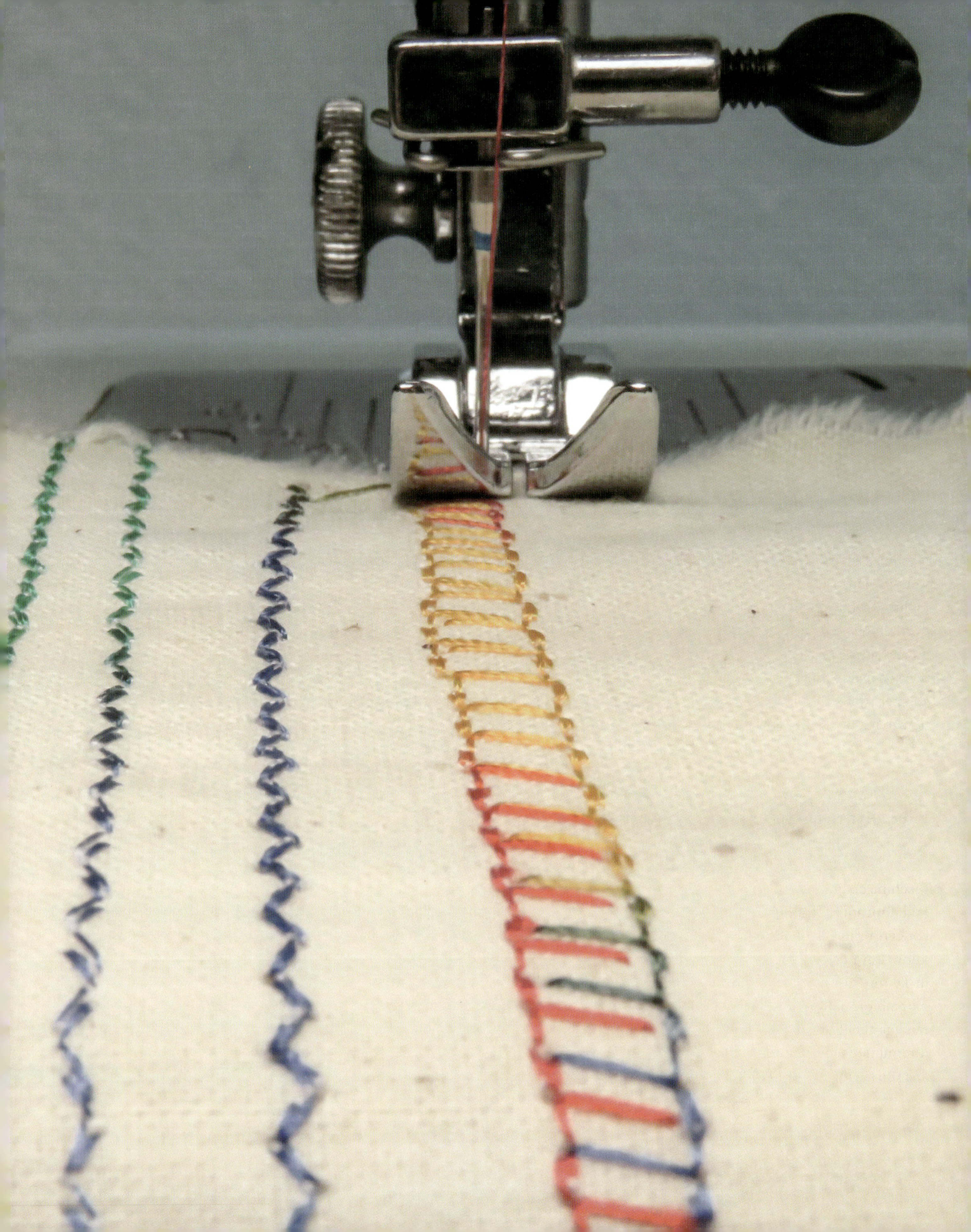

CHAPTER 2

Setting Up the Machine and Workspace

There are many things to consider before you begin stitching; in particular you need to find the right machine and set up a pleasant space to work in. This chapter also examines how to thread the machine and test the tension by stitching a sample with the presser foot on and feeder teeth up. As you begin to sew you may encounter problems, so this chapter shows how to resolve them and how to maintain the sewing machine.

Getting the Mindspace Ready

Machine embroidery needs a lot of focus and unwanted thoughts can disrupt concentration. I prefer to sew when I know I'm not going to be disturbed. I make sure all the bitty jobs are done so my embroidery time is not interrupted by random thoughts, needs or people. Little interruptions can alter the way you sew, and you may find yourself rushing to finish an embroidery or getting annoyed because you have to do something else in a minute.

Machine embroidery is a partnership between the machine and you. Relax – being creative and discovering new skills should be enjoyable. The machine will know if you are not in the mood so there is no point in trying to embroider if you are in the wrong frame of mind. Just walk away, do something else and come back to it later; you will be more productive after taking a step back.

Getting the Workspace Ready

The workspace is as important as the mindspace; you need to feel happy there. You need adequate lighting and comfortable furniture because you will be sitting in the same position for some time whilst using the machine, so it's essential that the table and chair are at the correct height for your body.

Chair

I use a wheeled office-type chair because the height can be changed. I can also push myself away from the machine without having to lift the chair. If you don't have an office chair you can use cushions to adjust your sitting height. Sitting puts stress on the back so remember to have regular breaks from using the machine. If sewing for more than an hour it is important to get up and walk around or do some stretches and make a drink to keep yourself hydrated.

You should not sew whilst hunched over the machine. I have the bad habit of sewing with my back slouched so my head is really close to the machine; this posture is really bad for neck and back tension and the moving thread lever has hit my glasses on a few occasions.

Work Surface

Your desk or table needs to be large enough to accommodate your machine, threads, scissors, notebook and so on. The height of the desk also needs to be tailored to you: I have a short back so I prefer to use a lower table. You need adequate space underneath the desk for your knees and legs to be comfortable. You also need enough space to position the foot pedal so it can be operated with ease.

Standing Up to Work

When I worked as an ecclesiastical embroiderer the workbenches were at breakfast bar height because the lady I worked for was much taller than me. I found that I was able to control the machine whilst standing and it was more comfortable to work this way because of the height of the tables. Working like this can reduce stress on the back but you may find that you are tilting the pelvis to operate the foot pedal.

Good Housekeeping

When I start a new project I clear my desk, removing as much clutter as I can. The hoop needs space to move; a messy desk is distracting and you end up knocking things onto the floor or losing them amongst the mess. Tools or threads should be placed to the right of the machine, where they are less likely to be knocked and mislaid; picking up a spilt tin of pins can be very annoying, as can chasing runaway thread reels or bobbins.

Lighting

The workspace needs adequate lighting because machine embroidery can be quite tiring for the eyes. If possible, choose an area that has a good supply of natural light. Sewing machine bulbs and regular household lighting can cast a warm light into the work area; daylight bulbs counteract this and help you see the true colour value of fabric and threads. Craft lighting can be expensive so a simple solution is to buy an anglepoise desk lamp and some daylight bulbs. If you have glasses for close work or reading make sure you wear them to prevent eye strain.

EXERCISE
Setting Up the Machine

YOU WILL NEED

Equipment
- Sewing machine
- Sewing machine manual
- Normal tension bobbin case
- Empty bobbin
- Presser foot
- Size 90/14 universal machine needle
- Screwdriver
- Fabric scissors
- Embroidery scissors

Materials
- Top thread
- Bobbin thread
- Scrap of cotton or calico
- Old towel

Machine used
- Bernina 801
- Feeder teeth up
- Normal tension

Sewing machine diagram; your machine may be slightly different, so refer to your manual. 1 needle, 2 straight-stitch presser foot, 3 feeder teeth (or feed dogs), 4 needle plate, 5 bobbin case, 6 shuttle hook or hook race cover, 7 feeder teeth switch, 8 stitch length dial, 9 buttonhole dial, 10 stitch width dial, 11 needle position dial, 12 hand wheel, 13 hand wheel release, 14 bobbin winding spindle, 15 thread reel holder (not shown), 16 stitch type selector, 17 thread tension selector, 18 thread tension disc, 19 thread tension slot, 20 pre-tensioning winder, 21 thread take-up lever, 22 thread regulator, 23 needle holder clamp, 24 thread guide.

Fold the old towel and place it on your worktable. The towel needs to be folded so it's the right size for the machine to stand on. Get the machine out of its bag or box and place it on the folded towel. The towel acts like a non-slip mat and muffles some of the noise; most machines can be a bit noisy when sewing at high speed.

Connect the foot pedal and switch the machine on; turn the machine's light on so you can see what you are doing. Move the foot pedal so it is out of reach, as you don't want to accidentally press it whilst threading the machine.

The following exercise illustrates how to thread a Bernina 801 vintage sewing machine; your machine will be slightly different so be sure to refer to your own manual. If you are an experienced sewer it is still good to look at your manual because you may have overlooked something important.

Chapter 2 – Setting Up the Machine and Workspace

Winding a Bobbin

1. Release the hand wheel to stop the needle going up and down. This can be done by gripping the inner part and turning the outer part or by pulling one of these outwards. Refer to your manual to check how to do this.

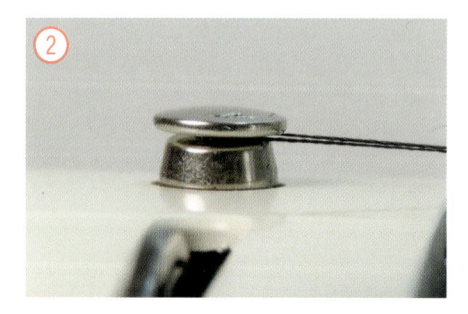

2. Place a spool of black or white thread onto the reel holder pin; the bobbin will be wound on this. Take the thread around the pre-tensioning winder; the thread slips into place under the mushroom-shaped part of the pre-tensioning thread winder.

3. Push the bobbin onto the bobbin spool and pass the thread through one of the holes or slots or wind it around the core of the bobbin a few times. Push the bobbin to the right so it clicks into place near the bobbin winder stopper. Keep hold of the end of the thread and press the foot pedal down gently to turn the winding spindle; the bobbin should start to wind.

4. The machine will probably stop automatically and click the bobbin spindle back to the left when the bobbin is full. Some machines don't do this but you can tell when the bobbin is full because the sound of the motor changes in pitch.

5. When the bobbin is filled insert it into the empty bobbin case so the thread reels off in a clockwise direction. Pull the thread through the slot and under the tension spring or as instructed by your manual.

6. Hold the bobbin case so the finger of the case is pointing upwards. Inset the case onto the spool pin so the finger fits onto the recess at the top. The bobbin should click as it slots into the correct position. Re-engage the handwheel so the needle moves up and down again.

Inserting the Needle

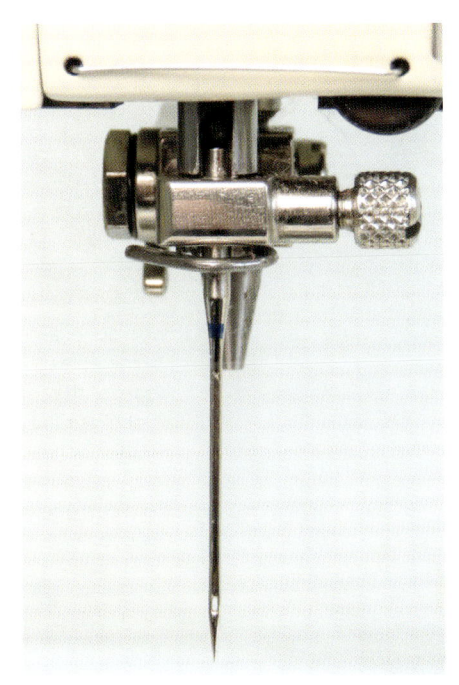

Insert a new size 90/14 universal needle into the needle holder, making sure the flat side of the needle shank is facing to the back of the machine. Tighten the needle holder clamp either by hand or with a screwdriver. You don't want the needle to become loose when you are sewing.

Attaching the Presser Foot

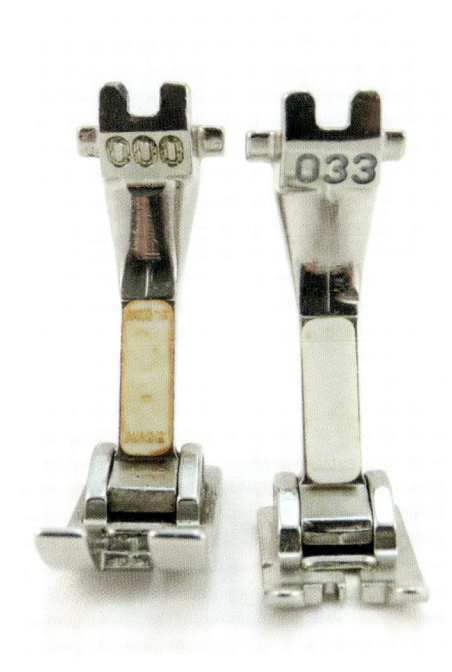

Raise the needle so it is in the up position and clamp or clip the straight-stitch presser foot in place. The buttonhole foot and the straight-stitch foot for the Bernina 801 look very much alike; check your manual to make sure you are using the correct foot for straight stitch.

Threading the Needle

1 Choose a strong no. 40 or no. 30 thread for the needle. The top thread can be made of viscose, rayon, cotton or polyester. Select a colour that will show up against the fabric scrap. Make sure the needle is in the up position by turning the hand wheel, then raise the presser foot so it is up.

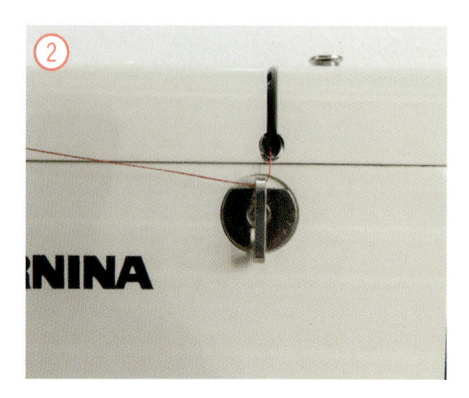

2 Place the chosen thread onto the reel holder pin and take the thread through the thread guide at the back of the machine. The rear thread guide keeps the thread in place as it travels through the tension slot and tension discs. If the thread comes out of the rear thread guide the stitches won't form properly.

3 Bring the thread over the top of the machine and into the tension slot so it passes through the tension disc.

4 Bring the thread down and pass it under the thread regulator; then bring the thread back up and pull it through the slot on the take-up lever. Bring the thread back down towards the needle and pass it through the thread guide (the metal loop just below the needle clamp).

5 Thread the needle so that it is threaded through the eye from front to back. Pull the thread so there is a length of top thread approximately 15cm (6in.) long.

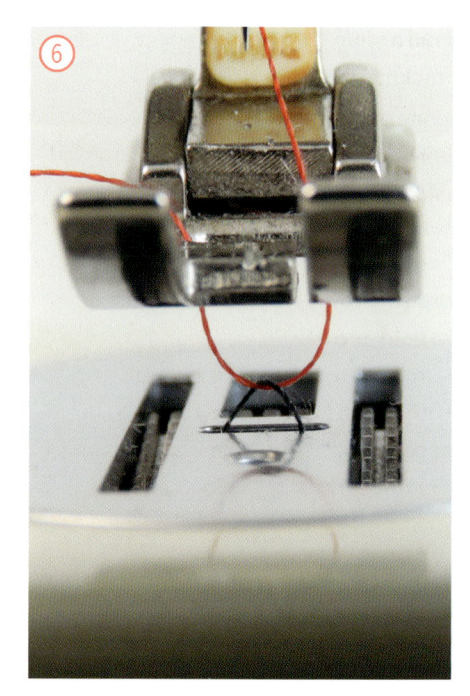

6 Hold the top thread tail and turn the hand wheel one revolution so the needle and thread take-up lever are in the up position. Pull the thread tail to bring a loop of the bobbin thread through the hole in the needle plate. Pull the bottom (bobbin) thread until the tail length is about 15cm (6in.) long.

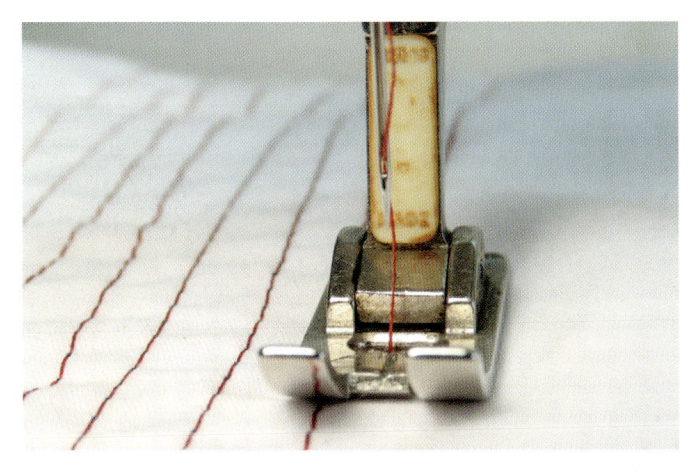

The line of straight stitch should lie flat with no looping or dots of thread on the top or bottom of the fabric. The stitches should not pull or gather the fabric. If the stitches are not forming properly have a quick look in the problem-solving section.

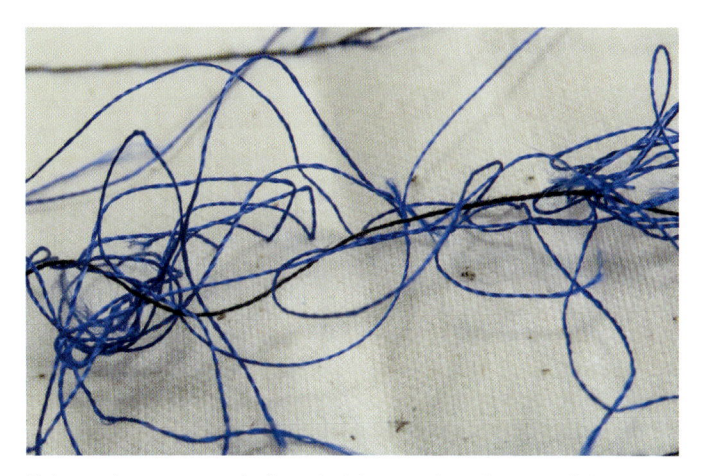

This tangle was created when the blue top thread came off the thread take-up lever. The blue thread was pulled to the bottom to create long loops and eventually caused the machine to groan and seize. Re-thread the machine and remove any threads caught in the bobbin chamber.

Testing the Stitch

Fold a scrap of calico in half so it is double thickness and position it under the presser foot. Lower the presser foot, check the feeder teeth are raised and set the stitch length to a medium-length straight stitch. Keep hold of both thread tails so they are behind the presser foot and apply gentle pressure to the foot pedal. The machine should feed the fabric through whilst stitching a perfectly balanced straight stitch. The fabric may need a little assistance to guide it but it should not be pushed or pulled over the needle plate.

Solving Machine Problems

In an ideal world the machine should sew perfectly as if it has just come from the factory but this may not be the case in reality. Machine problems can drive a person to distraction. The first task is to find out what is causing the issue: sewing machine problems can be caused by all kinds of factors, such as incorrect threading, poorly adjusted tension, a blunt needle, being dirty or needing a service.

I am ashamed to say that one of my machines made me cry once when it decided not to create perfectly balanced stitches. I sat for hours trying to sort the problem out – no wonder tension is called tension. I went back to the machine a few hours later with a calmer mind and resolved the problem in no time; working through problems one step at a time is the best way to solve them. If you are having trouble with your machine read through some of the solutions below.

Re-thread Everything and Try Again

Stitch issues can be caused by the machine not being threaded properly. The thread can sometimes slip out of the tension discs or thread guides and cause breakage or looping. This can happen whilst machining at high speed so be mindful of any changes in tension or strange machine noises; an unusual noise usually indicates something is not right, so stop sewing immediately and check everything.

Change the Needle

Missed stitches, thread breakage or pulled fabric can be caused by a blunt needle. Is the needle an old one? Has it been used for a different type of thread? Thread can wear a groove in the eye of the needle and when you swap to a different thread type it can become damaged as it passes through the eye of the needle.

Using the wrong needle can also cause the thread to break. Check the size of the needle. If the needle is too small the thread won't have enough room to pass through the eye, which causes friction leading to shredding and breakage. If using specialist thread types or weights be sure to use the correct needle designed for them.

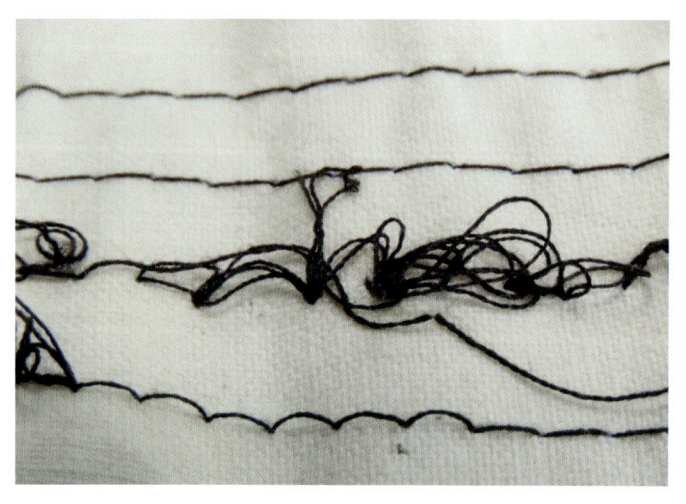

This loopy bobbin thread was caused by a bobbin not being threaded correctly. If you have a problem with loopy stitches the first step is to re-thread top and bottom and double-check everything.

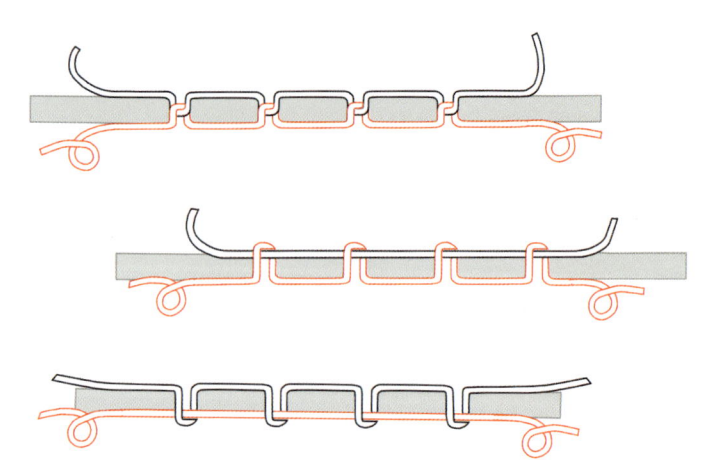

If the tension is correct the threads should meet in the centre of the fabric to make the stitch. When the top tension is too tight the upper thread becomes taut, pulling the bobbin thread to the top of the fabric to form dots. If the top tension is too loose the top thread makes loose stitches that are pulled to the bottom of the fabric.

Check the Foot

Forgetting to lower the foot causes stitch problems. This mistake is quite common when using a darning or embroidery foot because the foot looks lowered when it's actually in the raised position, so always check the foot is lowered before you begin sewing.

Check the Bobbin and Under the Feeder Teeth

Some stitch problems can be caused by the bobbin not being wound or inserted properly. Are there any threads caught in the race or around the bobbin spool holder? Loose threads, no matter how small, can interfere with the movement of the bobbin and race, so make sure the area is clean and free of fluff or threads.

I have known a knot of thread to become lodged in between the tension spring and the bobbin case, making the gap larger and causing the bobbin tension to go awry. Are there threads or fluff caught under the feeder teeth? Clogged feeder teeth can hinder the formation of stitches; a good clean should remedy the problem.

Adjust the Tension Settings

Thread breakage, puckering fabric and loose or tight stitches can all be caused by thread tension. Tension can go awry for many reasons: you may have forgotten that you altered the bobbin tension or you may have changed the top tension to suit a previous thread or stitch. It may be that the thread is of a different thickness or simply that the machine does not like working with that type of thread. The best way to resolve tension problems is to understand a bit about how the machine makes the stitches.

As the threaded needle passes through the fabric and the hole in the needle plate the needle thread is caught on the hook of the bobbin shuttle hook. The loop of needle thread is then carried around the bobbin case by the shuttle hook until it loops around the bobbin thread to form an interlocking knot. (To add to the confusion the sewing machine's shuttle hook can also be called a hook race.)

If the tension problems are not resolved, the stitch balance can be further tested by setting the stitch type to a medium-width zigzag. Incorrect tension is more noticeable with zigzag because the fabric pulls in to create a tuck or tunnel below the stitch, or the top thread is pulled to the bottom or vice versa.

Thread tension should be adjusted carefully: move the top tension dial a tiny bit or tighten or loosen the tension screw in the bobbin case a small amount. When altering the thread tension screw think about minutes on a clock; only turn the screw so it is like moving the clock hand five, ten or fifteen minutes.

When the top tension is too tight the bobbin thread is pulled to the top to create dots or loops along the line of the straight stitch. Tight tension can pull the fabric in and spoil an embroidery. It is worth persevering with the thread tension to get the stitch balance right.

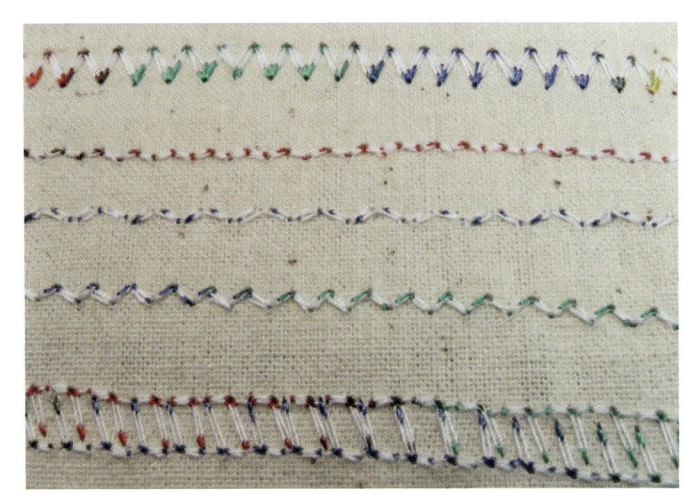

If the bobbin tension is too tight loops or dots appear on the bottom of the fabric. This does not spoil the appearance of the embroidery but it might mean the top thread is looser than it should be.

This sample of zigzag was stitched with blue through the needle and black on the bobbin. The blue top thread has pulled the fabric and the black bottom thread has come to the top, which means the upper thread tension is too tight; this can be remedied by loosening the top tension.

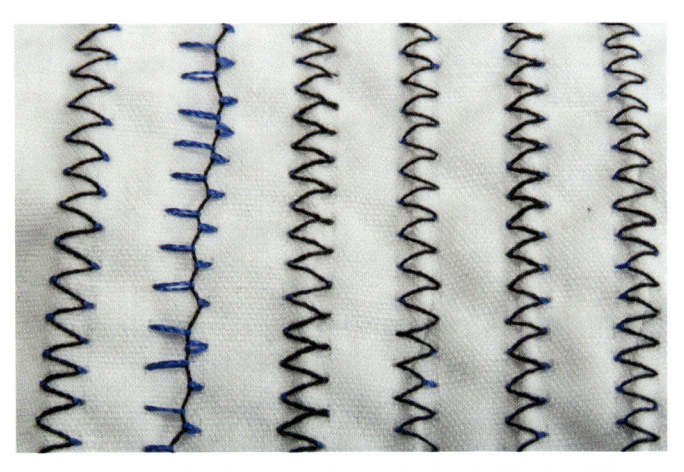

The underside of the zigzag sample reveals that the black bobbin thread is too tight. This can be solved by loosening the tension screw on the bobbin case.

Change the Top Thread

If the solutions above don't solve the thread or tension problems, it may be because the machine does not like that brand of thread. Through experience I have learnt not to use certain colours or brands. If you really like the threads and want to use them the only solution may be to use them on the bobbin for under-thread embroidery stitches such as moss, feather or whip stitch.

Chapter 2 – Setting Up the Machine and Workspace   **35**

EXERCISE

CLEANING THE MACHINE

If all else fails, carry out some basic machine maintenance. Cleaning the machine acquaints you with the parts and helps it to perform at its best. For this demonstration I will be cleaning the Bernina 801 because it's become really dirty beneath the feeder teeth. This exercise shows where lint collects and where to put drops of oil. Refer to your manual for instructions about removing the needle plate, bobbin case and race because your machine may be slightly different.

YOU WILL NEED

Equipment
- Sewing machine
- Sewing machine manual
- Soft brush
- Sewing machine oil
- Soft rag
- Screwdriver

Machine used
- Bernina 801
- Feeder teeth up
- Normal tension

1 If you open the hinged cover over the bobbin and race to find lots of fluff, it's time to clean the machine. Always turn off the power if you are doing any maintenance or cleaning.

2 Remove the needle plate that covers the feeder teeth. Some needle plates are secured with screws whilst others are removed by unclipping. Refer to your machine manual for instruction on how to do this. Most of the lint accumulates under the feeder teeth; brush it away with a soft brush (you may need to lift the feeder teeth slightly to remove all the lint).

3 Remove the bobbin case by gripping and pulling the latch; unclip the bobbin shuttle hook cover and take out the shuttle hook. Brush the lint from under the feeder teeth and where the race fits. Never blow the lint away as it can fly into your eyes and make them sore.

④ Look at the shuttle hook. Is the curved edge smooth and free of abrasions? Is the hook point sharp with no nicks or grooves? Small amounts of lint can collect inside the shuttle hook and shuttle hook cover so use the soft brush to clean them.

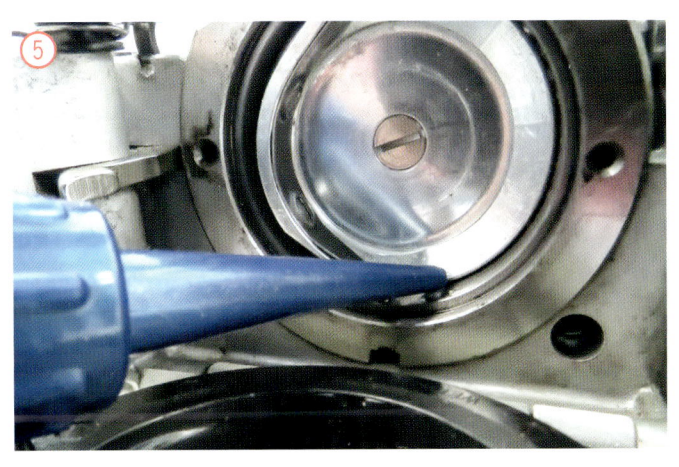

⑤ Put one drop of oil on the bottom of the innermost curve where the shuttle hook fits. This is where two metal surfaces are in contact, so oiling this area prevents the machine seizing. If too much oil comes out use a cloth to wipe away any excess.

⑥ Put the shuttle hook back in, making sure it is in the right position. Clip the bobbin shuttle hook cover into place and push the bobbin case into position (it should click as it engages), then replace the needle plate.

⑦ Once clean, turn on the power and sew a few stitches to remove the excess oil and make sure the machine is working properly. Your machine should be much quieter to use; a noisy machine probably needs cleaning and oiling. (This photograph shows the cleaned area without the needle plate in position.)

Chapter 2 – Setting Up the Machine and Workspace **37**

Here, sewing over a pin caused the needle to hit the needle plate and cut a deep groove in it. The groove kept damaging the thread, causing it to shred and break. The damaged area was smoothed with filing and burnishing but it can still be seen.

Rear view of the Bernina machine showing the mug placed directly below the reel holder. The troublesome thread can roll around in the mug without getting wrapped around the reel holder pins. You may need to re-position the mug to find the optimum position for the thread to spool off the reel.

Check the Manual

Many solutions can be found in the manual: something simple may have been overlooked. You can check online for further advice or instructional videos. If all else fails, take a break and try again later. Machines, like people, do have their off days and it may decide to work perfectly fine in a few hours' time.

Solving Thread Problems

Metallic threads have a rough coarse texture so if they keep breaking, switch to a metallic needle. Such needles have a large eye and are designed to handle the rough surface of this type of thread. If your metallic threads continue to break, it could be due to the quality. Also, note that some metallic threads work best when used on the bobbin.

If the top thread keeps breaking the problem could be linked to the needle plate or foot. Check both for burrs or scratches: if the machine needle has accidentally hit the needle plate or foot it may have cut a groove into the metal. Shallow marks can be sanded smooth but deeper burrs may need filing with a needle file before being sanded smooth.

The thread may keep twisting or knotting. Some threads are springier than others, and it could be the way it has been manufactured or the fibre content. Springy threads have a tendency to come out of the thread guides or tangle around the thread spool holder. This can cause real problems when sewing at high speed, as the top thread can knot around itself and bring the bobbin thread to the surface; in extreme cases the tension change can break the needle.

The twisty thread problem can be easily solved with the help of an old mug. If the thread reel is small enough, place it in a mug located directly below the reel holder. The mug keeps the thread contained and stops it from knotting. Thread the machine as normal but take thread in front of the reel holder; this ensures that the thread stays in the tension discs and thread guides.

If the thread cone is too large or heavy to fit on the machine's thread holder, wind some of the thread onto bobbins and use these on the top. Bobbins are lighter so remember to put an empty thread reel on top to add some weight, then the bobbin should unwind without causing any tension problems.

Fabric-eating Problems

Other problems can seem more alarming: for example, sometimes the fabric can be pulled into the hole in the needle plate. This can happen if the fabric is too thin or held stationary in one place when doing free machine embroidery work. As the stitches build up the needle forces their bulk and the fabric into the needle plate hole. This problem can be easily solved: move your foot away from the foot pedal and trim the top thread. Gently pull the fabric out of the hole in the needle plate and trim the threads off the bottom. If the fabric won't budge you may need to cut more thread from underneath before you can pull the fabric free. When the fabric has been released, remove the bobbin case to make sure there are no threads trapped underneath.

This tangle of blue thread was removed from under the belt that drives the major parts of the machine. Only take the machine apart if the power is off and you know what you are doing. If in doubt take it to a reliable sewing machine repair shop.

Unexpected Noises

If your machine makes an unusual noise it may indicate there is a problem. At one point my vintage Bernina was stitching slower and it was labouring; if you can drive, think of going up a steep hill in the wrong gear. I continued to sew but the machine really began struggling. My desk was a bit of a mess with a few reels of thread close to the machine. On closer inspection I realized that a thread from the blue reel had been caught and taken into the machine near the hand wheel.

I turned the machine off and removed the back panel. To my dismay the thread had been caught in the belt and wound itself around the belt and gears. The only option was to rotate the hand wheel manually to free the trapped thread, which just kept coming. The moral of the story? Listen to your machine, keep the workspace tidy and remember that human error accounts for most machine issues and problems.

Don't worry, it's not all doom and gloom. I have tried to list as many problems as I can think of so they can be solved and you won't be put off having a go at machine embroidery. As you become more familiar with using the machine you will be able to anticipate issues with the machine or threads. You become accustomed to the quirks of the machine and be able to tell if something is not right by the way the machine stitches or the sound it makes. Listen to the machine – it is trying to work very hard for your enjoyment.

Chapter 2 – Setting Up the Machine and Workspace

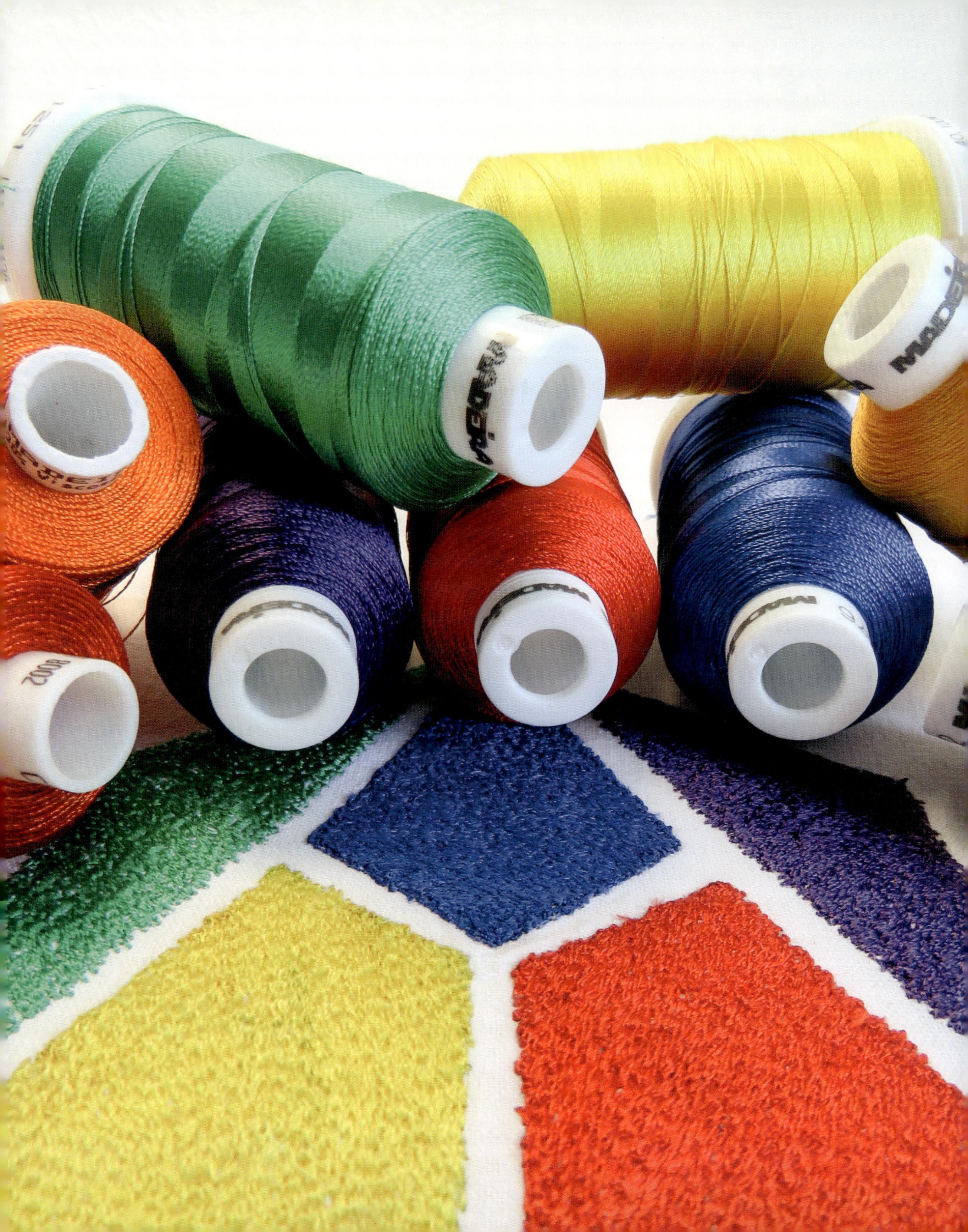

CHAPTER 3

Designing for Machine Embroidery

Before you begin any design work you must find inspiration and decide what the embroidery will become: for instance, is the finished embroidery destined to become a image, a functional item or wearable art? These decisions need to be made at the start of the process because how the project is planned is influenced by the subject matter and what the embroidery will be turned into.

The basic process of designing for machine embroidery can be broken down into stages:

- finding inspiration
- choosing what to make
- creating the design
- sourcing materials
- planning how to do the work
- making up the finished embroidery.

Some people don't bother with a structured design process and jump straight into making the project. This method can be productive if the designer is flexible and has the confidence to make important decisions along the way. Other design methods use much forethought: some people need the stability of meticulous plans, and they make detailed working drawings or sketches and test the threads and fabrics by stitching samples before starting the final piece. Careful balance is needed because too much preparation may create a project that is stilted whilst not enough may mean making mistakes that are difficult to rectify.

The methods I use depend on my mood and the type of project I am undertaking. I tend to use less planning for simple abstract designs and choose threads or materials as I go along. If the design is complex I like to use working drawings to remind me which colour or stitch to use. There is no wrong or right way to design or plan an embroidery because the way we create is unique to each of us. Embroideries are organic, they grow and change as they near completion and they may turn out very different from the initial idea.

Inspiration

Finding inspiration is the key to a successful embroidery; if you choose something that appeals to you or something that you feel passionate about, the design process

This figurative embroidery needed careful planning. For complicated designs it's useful to have a working drawing and a swatch of the thread shades used so the colours are stitched in the correct places.

becomes much easier. You may wish to embroider purely for pleasure or to make a comment about something you feel strongly about.

Lots of subject matter is suitable for embroidery. Subject matter can be found all around you: think about objects around the house, favourite fabrics or the view outside. Popular subjects for embroidery include flowers, decorative patterns, animals, birds, people or landscapes. When you have decided what the embroidery is going to be about you can explore the subject matter more by looking at magazines, books, photos or the internet. Further research can trigger an idea so it becomes a potential embroidery design.

Choosing What to Make

When you have found inspiration you need to choose what to make. The function of the embroidery could be set by the design, method of stitching, materials used or the desire to make an embroidery with a specific use. Complicated projects require more planning to be carried out; this can be done on paper or in your head. Planned stages can always be restructured or changed whilst making the project; nothing is set in stone.

The method or thought process does vary slightly for each type of embroidered item: for instance, when designing an embroidered cushion more thought must be given to the construction and durability of the fabrics and threads used. In addition to construction the cushion needs designing so that it is practical. Asking yourself questions about the future project helps you to find solutions and structure the method of working.

Is the design suitable for a cushion? Do the colours and fabrics complement the rest of the furnishings? Can the cushion be used or is it really just for ornament? Are the materials and threads durable? Does the cushion cover need to be removable for washing? Will the fabric and threads withstand washing? How will the cover be fastened so it can be removed?

How the embroidery is going to be finished or made up needs careful consideration. If the embroidery is going to be mounted on a readymade box, the box needs to be sourced before the embroidery is made so the design can be scaled to the correct size. The design should be stitched onto fabric that complements the style of the box and the embroidery threads need to be durable if the box is going to be handled a lot. Thought needs to be given to how the embroidery is mounted onto the lid. There must be enough fabric for folding over seams, glue or card may be needed for mounting the embroidery and the box may need to be lined with fabric to hide raw edges. Thinking about these solutions helps you choose the right materials for the project and put the stages of work into the correct order.

Two-dimensional embroideries such as images require a completely different approach; more emphasis should be placed on the design. The design should be composed so it is visually pleasing and the colours and stitches used need to complement the subject matter. The background fabric must be appropriate for the design and stable enough to support the embroidery. The placement of the design needs to be taken into account, the design should not be obscured by the frame and there needs to be enough fabric for lacing or mounting over card so the finished embroidery can be displayed properly.

Creating the Design

It is helpful to remember some of the following questions when producing the initial working drawings because the answers influence how the design is drawn.

Will the embroidery be stitched with line work, solid thread-painting or a combination of both? Is the colour theme going to be cool, warm or a mix of colours? What type of threads and fabrics will be used and are they suited to the subject matter? How will the design be transferred? How will the fabric be stabilized for embroidery? Which parts will be stitched first? How will the embroidery be mounted or finished?

Thinking about the stitch types and threads whilst drawing helps you translate the design into stitch types. If you prefer line drawing you may choose to stitch a minimal embroidery using simple outlines or set patterns. You may like to replicate painting and stitch your design with thread-painting. You may choose to experiment with mixed media and produce an embroidery with a variety of techniques including appliqué, embroidery and paint.

Line, Form and Stitch Type

If you draw or sketch, use line to put down what you see on paper. Lines can be used to describe form, texture and light or shade. Lines of stitchery can be used descriptively in realistic embroideries or to create patterns such as vermicelli stitch in abstract embroideries. If the embroidery is realistic or figurative you need to think about line and form and how to represent them with stitches or fabric. The best way to use line in embroidery is to use straight stitch to draw or sketch the outline of the subject matter onto the fabric.

If you like making line drawings you can replicate your drawing style with straight, zigzag or cable stitch. Each stitch type leaves a different mark: straight stitch is the finest, satin stitch is bold and cable stitch creates a raised texture. Varying the weight or thickness of the thread alters the density of the stitches: thin threads produce fine delicate lines whilst thick threads produce a chunkier stitch.

Composition and Negative Space

A design that is realistic or contains elements of pattern needs careful composition. Think about how large the fabric needs to be so you can position the elements of the design within a frame; in this case the frame is the edge of the fabric or paper used to make the embroidery or design. Traditional embroideries such as flower, pattern or bird motifs are best suited to being placed in the centre of the fabric with space all the way round them; the distance to the edge of the frame or mount should be equal on all sides of the embroidery.

Abstract designs may need areas of negative space or texture to add more interest to the design; contrasting rough threads or fabrics against smooth ones can make the embroidery more engaging. A good example of this is the way quilters leave areas plain to add emphasis to parts of the design. Tonal values or colour can be used in negative and positive spaces to provide a strong contrast between different areas of the design: for example, cool colours can be used next to warm ones or dark shades can be placed next to pastel tints. All of these methods can be used to make the design visually interesting. More information about composition and negative space can be found in Chapter 10, which deals with landscapes.

This embroidery of a beach hut was stitched with three weights of thread. The heavy outline was stitched with no. 12 thread, the details are stitched with no. 40 (medium) thread and the cross-hatched areas were built up with no. 60 (thin) thread.

Embroidered line work needn't be limited to black and white; it also works well when colour is introduced. This beach hut sample shows how straight stitch has been used to secure and decorate heat-bonded fabric to create a naive appliqué design.

This simple beach hut design is a bit plain because it is centred in the middle of the paper. It needs to have texture, colour or detail added to make it more interesting.

This design has been improved by the addition of more beach huts and some bunting. The added elements break up the blank spaces and help the viewer's gaze move around the composition.

Chapter 3 – Designing for Machine Embroidery 43

EXAMPLE
DESIGNING A PAISLEY PATTERN

This example shows how the paisley pattern evolved to become the design used for the pennant project in Chapter 6. You can follow how the design was created from the initial pencil sketches right through to the final design.

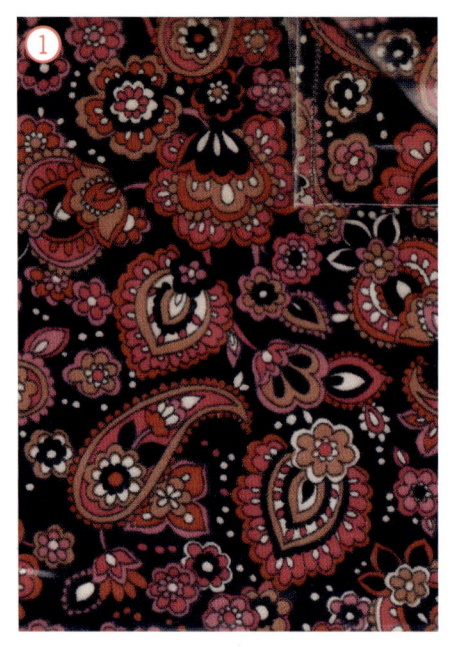

The paisley design was inspired by a scrap of vintage waterproof cotton. I liked the colour and texture of the fabric and imagined the pattern enlarged and thread-painted with rich warm colours on a cream background.

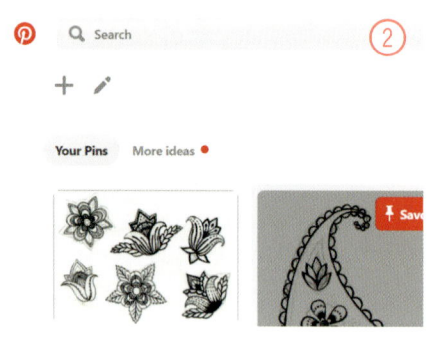

To help me create my design I found more styles of paisley on the internet. I saved the ones I liked to Pinterest, a cloud-based scrapbook which can also be used to store your own designs. However, be sure to make your board private if you don't want others to access it.

I made my initial sketches on white paper with pencil and ballpoint pen. It can be very hard to get the image down on paper so the sketch can end up being very different from the image in my head.

The next stage is to refine the individual elements of the design. At this point I was not sure if I wanted the design to be filled with colour or be outlined with contrasting black and white areas.

⑤

I made more drawings of the individual motifs. I felt these would work well with one or two thread colours but they would not be suitable for this project. These designs will be kept and developed for use in another project.

⑥

I drew many variations of the central paisley motif using pencil and black permanent pen. I felt the elements of this design didn't match so I discarded this version.

⑦

I took individual motifs from different drawings and swapped the placement of the central motifs to get the balance right.

⑧

The final drawing was traced onto white paper with pencil and defined with a black permanent pen. Some of the drawn lines had wobbles: these needed to be corrected before the design could be transferred to fabric.

⑨

The final rendition of the pattern was made on the computer using a design programme. I used a computer to enhance the drawing because I wanted the tear drop pattern to be repeated accurately.

⑩

I felt the lone central image lacked impact within the frame of the design so plotted some simple shapes on the computer and positioned them around the central motif. The design is now ready to be transferred onto the fabric.

Chapter 3 – Designing for Machine Embroidery **45**

Using Colour

Colour theory is one of the most important elements of design; it is usually the first thing taught in art lessons. Whilst making the working drawings you need to think about how colour is going to be introduced into the embroidery. Are the colours going to come from threads, fabrics or paints? When using fabric or thread the colour has already been set by the manufacturer during the dyeing process. Fabric and threads can't be mixed to create different shades like paint can but they can be blended into one another with careful stitching or layering.

To blend thread colours you need to choose a range of shades and tints to create an even graduation of light to dark. Graduation is needed to add form or dimension to a realistic thread-painted embroidery. To get a good blend choose at least three shades of thread; the more shades you use the more sophisticated the blend.

You need to think about the weight of thread and stitch type when blending or mixing threads. Thicker threads produce a coarser blend and the stitch type or direction affects how the threads blend together. Free machine embroidered straight stitch can be used like long and short stitch to blend colours together, and layers of different stitch types can also be used to create a textured effect to the blend.

The colour of the threads and fabric can be altered by painting or dyeing them; this can be done before or after the embroidery is done. If your embroideries are going to contain a lot of colour you will need to learn basic colour theory so you know how to use, mix and change colours successfully.

Colour Theory

Colour theory is simply a set of basic rules followed by artists to help them mix and use colours in their work. To use colour successfully you need to know the basic rules, such as what the primary and secondary colours are and which is the cool side and warm side of the colour wheel.

Don't be scared of colour; look around you for ideas. If you are embroidering a realistic subject look at the reference photo for clues. The subject matter can influence the choice of colour scheme; for example, embroidering a tulip flower with pastel shades would create a calm feeling whilst pure colours would give the embroidery a bright happy mood. If the subject of the embroidery is more imaginative or

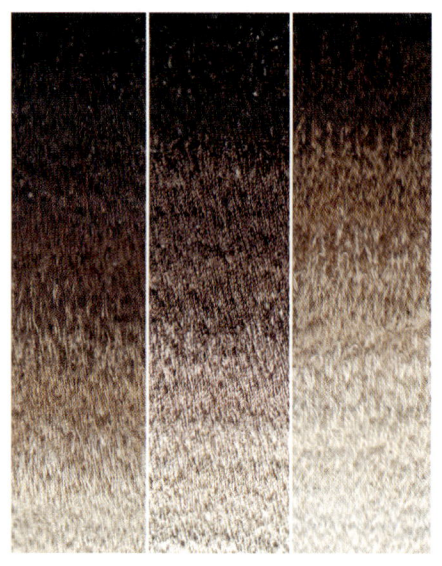

The weight and type of thread used can change the look of colour graduation or blending. These samples have been embroidered with straight stitch to replicate graduated long and short stitch. L to R: five shades of Madeira Cotona no. 50; seven shades of Madeira Classic no. 40; six shades of Madeira Lana no. 12.

Stitch types change how colours blend or graduate into one another. L: six shades of Madeira Cotona blended horizontally using straight stitch; centre: overlapping grids of straight stitch sewn with six shades of Madeira Classic; top R: scribble vermicelli sewn with five shades of Madeira Lana; bottom R: long scribble stitches sewn with five shades of Lana.

Column 1 shows how complementary colours react when stitched next to each other. Columns 2, 3 and 4 show how staggered blending of straight stitches can be used to graduate one colour into another. Column 5 shows how overlapping grids of straight stitch can be sewn to roughly blend two different thread colours together. In column 6, two different thread colours are be used in the needle to create a marled blend.

The black background increases the contrast of the bold warm colours to create a vibrant punchy paisley pattern.

The cream background and gold outline give this version of the paisley design a classic traditional theme.

This version of the paisley design has been stitched on bed linen; the pale blue colour complements the delicate straight-stitch embroidery.

The tulip was stitched with white Cotona thread and then hand-painted with Chromacolour acrylic paints. No coloured threads were used for this embroidery: all of the colour comes from the painting.

abstract, look in your fabric stash or thread collection for ideas and pull out colours that appeal to you; the selected colours could become the colour scheme for the embroidery.

The way colours are grouped together can set the tone or mood of the embroidery, whether it is realistic or abstract. Colours can be grouped together to create different colour schemes, the most popular ones being primary, secondary, warm, cool, complementary, triadic, split complementary, analogous, monochromatic or achromatic (greyscale).

Chapter 3 – Designing for Machine Embroidery **47**

This thread colour wheel is based on one designed by Johannes Itten. The primary colours are in the central triangle: blue, red and yellow. Primary colours cannot be made from mixing any other colours together. The secondary colours are on the outside of the triangle: purple, orange and green. The placement of the secondary colours illustrates how they are mixed from the primary colours. Yellow + blue = green; yellow + red = orange; blue + red = violet.

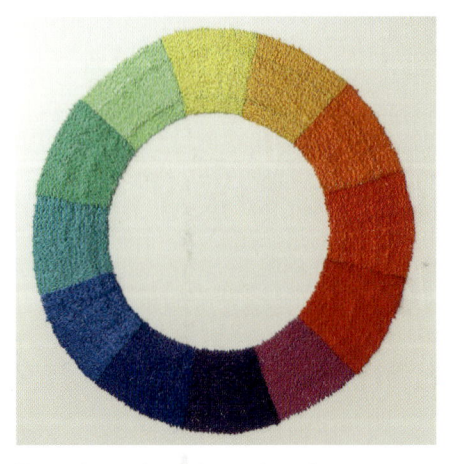

This colour wheel shows the primary, secondary and tertiary colours positioned in the correct order. The colour wheel can be divided into a cool side and a warm side. The cool half contains yellow-green, green, green-blue, blue, blue-violet and violet; the warm side contains red-violet, red, red-orange, orange, orange-yellow and yellow.

A printer would use yellow, cyan and magenta as their primary colours: yellow + cyan = green; yellow + magenta = red; magenta + cyan = purple. I often use the printer's combination when mixing colours for painting because it produces a vibrant colour key.

Grouping fabric and threads together can help you to choose your colour scheme. This selection of analogous colours are near each other on the warm side of the colour wheel.

Sourcing Materials

When choosing fabrics, threads and stabilizers you need to think about the design, how it will be stitched and the methods used to turn it into a finished item. Ask yourself lots of questions about colour, texture, quantity and quality. Does the colour suit the design? Does texture or the pattern work well with the design? Does the fabric handle well? Is the fibre content suitable for the design? Are the materials and threads of good quality? Do the threads need to be thick, thin, shiny or matt? Do you have enough supplies to finish the embroidery? Will the machine stitch the chosen threads and fabrics nicely? How do you need to prepare the fabrics? How will you transfer the design? Should you stitch samples?

For instance, fabrics chosen for chopping and inclusion in water-soluble film embroideries would be very different from those chosen for a thickly embroidered design. When the fabric is chosen think about how it is going to be supported during the embroidery process. Does it need backing with an iron-on or tear-away stabilizer? Would it stitch better backed with a layer of cotton? Will the fabric need hooping to prevent shrinkage?

Fabric that needs bonding to interfacing or heat-fusible glues needs to withstand heat. Some fabrics can shrink or scorch when subjected to heat, and this can spell disaster for a finished embroidery. If in doubt, stitch a small sample with the chosen fabric to test how it reacts to being embroidered, ironed and immersed in water.

Eagerness can lead to mistakes. I once completed an embroidery to find out the

A primary colour scheme uses red, yellow and blue or various tints, tones or shades of these colours. This simple mix can be used to add a happy mood to embroideries.

Secondary colour schemes use orange, violet and green. Primary and secondary colour schemes are triadic, meaning the colours are evenly spaced from each other on the colour wheel.

A warm colour scheme is taken from the warm side of the colour wheel. Warm colours include yellow, orange and red, plus various tints, tones or shades of these colours including peach, pink, purple, burgundy, etc.

A cool colour scheme uses the green, blue and violet hues found on the cool side of the colour wheel. The hues on this side must contain some blue for them to be considered cool.

A complementary colour scheme uses colours that are opposite each other on the colour wheel. In this case blue and orange have been used to create a combination that is both calming and vibrant.

Split complementary schemes use a colour from one side of the colour wheel and two from the opposite side. Imagine an elongated triangle placed on top of the colour wheel; the split complementary colours are located near the points of the triangle.

Monochromatic colour schemes use tints, tones and shades of one colour. This simply means that white, grey or black are added to the base colour to alter the hue. Tints are made with white, tones have grey added and shades are made by adding black.

Achromatic colour schemes are made up of neutral whites, greys and blacks. Greyscale schemes can be overpowering and dramatic; adding a few pastel shades can lift the embroidery and make it a bit more joyous.

fabric shrank when ironed, and it is upsetting to make a mistake like this when a project is nearly complete. Errors can be remedied; in this case the embroidery was cut from the fabric and appliquéd onto another background.

When you have chosen your fabric you need to decide how to transfer the design. Is the fabric translucent enough to trace the design? Does the design need to be transferred with dressmaker's carbon or would it be easier to use a layer of water-soluble film with the design traced onto it? Can the design be printed onto paper so that the outlines can be stitched through to the fabric?

Choosing Thread

Thread choice is dictated by the theme or subject matter of the embroidery; some projects require careful colour-matching whilst others allow for creative colour schemes. When choosing thread you need to think about weight, colour, composition, type and quality. It is wise to select threads in person or use a wrapped shade card because colours can be very different when seen in print or on the screen.

The weight of the thread dictates how detailed the stitching can be. If the design contains lots of detailed line work it would be best to choose a fine lightweight thread such as no. 40 or no. 60: the first is a normal weight thread and the latter is extremely fine. The thinner the thread, the easier it is to stitch fine details. The only drawback with fine thread is that takes longer to stitch because the thread has less coverage. In most cases no. 40 is the best weight to choose; it stitches well when used for free machine embroidery and for set utility patterns, sewn with a presser foot and feeder teeth up.

Choose good-quality branded threads because you can't guarantee that cheap ones will work or be available to buy again if you run out. The chosen brand must have a wide range of colours; it can be annoying to find the manufacturer does not produce the shade you need. If you choose a colour from another manufacturer you may find that the thread has a different texture or sheen from the others used in the embroidery.

When choosing thread you should also think about fibre content because what the thread is made of influences the texture of the stitches. Cotton thread produces a matt stitch whilst rayon, viscose or polyester create a shinier stitch. If you use threads with a sheen you need to about think how the gloss affects the embroidery design. Changing stitch type or direction subtly alters the surface of the embroidery making the threads appear darker or lighter in colour. More information about choosing threads can be found in Chapter 6, which covers thread-painting, and Chapter 11, which looks at animals and birds.

The type of thread used also changes the style of the design: for instance, a peacock feather stitched with plain cotton threads could be bland and unexciting; if it were stitched with metallic threads it would instantly be transformed into an opulent embroidery which has more in common with its subject matter. You also need to learn to vary the threads used: some projects work better if a combination of threads are used and, for instance, areas of solid stitch used to embroider a pattern design could be lifted if they are outlined with metallic thread. Threads also help with composition if a design has references to distance, a combination of thick and thin threads can be used to create an illusion of space between things: for instance, in a landscape thinner threads could be used in the background whilst thick threads could be used to stitch objects that are close to the front of the design.

Planning the Work

All projects can be broken down into steps or stages of work. In order to complete the embroidery successfully you need to think about what needs to be done and how to order the method of working so the stages can be placed in the correct order.

The first stages involve preparation: this could include washing, measuring, cutting, ironing, stabilizing and transferring the design to the fabric. When cutting fabric for a project, seam allowances or flaps should be added to the measurements so there is enough fabric to allow for hooping, framing, lacing or sewing seams. If you have not included enough fabric you will find it difficult to complete a project without adding more fabric to finish it. Adding extra fabric at a late stage can create structural and visual weaknesses within the design.

If the project has a design or pattern this needs to be transferred to the fabric before any embroidery can be done. It is important to choose a method that suits the design or chosen fabric. For instance, it may be difficult to trace a design onto dark fabric so another method (such as using dressmaker's carbon or drawing the design onto water-soluble film) may be more suitable.

The next stages include supporting the fabric and setting up the machine. It may be helpful to revisit some questions asked during the design process because the answers decide how the machine is set up and how the fabric is supported during the embroidery process. Free machine designs need the feeder teeth to be dropped and a darning or embroidery foot attached whilst set stitches need the feeder teeth up and a straight-stitch foot attached. Fabric that is going to be heavily embroidered with straight stitch needs to be kept taut; hooping keeps the fabric in tension and prevents it from pulling badly.

The machine needs a needle inserted that is suitable for the type of thread and fabric. Most threads can be sewn with a size 90/14 universal needle whilst others, such as metallics, may require a specialist needle. Some stitches are produced with altered tension or a loose bobbin; if these stitches are used the machine will need setting up so that it is ready to create these special stitches. If your design uses stitches such as moss or cable you need to use a spare bobbin case or alter the tension spring of the one you are using. When the machine is set up it is advisable to test the stitch and threads on a hooped scrap of fabric; testing ensures that tension or thread problems can be corrected before the main project is started.

The next thing to plan is which part of the design to stitch first. Complex designs need to be broken down into areas of colour or stitch type; this ensures that individual parts of the design are stitched in the correct order.

Don't forget that the positioning of the hoop can also influence the order of stitching. It may be more economical to embroider the area within the hoop before moving it to another part of the design.

The order of stitching depends on the type of design. If a detailed subject is being stitched it is best to leave the intricate stitches until last so that they are not covered up by subsequent layers of stitching. I treat portraits differently: it's best to stitch the details first because getting eyes, noses or mouths wrong can result in a lot of wasted time and thread.

It is very difficult to unpick mistakes in detailed embroidery without catching the surrounding stitches. Once a colour is stitched you may find that you need to work into it with another layer of stitches to get an even colour blend, neater edge or better sense of realism. Landscape designs need to be stitched so the distant elements are stitched first: the background is stitched first, then the mid-ground then the foreground. More examples and projects about the order of stitching can be found in Chapter 6 (thread-painting), Chapter 10 (embroidering the landscape) and Chapter 11 (animals and birds).

When the embroidery is finished it needs to be checked to make sure it is ready to be made up into a finished image or item. It is advisable to leave the embroidery untouched for a few days so you can look at it with refreshed insight. You should check if any more work needs doing and trim or take the loose threads to the back of the fabric. If you have used water-soluble film the embroidery must be washed and dried before it's ironed. Pressing the embroidery removes the handling marks or bulges caused by stitching and gets it ready for the final stage of the process.

Finishing the Embroidery

Finishing or making up the project should be carefully planned; this is really important if the embroidery is going to be made into something like a bag or cushion. The embroidery needs to be measured and any markings should be made in an area that is not visible or done with a chalk pencil that can be brushed away. The measurements should be double-checked before any initial cuts are made into the fabric or embroidery; any mistakes could be disastrous at this stage. It may be helpful to make a pattern of the project with calico or paper before cutting into the actual embroidery.

If seams need sewing you need to decide how to secure the pieces and plan which ones need stitching together first. You need to think about how to trim or neaten the seams so they press neatly. The item may need to be turned through so you must remember to leave a gap in the seam for turning. If trimmings such as zips, ribbon or buttons are used you must add them at the right time: for example, ribbons may need to be added halfway through the process so raw ends are hidden inside seams; a zip needs to be sewn in before making the item up.

Embroideries that are going to be made into images need thoughtful preparation. More care must be taken with measuring the fabric so the embroidery is positioned correctly when it is framed. The type of mount or frame used must suit the style of embroidery: traditional embroideries may suit framing behind glass more than a modern work. A modern embroidery could be enhanced by using another method of display such as showing raw edges or turning it into a hanging. More ideas about how to finish and frame embroideries can be found in Chapter 12.

This working drawing for the paisley pennant has been coloured in to remind me what colours to use for the small teardrop shapes around the paisley design.

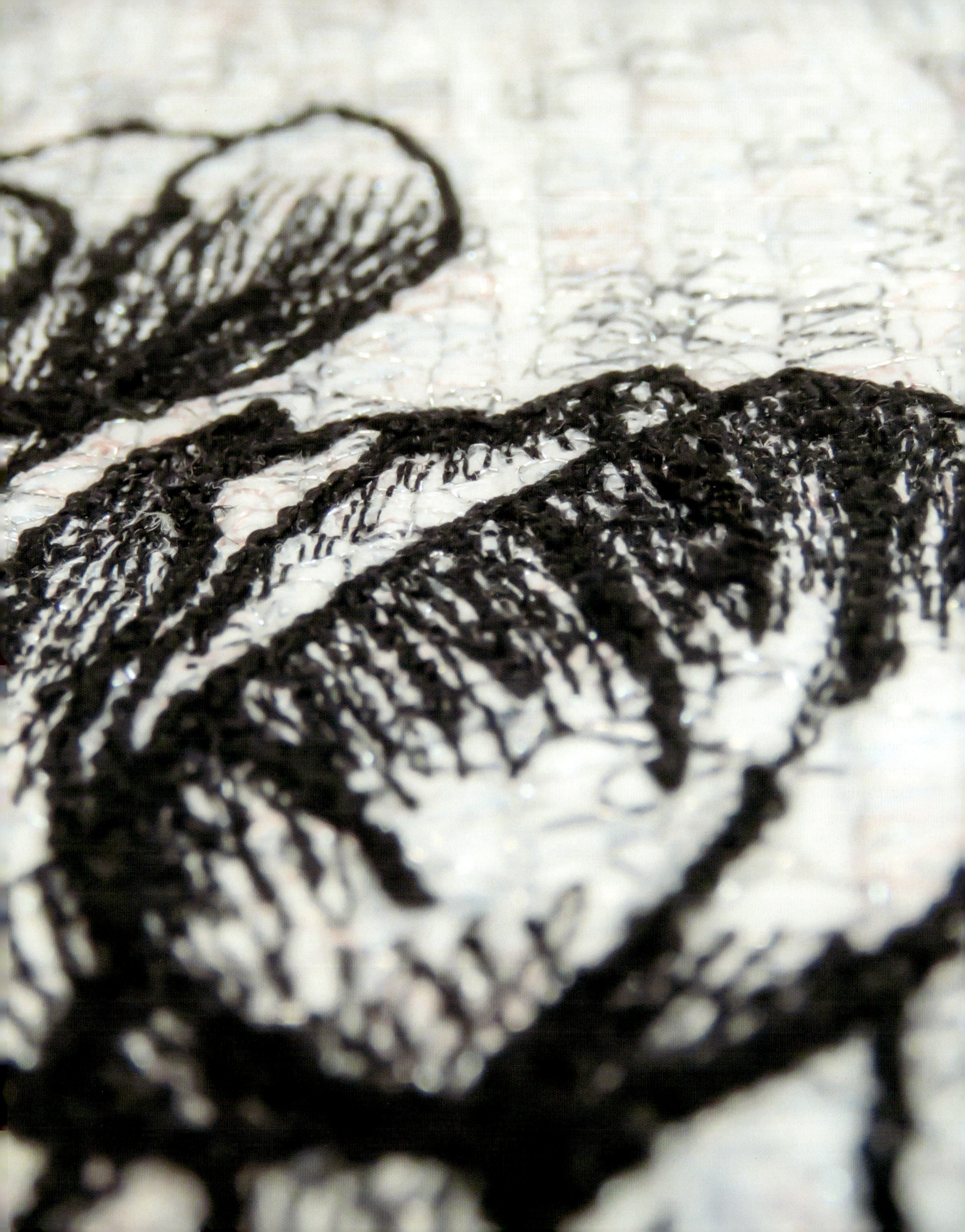

CHAPTER 4

Raising the Teeth – Using Set Stitches for Machine Embroidery

Creating a stitched line or design with a straight stitch presser foot means you are reliant on the feeder teeth to move the fabric. This chapter is about finding the optimal balance for stitch length and speed. You need to discover how much pressure needs to be applied to the foot pedal to make the machine work. For instance, using too much pressure with a long stitch makes the machine work fast and the fabric moves along quickly. If the stitch length is short or set to nil the fabric won't move at all and the stitching builds up to create a thick clump of thread.

The feeder teeth move the fabric when using a normal presser foot so it's important to learn how to guide the fabric so the needle follows the design, the previous row of stitching or the seam. Using simple straight stitch to embroider a project demonstrates how to move or turn the fabric so that the design is stitched accurately. Learning this level of control helps you become more confident and it will help you to become a more advanced embroiderer.

Machine Embroidery with the Feeder Teeth Up

Working in this way means the machine is in control of feeding the fabric over the needle plate to create the stitch. Some machines have thousands of set patterns; look at your machine or use the manual to locate the stitch type dial or selector. I will be using my basic Janome throughout this chapter; it has twenty set stitches. The first ten can be selected by moving the stitch pattern selector dial to A, B, C, D, E, F, G, H, I and J. Ten more patterns can be selected by moving the stitch length dial to S.S which stands for stretch stitch.

Lengthening, shortening, narrowing and widening stitches produce even more variations of these set patterns.

Simple machines have feeder teeth that move the fabric backwards and forwards; complex models may have teeth that move the fabric from side to side as well. Stitching the following samplers help you get used to how your machine moves the fabric under the presser foot. The best way to get neat stitching is to hold the fabric lightly and guide it so the stitching is straight; don't push or pull the fabric, just let the foot and the feeder teeth do their job.

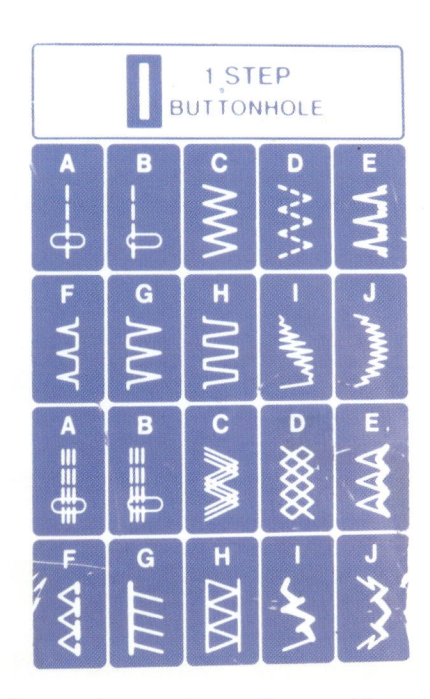

Your machine may have a diagram of the utility or fancy stitch patterns printed on it. It is important to actually use each utility stitch because the image on the machine can look very different from the sewn stitch.

SAMPLER

STITCHING SET PATTERNS

This sampler shows how to achieve variations of patterned utility stitches, including straight stitch, zigzag, satin stitch, tricot stitch, blind hem stitch, box stitch and other decorative patterns.

YOU WILL NEED

Equipment
- Sewing machine
- Straight-stitch presser foot
- Normal tension bobbin case
- Empty bobbins
- Size 90/14 universal machine needle
- Fabric scissors
- Embroidery scissors
- Ruler
- Dressmaker's chalk pencil or artist's watercolour pencil
- Pencil sharpener
- Eraser

Materials
- White thread for the bobbin
- Two variegated threads for threading the needle
- Two pieces of calico or stiff cotton approximately 32 × 23cm (12½ × 9in.) washed and ironed, ready for use

Machine used
- Janome JF 1018s
- Feeder teeth up
- Normal tension

1 Set the feeder teeth to raised and attach the presser foot used for straight stitch and zigzag. Wind a bobbin with white thread and insert it into the normal tension bobbin case, then slot the loaded case into the machine. Insert a size 90/14 universal needle into the needle clamp and secure. Thread the needle with a strong variegated thread, then turn the hand wheel to bring both threads through the needle plate and pull both threads to position them behind the foot.

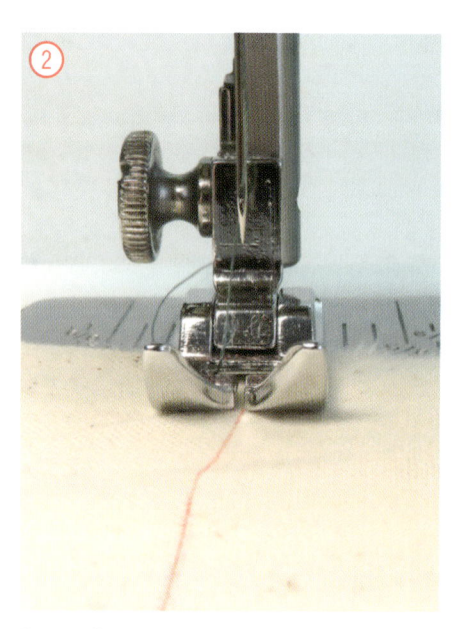

2 Draw a line along the width of the calico with a chalk pencil, position the ruler near the edge and keep the line straight. Place the calico under the presser foot so the drawn line lines up with the needle or the side of the foot; lower the presser foot when the fabric is in position.

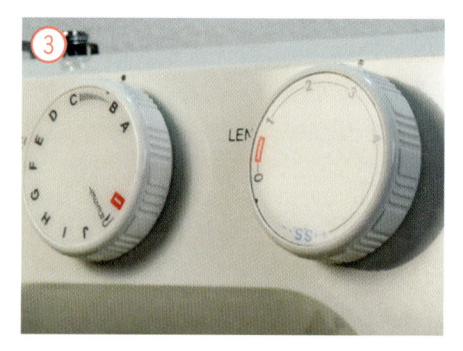

3 Set the stitch type to straight and the stitch length to medium. Sew a row of straight stitch along the drawn line, keeping the sewn line as straight as possible. Re-position the edge of the foot against the sewn line and sew another row of stitch. These rows of straight stitch teach you how to guide the fabric and to sew in straight lines, which are essential for surface decoration or seaming.

54 Chapter 4 – Raising the Teeth – Using Set Stitches for Machine Embroidery

④

Set the stitch type to narrow zigzag and line the edge of the foot up against the previous row of straight stitch sewing. Stitch a row of narrow zigzag then change the settings to sew one row of medium and one of large zigzag. As you stitch, notice how the needle moves from side to side to create the zigzag pattern.

⑤

Set the stitch type set to narrow zigzag and change the stitch length to satin stitch. Sew a row of narrow satin stitch, then reset the width to medium and sew another row. Continue experimenting with the width of the stitch to see how it alters the texture of the thread. I ended up sewing a few lines of satin stitch to try to get the tension right as the dots of bobbin thread indicated there was a problem somewhere.

⑥

Set the stitch length to medium and select another stitch; I chose setting D, tricot stitch. Sew a row at these settings (shown R), then shorten the stitch length and sew another row. Choose another pattern and sew one row set to medium stitch length and another row set to a shorter stitch length. Changing the length of the stitch alters the appearance of the patterned stitch.

⑦

Continue sewing until you have sampled at least ten set stitch patterns. Try to stitch two versions of each pattern, one with a normal stitch length and one with a shorter stitch length.

⑧

If there is enough space left on your calico, continue experimenting with the set stitches that appeal to you. Keep the fabric facing the same way because it could become confusing if patterns are rotated; some utility stitches have a definite left and right side.

⑨

The finished sample shows how versatile ten set stitch types can be. Patterned stitches can be used on their own or grouped together to make textured layers of stitch. The colour changes in the variegated threads enhance the decorative nature of the patterns and reveal the subtle changes in stitch direction.

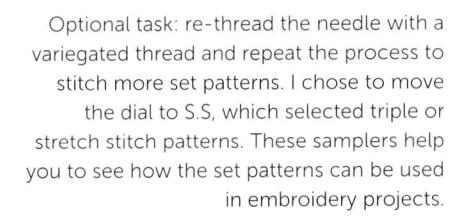

Optional task: re-thread the needle with a variegated thread and repeat the process to stitch more set patterns. I chose to move the dial to S.S, which selected triple or stretch stitch patterns. These samplers help you to see how the set patterns can be used in embroidery projects.

Chapter 4 – Raising the Teeth – Using Set Stitches for Machine Embroidery 55

SAMPLER

EMBROIDERING SET PATTERNS WITH A TWIN NEEDLE

Set stitches embroidered with a twin needle can be very striking. Contrasting or matching colours can be used to sew the parallel rows of stitch. Select a twin needle that is narrow enough to fit the hole in the presser foot and the hole in the needle plate. If zigzag or wide utility stitches are used, it is advisable to turn the hand wheel slowly to see if the twin needle has enough clearance; if the needle is too wide it will break. I used two needle widths for this sampler, the wide 4/80 needle is used for straight stitch and the narrow 1.6/70 needle is used for the wide patterned stitches. Don't turn or rotate the fabric whilst a twin needle is in the fabric because doing so breaks or twists the shaft of the needle.

YOU WILL NEED

Equipment
- Sewing machine
- Straight-stitch presser foot
- Normal tension bobbin case
- Empty bobbins
- Size 4/80 twin needle for straight stitch
- Size 1.6/70 twin needle for wide patterned utility stitches like zigzag
- Fabric scissors
- Embroidery scissors
- Ruler
- Dressmaker's chalk pencil or artist's watercolour pencil
- Pencil sharpener
- Eraser

Materials
- Black bobbin thread
- Red and black thread for the needles
- Calico or stiff cotton approximately 32 × 23cm (12½ × 9in.)

Machine used
- Janome JF 1018s
- Feeder teeth up
- Normal tension

1. Set the feeder teeth to the raised position. Insert a bobbin wound with black into the normal tension bobbin case and slot it into the machine. Insert a size 4/80 twin needle into the needle clamp and secure. Attach the presser foot and thread the left needle with black thread and the right with red thread. Turn the hand wheel to bring the bobbin thread to the top and pull the three threads to position them behind the foot.

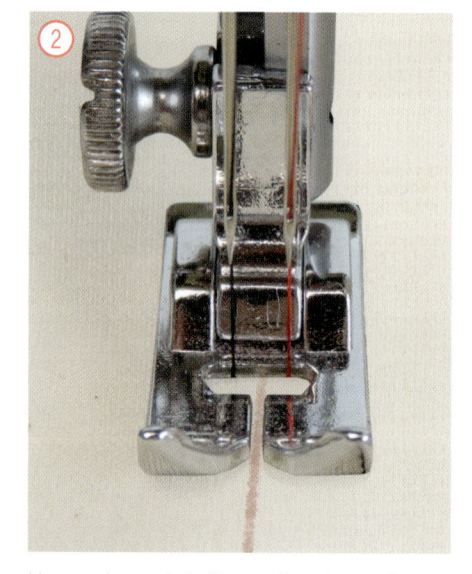

2. Use a ruler and chalk pencil to draw a line along the width of the calico near to the left edge. Place the calico under the foot so the beginning of the drawn line corresponds with the edge of the foot or the inside gap; when the fabric is in position lower the presser foot.

③

Make sure the needle is set to the middle position, select straight stitch and set the stitch length to medium. Stitch a row of straight stitch along the chalk line, remove the fabric and trim the thread tails. Re-position the fabric under the foot so the stitching lines up with the edge of the foot. Change the stitch length and sew two more rows of straight stitch. Sewing lines of straight stitch gets you accustomed to stitching with a twin needle.

④

Set the stitch type to triple stitch and stitch one row, then change the stitch length and sew another row of triple stitch next to the previous one. The difference in stitch length is more noticeable with triple stitch because the extra thread creates little bumps along the row of stitching.

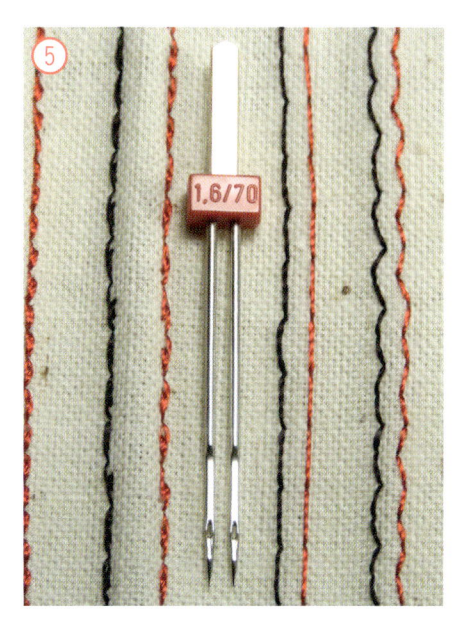

⑤

The 4/80 twin needle was too wide to produce the larger utility patterns, Testing the width of the needle by turning the hand wheel revealed that the needle would hit the side of the foot if used. If the needle is too wide swap it to a smaller size; I used a 1.6/70 twin needle for the rest of the sampler. The difference in width is clearly shown by the distance between the rows of straight stitch.

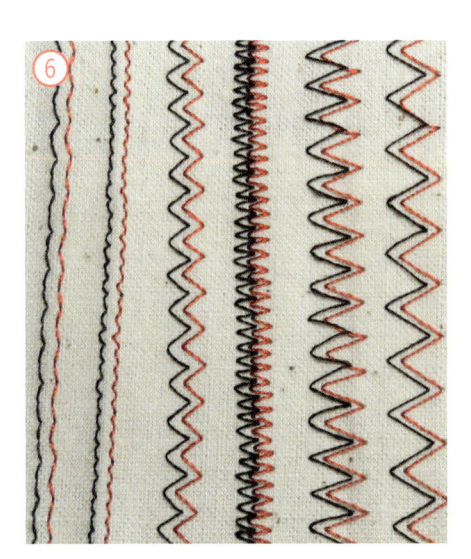

⑥

Set the stitch type to narrow zigzag and make the stitch length long. Stitch one row of zigzag at this setting, then sew more rows changing the width and length each time. You will see how using the twin needle adds more interest to plain zigzag stitch.

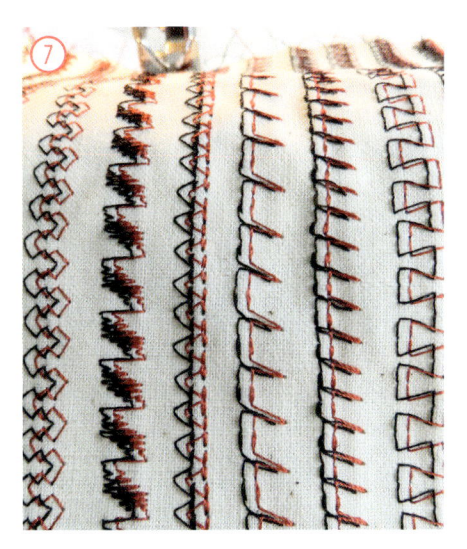

⑦

Continue testing the utility stitches until the calico is filled, choosing set patterns from the earlier sampler and stitching variations of them. Remember to check if the gap in the foot is wide enough for the needle to stitch the pattern.

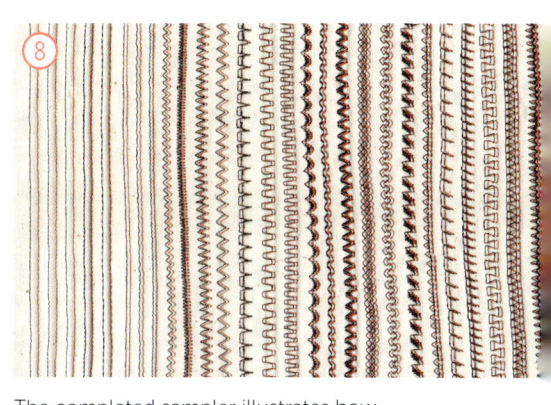

⑧

The completed sampler illustrates how effective set patterns can be when stitched with a twin needle. Some of the set patterns could be incorporated into crazy patchwork or appliqué projects to create bold stitched decoration.

Chapter 4 – Raising the Teeth – Using Set Stitches for Machine Embroidery

SAMPLER

Stitching Set Patterns with Cable Stitch

Cable stitch is sometimes called under-thread or bobbin embroidery because the best or right side of the embroidery is worked under the fabric instead of on top. Cable stitch is produced when a thicker thread or yarn is wound onto the bobbin. This stitch requires a loose bobbin case and normal top tension. If you are wary of altering the bobbin case tension, it may be necessary to purchase a spare bobbin case.

Cable stitch performs best when smooth flexible yarns are used as bumpy ones can get caught in the bobbin case causing the thread to break or get stuck. You may need to adjust the tension screw on the bobbin case for different thread weights: for example, thin no. 12 thread needs a different setting from that for thick cotton perle. Cable stitch works best for set stitches that are simple and spaced out; complicated patterns may create lumps of thread or unsightly tangles.

YOU WILL NEED

Equipment
- Sewing machine
- Size 90/14 universal machine needle
- Straight-stitch presser foot
- Spare bobbin case for loose tension embroidery
- Empty bobbins
- Small slotted screwdriver
- Embroidery scissors
- Fabric scissors
- Dressmaker's chalk pencil or artist's watercolour pencil
- Pencil sharpener
- Eraser
- Ruler

Materials
- Strong polyester, viscose or rayon top threads
- Various smooth yarns and threads for winding onto the bobbin: suitable yarns include cotton perle, stranded cotton, four-ply yarn, no. 12 machine thread, chainette yarn, thin viscose cord and double knitting yarn
- Calico or stiff cotton approximately 32 × 23cm (12½ × 9 in.)

Machine used
- Janome JF 1018s
- Feeder teeth up
- Loose bobbin thread tension

The colour of the top thread is important because of the tension differences; small dots of it are clearly visible along the stitch. For instance, if you want the dots to be an obvious part of the design, choose a contrasting top thread to make them stand out more; if you want the dots to be less noticeable, colour-match the top thread or use an invisible one. This sampler helps you discover how different yarns and threads influence the style of the cable stitch.

①

Wind a bobbin with variegated cotton perle. Thick thread can be wound by hand or machine; winding by machine produces better-quality bobbins. Insert the wound bobbin into the bobbin case and thread the cotton perle through the tension spring. You may need to loosen the tension screw with a screwdriver until the thread pulls out more freely.

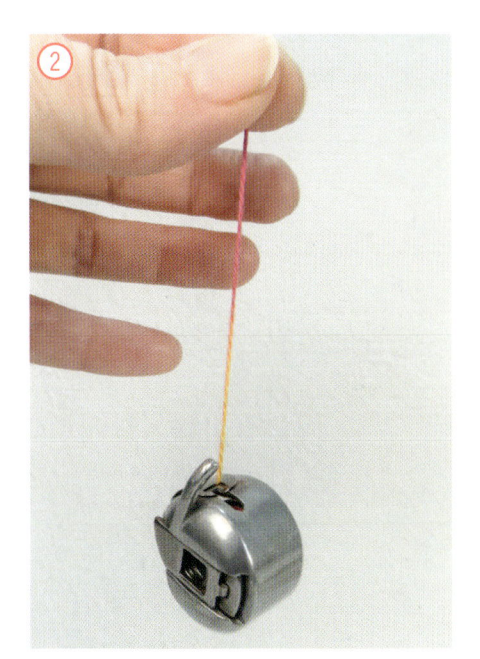

② Test the tension of the bobbin case by holding the end of the thread and letting the bobbin case dangle. Imagine you are holding a yo-yo and flick your hand downwards twice. If the thread stays in the same place the tension is too tight. If the threaded bobbin case drops 3 or 4cm (1 or 2in.) then the tension is correct. If the bobbin drops more than this the tension is too loose. Load the bobbin case into the machine. The best way to test the tension is to stitch a sample.

③ Attach a straight-stitch presser foot and insert a size 90/14 universal needle. Thread the needle with a strong plain thread and pull it through the eye until the thread length is approximately 10cm (4in). Turn the hand wheel so the needle lowers into the needle slot and bobbin race, then turn the hand wheel to bring the needle back up. Pull the end of the top thread until it brings the bobbin thread up through the needle plate. Pull both threads and position them behind the presser foot.

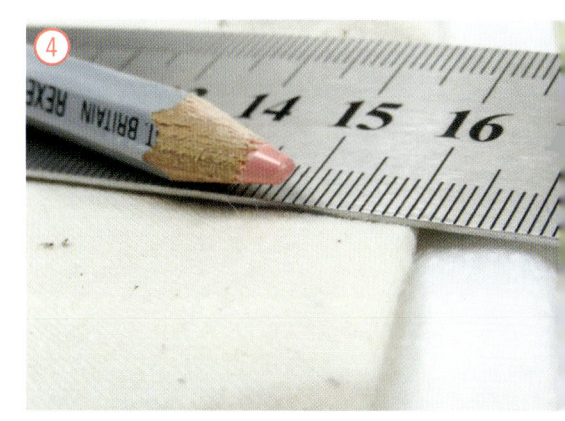

④ Use the chalk pencil and ruler to draw a line across the width of the calico near the left edge (I used a blunt pencil to draw a thicker line). Place the calico under the presser foot so the drawn line corresponds with the centre or side of the foot, then lower the foot. Set the stitch type to medium-length straight and start stitching a row of straight stitch along the drawn line; stop sewing when you have stitched 10cm (4in.) of straight stitch.

Chapter 4 – Raising the Teeth – Using Set Stitches for Machine Embroidery **59**

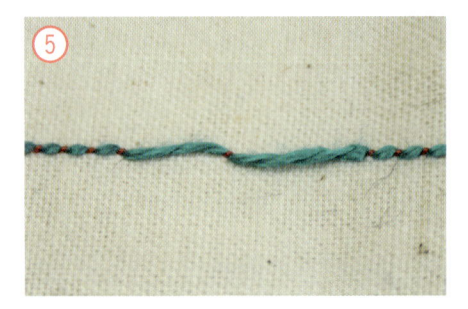

(5) Keep the presser foot lowered and carefully lift the corner of the calico to see if the cable stitch has worked. The cotton perle should be couched smoothly onto the underside of the calico; it should not have loops or missed stitches. If the cotton perle is loose, bobbin tension is too loose; if has pulled taut, the bobbin tension is too tight. You may need to adjust the top or bottom tension before you carry on stitching the sampler.

(6) When you are happy with the appearance of the cable stitch, finish off the first row. Stitch three more rows of straight stitch with the cotton perle. Vary the stitch length for each row of cable stitch: notice that changing the stitch length alters the spacing of the couching, thus changing the texture of the stitch.

(7) Change the stitch type to zigzag, set the stitch length to medium and sew a row of zigzag. Turn the calico over to see how the cable stitch has been sewn. The thinner top thread should only be visible as dots or tiny loops at the edge of the stitch. Sew three or four rows of zigzag, changing the stitch width and length settings, to experiment with the look of the stitching.

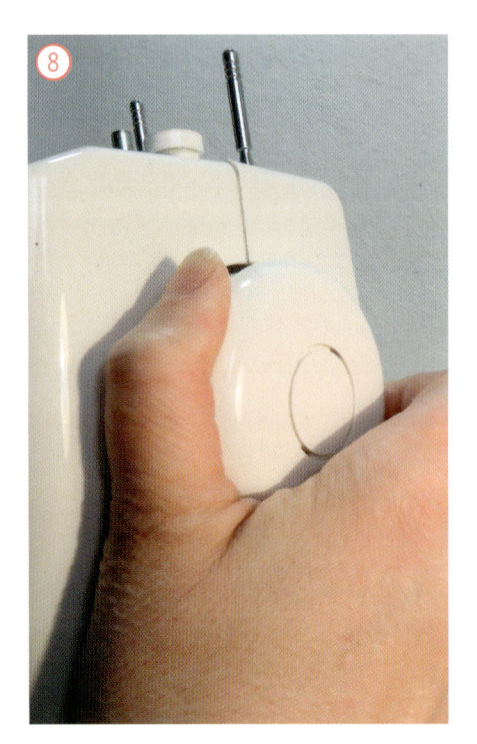

(8) Wind a heavy no. 12 weight machine thread onto an empty bobbin, then insert the wound bobbin into the loose bobbin case. Thread the needle with a strong colour-matched thread. Use the hand wheel to bring both threads to the top and pull the thread ends into position behind the presser foot.

(9) Set the stitch type to straight stitch and sew one row of cable stitch; turn the calico over to see how the stitch has formed. You may need to tighten the tension screw on the bobbin case because this thread is thinner than cotton perle. When you are happy with the tension sew a few more rows of straight stitch close to one another to create dense stitching.

60   Chapter 4 – Raising the Teeth – Using Set Stitches for Machine Embroidery

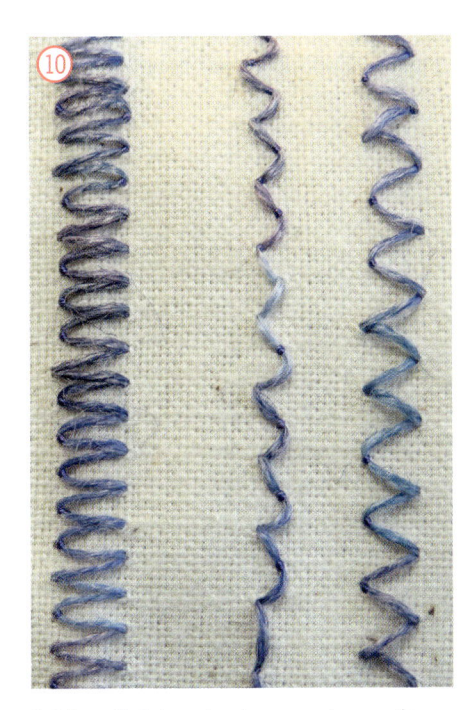

⑩

Set the stitch type to zigzag and sew a few rows to experiment with the width and length of this stitch. I started with a wide zigzag stitch set very near to the stitch length used for satin stitch. Madeira Lana can cope with close stitching and direction changes because it is finer and more flexible than cotton perle.

⑪

Choose some simple utility or set patterns and sew one row of each. Guide the foot along the edge of the previous row to keep the stitching straight. I chose to stitch two rows of tricot, then one row each of box, honeycomb and triple zigzag stitch.

⑫

Wind some stranded cotton onto an empty bobbin and place it in the loose tension bobbin case; insert the loaded bobbin case into the machine. Thread the needle with a strong colour-matched thread. Turn the hand wheel to bring both threads to the top. Reset the stitch type to straight and sew one line with straight stitch. The bobbin tension may need to be loosened because stranded cotton is thicker than the last thread used. Sew two or three rows of open utility stitches such as zigzag or tricot stitch to see how the thread copes with the changes in direction.

⑬

Wind a bobbin with chainette or knitted yarn; I chose metallic viscose for extra sparkle. You may need to lower the tension of the bobbin case because these knitted yarns have a rough texture. Thread the needle with a strong colour-matched thread and use the hand wheel to bring the bobbin thread to the top. Set the stitch to straight stitch and sew a row with a short stitch length, then reset the stitch length to long and stitch another row. Using various stitch lengths shows how the thin top thread couches or wraps the bottom thread to the fabric.

⑭

Reset the stitch type to zigzag and sew three or four rows with different stitch settings. Knitted yarns are not as flexible as cotton perle or stranded cotton so you may notice that they pull the top thread through to create spokes either side of the couched thread. If you don't like this effect you can try tightening the top tension but this might pull the fabric in, causing distortions.

Chapter 4 – Raising the Teeth – Using Set Stitches for Machine Embroidery **61**

⑮

Re-thread the needle with a variegated thread and wind some pale viscose cord onto an empty bobbin. Insert the wound bobbin into the loose bobbin case. Load the bobbin case into the machine and use the hand wheel to bring the bobbin thread to the top. Set the stitch type to medium-length straight stitch and sew one row of straight stitch. If the tension is okay, stitch three or four more rows of straight stitch with short and long stitch lengths. Straight stitch reveals how the top thread wraps the thicker bobbin thread to change the latter's colour and appearance.

⑯

Choose some simple utility or patterned stitches and experiment with these until you run out of space. You may notice that dots of upper thread are formed where the needle enters and exits the calico; this is most noticeable on the edge of the stretch stitch pattern shown R.

⑰

Turn the fabric over. The finished sampler shows how the thickness of the thread can alter the way the stitch is sewn: for instance, it is more difficult to sew utility or patterned stitches with a thick or stiff thread.

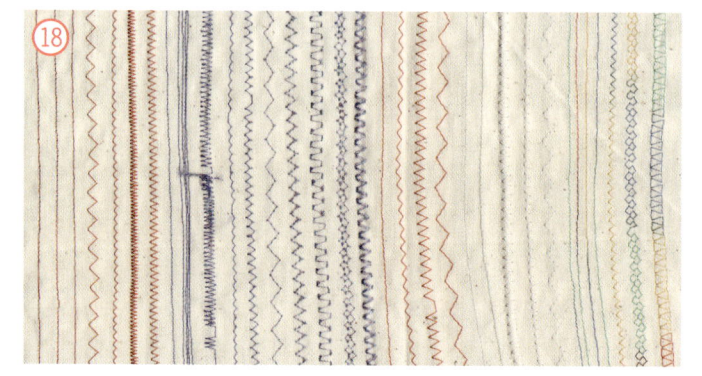

⑱

The front (working side) of the fabric reveals what colours were used through the needle, where the threads broke and where stitches were missed. Broken threads and missed stitches could indicate that the machine needs a new needle or a clean; they may also show that the tension settings were not quite right or it didn't like the choice of threads.

62 Chapter 4 – Raising the Teeth – Using Set Stitches for Machine Embroidery

SAMPLER

Couching Yarns onto a Background Fabric

Machine couching can be done with a normal presser foot or cording foot. Couching round yarns with a normal presser foot can be more difficult because the foot can push the yarn to one side before it has been caught by stitching. This sampler teaches you how to manipulate the yarn so it is couched neatly when using a normal presser foot. If you have a wobble, simply unpick and start again.

There are some advantages to using a regular presser foot; thicker, bulky or fluffy yarns can be couched with a normal presser foot, and these types of yarn may not fit through the channels in a cording foot. If the design requires precision or multiple rows of corded yarn you will get better results from a cording foot because the thread channels separate and guide the threads. If you decide to invest in a cording foot check your manual before you buy or ask a reputable dealer for advice.

YOU WILL NEED

Equipment
- Sewing machine
- Size 90/14 universal machine needle
- Straight-stitch presser foot
- Cording foot (if you have one)
- Strong polyester, viscose or rayon top threads
- Embroidery scissors
- Fabric scissors
- Scissors for cutting the yarn
- Dressmaker's chalk pencil or artist's watercolour pencil
- Pencil sharpener
- Eraser
- Ruler

Materials
- Various yarns, threads and ribbons: suitable yarns include four-ply yarn, cotton perle, chainette yarn, tape yarn and fashion yarns
- Calico or stiff cotton approximately 32 x 23 cm (12½ x 9in.)

Machine used
- Janome JF 1018s
- Feeder teeth up
- Normal tension

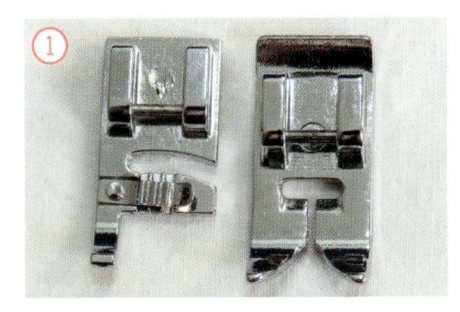

① Clip-on machine feet for a Janome sewing machine. The cording foot shown L has three channels through which to guide thread, cord or yarn; the straight-stitch presser foot shown R can also be used for couching threads.

② Set up the machine, make sure the feeder teeth are in the raised position and Insert a bobbin wound with white into the normal tension bobbin case. Attach the straight-stitch presser foot, insert a size 90/14 universal needle into the needle holder and thread the needle with strong variegated thread, then use the hand wheel to bring both threads to the top.

③ Use a ruler and chalk pencil to draw a line along the width of the calico near the left edge. Place the calico under the foot so the drawn line matches a reference point on the foot or the needle. Set the stitch to a narrow zigzag and position the yarn to be corded under the foot. Lower the foot and turn the hand wheel; the needle needs to pierce the fabric either side of the yarn, so alter the width of the stitch so that the needle enters the fabric close to the yarn.

④

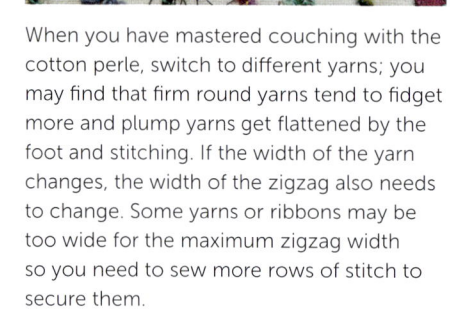

Sew a few stitches to secure the cotton perle. When it is secured you need to use one hand to pull it gently towards you to keep it taut; this makes it much easier to couch it under the zigzag. As you stitch you may discover the presser foot pushes the cotton perle out of line; try to anticipate this and guide the cotton perle back into position under the foot. Remember to keep your fingertips well away from the moving needle.

⑤

When you have mastered couching with the cotton perle, switch to different yarns; you may find that firm round yarns tend to fidget more and plump yarns get flattened by the foot and stitching. If the width of the yarn changes, the width of the zigzag also needs to change. Some yarns or ribbons may be too wide for the maximum zigzag width so you need to sew more rows of stitch to secure them.

⑥

Swap the normal presser foot for a cording foot; the Janome cording foot has three channels. Choose a thin yarn and cut three lengths slightly longer than the width of the calico. Thread one piece of yarn through each channel of the foot so there is about 2.5cm (1in.) of yarn behind the foot.

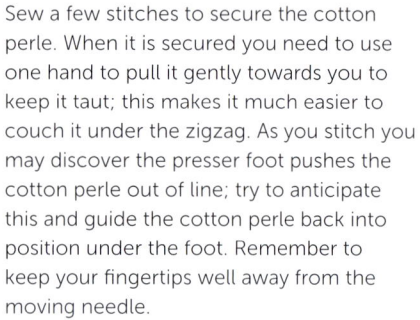

⑦

Change the stitch type to tricot and lower the cording foot. Keep hold of the thread tails at the rear of the foot and sew a few stitches to secure them. When the yarn is secured pull the yarns taut as you stitch; this keeps the yarn in the channels of the cording foot to produce straight, neatly couched threads.

⑧

Thread the cording foot with different types of yarn and stitch them to the calico background with tricot stitch. Mix thick and thin yarns together and change the top thread to see how it alters the appearance of the couched yarn. Some yarns don't flow as easily as others; the fluffy mohair and chenille did get stuck so they are not really suitable for use with this cording foot.

64 Chapter 4 – Raising the Teeth – Using Set Stitches for Machine Embroidery

⑨ Change the stitch type to medium straight stitch and lower the needle to see which cording foot channel is closest. Thread some four-ply cotton or similar weight yarn through the corresponding slot in the cording foot. Keep hold of the yarn tail behind the cording foot and straight-stitch down the centre of the yarn to secure it. This method of couching can be much harder to master but the stitches that hold the yarn in place are nearly invisible because they sink into the yarn.

⑩ Experiment with couching some more yarns and threads, varying the stitches and threads used to couch them. Try using some simple utility stitches or vary the number of yarns threaded through the cording foot. If you use a wide stitch, check the gap in the cording foot is wide enough for the needle to move without hitting the foot.

⑪ The finished sampler shows that a variety of yarns can be couched onto a background fabric. The yarns sewn with a normal straight-stitch foot have more wobbles than those sewn with a cording foot. The yarns sewn with a cording foot are shown to the right of the zigzagged ribbon.

Chapter 4 – Raising the Teeth – Using Set Stitches for Machine Embroidery **65**

SAMPLER
WRAPPING THREADS OR YARN BY MACHINE

Yarns are wrapped on the machine to make them stronger or thicker or to simply cover them with embroidery thread so that they match the colour scheme of an embroidery project. Wrapped yarns can be incorporated into projects to add extra dimension to a flat embroidery; they can be used to outline areas of stitching or to hide seams and raw edges. Wrapped yarns can be used to make trimmings such as bag handles or looped to make fastenings.

Yarns are wrapped with the feeder teeth up and a presser or cording foot attached. Zigzag or satin stitch is used because the width of the stitch can be set so the needle falls either side of the chosen yarn. The needle needs to enter the needle plate either side of the yarn because the stitch interlocks either side of the yarn to encase or wrap it with embroidery thread. Yarns wrapped with an open zigzag will reveal some of the central core whilst yarns wrapped with close satin stitch become completely encased in stitch so little or none of the yarn core is visible.

When choosing embroidery threads to wrap central yarn it is important to remember that both sides of the wrapped yarn will be seen. For instance, if the wrapped cord has to be one colour the bobbin needs to be wound with the thread that is used through the needle; if a strong contrast is required the bobbin can be wound with a different colour from the one used through the needle.

Yarns wrapped with a presser foot become slightly flattened by the stitching so they have an oval shape, whilst yarns wrapped with the cording foot remain more rounded. Yarns used with the cording foot need to be thin because if they are too fat you won't be able to pull the wrapped cord through the foot. Both feet have their own benefits or quirks; this sampler will help you experiment to see which one you prefer using.

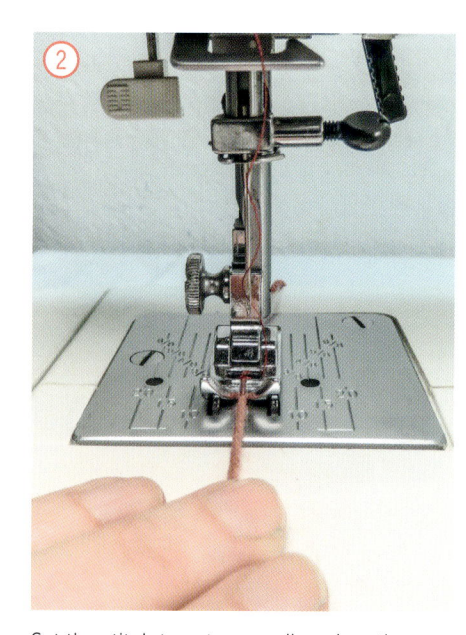

YOU WILL NEED

Equipment
- Sewing machine
- Size 90/14 universal machine needle
- Straight-stitch presser foot
- Cording foot if you have one and prefer to use one
- Empty bobbins
- Embroidery scissors
- Fabric scissors
- Scissors for cutting the yarn

Materials
- Strong viscose, rayon or polyester machine threads
- Metallic or glittery machine threads
- Various yarns, threads and wools for wrapping: suitable yarns include four-ply cotton, double knitting wool, chainette yarn and wrapped gimp

Machine used
- Janome JF 1018s
- Feeder teeth up
- Normal tension

① Insert a size 90/14 universal needle and attach the straight-stitch presser foot. When choosing a yarn to wrap it is best to begin with something smooth and round like cotton cord or cotton double knitting yarn. Wind an empty bobbin with strong embroidery thread and place it into the normal tension bobbin case, then thread the needle with a different shade of embroidery thread.

② Set the stitch type to a medium-length zigzag and turn the hand wheel to see where the needle falls. Place the yarn under the presser foot and lower it, leaving a tail of yarn measuring about 7.5cm (3in.) behind the foot. Adjust the width of the zigzag so it just about clears either side of the yarn.

③

Hold the thread tails and yarn behind the foot with one hand and keep the yarn taut in front of the foot with the other hand. Press down on the presser foot to sew the zigzag stitch and gently pull the yarn with the hand that is behind the foot. The yarn needs additional guidance because it is too thin for the feeder teeth to push it along. As the yarn passes under the foot the machine wraps it with an open zigzag.

④

The size of the cording foot channel does limit what kind of yarns can be wrapped. If the channel is too small it can catch on the zigzag or satin stitch making it harder to pull the yarn through the foot; this means the yarn could get stuck or be wrapped with uneven blocks of stitches.

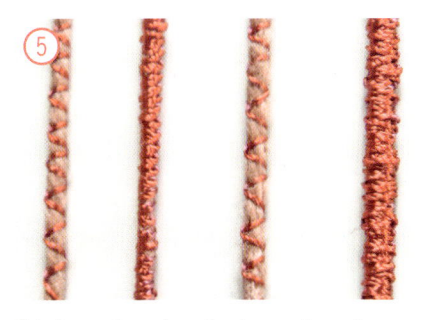

⑤

Stitch medium-length zigzag along the yarn; this setting creates an open stitch that reveals some of the central yarn. These are all cotton yarns: L to R: wrapped with one row of zigzag; wrapped with satin stitch; wrapped with two rows of zigzag; wrapped with three layers of satin stitch to create a thick wrapped cord.

⑥

Gold thread can be used to wrap plain cotton yarn. Yarn that is wrapped completely with satin stitch looks richly metallic, whilst open zigzag creates a subtle glittery effect. Layering metallic zigzag over previously wrapped yarn can completely change the look of the wrap; at R the green gimp is still visible below the metallic stitches.

Chapter 4 – Raising the Teeth – Using Set Stitches for Machine Embroidery **67**

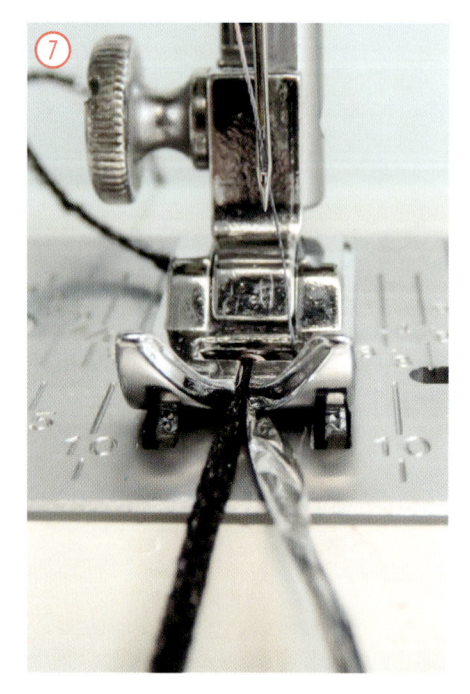

⑦ Two or three yarns can be wrapped together to create a thicker wrapped cord. This method is suitable for yarns or threads that are too fragile to be wrapped on their own. The yarns may need wrapping more than once to ensure they are all caught by the zigzag stitch. Rotating the yarn after the first wrap creates a rounder cord.

⑧ Cheap fluffy yarns like double knitting wool can be wrapped by machine. An open row of zigzag allows more of the fluffy yarn to show through. Building up layers of zigzag or satin stitch can tame the fluff and create an exclusive bespoke yarn. Once wrapped the soft flexible yarns can be plaited or twisted to make bag handles or cords for tassels.

⑨ The thread colour can be changed after each layer of open zigzag. Frequent thread changes can produce an ethnic styled wrap; the ends of the thread can also be cut close to the wrapped yarn to add to the rustic charm. This method is a great way to use up wound bobbins left over from other projects.

⑩ Thick bobbin thread can be used for wrapping. Swap the bobbin case for the loose tension one and insert a bobbin wound with thick thread. The thick thread appears on the underside of the wrapped yarn. The yarn needs more help because it's thicker; you may need to pull harder to get it to move under the foot. L: blue gimp wrapped with fine bouclé yarn; R: black double knitting wool wrapped with Madeira Glamour no. 12 thread Col. 3025 (pure gold).

STEP-BY-STEP PROJECT
Straight-stitch Tulip

YOU WILL NEED

Equipment
- Sewing machine
- Straight-stitch presser foot
- Size 90/14 universal machine needle
- Normal tension bobbin case
- Spare bobbin case for loose tension embroidery
- Empty bobbins
- Small slotted screwdriver
- Embroidery scissors
- Fabric scissors
- Glass-headed pins
- Hard pencil
- Pencil sharpener
- Eraser
- Set square
- Ruler
- Sharp hand-sewing needle
- Photocopier or scanner and printer
- Iron

Materials
- White A4 paper
- White non-woven mediumweight iron-on interfacing 23 × 18cm (9 × 7in.)
- Baking parchment
- White cotton or linen 23 × 18cm (9 × 7in.)
- Scrap of cotton fabric
- Madeira Classic thread nos. 40, 60 and 12 in black
- Madeira Classic thread no. 40 variegated in colour 2006 (pink, white and grey)
- Gütermann Sulky metallic thread in colour 7009 (pewter)
- Black and white bobbin thread

Design template
- Straight-Stitch Tulip

Machine used
- Janome JF 1018s
- Feeder teeth up
- Normal and loose bobbin thread tension

This project is ideal for learning how to do machine embroidery with the feeder teeth up; it combines set patterns overlaid with straight stitch. Machine embroidery with the feeder teeth up may be more suitable for projects that require an even stitch length or really straight lines. This project is done without a hoop because it is much easier to manipulate unframed fabric with the feeder teeth up.

Draw a rectangle measuring approximately 23 × 18cm (9 × 7in.) onto the cotton, using a ruler and set square to keep the lines straight. Cut the cotton out with the fabric scissors and use it as a template to cut out the interfacing. Place the interfacing glue side down onto the cotton and cover with a sheet of baking parchment. Set the iron to the recommended temperature and iron the interfacing onto the back of the cotton; the baking parchment stops the iron getting covered with interfacing glue.

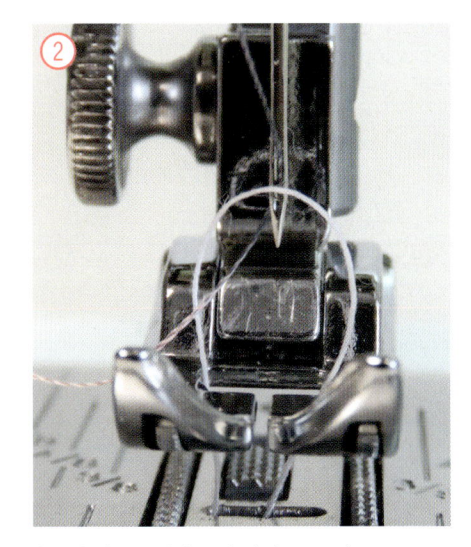

Attach the straight-stitch foot to the machine and insert a size 90/14 universal needle. Wind an empty bobbin with white bobbin thread, place it into the normal tension bobbin case and load it into the machine. Thread the needle with Madeira Classic no. 40, variegated colour 2006. Use the hand wheel to bring both threads to the top, pull out a short length of both threads and position them behind the foot.

③ Position a scrap of cotton under the foot and select a utility or fancy stitch. Look back at the stitches produced in the stitching set patterns sampler and choose one that appeals to you; I chose honeycomb stitch. Test the stitch on the scrap of cotton to check the tension; there should be no pulls or visible dots of thread if the tension is set correctly.

④ Position the prepared stabilized cotton under the foot and embroider twelve straight rows of set pattern. Stitch down the length of the fabric and vary the angle or distance of each row to make the background stitching more interesting.

⑤ Change the set pattern and embroider twelve more rows between the previous ones. Select a pattern that has a similar style; look at the set stitches sampler or test the stitches to choose one you like. I chose double overlock stitch because it has an open pattern similar to honeycomb stitch.

⑥ Change the set pattern and stitch twelve more rows between or slightly overlap them onto the sewn stitches. Keep changing and layering the set stitches until the cotton is evenly covered with patterned stitching. I used four set stitches to complete this stage: honeycomb, double overlock, overcast and tricot stitch.

⑦ Re-thread the needle with Sulky metallic thread in colour 7009 (pewter) and select one of the set patterns used before; I chose double overlock stitch. Sew ten rows of this over the previous embroidery, following the direction of the rows so that the thread change is not obvious. Change the set pattern and sew ten rows between the last ones; continue changing the thread pattern and sewing rows of patterned stitch to complete the embroidered background.

⑧ Print or trace a copy of the tulip template found at the back of this book. Pin the copy to the back of the cotton fabric; position it near the centre of the embroidered fabric.

⑨ Thread the needle with black thread and wind an empty bobbin with Madeira Classic no. 12 black thread. Insert the wound bobbin into the loose tension bobbin case and slot it into the machine. Use the hand wheel to bring both threads to the top of the needle plate, pull both threads and position them behind the foot. Set the stitch type to medium-length straight stitch.

⑩ Test the cable stitch on a scrap of cotton. The top or bottom tension may need altering until the desired result is achieved: cable stitch should not have any loops or missed stitches. See the section 'Stitching set patterns with cable stitch' for more information about setting up the machine for this stitch. Top: two rows sewn neatly with a long stitch length; centre: the third row has looped; bottom: two rows sewn with a shorter stitch length which has produced a smoother stitch.

⑪ Use this sampler to practise controlling the fabric under the foot. You may need to shorten the stitch length or slow down the speed of the machine so the fabric moves more slowly whilst it is being stitched. Practice rotating the fabric with the needle down and foot up. Stitching in reverse is more difficult to control; test the reverse lever or button so you get used to using it. This photo shows the foot raised: don't stitch with a raised foot.

Chapter 4 – Raising the Teeth – Using Set Stitches for Machine Embroidery   **71**

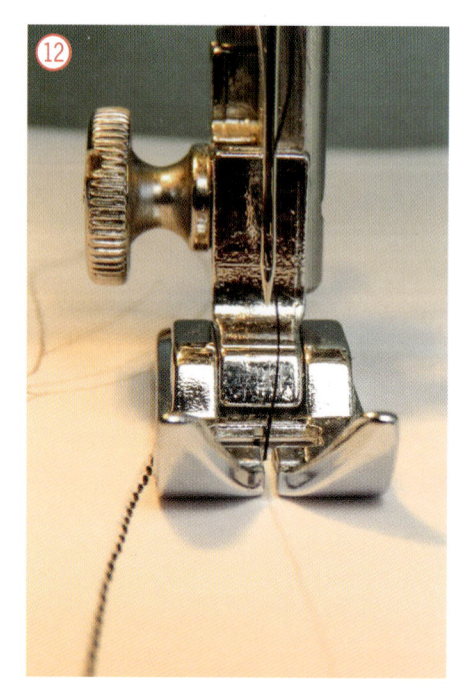

12 Place the cotton fabric under the foot so the pinned paper is facing upwards. Align the needle with the start of a drawn line and lower the foot. Use the hand wheel to bring both threads to the top of the paper. Apply gentle pressure to the foot control and manipulate the paper so the needle follows the drawn line. Stop sewing and lift up the cotton to check the cable stitch has been sewn correctly.

13 Continue sewing along the printed lines until each line has been embroidered twice with cable stitch. You may need to raise the foot to turn the fabric or use reverse to sew back along the line; use whichever method is easier. Stop and tie the thread ends before you begin stitching another part of the design; it is important to do this as you stitch because ends that are sewn in can get caught on the foot and add unwanted bulk to the back of the embroidery.

14 Check the embroidery to see if any parts of it need tidying up or correcting. You can leave the embroidery as it is and prepare it for framing or carry on with the following stages.

⑮ Wind a bobbin with black bobbin thread, place it into the normal tension bobbin case and insert in the machine. Thread the needle with black Madeira Classic no. 40 thread and set the stitch to short/medium-length straight stitch. Use the hand wheel to bring both threads to the top and pull them behind the foot. Turn the fabric over so the paper is against the bed of the machine.

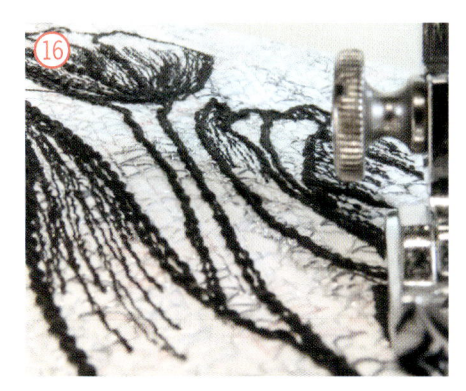

⑯ Add shading to the leaves and petals using the foot and feeder teeth to guide the fabric and trying to follow the curves of the design. Fill the dark areas with straight stitch, staggering or graduating the length of the stitched lines so they blend into the background. Do not overwork the stitched areas; rotate the fabric or use reverse to control the stitching. Continue stitching until the first layer of stitching is complete.

⑰ Thread the needle with Madeira Classic no. 60 in black. Stitch this thinner thread into the shaded areas, staggering the stitches so they blend further into the background embroidery. You need create a graduation of dark into light to create a sense of form. Think about how shading is done on an engraving; this effect can be replicated in stitch, with care and patience.

⑱ Trim the thread tabs or take them to the back and tie them off. (Tabs are the lengths of thread that remain when moving from one area of work to another.) Look at the embroidery to see if any more work needs doing to it. Peel away the excess paper and press the back of the embroidery, using a dry ironing cloth to protect the raised embroidery threads.

⑲

The embroidery is now ready to be mounted or used in another project. Look in Chapter 12 for more information about framing your embroideries.

Chapter 4 – Raising the Teeth – Using Set Stitches for Machine Embroidery 73

STEP-BY-STEP PROJECT
Monochrome Bag

YOU WILL NEED

Equipment
- Sewing machine
- Spare bobbin case for loose tension embroidery
- Normal tension bobbin case
- Small slotted screwdriver
- Twin needle size 1.6/70
- Size 90/14 universal machine needle
- Straight-stitch presser foot
- Iron
- Ironing cloth
- Fabric scissors
- Embroidery scissors
- Sharp hand-sewing needle
- Glass-headed pins
- Press studs
- Ruler
- Set square
- Dressmaker's chalk pencil
- Pencil sharpener
- Paintbrush or cotton bud for applying the glue

Materials
- Piece of thick calico 28 × 57cm (11 × 22½in.)
- Non-woven mediumweight iron-on interfacing 28 × 57cm (11 × 22½in.)
- Thin non-woven iron-on interfacing 28 × 57cm (11 × 22½in.)
- Patterned cotton for lining approximately 28 × 57cm (11 × 22½in.)
- Thin synthetic wadding 28 × 57cm (11 × 22½in.)
- Strips of black, white, patterned quilting and silver metallic fabrics including tissues, velvets and nets 28cm (11in.) in length
- Scrap of cotton fabric
- Black, white, metallic or pale pastel yarns for under-thread couching and wrapping
- Madeira Classic thread no. 40 in colour 2006 variegated (pink, white and grey)
- Gütermann Sulky metallic thread in colour 7009 (pewter)
- Black thread for the bobbin
- Strong black thread for machining seams and hand-sewing seams
- Impex Original Hi-Tack All-Purpose Very Sticky Glue or similar adhesive.
- Baking parchment

Machine used
- Janome JF 1018s
- Feeder teeth up
- Normal tension, loose bobbin thread tension

Creative embroidery need not be limited to framed images or hangings; making your own accessories is a great way to showcase your embroidery and design skills. This project takes you through the process of embroidering and making up an evening bag. The advantage of making your own accessories is that you can be experimental with embroidery, fabrics and colour to create items that can't be found elsewhere. You can create bags, brooches, jewellery or wraps so they match the style or colour of your outfit. I chose black and white because I don't use this colour scheme often and wanted to try something new and exciting.

1 Cut out pieces of calico and interfacing measuring 28 × 57cm (11 × 22½in.). Use a ruler and set square for accurate measurements. Iron the interfacing onto the back of the calico, placing the grainy glue side against the fabric. Use enough heat to fuse the heat-fusible glue and protect the surface of the iron with a sheet of baking parchment. Choose a selection of black and white fabrics, iron them and put them to one side.

2 Cut a wavy strip of patterned cotton measuring 6.5 × 28cm (2½ × 11in). This strip needs to be slightly wider for the seam allowance. Pin the strip to the calico right side up, positioning the strip so it is across the width and along the top edge. Cut a narrower, wavy piece of velvet and pin this on top of the patterned cotton; the edges should overlap so no calico is visible. Cut a piece of metallic tissue and tuck this under the velvet. If the tissue is too bright top it with a piece of metallic net and pin both in place.

Chapter 4 – Raising the Teeth – Using Set Stitches for Machine Embroidery

③

Insert a size 1.6/70 twin needle into the needle holder and attach a straight-stitch foot. Insert a bobbin wound with black into a normal tension bobbin case. Thread the right needle with metallic pewter thread and the left needle with variegated Astro thread. Use the hand wheel to bring the bobbin thread to the top, pull all three threads so a short length of each is behind the foot.

④

Choose a patterned utility stitch from the sampler on which you embroidered set patterns with a twin needle and set the stitch length and type to that stitch. Move the hand wheel to make sure the gap in the needle plate and the gap in the foot provide enough clearance for the twin needle. Test the chosen stitch on a scrap of cotton to check the tension and pattern formation.

⑤

Place the pinned fabric under the foot and align it so the velvet's wavy edge is in the centre of the stitch. Lower the foot and sew along the edge of the velvet, removing the pins before you reach them with either foot or needle. If you have chosen a wide utility stitch with a short stitch length it should cover the raw edges to prevent fraying.

⑥

Remove the fabric from under the foot and trim the thread. Make sure the needles are raised as they otherwise will break when turning the fabric. Rotate the fabric so the other side of the velvet's raw edge is under the foot and use the same patterned utility stitch to secure it to the background.

⑦

Continue cutting and layering the strips of fabric onto the calico background, positioning them so there is variety to the colour and textures used: for instance, light against dark, patterned against plain or matt against metallic. Use your hand to smooth the strips out as you pin them in place; this prevents movement or tucks when the fabric is sewn.

Chapter 4 — Raising the Teeth — Using Set Stitches for Machine Embroidery **75**

⑧ Use the same patterned utility stitch to secure the rest of the fabric strips. Sew down one side of each strip, then the other. Make sure the needle is raised before the fabric is turned and remove the pins before the foot reaches them.

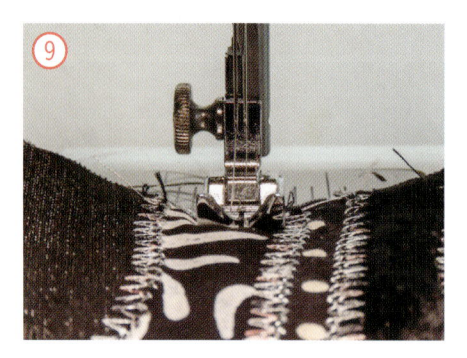

⑨ Change the patterned stitch to another; I chose triple zigzag because the angular pattern complemented the style of the previous pattern. To liven up blank areas embroider some more rows of stitch across the width of the bag. Align the foot against a previously sewn row to keep the line of stitch straight.

⑩ Choose some smooth yarns or threads to wind onto the bobbin for cable stitch. Remove the twin needle and insert a size 90/14 universal needle and set the stitch type to straight. Thread the needle with Madeira 2006 variegated thread. Wind the selected thread onto a bobbin and insert it into the loose tension bobbin case. Refer to the section 'Stitching set patterns with cable stitch' for further instruction.

⑪ Set the stitch type to medium-length straight stitch and test the cable stitch on a scrap of fabric used in the project. Remember that cable stitch is made on the underside of the fabric. I tested five yarns for colour and texture and chose three for this project. The chosen yarns were cotton perle no. 8 in pastel multicolour 1335, black metallic chainette and a silver mono filament foil yarn.

⑫ Wind an empty bobbin with each of the chosen threads and insert the first one into the loose bobbin case.

⑬ Turn the fabric so the right side faces upwards and choose where to stitch the first yarn with cable stitch. Mark about ten places with pins near to the edge of the fabric. Cable stitch is very versatile; it can be used decoratively or to hide fluffy raw edges if they show through the patterned embroidery.

Turn the fabric so the wrong side is facing upwards and place it under the foot so the needle is positioned over a pin. Remove the pin and re-position the fabric slightly so the needle is lined up with the edge of the patterned utility stitch. Sew down the length of the utility stitch so the cable stitch covers the fluffy sewn edge; repeat for the rest of the marker pins.

Insert the next wound bobbin into the loose bobbin case. Turn the fabric over so the right side faces upwards and select where to stitch the next yarn. You can stitch alongside the embroidered utility pattern or stitch across blank spaces. Mark eight to ten starting points with pins. Turn the fabric back over so the wrong side faces upwards and sew the lines of cable stitch with this yarn.

Swap the bobbin to the final yarn and stitch eight to ten rows of cable stitch with this yarn, using pins to mark the starting point of each row. Review the embroidery and use any combination of yarns already used to balance the design and fill in blank spaces. If threads broke or finished in the middle of the embroidery, take them to the back and tie them off or sew them into the back of the fabric.

Cut out rectangles of patterned cotton, thin iron-on interfacing and wadding. The pieces should be the same size as the stitched panel and measure approximately 28 × 57cm (11 × 22½in.). Iron the interfacing to the back of the patterned cotton, using baking parchment to protect the iron from stray heat-fusible glue.

Lay the stabilized cotton onto the stitched bag panel so the right sides face each other. Place the wadding on top of the bonded cotton and smooth out the layers. Pin the layers together round the edge, smoothing out the wrinkles or tucks as you pin.

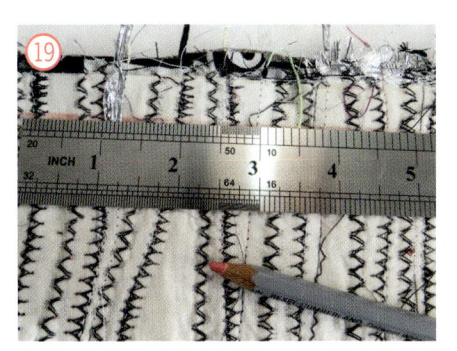

Turn the fabric over so the back of the embroidered panel faces upwards. Draw a rectangle with a chalk pencil to mark the seam lines, using a ruler and set square for accurate straight lines. My drawn rectangle measured approximately 23.5 × 49cm (9¼ × 19¼in.). Once sewn and turned through, the fabric folds over like an envelope to create the bag pocket and flap.

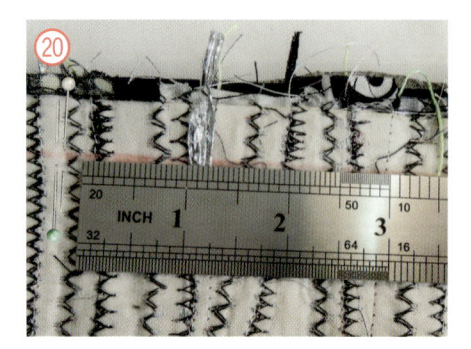

20. When the rectangle is drawn the pins may need re-positioning so they are pinned across the drawn line. The seam needs a gap for turning through, so mark an opening on one long side seam measuring approximately 11cm (4¼in.). Place an extra pin either side of the opening to indicate where to stop sewing. The gap needs to be large enough so the bag can be turned through without splitting the seam.

21. Wind strong black thread onto a bobbin, place it into the normal tension bobbin case and insert the bobbin case into the machine. Thread the needle with the same strong black thread and set the stitch to a medium-length straight stitch. Position the fabric under the foot so the needle lines up with the start of the seam, next to the double-pinned gap.

22. Lower the foot and sew a few stitches, press reverse to sew back over them, release reverse and continue sewing normally until you reach the first corner, then stop. Press reverse and sew backwards over a few stitches, release reverse and sew forwards until you reach the corner, then stop. This is called backstitching; it is used at the start and ends of seams and to reinforce corners.

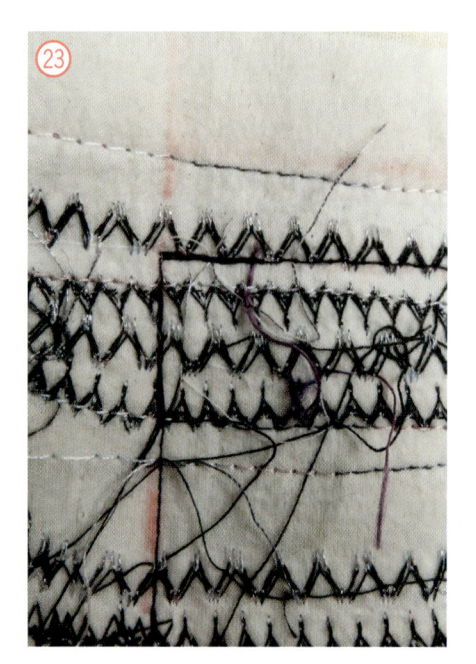

23. Leave the needle lowered in the fabric and rotate the fabric till the foot lines up with the seam line. Sew a few stitches forward then press reverse and sew back over the stitching but do not go beyond the corner point. Release reverse and continue stitching forwards until the next corner is reached, then stop and repeat the process.

24. Trim the thread tails and tidy up the back of the embroidery. Remove the excess fabric, trim the fabric across the corners close to the seam, then trim the side seams so there is a 1cm (⅜in.) seam allowance. If you have difficulty cutting straight lines it is okay to draw a cutting line or use a rotary cutter and cutting mat.

78   Chapter 4 – Raising the Teeth – Using Set Stitches for Machine Embroidery

25. Turn the bag though the opening so the right side is outside. Push the corners out with a blunt object to make sharp points. Ease the side seams out so they are straight and pin in place. Fold in the excess fabric around the opening and pin in place so it is level with the rest of the side seam. Cover the pinned bag with a dry ironing cloth and gently press along the seams. Remove the pins and re-press the whole thing; the final press flattens the wadding and produces crisp seams.

26. Pin the opening closed and thread a sharp hand-sewing needle with strong black or colour-matched thread. Sew the opening closed with slip stitch, then sew back along the opening for extra security. The hand stitching should be invisible or hidden within the seam. Fasten off and take the thread ends through to the middle of the fabric to hide them.

27. Fold the fabric over to create the bag pocket and flap; the folded fabric resembles an envelope. My pocket measured approximately 15.5cm (6in.) deep. The flap closure should not be longer than the bag or hang over the bottom of it. When you are happy with the shape of the bag, pin the sides in place and check the pocket has equal depth all the way along.

28. Lace the side seam of the pocket together, using two strands of strong colour-matched thread and a sharp hand-sewing needle. Try to keep the hand stitching neat and invisible. The seams need to be sewn twice to make sure they're secure. If you do not require a handle for the bag, skip the next five pictures and go to the steps about press studs.

29. Choose six strands of colour-matched yarn or cord; the yarns used for the cable stitch are an ideal choice. Cut a 193cm (76in.) length of each yarn and put them to one side. Thread the needle with Madeira Classic no. 40 colour 2006 and wind Sulky metallic pewter thread onto an empty bobbin and insert it in the normal tension bobbin case. Set the stitch to zigzag and wrap the six lengths of yarn by machine. Refer to the section 'Wrapping threads or yarn by machine' to remind yourself about how to wrap yarns.

30. Plait the wrapped yarns to make the handle. Use two wrapped yarns in each section of the plait. When the plait is finished pin the ends to stop them unravelling (I use pins because knotting could distort the shape of the handle). Pin the plait to the side seams of the bag to create the handle; check the length.

㉛ Unpin both ends of the plait and move them away from the bag. Paint the inside of the plait with Hi-Tack Very Sticky Glue (or a similar adhesive) and leave it to dry. You only need to paint the plait near the raw ends. Painting the back of the plait secures the wrapped yarns and stops them moving about whilst they are being sewn in place.

㉜ Cut off the messy part of the plait and paint the end of each wrapped yarn with fabric glue and leave to dry. The fabric glue stops the wrapped yarns coming undone when they are sewn into position behind the plait.

㉝ Bend the wrapped yarn ends under the plait, and re-pin the plait to the side seam. Thread a sharp hand needle with two lengths of strong black or colour-matched thread and sew the plait into place. Sew the plait more securely near the top of the bag where the handle will be placed under more stress.

㉞ To close the bag, measure the length of the opening and decide where to sew in the press studs. Fastenings should be positioned an equal distance apart either from the side or the middle of the bag. My bag measured approximately 23.5cm (9¼in.) across so I measured 6cm (2¼in.) in from both side seams and marked the spot with a chalk pencil.

㉟ Press the inside fabric together to transfer the marks to the other side of the bag lining. Check the transferred dots match up and re-mark them if necessary; if the positions don't match the press studs might not meet to close the bag.

㊱ Thread a sharp hand-sewing needle with a quadrupled length of strong black thread, tie a knot in the end of the thread and cut off the excess. Sew through the chalk mark to anchor the thread then position the male press stud over the sewn knot. Make sure the raised part is facing upwards. Sew on the press stud; don't sew through to the front of the bag and keep the stitching tidy. Fasten off and sew on the second male press stud.

80 Chapter 4 – Raising the Teeth – Using Set Stitches for Machine Embroidery

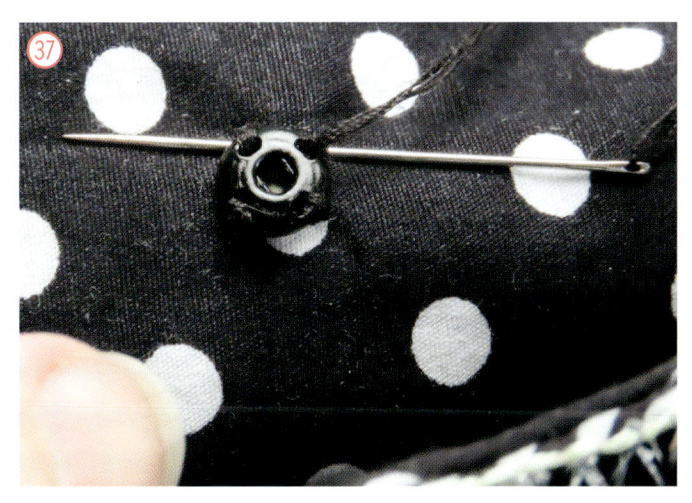

Sew the female half of the press studs into position: the circular recess should be facing outwards. Check that the sewn press studs line up and clip together without distorting or pulling the bag. If part of the press stud is out of line unpick it and sew it in place again.

Some fabrics are incredibly good at picking up lint or fluff. You may need to use a clothesbrush, lint roller or the sticky side of some masking tape to remove the unwanted threads and lint.

The bag is now finished. It can be embellished with beads if desired or have a brooch pinned to the flap.

Chapter 4 – Raising the Teeth – Using Set Stitches for Machine Embroidery   81

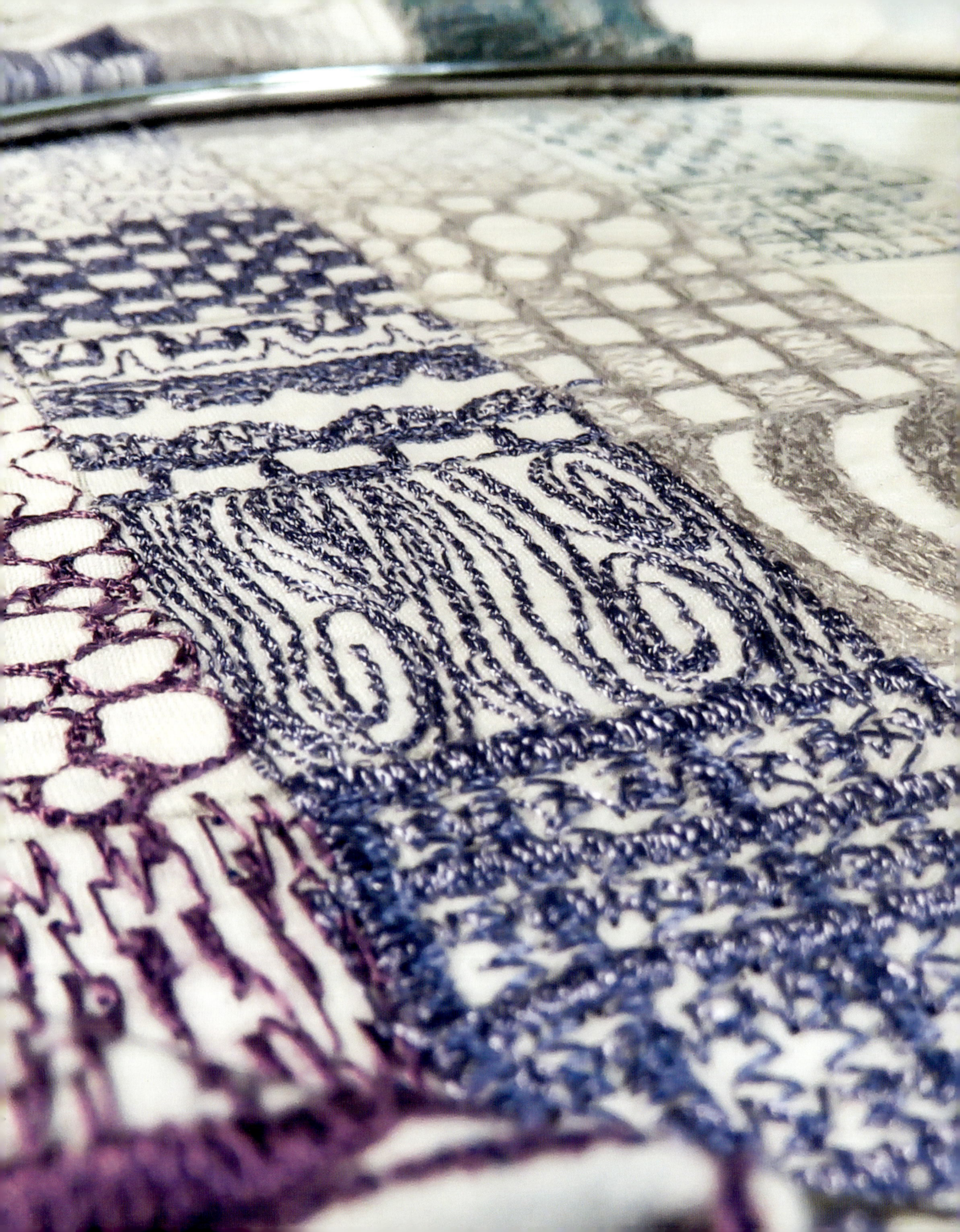

Chapter 5

Lowering the Teeth – Free Machine Embroidery with an Embroidery Foot

Free machine embroidery is done with the feeder teeth lowered and a darning or embroidery foot attached. When the feeder teeth are lowered, the machine is unable to move the fabric, so the embroiderer must move the fabric for the machine to stitch the design. The easiest way to get used to this concept is to think about keeping the pen still whilst moving the paper around to write or make a drawing. The person using the sewing machine controls the length and direction of the stitches by moving the hoop and operating the foot pedal at the same time. This may sound a bit like trying to rub your tummy at the same time as patting your head; I can assure you that free machine embroidery is not that difficult to learn.

A darning or embroidery foot is vital for machine embroidery because it stops fabric bounce and acts as a visual barrier to prevent needle injuries. The needle enters the fabric through the hole in the centre of the embroidery foot; it's like looking through a small target viewfinder, and with practice you know where the needle is going to pierce the fabric so you can follow the design with the needle to create the embroidery stitches. If a suitable foot can't be found, machine embroidery can be done with a spring needle. I don't recommend trying to do free machine embroidery without a foot or spring needle because it's not safe; my experience of trying to sew without a foot resulted in tension problems and the fabric was pushed into the hole in the needle plate.

Free machine embroidery requires co-ordination and the ability to judge where the stitching needs to be made. If you have completed some of the samplers or projects in the preceding chapter you will be ready to learn how to do machine embroidery. If the foot pedal is pressed at a steady rate, small movements create short stitches and big movements create longer stitches. Set patterns cannot be used for free machine embroidery because the feeder teeth are not in contact with the fabric to move it along and it would be difficult to judge the movement of the needle.

This close-up shows the hole in the centre of the embroidery foot. L: the sprung foot belongs to the Janome, where the clear plastic has been marked by the needle. R: the metal foot belongs to the Bernina and is more robust because it's made of metal.

The variety of stitches created by free machine embroidery are endless, as the hoop of fabric can be controlled to produce delicate line drawings or heavily embroidered textures. As you become more proficient you can create your own patterns to rival the beauty and complexity of the set ones.

This example shows straight stitch and zigzag used in their purest form. The fabric was simply moved backwards and forwards to create the lines of stitch and areas of dense embroidery.

Free Machine Embroidery Basic Stitch Types

Two set stitches are used for free machine embroidery: straight and zigzag. For machine embroidery to be successful the embroiderer needs to anticipate where the needle will pierce the fabric to form the stitch and create the design; this would be an impossible task if patterned stitches were used.

Straight Stitch

Straight stitch is the most basic stitch that can be found on the machine; it's usually used for seaming, joining fabrics or decorative topstitching. Straight stitch becomes more versatile when used with an embroidery foot because the hoop can be moved in any direction without distorting

This example of straight stitch shows how it is possible to get bolder marks by stitching over lines of stitch. Top R: a dense patch of machine embroidery sewn with straight stitch; bottom R: doodles. Note that straight stitch is not affected by changes in stitch direction.

the shape of the stitch. Straight stitch can be used to create open abstract patterns, make expressive line drawings or create densely embroidered thread-paintings.

The length or direction of the stitch is governed by how the hoop is moved. Moving the hoop backwards and forwards creates a straight line of stitch as does moving the hoop left or right. With practice you learn how to make small directional movements with the hoop to produce patterns such as vermicelli stitch, circles or scribbles.

The amount of pressure applied to the foot pedal controls how fast the needle enters and exits the fabric. This can influence the stitch length to some degree: for instance, if I needed to embroider solid areas of stitch, I could apply more pressure to the foot pedal so the area is stitched quickly with small stitches; if the design is detailed and delicate I could apply less pressure and move the hoop slowly so I have more control over the stitching. The tension of the thread can be altered to produce variations of straight stitch; these special stitches are discussed in Chapter 8, which looks at experimenting with stitches and tension.

84   Chapter 5 – Lowering the Teeth – Free Machine Embroidery with an Embroidery Foot

Zigzag

The zigzag setting creates a single row of angular jagged stitches. The needle moves from side to side to create the zigzag effect; most machines have variable width for zigzag stitch. Zigzag is traditionally used to sew seams on stretch fabrics or bind hems or edges to prevent fraying. Satin stitch is zigzag with a minimal stitch length and is used for stitching buttonholes and edging fabric appliqués.

Zigzag width is altered by moving the stitch width dial or button, but the length of the stitch is controlled by moving the fabric or hoop. Zigzag stitch can only be formed by moving the hoop vertically, back to front or front to back. It does not form properly in other directions; when the hoop is moved horizontally from left to right the resulting stitch looks like an untidy straight stitch. The textures made by zigzag are most suitable for use in landscape images: horizontal zigzag is very good for describing areas of scrub land whilst layered open zigzag is very effective for suggesting furrows.

Moving the hoop slowly forwards or backwards creates a closed satin stitch effect. Imagine using of an old-fashioned fountain pen when making satin stitch because it will help you move the hoop in the correct direction. Open zigzag with a fast-moving hoop can create rough random textures whilst close zigzag and a slow-moving hoop creates calligraphic marks. If your design requires straight lines of zigzag or satin stitch it is better to use a normal presser foot with the feeder teeth up because this method produces a neater stitch.

This example shows how hoop direction alters the zigzag pattern. L: rows of zigzag increasing in width; middle: thick satin stitch and a wavy line of zigzag made by moving the hoop side to side whilst stitching slowly; top R: dense stitching made with zigzag; bottom R: doodles stitched with zigzag.

Chapter 5 – Lowering the Teeth – Free Machine Embroidery with an Embroidery Foot

EXERCISE

FREE MACHINE EMBROIDERY WITH AN EMBROIDERY FOOT

Learning how to do free machine embroidery develops your ability to multi-task; as you become familiar with the process you will understand how to move the hoop in harmony with the machine. This method of embroidery sets creativity free; it's no longer about what the machine can do, it's about what you can do with the skills you have learnt. You will have 'wow' moments, 'eureka' moments, 'oh, no' moments and 'I wonder what will happen if I do that' moments.

YOU WILL NEED

Equipment
- Sewing machine with drop feed or darning plate
- 15cm (6in.) or 20cm (8 in.) wooden embroidery hoop
- Darning or embroidery foot
- Size 90/14 universal machine needle
- Normal tension bobbin case
- Empty bobbin
- Embroidery scissors
- Fabric scissors
- Small slotted screwdriver
- 2H or coloured pencil
- Pencil sharpener

Materials
- Cotton fabric approximately 30.5 × 37cm (12 × 14½in.)
- No. 40 viscose or rayon machine thread
- Black bobbin thread

Machine used
- Bernina 801
- Feeder teeth down
- Normal tension

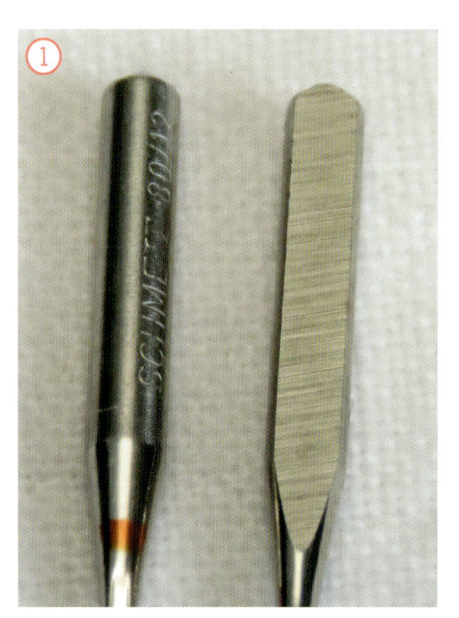

① Insert a size 90/14 universal needle into the needle clamp. The front of the needle's shank is curved and the back is flat. Make sure the needle is pushed all the way into the clamp with the flat side to the back, then tighten the needle clamp with a screwdriver. With some machines the needle can be set to the left, middle or right; make sure the needle is set to the middle because it's easier to control the stitches.

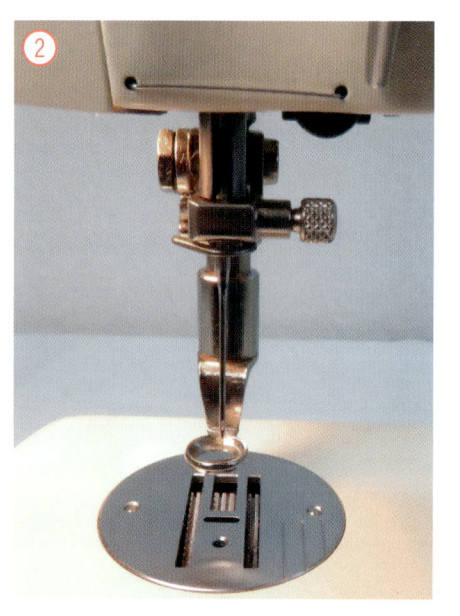

② Attach an embroidery or darning foot and lower the feeder teeth. Set the stitch type to straight; there is no need to alter stitch length because you will be controlling the length of the stitches by moving the hoop. (This photograph shows the Bernina 801.)

③ Your machine may have a slightly different set-up. Some have clip-on feet or feeder teeth that can't be lowered; if this is the case you need to remove the presser foot holder so you can screw the darning or embroidery foot into place and cover the feeder teeth with a clip-on darning plate. (This photograph shows the Janome.)

④

Wind a bobbin with black bobbin thread and place it into the normal tension bobbin case, then insert both into the machine. Thread the needle with rayon or viscose top thread and turn the hand wheel to bring both threads to the top, pull out a short length of both threads and position them behind the embroidery foot.

⑤

Undo the screw on the outer ring of the hoop and place the outer ring on a flat surface. Lay the fabric on top so it's positioned centrally, take the inner part of the hoop and press it onto the larger outer hoop. When both parts are lined up, pull the edges of the fabric so it begins to get taut, secure the screw by hand, then pull the fabric tighter and use a slotted screwdriver to do up the screw. Correctly hooped fabric should sound like a drum when flicked.

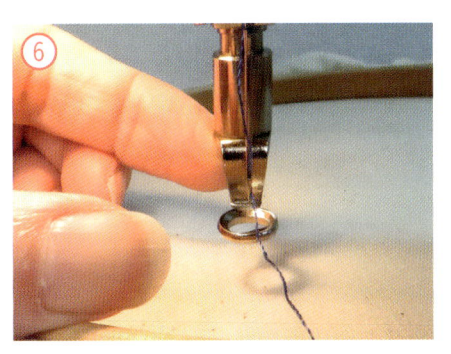

⑥

Position the hoop under the foot so the fabric is against the needle plate. You may need to push the darning or embroidery foot up with your finger so the hoop has enough room to slide underneath. Hold both thread ends whilst lowering the foot; this helps the top thread position itself in the tension discs correctly. If the foot is not lowered the stitches won't form properly and your fabric will have loops of stitch underneath.

⑦

Position your hands on the edge of the hoop (visualize twenty to and twenty past on a clock face). Experiment with moving the hoop around without pressing the foot down; don't tilt or rock the hoop but keep it flat against the bed of the machine. Once you have mastered moving the hoop you can begin sewing.

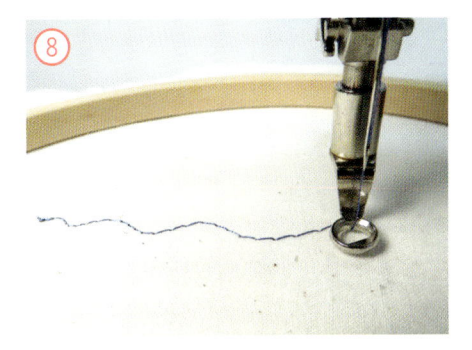

⑧

Press gently on the foot pedal and slowly move the hoop away from the starting point to create a line of stitch – you have just stitched your first line of free machine embroidery. Stop and cut the starting thread tail close to the fabric; if you leave loose threads they could be sewn into the work or you might be tempted to brush them out of the way and catch your finger on the needle.

⑨

Start embroidering again. Move the hoop around, overlapping the stitches so you get used to the balance between moving the hoop and pressing the foot pedal. Big movements at low speed create long stitches and small movements at fast speed make short stitches. To begin sewing somewhere new, trim the thread close to the surface, raise the foot and gently pull more top thread through the needle to create a longer thread tail. Lower the foot, hold on to the thread tail and start stitching again. Imagine some shapes or patterns and have a go at stitching them.

Chapter 5 – Lowering the Teeth – Free Machine Embroidery with an Embroidery Foot **87**

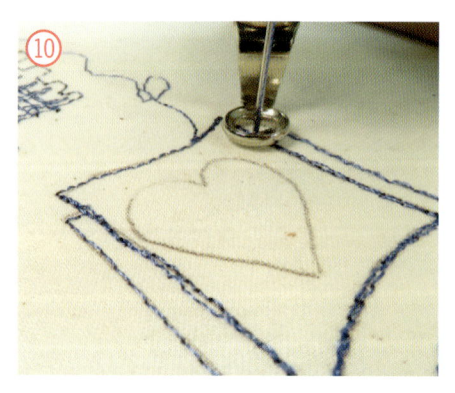

⑩ Draw a simple shape with a 2H or coloured pencil. Move the hoop so the needle follows the drawn line; don't worry if you wobble, draw another shape and try again. Stitch round the outline a few times to see how this changes the thickness of the straight stitch; finish by doing a few stitches in the same place and trim the thread close to the fabric.

⑪ You may need to move the hoop to a fresh area of the fabric. Stop sewing and turn the handwheel to make sure the needle is out of the fabric. Remove the hoop from under the machine. Loosen and re-position the hoop. Write your name on the fabric in joined-up script with an ordinary or coloured pencil. Try to follow your signature with stitch; light pressure on the foot pedal and moving the hoop slowly helps you to sew more accurately.

⑫ Move the hoop again so you have a fresh area of fabric to work on and set your machine to medium zigzag. Move the hoop in the same way to see how the zigzag is affected by stitch direction; move the hoop slowly to create satin stitch. Draw a simple shape and follow the outline with zigzag without rotating the hoop. Note how the vertical lines, backwards or forwards, are thicker and the horizontal lines, left to right, are narrow like messy straight stitch.

⑬ Write your name in 2H or coloured pencil and set the zigzag to a narrower width to stitch your name. Move the hoop slowly and keep it facing the same way; don't rotate it. Moving the hoop without rotating it keeps the vertical lines thick and the horizontal ones thin, here creating letters with a calligraphy style.

⑭ You have just completed your first sample of machine embroidery. Remove the embroidery from under the machine and remove the hoop and put it to one side. Trim the top and bottom threads. The fabric may have handling marks or be puckered a small amount, but ironing the embroidery on the back will remove the small wrinkles.

88 Chapter 5 – Lowering the Teeth – Free Machine Embroidery with an Embroidery Foot

EXERCISE

FREE MACHINE EMBROIDERY WITH A SPRING NEEDLE

If you can't find an embroidery foot for the machine a spring needle can be used instead. Sewing with a spring needle can be quite liberating as you can see where the stitches are being made without the foot hiding the stitched area. The feeder teeth must be lowered when using a spring needle because they are not needed to move the fabric.

It is important to properly tension the fabric in a hoop when using a spring needle because it's much easier and safer to stitch onto taut hooped fabric. The fabric may have a bit more bounce because the foot is not there to hold it down. The hoop also acts like a handle; to prevent injury your fingers should be kept on the rim of the hoop. Spring needles work best on fabric that has a smooth even weave.

YOU WILL NEED

Equipment
- Sewing machine with drop feed or darning plate
- 15cm (6in.) or 20cm (8 in.) wooden embroidery hoop
- Spring needle
- Normal tension bobbin case
- Empty bobbin
- Embroidery scissors
- Fabric scissors

Materials
- Scrap of cotton approximately 20 x 40cm (8 x 15¾in.)
- No. 40 viscose or rayon machine thread
- Black bobbin thread

Machine used
- Bernina 801
- Feeder teeth down
- Normal tension

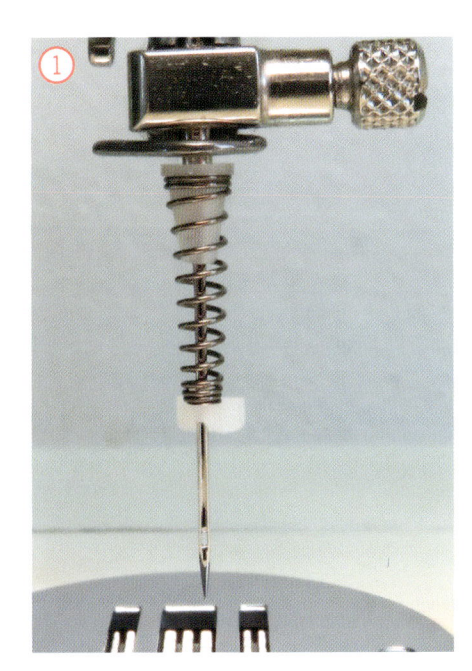

1. Insert the spring needle into the needle holder and tighten the clamp or screw to hold the needle in place.

2. Insert a bobbin wound with black into the normal tension bobbin case and click into place.

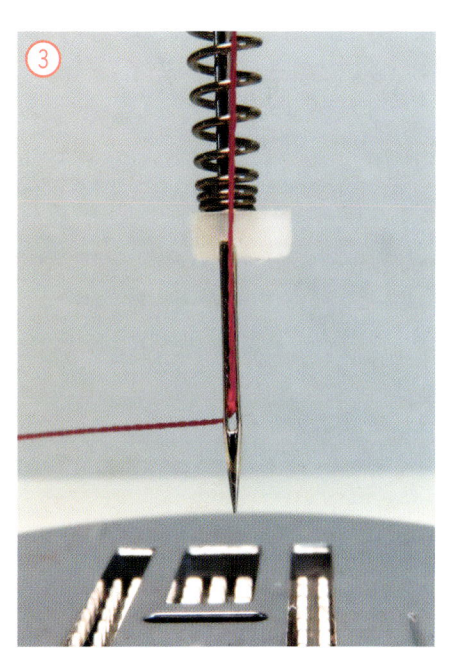

3. Thread the needle with strong no. 40 plain viscose or rayon machine thread.

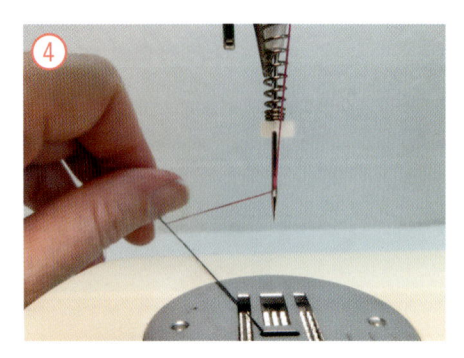

4 Turn the hand wheel to bring both threads to the top, then pull a short length of both behind the needle plate.

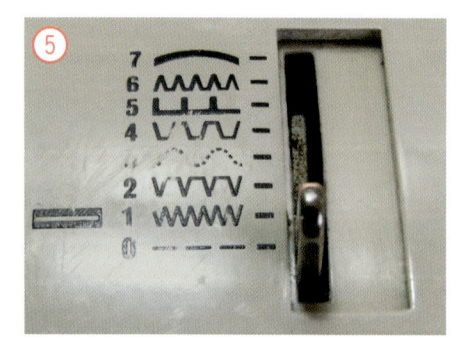

5 Lower the feeder teeth and set the stitch type to straight.

6 Fold the cotton to double thickness and place it in a hoop. Stretch it until it is taut and tighten the hoop. Place the hooped cotton under the needle so that the fabric is against the needle plate.

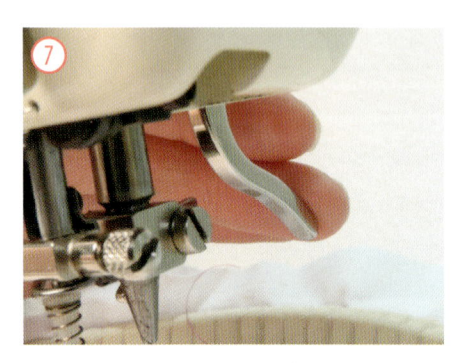

7 Use the foot raiser to lower the absent foot. This lever needs to be down because it affects the tension of the stitches; if it is left up the machine won't sew properly.

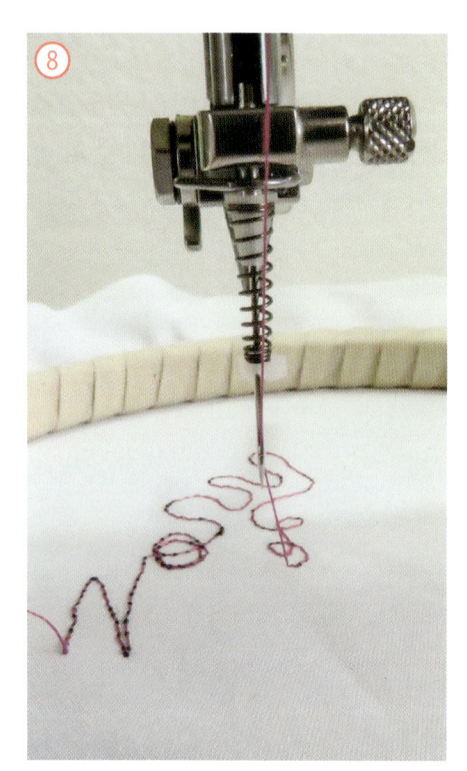

8 Apply gentle pressure to the foot pedal and move the hoop slowly, keeping your hands on the edge of the hoop away from the needle. Stop and check the tension; if black dots of bobbin thread are coming to the top, reduce the top tension until they disappear.

9 Keep experimenting with the stitching until you feel comfortable with using the spring needle.

STEP-BY-STEP PROJECT
Free Machine Embroidery Sampler

YOU WILL NEED

Equipment
- Sewing machine with drop feed or darning plate
- Embroidery foot, darning foot or spring needle
- Size 90/14 universal machine needle
- Size 110/18 wool Lana machine needle, for Lana no. 12 thread
- Normal tension bobbin case
- Empty bobbin
- 15cm (6in.) wooden or metal hoop
- Small slotted screwdriver
- Embroidery scissors
- Fabric scissors
- Iron
- Ironing cloth
- Baking parchment
- Ruler
- Set square
- H pencil
- Pencil sharpener
- Eraser
- Black ballpoint or gel pen (one that does not run into the fabric)

Materials
- White A4 paper
- White mediumweight iron-on interfacing 30.5 × 38cm (12 × 15in.)
- White cotton or calico 30.5 × 38cm (12 × 15in.)
- White tear-away interfacing 24 × 12.5cm (9½ × 5in.)
- Various machine embroidery threads; Gütermann Sulky rayon viscose no. 30 in colour 1076 Madeira Classic viscose no. 40 in colour 1033
- White bobbin thread
- Fujix Kingstar polyester thread no. 40 in colour 292
- Madeira Cotona cotton thread no. 50 in colour 688
- Madeira Polyneon polyester thread no. 40 in colour 1607
- Madeira Lana no. 12 thread (50 per cent wool, 50 per cent acrylic) in colour 3881

Design template
- Optional: Swirl Pattern

Machine used
- Bernina 801
- Feeder teeth down
- Normal tension

It's important to explore how moving the hoop creates the stitch pattern; this project will help you gain more confidence to explore your own vocabulary of stitches. How you stitch is personal to you: for example, when I embroider I make small controlled movements to produce short stitches whereas someone else may move their hands and arms more freely to create larger, more expressive stitching.

The idea is to try something different in each square. I certainly had fun doing this sampler, I had a few 'wow, I love that' moments, and the dotty line was one of those. If you are a doodler you should enjoy this project – think of Zentangles on fabric. If you find the number of squares too alarming, reduce the size of the grid; there are no set rules for making this sampler. If a grid does not appeal to you, use the Swirl Pattern template for inspiration.

Stitching this sampler is an ideal way to explore different types of thread; you need to find one that you enjoy working with. Trying different threads helps you see how the thread alters the appearance of the stitch: for instance, the matt sheen of cotton is very different from shiny rayon. It's vital to test threads before you invest in a selection of colours: contrary to manufacturers' advice, machines do have personalities and certain colours or brands are more prone to breakage or knotting than others. You don't need to rush out and buy the threads used for this sampler; I have listed them purely for guidance.

①
Heat the iron to the recommended temperature and place the interfacing on top of the cotton glue side down. Cover the interfacing with baking parchment and iron the interfacing to the back of the cotton. Using baking parchment stops the iron getting dirty. Poor-quality interfacing can shrink, causing the cotton to wrinkle; if this happens, press the front of the cotton to even out the wrinkles.

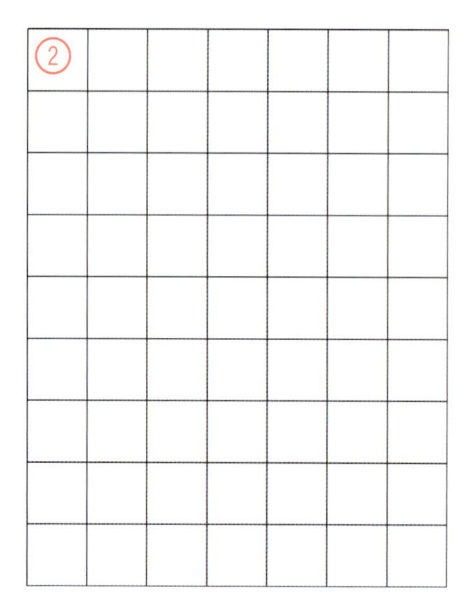

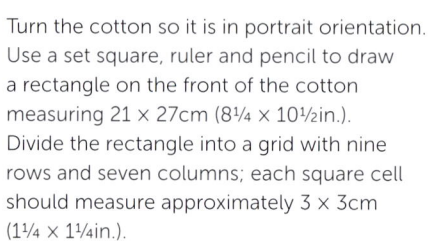

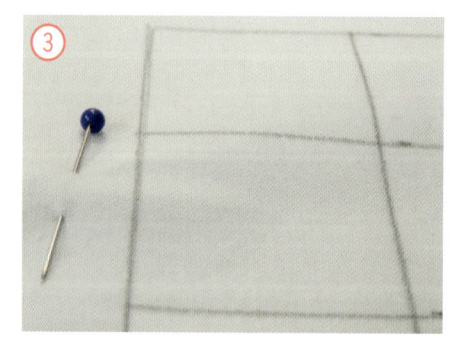

② Turn the cotton so it is in portrait orientation. Use a set square, ruler and pencil to draw a rectangle on the front of the cotton measuring 21 × 27cm (8¼ × 10½in.). Divide the rectangle into a grid with nine rows and seven columns; each square cell should measure approximately 3 × 3cm (1¼ × 1¼in.).

③ Fold the white tear-away interfacing in half and pin it behind the second row of squares. This extra layer of interfacing will reinforce the fabric behind the dense stitching to prevent shrinking and distortion.

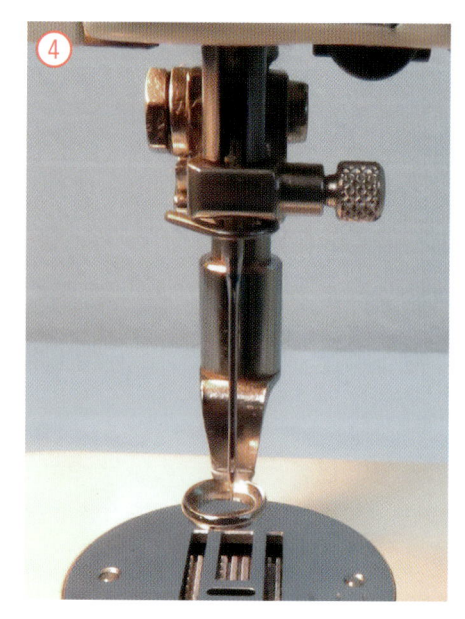

④ Set up the machine, lower the feeder teeth, insert a size 90/14 universal needle into the needle holder and tighten the clamp. Attach the embroidery foot, select straight stitch and change the needle position to central. Thread the needle with a strong plain thread; I used Sulky rayon no. 30 in colour 1076.

⑤ Insert a bobbin wound with white bobbin thread into the bobbin case, then load it into the machine. Turn the hand wheel to pull the bobbin thread to the top, then pull a short length of both threads across the needle plate towards the back of the machine.

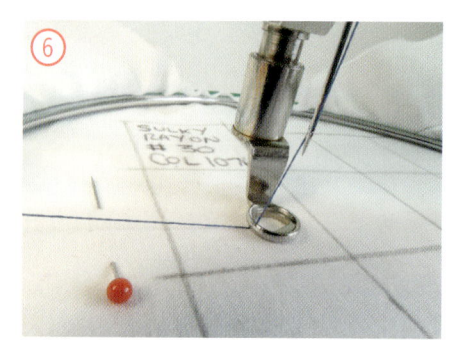

⑥ Place the fabric in a hoop so the left-hand corner of the grid is central. I am using a metal hoop because it's easier to re-position the fabric. Use a black biro or gel pen to write the brand name, weight, content and thread colour in the top left corner square. Position the hoop under the needle and lower the foot.

⑦ Divide the square below the writing into quarters. Stitch the first quarter densely, moving the hoop backwards and forwards until no background shows. Stitch densely left to right in the second quarter; this type of straight stitch is used to embroider dense thread-paintings.

92 Chapter 5 – Lowering the Teeth – Free Machine Embroidery with an Embroidery Foot

⑧

Stitch some shading in the bottom part of the square, graduating the closeness of the stitches so the background fabric shows through. These squares of dense stitch show how stitch direction alters the sheen and shade of the thread as it catches the light.

⑨

Move to the next square down. Imagine drawing lots of bubbles and practise moving the hoop in a slow circular motion. Use straight stitch to sew the outside of a circle, repeat the action a few times to create a thick line of stitching, and continue stitching adjoining circles until the square is filled. It does not matter if the bubbles are different – uneven shapes add interest to this stitch pattern.

⑩

Re-position the hoop so you are ready to stitch the next square. Start stitching from the top edge and move the hoop slowly to create a wavy line that meanders back and forth. Try to keep the stitching and meanders the same size; the stitching should not cross over itself. This stitch is called meandering vermicelli; it is useful for quilting backgrounds or for holding fabric snips together when making fabrics with soluble film.

⑪

Go to the next square. Move the hoop backwards and forwards quite quickly to create a patch of scribble, then change direction and stitch another patch of scribble. Keep stitching until the square is filled with directional scribble stitch. This is quite a fast stitch; don't snag the needle when moving the hoop because catching it at the wrong moment can break or bend it. This stitch is very useful for adding texture to the sky in large landscape pictures.

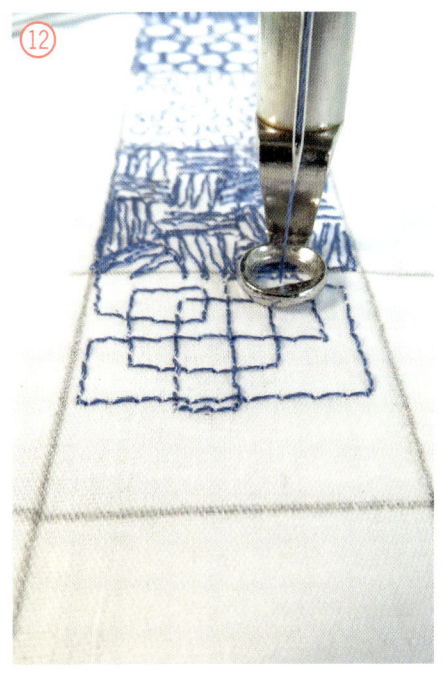

⑫

Move to the next square down. Angular straight stitch makes use of sharp left or right turns. This stitch is more attractive when less stitching is done; the gaps between the lines of stitch create tiny areas of negative space. This stitch can be sewn with cable stitch to add texture to abstract embroideries.

⑬

Re-hoop the fabric and rotate the hoop so the fabric is landscape. Set the stitch type to medium-width zigzag. Line the foot up with the edge of the square and move the hoop backwards or forwards very slowly to create a solid row of satin stitch. Move the hoop and sew another row of satin stitch. If you want the stitches to have more definition sew another row on top. Embroider some small blocks of satin stitch between the rows to create a brick pattern.

Chapter 5 – Lowering the Teeth – Free Machine Embroidery with an Embroidery Foot   93

⑭ Set the stitch type to narrow-width zigzag. Think about how you moved the hoop whilst embroidering vermicelli stitch. Move the hoop in a similar way to create a wavy line of zigzag. Zigzag creates an unpredictable pattern so it does not matter if the stitching overlaps. This stitch is very useful for creating rough scribbled textures.

⑮ Go to the next square down. Move the hoop back and forth to create regular lines of zigzag, stitching so they are very close together. Adjacent rows of zigzag create linear textures that could be used to describe distance in landscape pictures. Layers of this stitch could also be used to produce textured thread-paintings.

⑯ Re-position the hoop at the top of the second column. Re-thread the needle with the next chosen thread; I used Madeira Classic no. 40 in colour 1033. Use a black biro or gel pen to write the brand name, weight, content and thread colour in the top square.

⑰ Set the stitch type to straight, position the hoop under the needle and lower the foot. Thread-paint the square, creating an area of heavy stitch at the bottom. Remember to press more firmly on the pedal for this stitch and move the hoop a bit faster. (Moving the block of dense stitch to the bottom provides a nice contrast and prevents fabric shrinkage.)

⑱ Continue embroidering new straight-stitch patterns in the next four squares of this column. Change to zigzag and embroider zigzag or satin stitch patterns in the last three boxes.

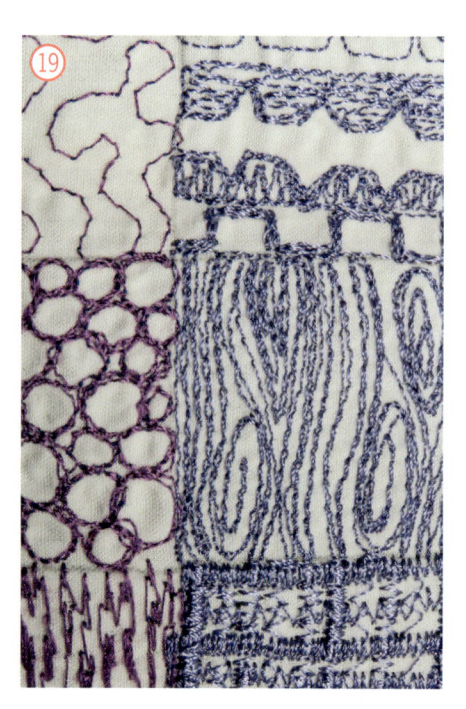

⑲ Re-thread the needle with a different top thread; I used Kingstar polyester in colour 292. Write the name of the thread in the top square, then embroider a block of dense stitching in the square below. Fill the four squares below with various straight-stitch patterns. Set the stitch type to narrow zigzag and stitch patterns in the last three boxes.

Thread the needle with a thinner thread; I used Madeira Cotona no. 50 in colour 688. Write the thread details in the top square. Set the stitch type to straight and embroider the first square densely, then embroider four more squares with various straight-stitch patterns. Set the stitch type to narrow zigzag and stitch patterns in the last three squares.

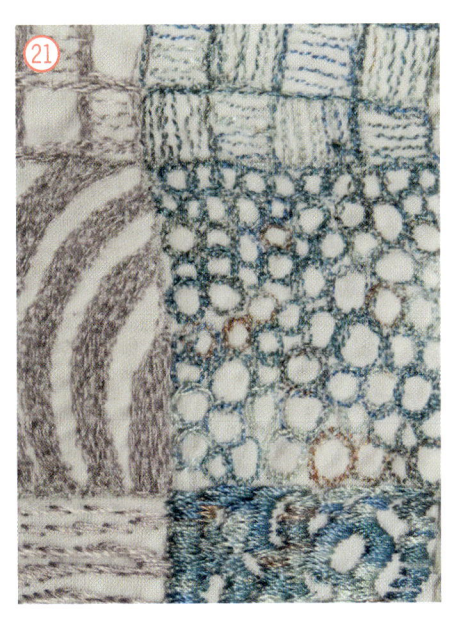

Repeat the process to stitch column five. This time thread the needle with a variegated thread; I used Madeira Polyneon no. 40 in colour 1607. Variegated, ombre or astro threads add colour changes to the pattern and trick the mind into thinking the embroidery is more complex.

Change the needle to a size 110/18 Lana needle and reset the stitch type to straight. Thread the needle with Madeira lana no. 12 colour 3881. Repeat the process to stitch column six. Lana thread is thicker; if you have problems with top tension or thread breakage lower the top tension. Machine embroidery with thick thread builds up quickly so less stitching is needed.

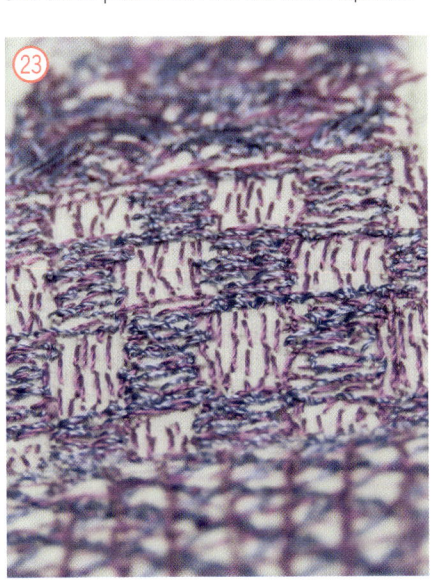

Change the needle back to a size 90/14 and set the stitch type to straight. Choose three colours used previously and embroider a base layer in one colour, swap the thread and work into the pattern with another colour, then stitch into some of the squares with a third colour. Thread colours can be mixed during the embroidery process to create some interesting effects.

Remove the embroidery from the hoop and trim off the loose threads. Cover the embroidery with an ironing cloth and press to remove marks left by the hoop. You may find that your fabric has shrunk with the density of stitching. The finished sampler will help you choose the right stitches for an embroidery or inspire you to discover more.

If the rigidity of the squares does not appeal to you, draw a random scribble onto cotton and fill each section with different stitch types and thread colours. The Swirl template for this version of the sampler can be found in the back of this book.

Chapter 5 – Lowering the Teeth – Free Machine Embroidery with an Embroidery Foot **95**

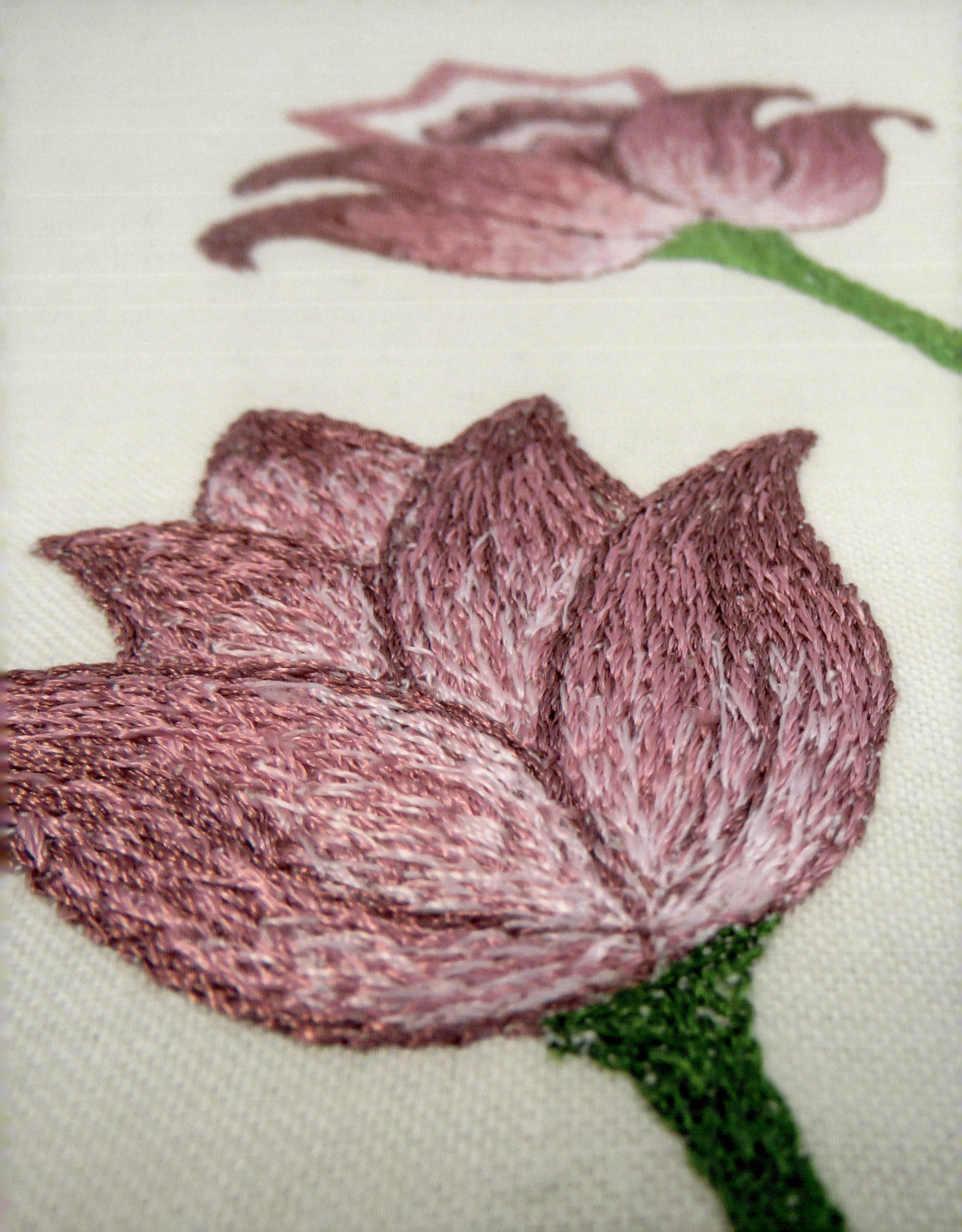

CHAPTER 6

THREAD-PAINTING

Free machine embroidery is sometimes called thread-painting. The needle becomes the brush, the threads transform into paint and the fabric is the canvas. The projects in this chapter will teach you how to paint with thread using straight stitch and a little bit of zigzag. I have chosen straight stitch as the main stitch type because it's the best stitch to use for thread-painting detailed embroideries. Straight stitch is easier to control, so the finished embroidery looks like a stitched version of the design. Another advantage of using straight stitch is that the thread direction is clearly visible; thread direction can be used to mimic brush marks if the design is carefully planned.

The process of thread-painting has many stages; the design or pattern needs to be translated into working drawings so that the embroiderer can make important choices about colour and stitch direction. The finished design needs to be transferred onto the fabric so that the embroidery can be stitched in the correct order. Good hoop control is vital for colour blending and keeping the stitches within the confines of the design. Once finished the embroidery needs careful preparation so it can be mounted for display or turned into functional art.

Transferring the Design

Some methods are more time-consuming and messy than others; I prefer to use quick, simple methods. You must consider the suitability of the fabric before you decide how to transfer the image: for instance, it wouldn't be possible to trace a design through thick dark material; fine synthetic materials may shrivel up with the heat of the iron when using transfer pencil; delicate hand-dyed fabrics may lose their colour when water-soluble film is washed away.

Tracing the Design onto Fabric

This is the most direct method of design transfer. Simply place a copy of the design underneath the fabric, pin it in place and trace. Pin the fabric so that it can't move whilst you are tracing the design. Tracing

If the fabric is too opaque to trace, use a light box or tape the fabric and design to a window. The extra light helps you to see the design so it can be traced more accurately. The design has been traced with pink watercolour pencil.

works well on fabrics which have a firm even weave.

When tracing use something that won't transfer to the embroidery threads; watercolour pencils or dressmaker's chalk pencils are a good choice because they can be colour-matched to the threads. Pencil is not a good choice because the soft graphite will show through the stitching or make the threads grey. If you must use pencil, choose a hard lead such as H2. Disappearing marker pens are best avoided because the design can fade before you have finished stitching it.

The easiest way to use transfer pencil is to print the design so it is the actual working size and trace the design on the back of the printed paper with the transfer pencil; this reverses the design for you so that it's facing the correct way for stitching.

Printed designs can be pinned to the fabric and outlined with straight stitch. Standard printer paper is robust enough to withstand stitching; it also stabilizes the fabric whilst the outline is stitched.

The paisley design was transferred onto Avalon water-soluble film with a blue Fineliner, then the embroidery was stitched with straight stitch using pale blue thread. The blue pen did not run into the white cotton when the film was washed away.

The beach hut design was transferred to the fabric using blue dressmaker's carbon paper. The design was traced with a ballpoint pen to ensure there was enough pressure to transfer it onto the fabric.

Transfer Pencil

The pigment in a transfer pencil is activated by heat. Draw the design onto thin paper, then pin the paper to the fabric, design side down. Press a hot iron onto the paper to activate the pigment so it is transferred to the fabric. If the iron has holes in the plate parts of the design may be not transferred. Double images can be accidentally made if the design is not pinned properly or if the iron is moved around too much.

This method of transferring the design creates a mirror image of the design. If the design contains text or numbers you must reverse the image because the transferred design will be the wrong way round. Transfer pencil is permanent; it cannot be removed from the fabric once fixed so all the transferred design must be covered with embroidery.

Dressmaker's Carbon

This comes in sheet form, which has a waxy inked side just like the sheet found a duplicate book. Dressmaker's carbon performs the same function but it's less messy and it's specially formulated for use on fabric. It is available in many colours including white, which is ideal for transferring designs onto dark fabric.

To transfer a design, pin the paper design to the fabric along two sides then slide the dressmaker's carbon underneath, inky side facing down. Place the fabric on a hard surface because the design is transferred more evenly. Trace the design with a hard pencil or ballpoint; pressing down hard transfers the ink onto the surface of the fabric. Unpin the paper and remove the carbon to reveal the design. This method is easier than using a transfer pencil because you don't have to worry about mirroring or reversing the design.

Paper or Tissue

One of the traditional methods of transferring a design is to draw it on thin paper. The paper design is tacked or pinned onto the fabric. The outlines are tacked by hand or machine. The paper can then be torn away to leave the tacked design. This method is time-consuming because it's difficult to remove the small pieces of paper without making a mess. Using paper does have some merits: it protects the fabric from dirt, it's not permanent and it's suitable for fabrics with uneven textures or weaves.

Water-soluble Fabric or Film

The most suitable film for design transfer is a transparent one such as mediumweight Avalon. Soluble film is suitable for use with fabrics and threads if they can cope with immersion in water. The transparent film is pinned over the design and traced using a permanent pen or colour-matched Fineliner. Water-based pens shouldn't be used because the ink does not dry and the colour can run into the embroidery when the film is washed away. The traced design is pinned to the fabric and the fabric is placed in a hoop. Extra pins may be required because soluble film is flimsy and it has a habit of moving whilst it is being sewn. The embroidery is stitched through the film which also stabilizes the fabric. When the embroidery is finished the excess soluble film is peeled away and the embroidery immersed in water. Once rinsed the embroidery is left to dry on an old towel. The finished embroidery may need extra pressing because it has been immersed in water.

Adapting a Design for Thread-painting

Beginners should choose a simple design. Look for one with a limited colour palette and simple outlines. Botanical patterns or historical flower drawings are an ideal subject to choose because they have already been designed for you. Artists' and illustrators' resource books are a good place to start looking for inspiration: the designs found in these publications are reproduced with the artist or crafter in mind.

There are a few things to consider when adapting a design. Do you want the embroidery to be a simple outline or made up of solid colours? What texture would you like to achieve with the stitches? What fabric and threads would you like to use? How are you going to blend colours? Will the design have graduated shading? The answers to these questions influence how you adapt the design.

The first thing to do is make a copy of the design to the actual working size of the embroidery. A scanner and printer are ideal for this because drawing to scale can be time-consuming. Make several copies of the design because you may want to alter part of the design to make it more personal; colouring copies with artist's pencils can help you choose the right colour scheme for the embroidery. More about designing for embroidery can be found in Chapter 3.

Choosing Fabric for Thread-painting

Have a fresh look at the design and visualize the type and size of material needed for the thread-painting. Material can be fickle. At first glance the fabric may seem suitable for the intended project but halfway through you may notice it pulling in or bubbling; this can even happen when the fabric has been stabilized. Natural cotton or canvas are the best materials to use for thread-paintings as natural fabrics are more responsive to being pressed after being put in a hoop and roughly handled.

Review the design to see if any elements could cause problems: for instance, spaces enclosed by embroidery can pucker and some shapes can cause fabric to distort when combined with stitch direction. Is the chosen fabric suited to your adapted design and method of transfer? Will it be able to cope with the type and density of stitching used? How will you stabilize the fabric and prevent it from pulling or shrinking with the stitches?

To combat potential problems it is advisable to rinse the fabric in water to remove the finishing agents and iron when dry. Washing and ironing reveals how the fabric reacts to water and heat; some poly cottons can shrink when ironed and it is better to discover that attribute before beginning an embroidery project. I have been caught out a few times by a fabric that has unexpectedly bubbled or scorched. It is important to learn from your mistakes and discover how to correct them.

This working drawing for the vintage flower project has been adapted ready for embroidery; it shows the colour changes and what stitch direction to use.

The fabric used for this finished embroidery shrank when ironed, leaving very noticeable bubbles and creases. This error highlights the importance of choosing and testing fabrics before starting the real project. However, all was not lost; the embroidery could then be appliqued on to another background.

Choosing Thread

Thread type alters the appearance of the stitching so it's important to choose the right thread for thread-painting. If you prefer your embroidery to have a textured surface you may prefer to use thick threads with a specialist needle. The individual stitches are easier to see but thick threads are clumsy when it comes to adding details or blending colours. Thin threads take a longer time to stitch but they are better for adding details and getting a smooth finish or blend when changing colours.

No. 40 thread is the best one to begin thread-painting with; because this weight is so popular it's available in a wide range of fibres and colours. The next thing to consider is fibre content; rayon, viscose or polyester produce a glossy sheen whilst cotton has a matt appearance. I would advise testing a few different brands to see which ones you prefer.

Thread Colour

Colour is one of the most crucial elements of thread-painting and knowing the basic rules of colour theory will help you choose the right colours for the embroidery threads. You need to think about the mood of the embroidery and the subject matter. It may be helpful to ask yourself a few questions to help you pick a colour scheme. Do the colours need to be realistic? Do you need to match the colours to the design? Do they need to enhance or reflect the meaning of the subject matter? Does your thread range have all the colours you need? Colour theory is discussed in Chapter 3.

If your design contains graduated colours you will need at least three shades of thread to produce a colour gradient. Add more shades to your colour palette or use a finer thread to obtain a smoother blend; some of my embroideries contain at least twelve shades, tones or tints of the same base colour. Graduating colours with machine thread-painting is a lot like using long and short stitches in hand embroidery; the two colours need to meet and mix and this can be achieved with the use of staggered stitching.

Stitch Type

When you have chosen the threads you also need to think about stitch direction and type. It is easier to thread-paint with straight stitch because zigzag is more difficult to control – it's harder to stay within the confines of a design because the needle is moving from side to side. Straight stitch is easier to control because the stitches appear to stay the same when the hoop changes direction but when stitched en masse hoop direction does alter the appearance of straight stitch: for instance, horizontal stitches have a different sheen from vertical ones, longer stitches produce a glossier embroidery whilst shorter ones create a matt texture. These effects are more noticeable when stitching with shiny thread such as rayon, viscose or polyester.

Imagine moving the hoop so the stitch direction and length suit the design. Stitching in a small space is harder than stitching in a larger one. Look at the design to see which direction is most suitable: for example, follow the length of a plant stem rather than trying to stitch horizontally across its narrow width. If the space is small we tend to produce smaller stitches which have a different texture from longer stitches; this only matters if you want the stitching to be uniform across the embroidery.

STEP-BY-STEP PROJECT
Whimsical Beach Hut

YOU WILL NEED

Equipment
- Photocopier or printer and scanner
- Sewing machine
- Darning or embroidery foot
- Normal tension bobbin case
- Empty bobbins
- Size 90/14 universal machine needle
- Embroidery scissors
- Fabric scissors
- Paper scissors
- Glass-headed pins
- Quick Unpick (seam ripper)
- Ruler
- Iron
- Ironing cloth for damp pressing
- Baking parchment
- Pencil
- Pencil sharpener
- Biro or ballpoint pen
- Disappearing fabric marker

Materials
- White A4 paper
- Dressmaker's carbon paper
- Cotton fat quarter with clouds printed on it
- Taupe- or sand-coloured lining fabric scrap
- Firm iron-on interfacing measuring approximately 15 × 20cm (6 × 8in.)
- Stitch 'n' Tear or similar tear-away stabilizer
- Bondaweb heat-fusible webbing
- Madeira Bobbinfil or white cotton thread
- Madeira Classic no. 40 thread in colours 1028 (blue), 1023 (lemon), 1296 (deep ocean blue), 1125 (saffron yellow), 1336 (saddle brown), 1170 (fern green), 1132 (clear blue), 1066 (cornmeal); variegated thread with brown, grey, beige or taupe overtones

Design template
- Whimsical Beach Hut

Machine used
- Bernina 801
- Feeder teeth down
- Normal tension

I have fond memories of the blue and yellow beach huts on Felpham sea front – their pastel colours make them an ideal subject for thread-painting. Landscapes don't have to be serious; you can use a bit of artistic licence to create something fun and personal to you.

This project demonstrates how to use heat-fusible webbing to add extra detail to the background fabric. Dressmaker's carbon paper is used to transfer the design and a combination of satin stitch and straight stitch is used to embroider the beach hut and its setting. Thread painting with satin stitch teaches you how to control the hoop and foot pedal speed and produce even spacing between the stitches. When the embroidery is finished you will be shown how to press it and mount it in a simple frame.

① Iron the fat quarter to remove the creases, then iron interfacing to the back. Make sure the glue side is against the fabric and use a sheet of baking parchment to protect the iron. The iron glides over the baking parchment to create a firmer bond between the fabric and interfacing. Cut away the excess fabric to leave a small 1cm (3/8in.) strip round the interfacing.

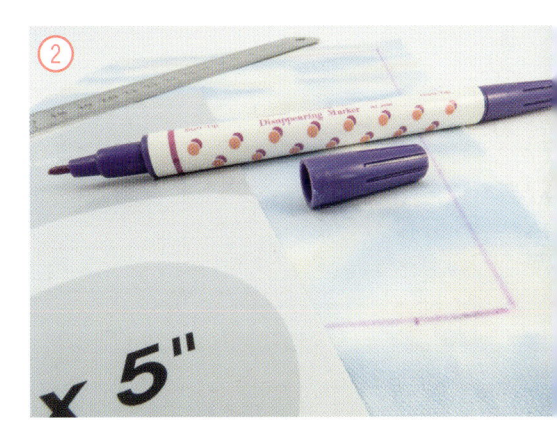

② Turn the bonded fat quarter so the right side is facing upwards. Remove the paper insert from the frame and position it in the centre of the fabric. Pin it in place and draw round the insert with the disappearing fabric marker; use a ruler to keep the lines straight. This guideline indicates where the frame will be on the embroidery.

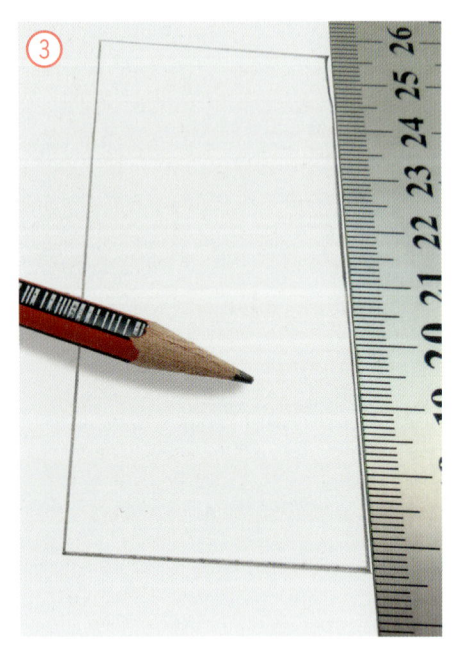

③

Use a pencil and ruler to draw a rectangle measuring 15 × 5cm (6 × 2in.) onto the paper side of the heat-fusible webbing. Cut it out with paper scissors so there is a small border around the drawn lines.

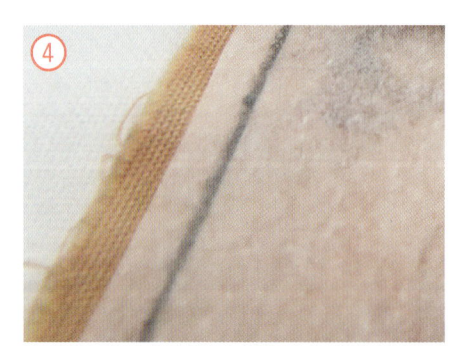

④

Place the cut webbing on the back of the taupe lining scrap, glue side down. Cover with baking parchment then iron the webbing to the lining. Cut out the bonded fabric rectangle, using the lines for guidance, then peel off the backing paper.

⑤

Position the rectangle of bonded lining near the bottom of the cloud fabric so it covers the base of the drawn rectangle. Make sure the bonded glue side is against the fabric, cover with backing parchment and iron to fix in place.

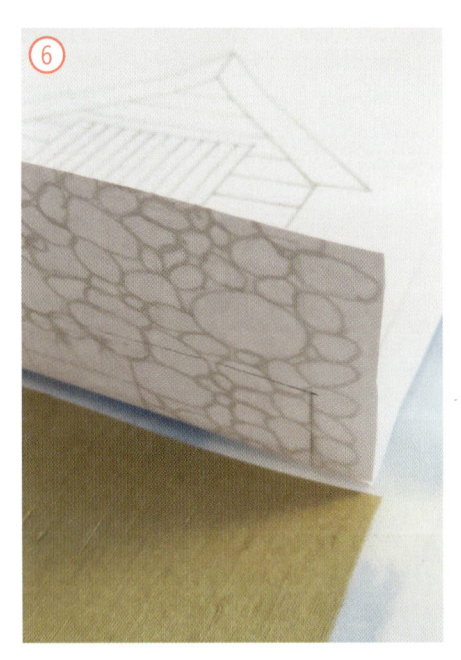

⑥

Print a copy of the design and fold the paper along the top of the pebble beach. Align the fold with the top of the bonded lining fabric. Pin the paper to the fabric across the top so the paper can be folded up without changing the position of the design.

⑦

Put the fabric on a hard surface and position the dressmaker's carbon underneath the printed design, making sure the inky side is against the fabric. Use a ballpoint pen to trace the design; you may need to use a ruler to keep the lines straight. Working on a hard surface helps the ink to transfer to the fabric more effectively.

⑧

Lift up the carbon paper to check the design has been successfully transferred. Unpin the design and put the dressmaker's carbon back into the packet. Pin two layers of Stitch 'n' Tear (or similar tear-away stabilizer) to the back of the design; the fabric needs extra support because of the density of the satin stitch.

102   Chapter 6 – Thread-painting

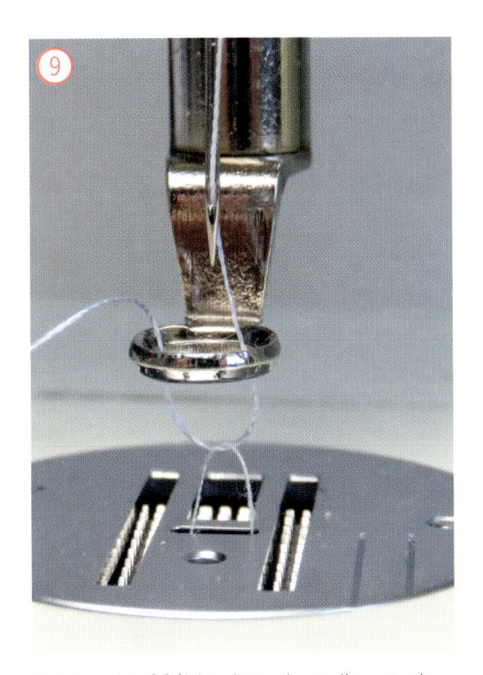

⑨ Insert a size 90/14 universal needle, attach the embroidery foot and insert a bobbin wound with white Bobbinfil or cotton. Thread the needle with Madeira 1028 (blue), then turn the hand wheel to bring the bobbin thread to the top, pull out a short length of both threads and place them to the rear of the needle plate. Set the machine to the widest zigzag and lower the feeder teeth.

⑩ Position the fabric under the embroidery foot and lower it. Move the fabric so the needle is over the start of a wall slat. Rotate the hand wheel to check if the needle is in the correct position; the needle should puncture a traced slat line so alter the width of the stitch to match the width of the wall slat. If the fabric is in the wrong position think about where the stitches form and move the fabric to the correct position.

⑪ Start embroidering the wooden wall with satin stitch. Keep one edge of the stitch lined up with the traced line and move the fabric with slow uniform speed. Continue sewing until all the wall slats are stitched; you may need to embroider another layer of satin stitch to fill in gaps. Take the thread ends to the back and tie them off (the ends need tying because satin stitch is more likely to fray if it's trimmed without knotting).

⑫ Thread the needle with Madeira 1023 (lemon). Reset the width of the zigzag so it matches the width of the vertical door slats; rotate the balance wheel by hand to test the width of the stitch. Sew the door with satin stitch; uneven stitching can be neatened by sewing another row of satin stitch on top. Take the ends to the back and tie them off. Variations in stitch direction may cause the fabric to warp; minor warping eases when the embroidery is damp pressed.

⑬ If the stitches have hidden the roof redraw the lines with a dressmaker's disappearing marker. Line the needle up with the edge of the roof's eave and widen the stitch so it matches the width of the roof. Move the fabric so the satin stitch matches the slant of the roof. When the roof is stitched take the threads to the back and tie them off. Set the stitch type to straight and fill in the parts of the roof that have been missed; match the length of the stitches to the zigzag embroidery so they blend in better.

⑭ Thread the needle with Madeira 1296 (deep ocean blue) and keep the stitch set to straight. Embroider the divisions between the wall slats, then sew round the roof, door and sides of the beach hut. Embroider three or four rows of straight stitch to make the outline bold enough. Stitching in the gutter raises the surface of the satin stitch to give the embroidery a fun sense of naivety.

Chapter 6 – Thread-painting **103**

⑮

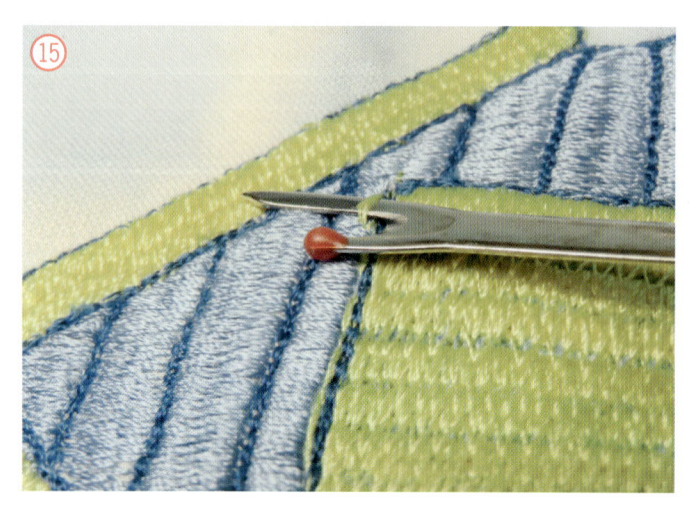

Trim away the thread tabs and inspect the embroidery; noticeable wobbles need to be corrected by unpicking and re-sewing. In this example I have not been very neat with the straight stitch around the door; the yellow satin stitch needs to be removed. It is easier to catch large stitches with the point of a quick unpick; care needs to be taken because the cutting edge is very sharp and it can easily rip a hole in the fabric. Use embroidery scissors to tidy up the tufts left by unpicking.

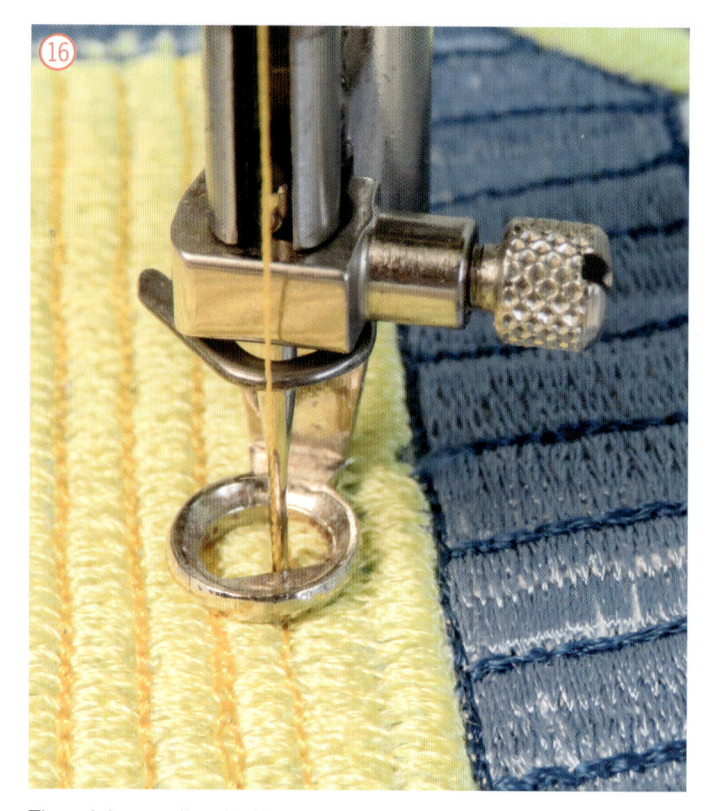

⑯

Thread the needle with Madeira 1125 (saffron yellow) and use straight stitch to outline the door slats. Find the gap between the rows of satin stitch and sew two or three rows of straight stitch to fill it in.

⑰

Thread the needle with 1028 (blue) and set the machine to medium-width zigzag. Sew a door handle and two door hinges with satin stitch, varying the width of the satin stitch to add interest to the hinges. Take the threads to the back and tie them off. Set the machine to straight stitch and thread the needle with 1296 (deep ocean blue). To make the details stand out, sew around the door handle and hinges with two rows of straight stitch, then trim the thread ends close to the embroidery.

⑱

Thread the needle with a variegated rayon or viscose thread, which needs to have brown, grey, beige or taupe overtones. Stitch the outline of the pebbles with straight stitch; sewing round them several times, then fill them in with straight stitch. Sew each pebble in different directions. Don't stitch too closely; allow some of the background fabric to show through. Trim the thread ends with embroidery scissors.

Thread the needle with Madeira 1336 (saddle brown) and outline the pebbles with straight stitch. One or two rows of stitching should provide enough detail because the pebbles have already been outlined. Re-thread the needle with Madeira 1170 (fern green) and add some patches of foliage between the pebbles; try to stitch these patches randomly so they represent tufts or grass or weeds. Trim the thread tails close to the embroidery.

Add some shading to the blue slats with Madeira 1132 (clear blue). Use straight stitch and sew in the same direction as the satin stitch; the threads will blend together to create subtle shading. Thread the needle with Madeira 1066 (cornmeal) and add some highlights to the door slats with straight stitch; don't stitch into the outlines. Trim the thread ends close to the embroidery.

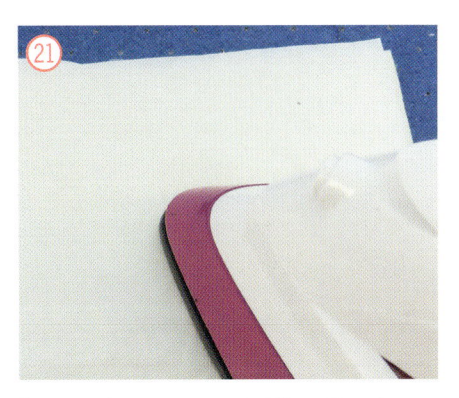

Remove the tear-away stabilizer, then iron the embroidery on the reverse with a damp cloth. Manipulate the iron to remove the creases and bulges. If the creases won't budge you need to remove the iron-on interfacing; gently heat it with the iron and peel it away from the fabric whilst hot. Cut the interfacing from the embroidery.

Press the back of the embroidery and fabric with a scrap of cotton; this removes the remnants of fusible glue. Press the front of the background fabric with a clean iron to remove the remaining creases; press close to the embroidery but do not iron the surface of it.

The embroidery is now ready to be framed. See Chapter 12 for information on this.

Chapter 6 – Thread-painting   **105**

STEP-BY-STEP PROJECT
Paisley Pennant

YOU WILL NEED

Equipment
- Photocopier or scanner and printer
- Sewing machine with drop feed or darning plate
- Size 90/14 universal machine needle
- Straight stitch presser foot
- Embroidery or darning foot
- 15cm (6in.) wooden or metal embroidery hoop
- Normal tension bobbin case
- Empty bobbins
- Dressmaker's chalk pencil or artist's watercolour pencil
- Pencil
- Pencil sharpener
- Ruler
- Set square
- Measuring tape
- Iron
- Ironing cloth
- Soft towel
- Baking parchment
- Glass-headed pins
- Sharp needle for hand-sewing seams and braid

Materials
- A4 paper
- Two pieces of thick black cotton 29 × 43cm (11½ × 17in.)
- Thin iron-on black interfacing 29 × 43cm (11½ × 17in.)
- Stitch 'n' Tear or similar tear-away stabilizer
- Scrap cotton to test stitches
- Dry glue or double-sided tape
- Pompom braid
- Black bobbin thread
- Strong black thread for the seams
- Red or black thread for hand-sewing
- Seven thread colours to embroider the design, plus black; I used Madeira Classic no. 40 thread in colours 1064 (yellow), 1137 (deep yellow), 1078 (orange), 1147 (red), 1081 (azalea), 1310 (magenta), 1033 (purple), 1007 (amber black)
- Dowel about 5cm (2in.) longer than the finished pennant

Design templates
- Paisley Motif
- Paisley Flowers

Machine used
- Bernina 801
- Feeder teeth down for embroidery
- Feeder teeth up for making up
- Normal tension

This project shows how to transfer a design using the paper method. The paper technique is the best one to use for this embroidery because the background fabric is black. Tracing the design through black fabric is impossible and it's difficult to see a soluble film design against a dark background.

The paper stabilizes the cotton whilst the outlines are embroidered with straight stitch. This design has lots of thread changes; it's more effective when different colours are sewn next to each other. All of the stitching is done with straight stitch so you need to decide how to use stitch direction to fill in the central design and small motifs.

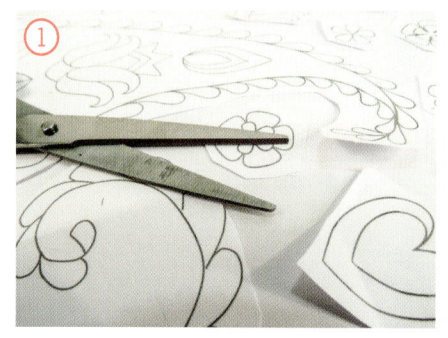

① Look in the back of the book to find the Paisley Motif and Paisley Flowers templates; trace or photocopy them onto plain paper. The central motif should measure 20 × 15cm (8 × 6in.). Cut out the flower motifs and arrange them on A4 paper to create your version of the design. When you are happy with the design, secure the pieces with dry glue or double-sided tape and make a photocopy or tracing of it.

② Draw a rectangle measuring 29 × 43cm (11½ × 17in.) on the black cotton with a chalk or watercolour pencil. Always use a ruler and set square, as careful measuring makes a project much easier to finish.

3 Cut the fabric out and use it as a template to cut out the interfacing. Iron the interfacing onto the back of the cotton, making sure the glue side is against the fabric and protecting the iron with a layer of baking parchment. Cut out the back panel using the prepared fabric as a template.

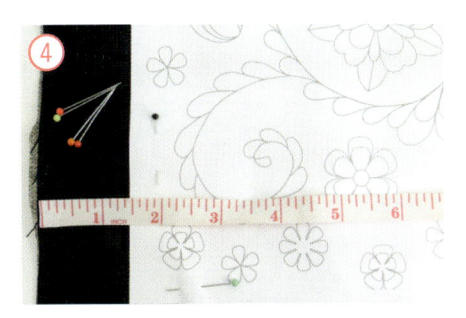

4 Pin the printed design to the front of the cotton so there is a 4cm (1½in.) seam allowance at the bottom and both sides of the paper. The paper needs lots of pins to stop the fabric shifting underneath it. The seam allowance at the top of the paper is larger because the fabric needs to fold over to form a tube for the hanging rod to be inserted.

5 Set up the machine, insert a size 90/14 universal needle, tighten the needle clamp and thread the needle with Madeira no. 40 thread 1147 (red). Attach an embroidery foot, lower the feeder teeth and set the stitch type to straight. Insert a bobbin wound with black into the normal tension bobbin case and click into place. Turn the hand wheel to bring the bobbin thread to the top, then pull a short length of both threads behind the needle plate.

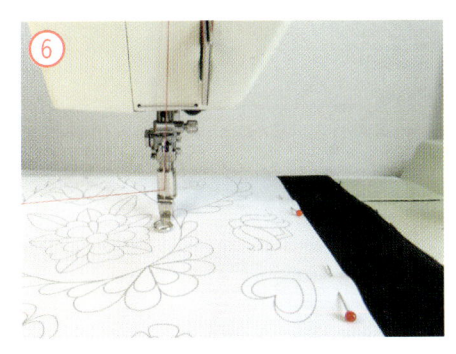

6 Slide the paper-topped cotton under the foot and lower the foot lever. There is no need to use a hoop because the paper acts as an additional stabilizer and attempting to hoop a paper design will tear it.

7 Stitch the outline of each motif with one row of straight stitch. When the tacked outline is complete remove the pins and cut the thread tabs from the top of the paper. Peel the paper away to reveal the tacked design, although it may be useful to leave some paper inside the motifs because the initial of the chosen thread colours can be written on them.

8 Pin one layer of tear-away stabilizer to the back of the tacked cotton and place the cotton in a hoop so the large paisley motif is central. Choose a colour and remove the paper from the area so it's ready to stitch. Embroider the design with straight stitch, sewing a foundation grid and then stitching more densely in one direction to give the embroidery a raised effect.

Chapter 6 – Thread-painting

9. Continue stitching the largest section of the design, changing colours as you stitch. Trim the thread tabs between each colour change to stop the foot or needle getting caught on them. Remove the paper before you stitch because sewing through paper makes the needle blunt.

10. Re-position the hoop when the area within is stitched. Keep swapping thread colours and stitch direction to add variety to the design. Continue stitching and moving the hoop until all of the motifs are embroidered. I used a metal hoop because it is easier to reposition when stitching is not dense.

11. Re-thread the needle with two black threads and make sure both are engaged in the tension discs. Using two threads through the needle can cause loops, so stitch a sample on scrap cotton to check both threads are stitching neatly. Outline the motifs with black straight stitch to redefine the design.

12. Examine the embroidery and trim the thread tabs from the front. Give the embroidery a good shake to remove the scraps of perforated paper.

13. Take one of the black threads out of the needle and stitch the background of the main motif with open straight stitch. Stitch horizontally and allow the background fabric to show through the embroidery. Cut the thread tabs away from the front and back, then peel away the tear-away stabilizer.

14. Place the embroidery on a soft clean towel and cover it with a dry ironing cloth. Iron the back of the embroidery; dry pressing should remove handling and hoop marks. If the stitching has distorted the fabric, damp press the embroidery on the back or mist the fabric with a fine spray. Damp pressing should flatten the fabric whilst leaving the embroidery stitches raised.

15. Turn the embroidery so the wrong side is facing upwards. Find the bottom of the lowest motif and make a line 4cm (1½in.) below it with a chalk pencil. Use a ruler to draw the bottom horizontal seam line; the rest of the rectangle is measured and drawn from this baseline.

16. Find the motif nearest the left edge of the fabric and make a mark 4cm (1½in.) from its left (outer) side. Locate the motif closest to the right edge of the fabric and make a mark 4cm (1½in.) from its right (outer) side with chalk pencil.

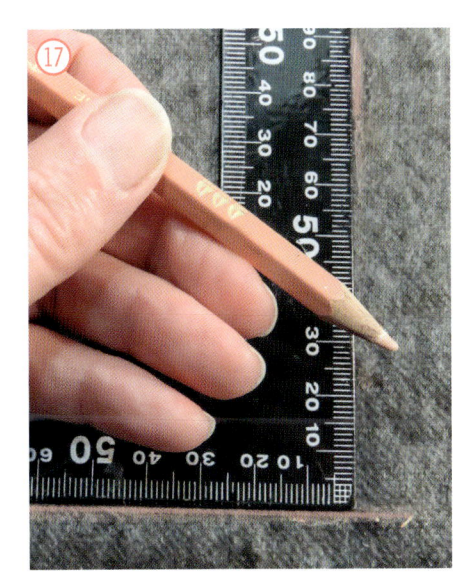

⑰ Align the set square with the bottom seam line and left mark. When the marks line up with the set square to make a right angle, draw the left side seam. Flip the set square and position it against the bottom seam line and right mark. When the marks line up to make a right angle, draw the right side seam.

⑱ Measure the distance between the side seams at the bottom, middle and top. The measurements should be the same; if they are not, one of the side seam lines is wrong. Redraw the seam lines and mark the wrong one with a cross. Align the set square with a side seam and draw a line across. My rectangle measured 25.5 × 42cm (10 × 16½in.).

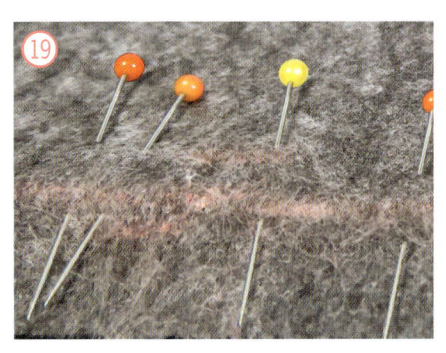

⑲ Lay the embroidered panel onto the back panel so right sides face each other. Pin the pieces together so they have matching seam allowances and position the pins so they cross the drawn chalk lines. Leave a small gap on the bottom seam for turning through. It is helpful to mark the start and end of the seam with two pins so that you remember where to start and stop sewing.

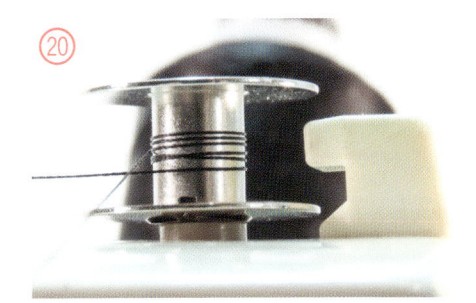

⑳ Wind a bobbin with strong black thread, load it into the bobbin case and insert in the machine. Thread the needle with strong black thread. Attach the straight-stitch presser foot, set the stitch type to medium-length straight stitch and raise the feeder teeth.

㉑ Back stitch the seams. Position the fabric under the foot and line the start of the bottom seam up with the needle, then lower the foot. Follow the drawn line with the needle, sew a few stitches forward, then press reverse to sew back over them. Release reverse and sew forward. Stop when you reach the corner; do not stitch beyond the corner. Remove the pins just before the foot reaches them.

㉒ At the corner, press reverse and sew backwards for a few stitches, then release reverse and sew to the corner, then stop. Lift the foot and rotate the fabric so the side seam lines up with the needle. Lower the foot and sew a few stitches forward, stop, press reverse and sew a few stitches back to the corner. Release reverse and stitch forwards, following the drawn line till you reach the next corner. Repeat the process to stitch all of the seams. When you reach the bottom seam remember to leave a gap for turning through.

Chapter 6 – Thread-painting **109**

㉓

This illustration shows where to use backstitch to reinforce the seam; using backstitch strengthens the seam so it does not come undone when turning through. Backstitching is usually situated at the start and end of seams; it can also be found where stitching changes direction, such as at corners or where the fabric is thicker.

㉔

Check the seams are straight and tuck-free; an easy way to do this is to fold the fabric so the side seams lie one on top of another. There should be no difference in the width between the seams. If there is a noticeable difference or wobble, mark where it starts and finishes with pins. Measure and redraw the seam line and re-sew it, then unpick the wobbly part. Turn the embroidery through to check the positioning of the embroidered design.

㉕

Turn the embroidery back through the opening so the raw seams are exposed. Cut the corners so the angled cut is close to the sewing line but not through it. Trim the rest of the seam allowance to about 1.5cm (¾in.). You may need to use a ruler to draw the cutting line because wobbly cutting can show through the fabric when the finished embroidery is pressed. Turn the embroidery back through so the right side is on the outside.

㉖

Use your fingers to ease the side seams out then use the point of a pin to tease the corners out carefully. Do not apply too much pressure when pulling the corners out because you do not want the fabric to split or fray near the seam.

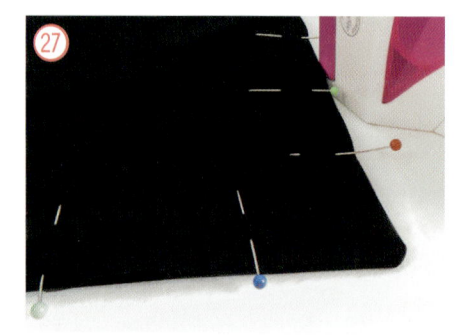

㉗

Pin the opening closed; the easiest way to do this is to fold the fabric inwards along the drawn seam line and pin in place. Fold the other side inwards to match and pin the sides together to close the opening. Pin the edge of the pennant to keep the side seams in position. Damp press the seams, then remove the pins and press again to get nice crisp edges.

㉘

Thread a sharp hand-sewing needle with black thread and use slip stitch to sew up the opening, then press the sewn seam to remove the handling marks.

110   Chapter 6 – Thread-painting

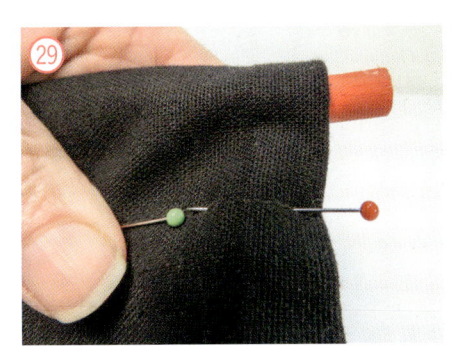

29 To make the hanging loop, fold about 5cm (2in.) of the excess fabric over to the back and pin in place. Make sure the pinned flap is wide enough to accommodate the dowel. The depth of the tube needs to be the same all the way along; if the tube is not level the pennant will be crooked when hung.

30 Turn the pennant so the embroidery is facing upwards and mark 4.5cm (1¾in.) down from the top of the fold with a chalk pencil; make three or four marks using the same measurements and join them up using a ruler and pencil. Measure to check the drawn seam line is accurate. The seam should secure the flap to the back without stitching through the embroidery. Sew the seam line with black thread using straight stitch, reversing at the beginning and end. Take the threads to the back and tie them off, threading the ends into the fabric to hide them. Check that the dowel fits.

31 Pin the pompom braid to the back, making sure the decorations are evenly spaced and match side to side. It may be easier to turn the fringe at the corners to make a mitred corner rather than cutting and folding the braid under. Hand-sew the braid in place with black or red cotton; black cotton does not look as neat on the back but it blends in better if you accidentally sew through to the front. Finish off by pushing the dowel or rod through the tube and add the decorative end caps.

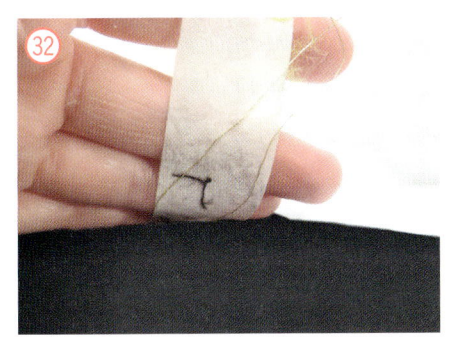

32 Brush off the thread tails and fluff; some fabrics are notoriously good at picking up fluff. A quick way to de-fluff your finished work is to roll some masking tape around your hand so the sticky side is facing outwards and gently pat the fabric with it.

33 The pompom braid picks up the bright colours of the embroidery. If the bold pompoms don't appeal to you the pennant can be left as it is, finished with a simple fringe or decorated with a matching ribbon garland.

Chapter 6 – Thread-painting **111**

STEP-BY-STEP PROJECT
Vintage Flower

YOU WILL NEED

Equipment
- Photocopier or scanner and printer
- Sewing machine with drop feed or darning plate
- Embroidery or darning foot
- Size 90/14 universal machine needles
- Glass-headed pins
- Normal tension bobbin case
- Empty bobbins
- 15cm (6in.) wooden hoop
- Ironing cloth
- Iron
- Baking parchment
- Clover mini-iron (optional)
- Fabric scissors
- Embroidery scissors
- Dressmaker's chalk pencil or artist's watercolour pencil
- Pencil
- Pencil sharpener
- Eraser

Materials
- White A4 paper or tracing paper
- Cream or ivory finely woven cotton canvas or natural fabric with an even weave measuring 38 × 46cm (15 × 18in.)
- Iron-on white non-woven interfacing
- White Stitch 'n' Tear or similar tear-away stabilizer
- White Madeira Bobbinfil
- Kingstar polyester thread no. 40 in colour 73 (dark pink)
- Madeira Classic thread no. 40 in colours 1108 (medium pink), 1120 (pale pink), 1071 (antique white), 1170 (dark green), 1049 (medium green), 1169 (pale green)

Design template
- Vintage Flower

Machine used
- Bernina 801
- Feeder teeth down
- Normal tension

Machine-embroidered straight stitch can be controlled to achieve blended stitches similar to those found in crewel work or traditional long and short stitch embroidery. This project is definitely influenced by my ecclesiastical embroidery training when I helped to restore some wonderful hand embroideries. The design is very traditional and the finished embroidery would look lovely outlined with traditional handsewn goldwork jap thread.

To obtain a pleasant gradient of shaded stitches you will need at least three shades of thread per colour group: for example, light pink, medium pink and dark pink. It is acceptable to mix brands (for example, Madeira and Sulky) but not thread type (for example, rayon and cotton) as this would affect the texture of the design. It is best to avoid mixing thread weights when blending colours because the thicker threads will stand out more.

①
Copy or trace the design in the back of the book. The design should measure approximately 23cm (9in.) tall when printed onto A4 paper.

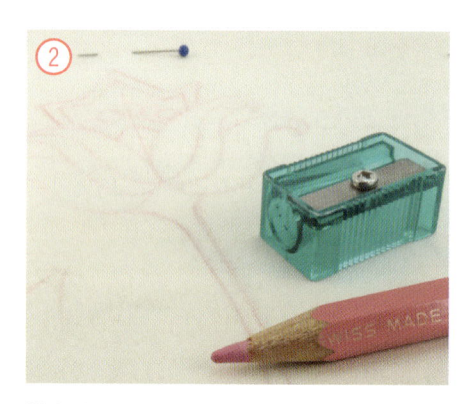

②
Slide the printed design under the ivory cotton so it's positioned in the centre of the fabric and pin in place. Use a dressmaker's chalk or watercolour pencil to trace the design, picking a colour to match the threads. If you can't see the design through the fabric, tape it to a window with masking tape; the natural light acts like a light box to help you to see the design more easily.

Chapter 6 – Thread-painting

③

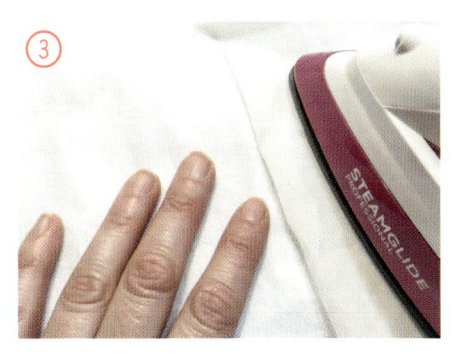

Iron the mediumweight interfacing onto the back of the cotton fabric, remembering that the glue side has a rougher surface. Put a sheet of baking parchment between the iron and interfacing; this helps the iron move over the interfacing without getting glue stuck to it. Iron-on interfacing can shrink with dense stitching; if you are worried about this happening use tear-away stabilizer instead of an iron-on one.

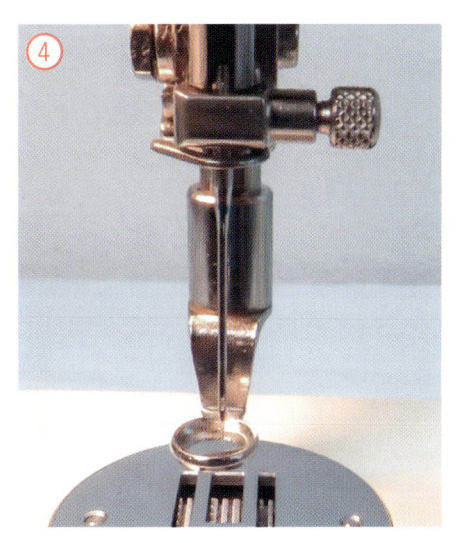

④

Set up the machine, drop the feeder teeth, attach an embroidery foot, insert a size 90/14 universal needle and set the stitch type to straight. Wind an empty bobbin with white Madeira Bobbinfil and insert it into the normal tension bobbin case, then load into the machine.

⑤

Pin a layer of tear-away stabilizer to the back of the design. Place the fabric in a hoop so the largest flower is central and pull the fabric to tighten it; hooped fabric should be drum-tight. Slide the hoop under the embroidery foot and thread the needle with dark pink; I used Kingstar polyester no. 40 thread in colour 73.

⑥

Stitch the dark parts of the large flower head. Follow the curve of the petals and fill the tips with dense straight stitch. Stagger the stitches into the area where the next colour change will be sewn and outline some of the petals with straight stitch. Trim the thread tails from the front of the embroidery.

⑦

Thread the needle with Madeira 1108 (medium pink) and embroider the next part of the flower. Imitate hand-sewn long and short stitches, staggering the stitches so they blend into the dark pink embroidery. Try to produce a gentle graduation. Keep the stitches flowing so they follow the direction of the petals; you may need to curve the stitching to get the right effect. Embroider the spiky flower head with straight stitch. Cut the thread tabs from the front of the embroidery.

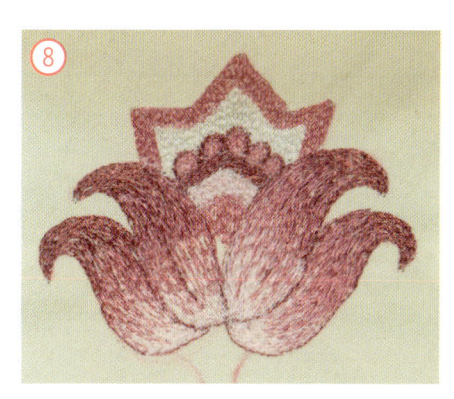

⑧

Thread the needle with Madeira 1120 (pale pink) and embroider the pale part of the petals. Stitch into the medium pink embroidery to get a graduated effect. Re-thread the needle with Madeira 1071 (antique white) and stitch the gap between the spiky flower head and the petals; use up-and-down straight stitch to fill this area in. Trim the thread tails from the front of the embroidery.

Chapter 6 – Thread-painting   **113**

⑨ Stitch the remaining parts of the flower head with the colours already used. Look at the flower to see if anything needs changing or refining. In my example the dark outlines between the petals had been lost; they were re-stitched with Kingstar 87 (dark pink). Some of the colour blending needed improving, there were gaps to be filled and edges to be neatened. Trim the thread tails between each colour change to stop them being sewn into the embroidery.

⑩ Remove the embroidery from the hoop and re-position it over another flower head. Stitch this flower head in a similar way using straight stitch, starting with the darkest thread, then blending in the medium and light threads to produce the graduated shaded effect. Use a combination of the colours already used: 73 (dark pink), 1108 (medium pink) and 1120 (light pink). Trim the thread ends, re-position the hoop over the final flower head and embroider this using the same method.

⑪ Re-position the hoop so the green foliage is within it. Thread the needle with Madeira 1170 (dark green) and use straight stitch to embroider the stem and calyx. Make the stitches follow the length of the stalk and keep within the drawn guidelines. Use longer stitches for the foliage because this gives the leaves a glossier appearance when compared to short stitches. Stagger the stitching for the next colour to blend in, then trim the thread tails.

⑫ Thread the needle with Madeira 1049 (medium green) and stitch the paler parts of the stalk and leaves with straight stitch. Embroider into the dark green to obtain a smooth graduation of colour and curve the stitches so they follow the shape of the leaves. Trim the threads tabs from the front of the embroidery.

⑬ Re-position the hoop so the big leaf is central and thread the needle with Madeira 1170 (dark green). Stitch the stalk, veins and outline, sewing rows of straight stitch one on top of another to produce thick defined embroidery. Change the thread to 1049 (medium green) and use straight stitch to fill the areas between the veins. Thread the needle with Madeira 1169 (pale green) and stitch the palest part of the leaf, stitching into the medium green areas to get a smooth blend of colours. Cut the thread tabs between each colour change.

⑭ Continue re-positioning the hoop to stitch the rest of the foliage, using any combination of dark, medium and light green. Start with the dark colours, then stitch the paler colours into them. Look at the embroidery and decide if it needs any more stitching to finish it. When you are sure the embroidery is complete cut the thread tabs from the front and back.

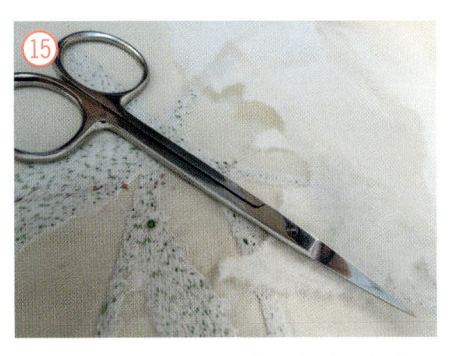

⑮ Use a low heat setting to iron the back of the embroidery, protecting the fabric with an ironing cloth. If the wrinkles do not resolve themselves turn up the heat and press with a damp cloth. Excessive pressing with a damp cloth can make the interfacing shift and wrinkle more; if this happens the only option may be to remove it.

⑯ Optional stage: removing the interfacing. Heat the interfacing with the iron to melt the glue and peel the interfacing off the fabric whilst warm. Interfacing can be tough and usually tears in one direction; you may need to use scissors to cut it away from the embroidery.

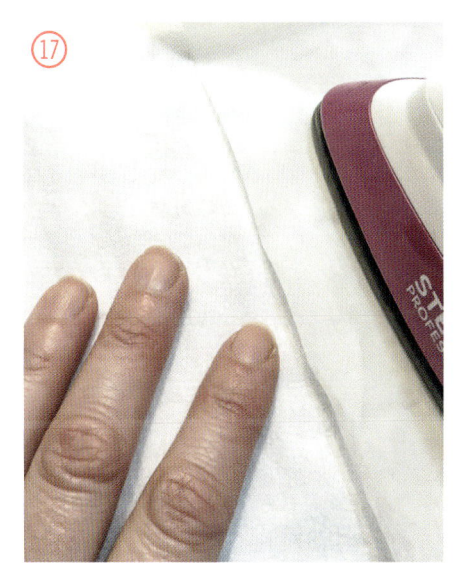

⑰ Optional stage: cover the back of the embroidery with a scrap of cotton and press it to remove the glue and handling marks. There may be creases in the spaces between the embroidery; the head of a mini-iron can reach these small areas more easily than a regular iron. Check the tip of the min-iron is clean and iron the embroidery on the back without using a protective cloth.

⑱

The embroidery should now be lying nice and flat; it is ready to be laced and framed. See Chapter 12 for suggestions about how to lace, mount or frame the embroidery.

Chapter 6 – Thread-painting **115**

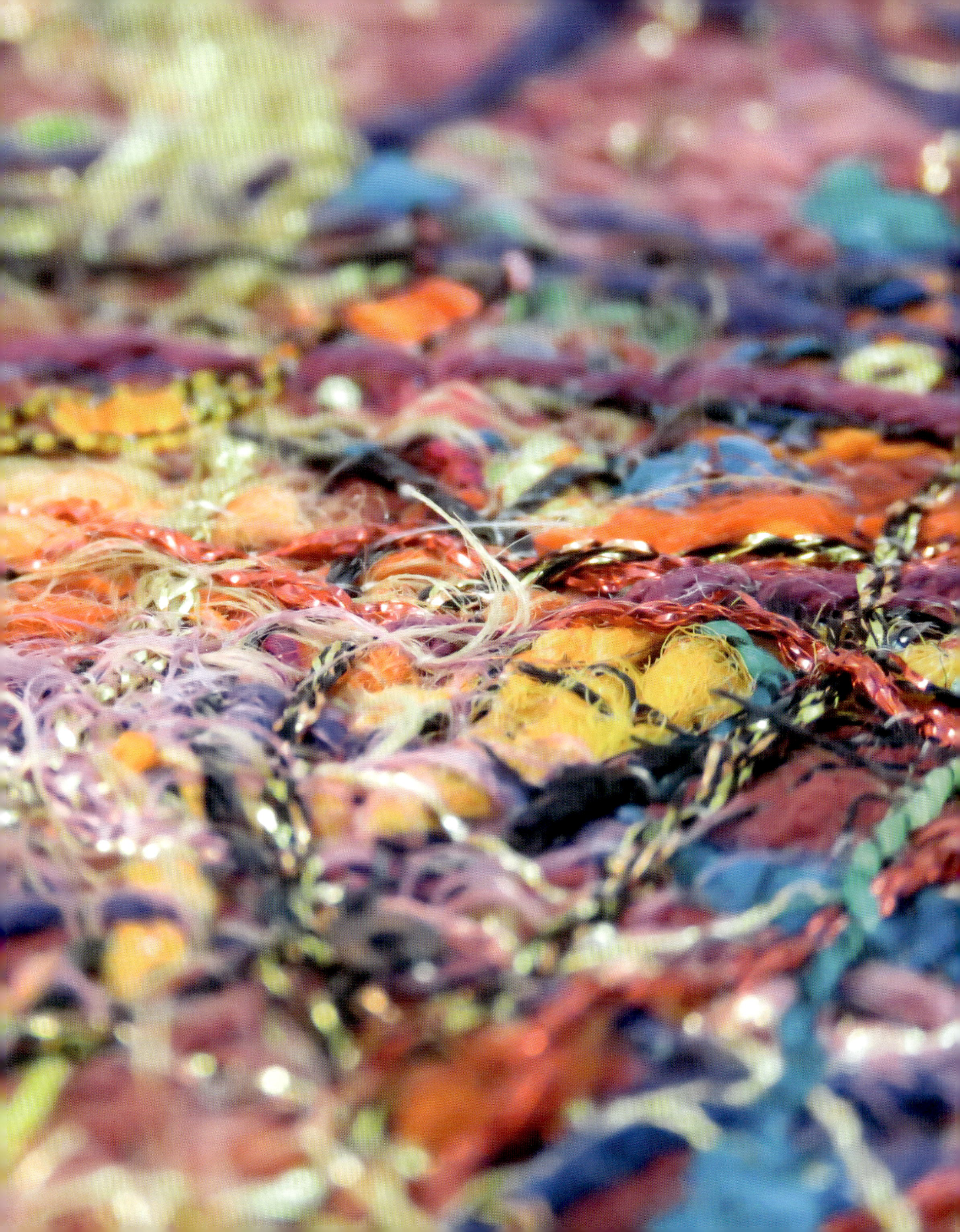

CHAPTER 7

Using Water-soluble Film

Soluble film has unique properties that enable the embroiderer to push the boundaries of what's possible with traditional machine embroidery; it has become an essential addition to my embroidery supplies and I often wonder how I managed without it. I hope you will be inspired to try some of the projects in this chapter and have your own 'wow' moment like I did when I first used it.

Water-soluble Film

Soluble film was originally developed in the 1960s and is used for many applications such as packaging detergents, personal care, laundry bags, medicinal dressings, food protection and the textile industry. It is made from plant cellulose or polyvinyl alcohol; manufacturers claim that dissolved film has little or no impact on the environment because the dissolved residue is consumed by bacterial micro-organisms.

The most common soluble embroidery stabilizers are clear film and non-woven opaque fabrics; other specialist solubles come in the form of woven fabrics or sheets of paper. Film weight is usually described as light, medium or heavy. Soluble film and fabrics can be brought in packets or loose by the metre or yard. Widths vary, depending on what the film was developed for: some films are manufactured to fit industrial hoops whilst others are packaged for textile artists to use.

Clear Water-soluble Film

Glossy soluble film looks and feels like food wrap. Some brands come wound onto cardboard tubes for easy dispensing whilst others are packaged in grip-seal bags. Glossy brands can be quite clingy and care must be taken to separate the film so the correct amount is used. The dimpled kind has a matt surface that is more manageable and easier to separate.

Clear soluble film is available in various weights and widths. Some dissolve in cold water, others in hand-hot water; refer to the packaging for the correct temperature. Some clear brands can smell of acetic acid when the packet is first opened; this is due to the ingredients of the film. If you have sensitive skin it may be advisable to wear

The transparency of Romeo and Avalon makes them ideal for transferring designs; when the embroidery is finished the film is simply washed away. Top: shown slightly rumpled, thick glossy Romeo is suitable for flat and three-dimensional embroideries. Bottom: Avalon is a dimpled lightweight film suitable for flat machine embroideries.

gloves whilst dissolving the film because it can feel very sticky or slimy when it begins to break down.

Popular brands of transparent water-soluble film are Avalon, Romeo, Sulky Solvy and Badgemaster. Avalon is a lightweight film made by Madeira and has a dimpled surface that reflects less light; this is helpful when embroidering because bright light from the machine can be distracting. Romeo is a heavyweight film also made by Madeira; it is slightly shiny and has

Rear: Aquasol non-woven water-soluble fabric has a soft dimpled surface and remains very stable when embroidered. Front: woven hotwater-soluble fabric acts like traditional fabric and handles like cotton organza; it's very flexible on the bias so drawn designs can become easily distorted.

Woven soluble fabric needs to be placed in a hoop because it's so flexible; these circles were stitched with straight stitch using metallic and plain embroidery threads. When the fabric is dissolved it leaves the stitched circles behind to create abstract machine lace.

a slight yellow colouration when folded. Sulky Solvy is a thin film made by Sulky which has a textured surface. Sulky Ultra Solvy is a thicker version from the same manufacturer. Badgemaster, made by Aquafilm, is a very thick film, sometimes called 'super film'. Heavyweight or thick films like Badgemaster and Romeo can be used to make three-dimensional embroideries.

Opaque Water-soluble Fabric

Opaque soluble fabrics can be woven or non-woven; some have a soft feel whilst others can be firm like paper. If you can't get used to the 'plastic' feel of water-soluble film, you may prefer using soluble fabric because it's like sewing on normal material. Some brands of opaque water-soluble have a temporary sticky surface making them ideal for positioning yarns and fabric snips. These types of film have a wax paper backing to protect the glue, which is water-soluble so that it disappears when the soluble fabric is washed away.

Non-woven Water-soluble Fabric

This is made from soluble fibres; it is usually white and handles like interfacing or thin fleece. Non-woven solubles are less likely to distort when stitched because they are firmer than woven water-solubles. Popular brands of non-woven water-soluble fabrics are Aquasol, Solufleece, Soluvlies and Sulky Fabri-Solvy. The first three are different names for the same product made by the manufacturers of Vilene. These soluble fabrics have a soft feel like interfacing; because they are non-woven they are very strong and do not distort when sewn.

Opaque water-soluble can be used to stabilize fine fabrics, as a topper to secure fabric snips or as a medium to transfer designs, and it's transparent enough to see bold black and white designs or pencil drawings. It's nice to use opaque soluble if you don't want to see the fabric beneath. Colours become muted so you can concentrate on the stitching; you get a lovely surprise when you wash the soluble away to reveal the finished embroidery.

Sticky Water-soluble Fabric

Sticky films have a layer of temporary water-soluble glue on one side to aid the positioning of fabrics or designs. These types of films reduce the amount of pins needed to secure a design, and they are very handy for abstract designs or for projects that use tiny snips. Aquabond by Aquatics and Sticky Fabri-Solvy by Sulky have a sticky side for easy positioning of fabrics and yarns.

Opaque Woven Soluble Fabric

Woven soluble fabric is made from soluble fibres that are spun and woven into a plain weave fabric which looks and feels like coarse silk lining or cotton organza. Woven soluble fabric can be tricky to use because it has a flexible warp and weft. Designs can distort when the soluble fabric is placed in a hoop and intense stitching can make holes in it. Care needs to be taken when transferring designs because ink-based pens run into the warp and weft and graphite pencils mark the stitched threads. Woven soluble is dissolved in hot water, which can be a problem if the fabrics or threads are sensitive to heat. The dissolved embroidery needs more blocking and shaping because the soluble fibres shrivel up as they dissolve, causing the embroidery stitches to shrink with them.

Water-soluble Paper

If you like the texture of paper and working without a hoop, this could be the soluble for you. Water-soluble paper looks and feels like a stiff non-woven tear-away such as Stitch 'n' Tear. It's ideal to use for organza cut work because it is firm enough to use without a hoop. A layer on the top and bottom secured with pins is sufficient

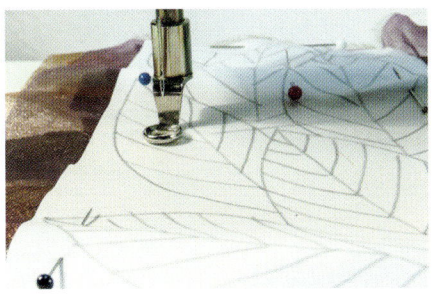

Two layers of soluble paper are firm enough to support these layers of organza. The pencil lines will be stitched over with straight stitch; the design will be finished with satin stitch, then layers of organza are cut away to create the cut work design.

The organza was stabilized with two layers of lightweight soluble film, one piece of film having the design drawn onto it with a permanent black pen. The leaf was embroidered onto two layers of shot organza with straight stitch; metallic thread was used top and bottom to stitch the embroidery. Here the film has been washed away.

to hold the fabric in place. Soluble paper is lovely to draw on because it feels like paper, and designs can be drawn with pencil when using dark threads or fabric. Aquatics manufacture a soluble paper just called Paper and Sulky produce one called Paper Solvy; both are supplied in sheet form.

Water-soluble Film Weights

Film weights have different properties, the weight and type chosen depends on the project and what you need the film to do.

Lightweight film can be used to:

- stabilize fine fabrics like organza (use one layer of film top and bottom)
- transfer designs (trace the design onto the film then pin on top of the fabric)
- prevent stitches sinking into deep pile of fabrics like velvet (use one layer on top of the fabric)
- keep layered fabric snips or yarns in place (use one layer on top)
- create fabrics (sandwich snips or scraps between two layers of film)
- embroider appliqué designs (use one layer of film and a layer of fabric).

Mediumweight film can be used to:

- stabilize fine fabrics (use one or two layers for support)
- transfer designs (trace the design onto the film then pin on top of the fabric)
- keep layered fabric snips or yarns in place (use one layer on top)
- create fabrics (sandwich snips or scraps between two layers of film)
- embroider appliqué designs (use one layer of film and a layer of fabric).

Heavyweight film can be used to:

- transfer designs (trace the design onto the film then pin on top of the fabric)
- create fabrics (sandwich snips or scraps between two layers of film)
- create machine lace or embroideries for appliqué
- create three-dimensional embroideries (partially dissolve the film and mould the embroidery around a former then leave to dry).

Stabilizing Fine Fabrics

A layer of film on the top and bottom will support fine fabrics to prevent them being damaged by the embroidery process. Water-soluble is very useful if you don't want white or black interfacing to be visible through transparent fabrics like organza. Removing traditional tear-away can pull the embroidery or delicate fabrics, whereas water-soluble film is easy to remove; simply cut or tear away the excess film and immerse the embroidery in water to dissolve the remaining film.

Using a Topper to Add Definition to the Embroidery

When used on tricky fabrics like velvet or felt soluble film acts like a barrier to prevent the stitches drowning in dense pile. Fabrics with pile or bounce can cause stitches to shift, which can create problems with detailed designs, and soluble film flattens the surface so that designs can be stitched more accurately. The finished embroideries are more defined because they are stitched on top of the fabric instead of being lost amongst the surface fibres.

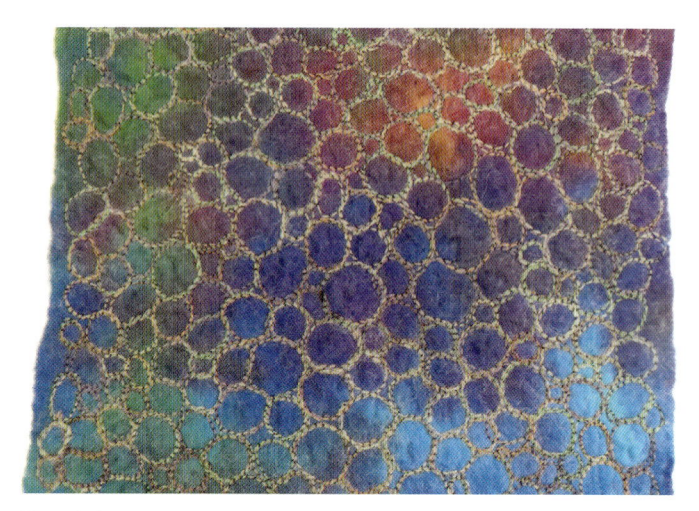

The circles were drawn onto opaque soluble fabric which was pinned on top of the hand-dyed felt. The felt needed to be supported by two layers of tear-away stabilizer because it was embroidered without a hoop. The circles are stitched with straight stitch using Madeira Lana; the visible dots of bobbin thread create a marl effect.

The snips of organza and metallic tissue were sprinkled onto the film so they overlapped each other. The spiral design highlights the nautical theme of the blue, green and iridescent fabric scraps. The embroidery was stitched freehand with straight stitch using metallic thread.

Creating Fabric with Two Layers of Film

Soluble film can be used as a medium to create your own fabrics with scraps of material or yarn. The method can be likened to making a sandwich; the soluble film becomes the bread and the fabric scraps become the filling. This simple process can produce stunning results and embroiderers who have never used this method often enjoy the magical 'wow' moment.

To create the design scraps of fabric or yarn are sprinkled or arranged on a base layer of soluble film, then another piece of film is laid over the fabric scraps to cover them and stop them moving around too much. The film sandwich is placed in a hoop to keep the film taut and free machine embroidered; any straight-stitch pattern can be used, as long as each scrap is connected to its neighbour with stitching.

If the stitches don't interlock with the scraps or each other the embroidered fabric will fall apart when the film is dissolved. If you want to create a lacy fabric sprinkle the snips so there are more gaps; if you want the fabric to be dense with smaller gaps sprinkle the snips so they are layered on top of one another.

Making your own fabric gives you total control over the colour and texture of the project. When choosing snips you can go down the multicolour route or stick to harmonious colour combinations; there are no rules, so let your imagination run wild. Yarns, wool and threads can be used on their own or with fabrics; fine mohair, tape or Lurex fashion yarns can add further texture to the embroidery. Organza, metallic tissue, net or lining fabrics work well because they are thin; if they have sparkle they will add extra glamour to the finished embroidery. The fabric design can be stitched with any type of embroidery thread: plain colours blend into the snips whilst metallics stand out and add even more glitz.

Using Water-soluble Film to Transform a Base Fabric

Water-soluble film can be used to transform a boring base fabric. Simply sprinkle yarn snips or small fabric scraps onto the fabric base to create the design, then cover it with a layer of light- or mediumweight soluble film to keep the pieces in place. The film keeps the snips in place and prevents them getting caught in the embroidery foot. If the film has no glue it needs to be secured with lots of pins. Imagine how tedious it would be to position each fabric piece without the film – how would you keep them in place without sewing your fingers?

If you don't have time for pinning use temporary spray glue to keep the snips in place. Spray glue must be used in a well-ventilated area because it is very smelly and messy to use. Sticky soluble fabrics are the ideal solution for creating

This example shows the importance of interlocking stitches. The fabric scraps here were sprinkled too sparingly and the embroidery did not join up properly, resulting in a fabric that fell apart when the soluble film was washed away. This is not a total disaster as the fragile pieces can still be used in another project.

Fabrics made with water-soluble film can be formal in design. This example was created using thick soluble film. The cotton velvet squares were held in position by wetting the film with a damp cotton bud, then pressing them onto the damp, sticky film and leaving them to dry. The velvet was covered with another layer of film and the squares were joined with free-motion straight stitch.

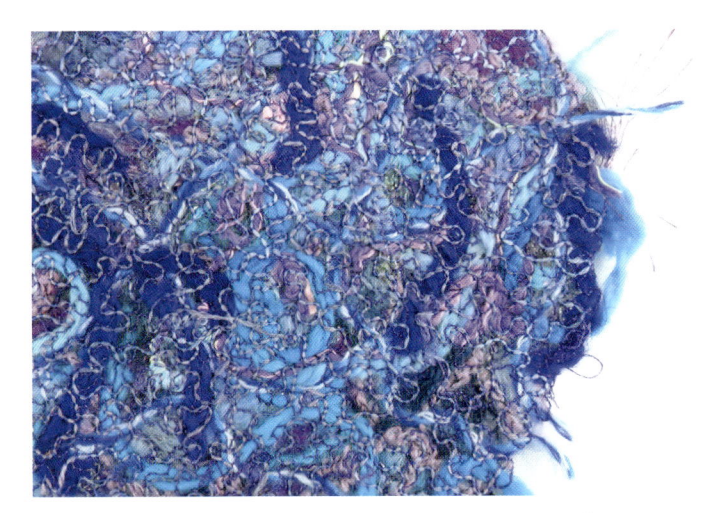

These scraps of fancy yarn were secured with two layers of meandering vermicelli. Two layers of stitch ensured the fabric did not fall apart: the first layer was completed with lilac Kingstar polyester and the second was stitched with variegated Lana thread which complemented the colour and fibre content of the yarn snips.

If an item can be sewn and withstand immersion into water it can be used in conjunction with water-soluble film. This embroidery contains feathers and snips of organza, the straight-stitch circles being stitched with metallic thread.

abstract designs on a base fabric, the only drawback being that they are opaque so you can't clearly see what is below. Using a fabric base means the embroidered fabric is more stable and it can be used to create images, bags, cushions or garments. The step-by-step velvet cushion project shows how to create a yarn- and thread-topped velvet cushion using sticky water-soluble fabric.

Chapter 7 – Using Water-soluble Film **121**

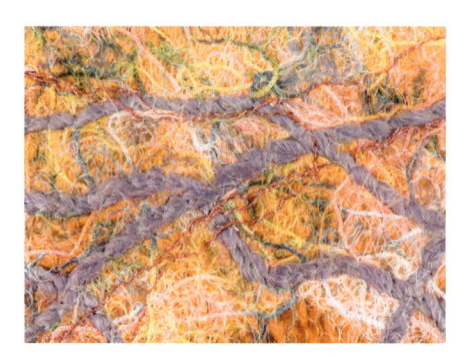

Furnishing velvet was sprinkled with chunky yarn rovings, two-ply mohair, glittery threads and feather yarn. The yarns scraps were held in place by soluble film and embroidered with invisible thread. A meandering vermicelli stitch was used to complement the softness of the yarns.

This background was created by sprinkling thin fashion yarns and snips of embroidery thread onto batik quilting fabric. Cotton quilting fabric is ideal for crazy patchwork projects because it does not add bulk when folded or quilted.

A limited colour palette of black and white can create stunning monochrome fabrics. The scraps of velvet, net, mesh and snips of yarns were secured with open vermicelli stitch using plain black thread.

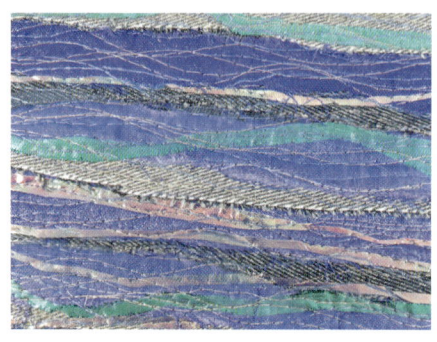

A denim base was layered with strips of denim, metallic tissue, organza and iridescent lamé. The strips were covered with one layer of Sulky Fabri-Solvy and secured with pins. The strips were stitched with gold metallic thread, transforming the plain scraps into luxurious embroidered fabric.

Embroidered yarn-topped fabrics can be embellished with cable stitch. This can be done before or after dissolving the film away. If you decide to remove the soluble film before adding cable stitch, the embroidery needs to pressed and stabilized before adding cable stitch.

Transferring a Design

All weights of transparent soluble film can be used for design transfer. Choosing soluble film saves time and materials because the soluble film becomes the stabilizer and transfer agent. Using film for design transfer is easy: pin the film onto the design and trace it with a permanent, gel or Stabilo fineliner pen, then pin the traced film onto the fabric ready for embroidery.

Biro ink can rub off onto your threads as you sew and some pens can dye the thread when the film is washed away or make ghostly lines. Always do a sample to test if the pen marks the thread or fabric. When the embroidery is complete tear away the excess film and soak the embroidery to remove the rest of the film. Leave the embroidery to dry facing upwards on an old towel, then damp press on the reverse when dry to remove handling or hoop marks.

This sheep embroidery is not finished. The permanent pen drawing is clearly visible on the supporting layer of soluble film. As the embroidery reaches completion the pen lines become completely covered by stitching.

Cut Work

Cut work is sometimes called reverse appliqué. Several layers of thin fabrics such as organza or lining material are embroidered with a simple design. The upper fabric is then cut away to reveal the layered fabric below. Water-soluble paper is ideal for cut work because it does not get stuck to the foot and it is firm enough to be used without a hoop. Heavyweight soluble film can also be used for cut work but it is more difficult to manoeuvre without a hoop because it is flexible.

To produce a cut work project, use one piece of soluble paper as a base, then layer several sheets of fine fabrics like organza, metallic tissue or chiffon on top. Draw the design onto another piece of soluble film and place on top, then pin through all the layers to secure them. Stitch the design with a few rows of straight stitch or narrow satin stitch. The embroidery can be done with an embroidery foot and lowered feeder teeth or a presser foot and raised feeder teeth; using a presser foot produces a neater satin stitch.

The film is washed away from the completed embroidery. Soluble paper must be cut away before it's dissolved because it leaves a white halo around the stitches. The dry embroidery is pressed and some of the fabrics are cut away to expose the different layers. This technique is very useful for creating a stained glass effect.

Two layers of soluble paper were used to support the brown and rust organza pieces. The design was embroidered with straight stitch and some areas stitched in satin stitch. The design was sewn with Madeira FS no. 20 metallic thread. The soluble paper was cut away and the embroidery was soaked to remove the remaining bits. When dry, the top layers of organza were then cut away to reveal the base layer of organza.

Creating Motifs Ready for Appliqué

Soluble film can be used to create embroidered motifs that can be sewn onto another background. The advantage of appliquéing an embroidery is that the background fabric is less likely to pucker or distort with heavy stitching. The embroidery should be stitched on a colour-matched base fabric because it is easier to blend the fixing stitches into the embroidery or the fabric. Organza or synthetic lining work well because they do not add bulk to the embroidery.

To create an appliqué, trace the design onto soluble film and pin it onto a base fabric, embroider the motif and dissolve away the soluble film. Dry the embroidery and damp press it, then cut the embroidery out from the base fabric. Appliqué the motif to the new fabric background; this can be done by hand or by machine. Heat-fusible glue can be used but it will flatten the embroidery.

Heavyweight soluble film can be used without fabric to produce appliqué motifs. This method is very time-consuming because a base grid needs to be stitched first. The base grid is made of rows of straight stitches sewn horizontally and vertically, like warp and weft. The stitched appliqué needs a base to anchor the stitches, otherwise the embroidery will unravel and fall apart.

The bottom thread will be visible so it is important to colour-match the top and bobbin thread with each colour change. Lots of stitching must be done for this technique to work; hold the embroidery up to the light to check the stitching and if you can see light through it more embroidery needs to be done because the pinpricks of light become holes when the soluble film is dissolved.

Warp and weft appliqués are not the best choice if accuracy is important. Heavy

The butterfly was sewn onto organza and partially cut out to show how close the fabric needs to be trimmed ready for appliqué. Delicate appliqués need careful handling; this one should be hand-sewn to the background fabric.

Layered organza created the colour changes in this floral appliqué. The design is stitched with Madeira FS no. 20 metallic thread. The embroidery was cut out with a soldering iron to create an edge that does not fray. Extra care must be taken when using a soldering iron because some fabrics are flammable and the fumes can be toxic.

stitching can shrink the design by about 10 per cent and the embroidery may not lie flat due to the pull caused by stitch direction. Also, dense stitching can also cause parts of the embroidery to undulate, resulting in an uneven surface.

Machine Lace

Heavyweight soluble film can be used to create fabric with stitching alone; the film supports the stitches so no fabric is needed. Machine lace is associated with computer machines because they can produce designs quickly. It is possible to make machine lace with free machine embroidery but it won't be as neat as the designs stitched by computer machines.

The stitches must interlock with each other otherwise the lace will fall apart when the film is dissolved away. The grid of stitches can be made of warp and weft straight stitch or interlocking circles; satin stitch can be used to add definition to designs but it must be stitched on top of rows of straight stitching, otherwise it will unravel when the film is dissolved.

Three-dimensional Embroidery

Flat soluble film embroideries can be made into three-dimensional pieces such as bowls, masks, flowers or sculptures. Heavyweight films such as Romeo or Badgemaster are used for three-dimensional work because some film residue needs to be left in the embroidery. The embroidery is left in the water just long enough for it to become sticky, the wet embroidery is placed over a mould covered with cling film and left to dry, and the film residue hardens the embroidery as it dries. Embroideries moulded with soluble film are reactive to the environment: if it's damp they will become soft; if they get wet the film residue will dissolve and leave a soggy mess.

Extra Tips and Hints

Transparent soluble film is adaptive to the environment: for example, if your studio is damp or you work on a rainy day the texture of the film changes; it becomes a bit softer or stickier, making it more difficult to work with. A hairdryer can be used to remove some of the moisture from the film; it is best to use a low heat setting so the film does not become brittle. Soluble film should be stored in plastic packets or containers to prevent it picking up moisture from the environment.

Some transparent heavy films can be joined together with a damp cotton bud; care must be taken as you don't want to dissolve the film. Larger pieces of film can be joined by stitching them together; when the film is embroidered simply unpick the stitches that joined it together.

Chapter 7 – Using Water-soluble Film

No fabric is used to support the fox embroidery; it is stitched onto Romeo soluble film with Sulky viscose threads. The left side of the embroidery is unfinished to show how the straight-stitch grid supports the detailed thread-painting.

The butterfly design was traced onto one layer of Romeo soluble film. The stitches must interlock so that the embroidery does not fall apart when the soluble film was washed away. The stitching was done with shaded thread. I did not like the colour of the body so I painted it with black acrylic paint.

Woven soluble is more suitable for abstract lace designs because the pull of warp and weft can distort the embroidery. The design was stitched with simple circles and grid patterns using straight stitch; a combination of threads adds interest to the design.

The bowl was made using Badgemaster. Two layers of soluble film were used to trap scraps of organza. The film was embroidered with metallic threads using straight-stitch patterns such as circles or grids. The wet embroidery was shaped inside a bowl that had been covered with cling film. The embroidery was left to dry. Using cling film ensures the embroidery does not stick to the bowl.

Chapter 7 – Using Water-soluble Film   **125**

STEP-BY-STEP PROJECT
Scraps and Snippets

YOU WILL NEED

Equipment
- Sewing machine with drop feed or darning plate
- Darning or embroidery foot
- Normal tension bobbin case
- Empty bobbins
- 15cm (6in.) wooden or metal embroidery hoop
- Small slotted screwdriver
- Size 90/14 machine needle for metallic thread
- Glass-headed pins
- Fabric scissors
- Embroidery scissors
- Iron
- Ironing cloth
- Bowl or sink to wash the film away
- Old towel on which to dry the embroidery

Materials
- Avalon water-soluble film
- Madeira Supertwist thread no. 30 in colour 290
- Lightweight synthetic fabric scraps including organza, lining and metallic tissue

Machine used
- Bernina 801
- Feeder teeth down
- Normal tension

This project shows how to make fabric by trapping scraps of lining, organza and metallic tissue between two layers of Avalon soluble film. The trapped scraps are then sewn together with meandering vermicelli stitch or another straight-stitch pattern. Producing this scrap embroidery is a good way to recycle fabric scraps that are too precious to be thrown away but too small to be used for anything else. The finished embroidery can be mounted and framed or used in other projects.

Iron the fabric scraps to remove the creases or folds; this helps the snips lie flat between two layers of soluble film. Cut your fabric scraps into squares or rectangles measuring about 1.5cm (⅝in.) along one side. I chose warm shades of organza, synthetic lining and metallic tissue; these will be embroidered with Madeira Supertwist colour 290 to add more sparkle.

Choose the hoop size; this determines the size of the embroidery. A 15cm (6in.) hoop has enough space to create a 12.5cm (5in.) piece of embroidery. Lay one piece of film onto the work surface; place the smaller part of the hoop onto the film. Sprinkle the snips inside the hoop.

Remove the small part of the hoop and lay a second piece of soluble film on top of the snips. Slide the large outer part of the hoop under the layers so the snips are in the centre of the hoop. Press the small inner hoop into place and pull the film taut. Tighten the screw on the hoop and make sure the film is drum-tight. The film needs to be tightly stretched to keep the snips in place; taut film is also easier to stitch.

Set up the machine, lower or cover the feeder teeth, insert a size 90/14 metallic needle, set the machine to straight stitch and attach a darning or embroidery foot. Wind an empty bobbin with the same thread used for the needle; it's important to use colour-matched threads because the bobbin thread is visible through the gaps between the snips. Insert the wound bobbin into the normal tension bobbin case and load into the machine.

5 Thread the needle with Madeira Supertwist no. 30 in colour 290. Turn the hand wheel to bring the bobbin thread to the top and pull a short length of both threads behind the needle plate. Position the hoop under the foot; you may need to raise the embroidery foot with your finger to give the hoop enough clearance. Sliding the hoop under the embroidery foot is more problematic when a darning plate is used because it decreases the space between the foot and the bed of the machine.

6 Lower the foot and position the hoop so it is near the foot but not touching it. Hold both of the thread tails and begin sewing a wandering vermicelli. After a few stitches, stop sewing and trim off the thread tail to stop it getting caught and ruining the embroidery. Continue stitching the vermicelli; do not stitch too densely but make sure all the fabric snips are caught with stitch. If the thread breaks just cut the ragged end, re-thread the needle and start sewing in the spot just before the thread broke. Continue embroidering until the area inside the hoop is filled with stitches.

7 Remove the hoop from the machine, loosen the hoop and take out the finished embroidery. Trim the loose thread ends close to the embroidery and cut away the excess soluble film. Do not throw the offcuts of water-soluble film away as they can be reused to patch a hole in a larger piece of film or to trace a small design for embroidery.

8 Fill an old bowl or sink with warm water, place the embroidery in it and leave it to soak. If you have used Avalon you will see the film lifting away and dissolving instantly because it's a lightweight film. Gently swirl the embroidery in the water and place it on an old towel to dry. Don't wring out the embroidery because it could damage the delicate stitches.

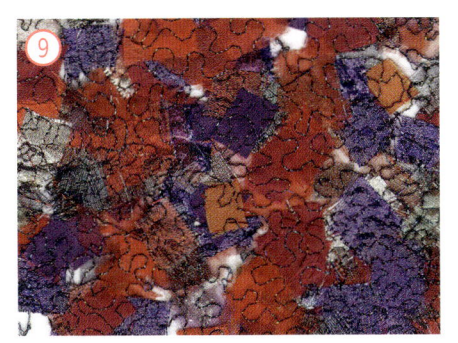

9 If the embroidery has not dried flat you need to iron it. Use a low heat setting and an ironing cloth to protect the finished fabric. You can now decide what to do with the fabric. It could be left as a sampler or transformed into something more exciting; see the projects at the end of this chapter for more ideas.

10 Other straight-stitch patterns can be used to make up scraps and snippets. Top L: spirals stitched with Madeira FS no. 20 thread in colour 465 (turquoise). Top R: circles stitched with Madeira Supertwist 360 (black opal). Bottom L: squares stitched with Coats Reflecta gold 300. Bottom R: scribble stitching with Madeira FS no. 20 in colour 483 (coral fish).

Chapter 7 – Using Water-soluble Film **127**

STEP-BY-STEP PROJECT
Wooden Trinket Box

This project shows how to transform a plain wooden box using the fabric made from the scraps and snippets project. Small wooden boxes with laser-cut lids are readily available from craft shops or online suppliers. Some boxes have intricate patterns cut into the lid, others have a simple recess or hole for a photo; both types are suitable for making a trinket box. You do not want the box to overpower the embroidery so choose the right style to show off the finished embroidery.

YOU WILL NEED

Equipment
- Sandpaper
- Sharp hand-sewing needle
- Pencil
- Pencil sharpener
- Paintbrush for paint or varnish
- Old paintbrush for glue
- Craft knife
- Ruler
- Tape measure
- Cutting board
- Fabric scissors
- Paper scissors
- Cotton buds
- Clothes pegs
- Iron
- Weight

Materials
- Finished scraps and snippets embroidery
- Small wooden box with laser-cut finish
- Impex Original High-Tack All-Purpose Very Sticky Glue or similar adhesive
- Pelmet Vilene
- Baking parchment
- Heat-fusible glue
- Strong thread for hand-sewing and gathering
- Quilt wadding scraps
- Fabric to line the box
- Holographic card
- Mount board or grey board offcuts
- Acrylic paint
- Varnish

① You can leave your wooden box as it is or paint it to change the colour. If your box has hinges remove them before painting. The pattern on the round lid reminded me of a rose window so I stained the box with brown acrylic paint and varnished it to seal the paint. To give the box a professional finish you also need to paint the inside; if you intend to line the inside just paint the visible parts.

② Measure inside the box lid. If the shape is difficult to measure use a thin piece of paper and a crayon to make a rubbing. Cut out the template with paper scissors and check that it fits the lid recess. Use the template to cut out a piece of holographic card and check it fits the lid. Select part of the scraps and snippets embroidery, using the box lid and moving it around to find the part that looks right. Use the template and cut out that part of the embroidery with fabric scissors.

③ Dot glue inside the box lid; don't get glue near the fretwork gaps. Press the cut embroidery into the lid, best side against the glue. Paint glue near the edges of the holographic card, making sure the glue is applied to the holographic side. Dot spots of glue onto the back of the embroidery, making sure it won't show through the fretwork. Press the holographic card into place so the glued holographic side is against the embroidery.

128   Chapter 7 – Using Water-soluble Film

④

Use the template to mark the grey board inserts for the lid and base. Cut the card inserts 0.3cm (⅛in.) smaller so they fit into the box when covered with fabric. Use a pencil to trace the template and a craft knife to cut the grey board. Remember to protect the work surface with a cutting mat. The edges of the card can be reshaped with sandpaper to improve the fit. Cut two pieces of wadding the same size as the grey board insert. Cut two pieces of lining fabric, making sure they are large enough to be gathered around the grey board inserts.

⑤

Make the lid and bottom lining by threading a sharp hand-sewing needle with a doubled length of strong thread and tacking round the edge of the fabric. Place a piece of wadding in the centre of the fabric then put a grey board piece on top of the wadding. Hold the grey board in place whilst pulling both ends of the tacking thread so it gathers tightly around the grey board and wadding. Tie the ends of the tacking thread with a secure knot to keep the wadding and card in place and trim the loose thread.

⑥

Line the inside of the box to match the lid and base. Measure the circumference and height of the inner wall with a tape measure. This box is circular so the lining needs to be pliable; use pelmet Vilene instead of card. The pelmet Vilene should be cut so it matches the circumference measurement. Alternatively, to give the box a neater finish you could make it shorter in height so the box wood shows above it.

⑦

Paint the inside of the box lid with glue; don't get any near the edges because it could mark the lining fabric. Press the covered lining into place and press down firmly to encourage the glue to stick. Remove stray blobs of glue with a wet cotton bud (check the fabric doesn't watermark before doing this). Use a weight to press it down whilst the glue dries (I used a floral paperweight). Repeat this stage to line the base of the box.

⑧

Cut a piece of lining fabric to cover the pelmet Vilene, adding a 2cm (¾in.) seam allowance to both edges. Cut a piece of heat-fusible glue the same size and bond it to the back of the lining, using baking parchment to protect the work surface and the iron. Peel the backing paper off the bonded fabric. Position the Vilene in the centre of the bonded lining so it is against the heat-fusible glue.

⑨

Fold the long edge of the fabric over the pelmet Vilene and bond it in place with the iron; repeat for the other side. Fold one short edge over to the back and insert an extra bit of heat-fusible glue, then iron to fix the flap in place. Leave the other flap alone because it creates a neat overlap when glued into position. Turn the lining over and cover with backing parchment; iron the front to fix the Vilene in place.

Chapter 7 – Using Water-soluble Film 129

⑩ Paint the inside of the box wall with glue, avoiding the exposed wooden lip near the lid. Position the loose fabric tail first, then ease the rest of the long strip into position. Keep pressing the lining against the box wall until you reach the folded end, then press this into place. Check the lining is level; if it isn't, re-position it. Use a damp cotton bud to remove stray spots of glue before they dry. Keep the lining in place with clothes pegs but check they don't mark the wood before using them.

⑪ Remove the clothes pegs and check the lining has stuck. Smooth out the lining fabric to remove the indents made by the pegs. Screw the hinges back in place and make sure the lid closes properly. Check the box over for stray spots of glue and give it a final polish with a scrap of muslin or cotton. These little boxes make ideal presents and you could hide an additional gift inside.

STEP-BY-STEP PROJECT
Embroidered Greetings Card

This project shows how to make a personalized card with a small piece of embroidered fabric. Abstract scrap embroideries can be adapted to suit any occasion: they can be embellished with peel-off stickers or stick-on gems or decorated with beads and hand embroidery.

YOU WILL NEED

Equipment
- Cutting mat
- Craft knife
- Metal ruler
- Rotary cutter
- Pencil
- Pencil sharpener
- Eraser

Materials
- Scraps and snippets embroidery
- Acid-free double-sided tape
- Sticky double-sided foam pads
- Card stock including mirror or holographic
- Folded greetings card blanks
- Gold outline peel-off stickers (I used a JeJe brand butterfly design)
- Outline peel-off stickers (various designs)
- Hand-sewing needles
- Metallic gold threads or thin gold cords

1. Choose a scraps and snippets embroidery and iron it flat, using an ironing cloth or baking parchment to protect the delicate fabrics. Select a gold peel-off butterfly sticker and position it on the embroidery, making sure there is enough room around the butterfly to allow for a a rectangular border, then press the sticker down firmly.

2. Place the embroidery on the cutting mat and move it so the butterfly is level with a grid line. Use the grid lines to visualize where to cut the rectangle so that there is an even border around the sticker. Position the metal ruler onto the embroidery and use a rotary cutter to cut the first line. Turn the embroidery and align the cut edge with a grid line, use the grid lines to position the ruler and cut the rest of the rectangle.

3. Stick double-sided tape to the back of the embroidered rectangle. Use a small amount near the edge and make sure it's not visible through the gaps. Choose the backing card for the embroidery: holographic or metallic finishes often bring embroideries to life.

④ Peel the backing off the double-sided tape and stick the rectangle of embroidery to the card, making sure there is enough card to make a border around the embroidery. Decide how large the border is going to be, then cut the excess card away with a craft knife and ruler, using a cutting mat to protect the work surface. Don't use the rotary cutter on card because it blunts the blade.

⑤ Choose another piece of card to layer under the embroidery. Decide how large to make the border then use the metal ruler and craft knife to cut it out. Cut by eye or use a pencil to draw on the card before cutting. Stick foam pads onto the back of the card-backed embroidery and position it onto the large card rectangle, then press down to secure. The foam pads add extra dimension to the matting and layering.

⑥ Continue layering with card until you are happy with the design. The card rectangles can be offset to add interest to the design and border stickers can be used to enhance the edge of plain card. Mount the finished embroidery on the greetings card blank with double-sided tape or foam pads.

⑦ These cards have been produced from the same scrap and snippet embroidery. Notice how the choice of backing card and sticker alters the appearance of the embroidery. The butterfly has pink holographic card behind it for a tropical feel and the birthday card has a gold background to enhance the blue tones.

⑧ Hand embroidery can be used to decorate cards. The embroidery was bonded onto green metallic paper with heat-fusible glue then cut into a triangle shape. The triangle was stuck to white card with double-sided tape and a holographic star and trunk were added. The tinsel decorations were hand-sewn through the card, and the ends taken through to the back and hidden. The embroidered tree was mounted onto a greetings card blank and finished with peel-off sticker borders.

132   Chapter 7 – Using Water-soluble Film

STEP-BY-STEP PROJECT
Velvet Cushion

YOU WILL NEED

Equipment
- Sewing machine with drop feed or darning plate
- Size 90/14 universal machine needle
- Straight-stitch presser foot
- Zip foot
- Embroidery or darning foot
- Normal tension bobbin case
- Empty bobbins
- Fabric scissors
- Embroidery scissors
- Glass-headed pins
- Sharp hand-sewing needle
- Ruler
- Set square
- Dressmaker's chalk pencil or artist's watercolour pencil
- Pencil sharpener
- Iron
- Ironing cloth
- Baking parchment
- Sink or bowl of water to wash the embroidery
- Old towel on which to dry the embroidery

Materials
- Gütermann Sulky Invisible polyamide or colour-matched machine thread
- White bobbin thread
- Black bobbin thread
- Colour-matched Gütermann Sew-All polyester thread
- White thread for tacking
- Cotton furnishing velvet
- Thin iron-on interfacing
- Zip
- Cushion pad measuring 30.5 × 30.5cm (12 × 12in.)
- Aquabond soluble fabric or similar soluble with a sticky side
- Scraps of yarn, wool and fancy threads

Machines used
- Bernina 801 and Janome JF 1018s
- Feeder teeth down for embroidery and feeder teeth up for making up
- Normal tension

This project shows how to transform plain furnishing velvet into a luxuriously textured cushion. Learn how to layer yarns and threads onto a velvet base and keep them in place with a layer of sticky soluble fabric. You will discover how to use simple vermicelli stitch to secure the snips before dissolving the soluble film in water to reveal the embroidered design. You will turn the embroidery into a zipped cushion cover: the addition of a zip means the pad can be removed so the cover can be laundered.

Cotton furnishing velvet is the best choice for the beginner because it has no stretch and is firm to sew. The colour scheme is dictated by the colour of the velvet. My furnishing velvet was a deep wine colour so I chose warm colours including pink, orange, yellow, purple, red and metallic gold. You can choose a less vibrant colour scheme or pick one to match your home furnishings. If you can't find a cushion pad the same size as mine, make your own and fill it with fire-retardant wadding. Whatever size you choose the velvet pieces need to be bigger on all sides to allow for seams, shrinkage and the inevitable fidgeting.

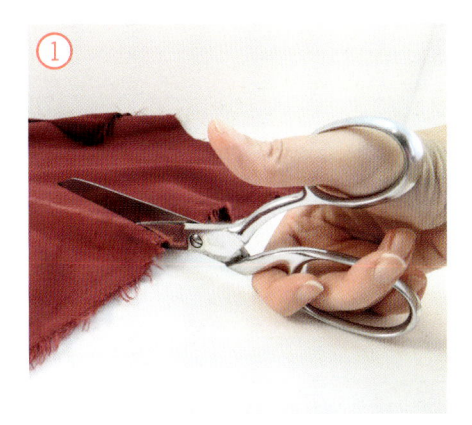

①
Lay the velvet onto the work surface, pile side downwards, then smooth it out. Use a ruler, set square and chalk pencil to draw a square measuring 38 × 38cm (15 × 15in.). Cut out the square with fabric scissors; put the front panel to one side.

Chapter 7 – Using Water-soluble Film 133

Measure and cut two more rectangles of velvet for the back panels, making sure first that the pile runs in the same direction as shown. Using a chalk pencil, ruler and set square to draw the pieces accurately, cut one 14 × 38cm (5½ × 15in.) and the second 28 × 38cm (11 × 15in.). Put the two cut back panel pieces to one side.

Keeping the front panel pile side downwards, use a chalk pencil, ruler and set square to draw a square in the middle of the velvet measuring 32 × 32cm (12½ × 12½in.). If you have cut out your square accurately your cushion should have a seam allowance of at least 2.5cm (1in.) to allow for movement and shrinkage.

Attach a straight-stitch presser foot, raise the feeder teeth and set the stitch to a long straight stitch. Insert a size 90/14 universal needle and thread the needle with white cotton. Insert a white bobbin into the normal tension bobbin case and load into the machine.

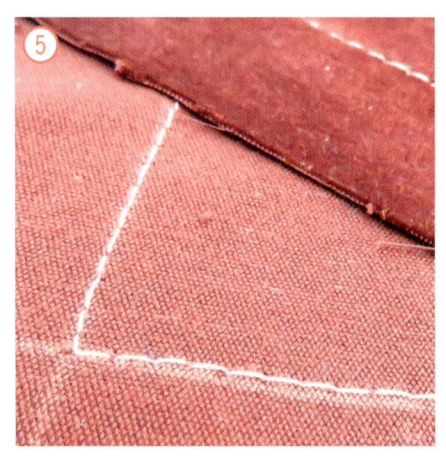

Position the velvet under the foot and align the needle with the chalk guide line, then lower the foot and sew along the chalk line to tack the perimeter of the square. The tacked line becomes the guide for positioning the yarn and thread scraps. Iron some lightweight interfacing onto the back of the three velvet pieces, using baking parchment to protect the iron; the interfacing stiffens the velvet so it is easier to sew.

Turn the velvet square so the right side is upwards. Choose a variety of yarn scraps to embellish the velvet, selecting different colours and textures. Sprinkle the yarn onto the velvet one piece at a time, letting the yarn fall into place when it's dropped. Position the yarns so they cover the surface evenly, slightly overlapping the tacked guide. If you are not happy with the design, start again.

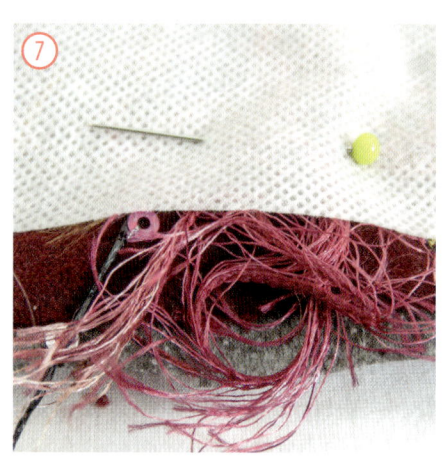

Cut a piece of Aquabond soluble fabric large enough to cover the velvet square. Peel away the backing paper and position the fabric so the sticky side is against the yarn snips; press down with your hands to secure it. The film should be sticky enough to hold the yarn snips in place. Pin the edge of the soluble fabric because the velvet will fidget whilst it's being embroidered; movement could shift the yarns whereas pinning keeps them in place.

134   Chapter 7 – Using Water-soluble Film

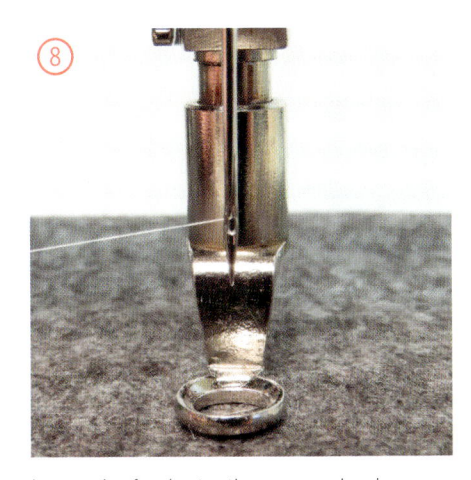

⑧ Lower the feeder teeth or use a darning plate. Attach an embroidery foot and set the stitch type to straight. Thread the needle with Sulky Invisible thread and insert a bobbin wound with black. (If you don't have invisible thread you can stitch with a colour-matched plain polyester, viscose or rayon thread.) There is no need to use a hoop as the interfacing and soluble fabric provide enough support for the embroidery.

⑨ Start sewing a meandering vermicelli stitch in the centre of the velvet and work towards the edges. If the velvet decides to fidget, smooth out the tucks as you sew. Continue stitching until the whole square is filled with meandering vermicelli stitch; the needle leaves small holes in the soluble film so you can see where you have sewn. Take the threads through to the back and tie them off.

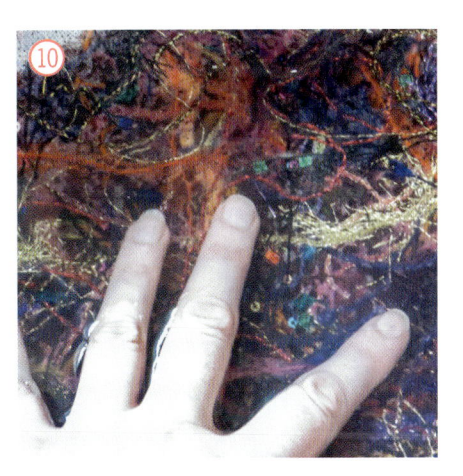

⑩ When the embroidery is complete, soak the embroidery in a bowl of warm water. Soluble fabric becomes transparent as it begins to dissolve. Gently work the surface of the embroidery with your fingertips to help the soluble glue dissolve; leave the velvet to soak. Rinse the velvet to remove the residue; you don't want it to dry hard. Do not wring out the velvet; leave it to dry face up on an old towel or hang it on the washing line.

⑪ To position the zip, take the larger back panel and place it on the work surface, pile side down. Use a chalk pencil to mark the middle of the long edge then mark the middle of the zip (on its wrong side). Place the zip along the long edge so the middle marks line up and mark the position of the metal zip stops onto the velvet; these can be found at each end of the zip. (If the zip is an open-ended one, mark where you want the zip opening to start and finish.) Remove the zip and use the chalk pencil and ruler to draw the seam line 1.5cm (⅝in.) in from the edge of the velvet; the seam line should pass through the middle and end zip marks.

⑫ Put the two back panels together so the right sides face each other; make sure the pile runs in the same direction for both panels. Pin the two pieces together along the drawn line, using lots of pins because velvet fidgets when it is sewn.

⑬ Wind a bobbin with colour-matched Sew-All thread and insert it into the normal tension bobbin case, then load into the machine. Thread the needle with the same thread and set the stitch type to normal-length straight stitch. Raise the feeder teeth and attach the straight-stitch presser foot.

Chapter 7 – Using Water-soluble Film

⑭ Position the velvet under the foot so the start of the seam is in line with the needle, then lower the foot.

⑮ This shows where to do the backstitching for the zip opening (placket). Sew a few stitches, press reverse and sew back over them, then release reverse and continue sewing towards the zip stop mark. Stop there. Press reverse and sew a few stitches, release reverse and sew a few stitches, then stop. Change the stitch length to long and sew to the next zip stop mark, then stop. Shorten the stitch length, press reverse and sew backwards for a few stitches, release reverse, continue sewing to the edge of the velvet, then press reverse to sew a few stitches backwards. Stop and trim the threads close to the velvet.

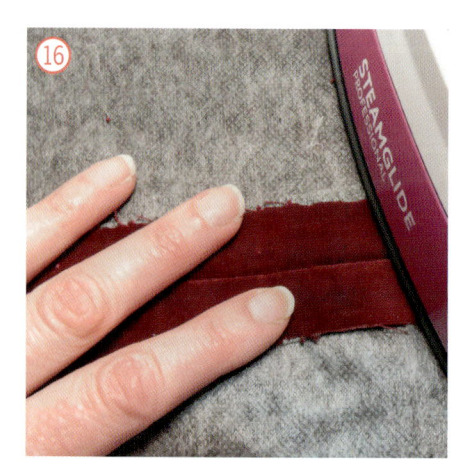

⑯ Open the seam and damp press it on the back. Lift the seam allowance to find the top and bottom chalk marks for the zip stops and re-mark them on the pressed seam with a chalk pencil.

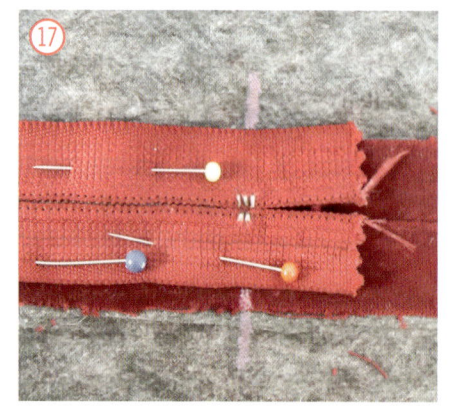

⑰ Position the closed zip along the seam so the front side of the zip faces the back of the velvet (that is, the interfacing side). The metal zip stops should be positioned over the chalk marks and the zip teeth should be positioned exactly along the central seam opening (placket). Pin the zip to the velvet, then tack it in place by hand. If the zip moves push it back into position whilst hand-sewing.

⑱ Remove the presser foot and attach the zip foot. (I swapped machines because I didn't have a zip foot for the Bernina.) Change the stitch length to medium straight stitch. Move the needle position so it's set to the right of the zip foot. Turn the fabric so the right side is upwards and align the left side of the zip foot with the beginning of the central seam.

⑲ Sew down the length of the seam to attach this side of the zip to the velvet. You might feel the fabric push aside when the foot reaches the zip pull. If this happens keep the needle in the fabric, lift the foot and re-position the zip pull so it's not in the way. When this side of the zip is sewn, rotate the fabric and re-position the foot so the left side is in line with the central seam. Sew down the entire length of the velvet to stitch the other side of the zip, then trim the threads close to the velvet.

136   Chapter 7 – Using Water-soluble Film

20 Check the zip is sewn to the back panel neatly. If there are gaps or tucks, unpick and re-sew the messy parts of the seam. Remove the tacking stitches carefully; don't cut into the machine-sewn seam. Re-position the fabric and sew across the zip tape just after the metal zip stops but don't sew over the zip teeth. Sewing the ends of the zip secures the central seam and holds the end of the zip in place. Take the threads to the back and tie them off.

21 Iron the wrong side of the embroidered panel and place it on the work surface so the wrong side is facing upwards. Use a set square, ruler and chalk pencil to draw a square measuring 32 × 32cm (12¾ × 12¾in.). The embroidery should fill the inside of the drawn square; if there are gaps turn the velvet over to see if they are noticeable on the embroidered side. If you decide to fill the gaps you need to add more yarn and embroider it with vermicelli to match the rest of the cushion.

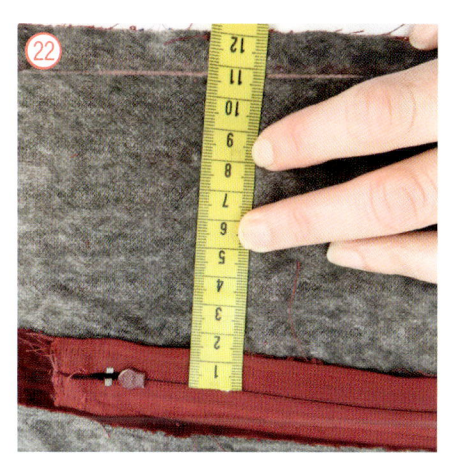

22 Place the back panel on the work surface so the wrong side faces upwards and the narrow panel is at the top. Measure 11cm (4¼in.) up from the centre line of the zip and mark the measurement with a chalk pencil. Mark again in three different places along the length of the zip and join the marks up with a chalk pencil and ruler. This line is the starting point for measuring the rest of the seam lines.

23 Locate the two tabs of straight stitch that secure the end of the zip tape. Measure the length between them and divide this by two, then mark the middle point with a chalk pencil or pin. Measure 16cm (6¼in.) either side of this central point and mark each point with a chalk pencil or pin. It is important to make the seam allowance even on either side of the zip ends because uneven seams make the back of the cushion look untidy. Use a set square to draw the two sides of the square; when finished the square should measure 32 × 32cm (12¾ × 12¾in.).

24 Position the two panels of velvet together so the right sides face each other and align the four drawn corner lines. Push a pin through the layers so it pierces the corner point of both front and back pieces. Handling may have faded the drawn lines; to find the corner points look for scuff marks on the interfacing or redraw the seam lines. Pin all four corners, then undo the zip; this makes an opening for turning the cushion through when all the seams are sewn.

25 Continue pinning the front and back pieces together. Push the pins through the chalk guidelines so the pins follow the seam line. The pins should pass through the drawn line on the back and front of the cushion; this ensures the velvet is pinned accurately and there is enough velvet left for a seam allowance. Pin across one of the first pins to make a cross, remove the pin that is lined up along the chalk line, and leave the one crossing it. Continue changing the pins and manipulating the velvet until it is pinned all the way around.

Chapter 7 – Using Water-soluble Film   **137**

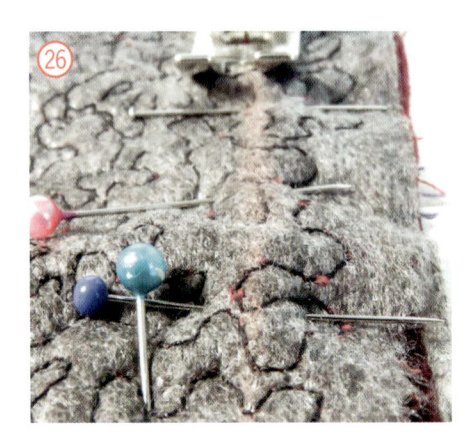

26 Attach a straight-stitch presser foot and raise the feeder teeth. Thread the needle with colour-matched Sew-All thread and load a bobbin wound with the same thread. Set the stitch type to medium-length straight stitch and position the needle so it's over the drawn chalk line. Lower the foot and stitch the seam, following the chalk line and keeping the line of sewing straight. Remove each pin just before the foot reaches it. Stop sewing when you reach a corner. The corners need backstitching to strengthen them; this stops the seam splitting when the corners are turned through.

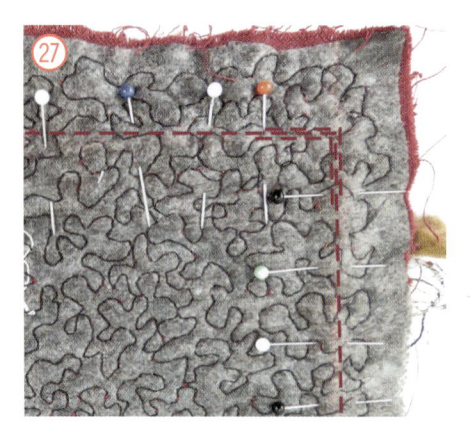

27 At the corner press reverse and sew a few stitches, release reverse and stitch forward to the corner. Do not go past it; leave the needle down and turn the velvet so the foot follows the next seam line. Sew a few stitches, then press reverse without going beyond the corner. Release reverse and sew until you reach the next corner. Repeat the process until you meet the starting point, where you press reverse and sew a few stitches; cut the thread close to the work.

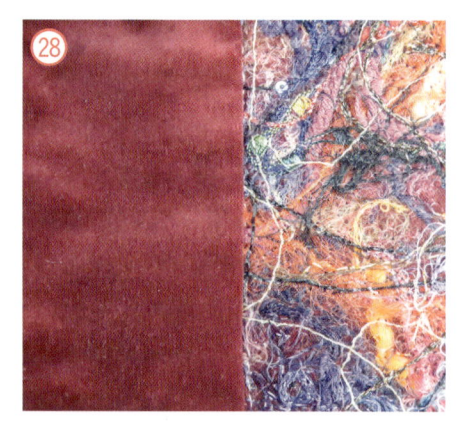

28 Turn the cushion through the zip so the right side is outside, check the placement of the embellished panel and examine the seams for tucks or bumps. If you find a tuck, turn the cushion back though, unpick that part of the seam and re-sew.

29 Turn the cushion back through so the raw seams are exposed. Use sharp scissors to cut away the corners, cutting close to the backstitching but not through it. Cutting the corners this close produces neat corners when the cushion is turned through to the right side. Cut away the frayed edges so the seam allowance is approximately 1.5cm (⅝in.). Turn the cushion cover back through so the right side is on the outside. Take care when pushing the corners through that you do not pop the seam stitches at this stage.

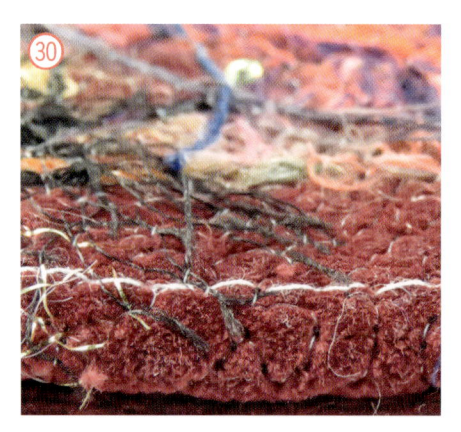

30 Unpick the visible white tacking stitches, taking care not to cut the yarns or embroidery stitches. If the velvet is creased, damp press it lightly; this final press neatens the seams and makes the cushion look professional. Insert the cushion pad, taking care not to split the zip seam. Close the zip, ease the metal fastening into the invisible seam and plump the cushion to move the padding into the corners.

138   Chapter 7 – Using Water-soluble Film

㉛

Furnishing velvet is notoriously good at picking up bits of fluff; remove these with some masking tape or a clothesbrush. The finished cushion can now take pride of place in your home. The furnishing velvet and yarns create a soft cushion perfect for snuggling into on a cold night!

Chapter 7 – Using Water-soluble Film **139**

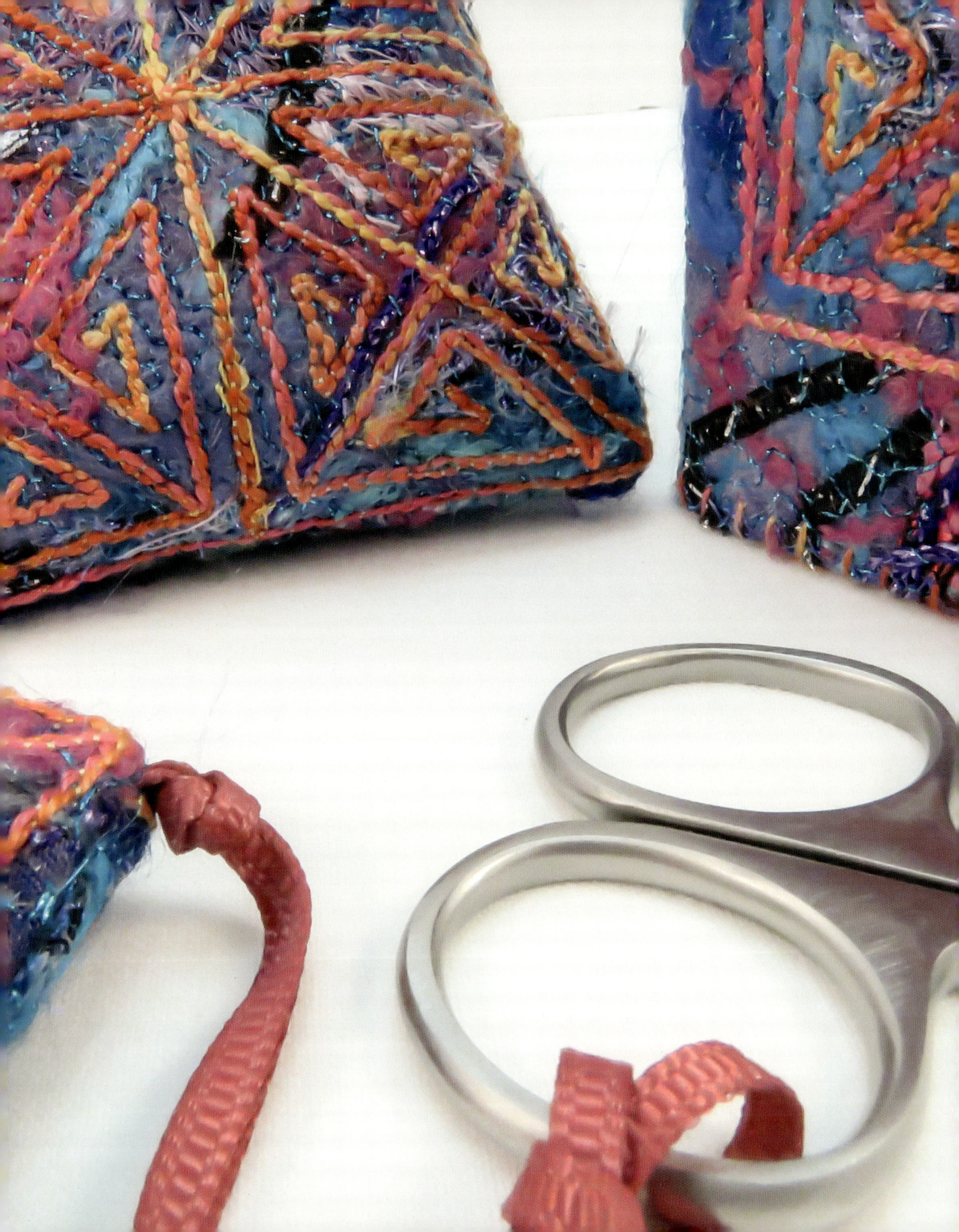

CHAPTER 8

EXPERIMENTING WITH STITCHES AND TENSION

Altering the tension may feel scary at first; the projects and examples in this chapter aim to show that changing the thread tension can be creative and fun. During normal sewing the threads interlock in the middle of the fabric to create the stitch. Slight changes to the top or bottom thread tension moves where the stitch interlocks, thus changing the appearance of the stitch.

Tight top tension brings the bobbin thread up so that the stitch interlocks on the surface of the fabric, creating loops or dots. This stitch is called whip stitch because the bobbin thread is whipped around the tight top thread. The bobbin tension and sewing speed can be altered to create variations of this stitch: these are called moss and feather stitch.

Cable stitch is produced when thick thread is wound onto a bobbin and the bobbin case tension screw is loosened to allow the thick thread to unwind. The bobbin thread is too thick to be pulled into the fabric so the stitch interlocks on the underside of the fabric, thus couching the thick thread to the bottom of the fabric. The only problem with cable stitch is you can't really see what is happening underneath the material. As you become more experienced you will begin to notice subtle changes in tension or machine noise; these are signals to stop sewing and check what is happening underneath the fabric.

The samplers at the beginning of this chapter show how to create whip, moss, feather and cable stitch. Remember that your machine may need different adjustments to obtain the correct results; experimenting is the key to success. If you are worried about altering the bobbin case tension it's wise to invest in a spare case because it won't need resetting. For example, I once forgot about altering the bobbin case and wondered why the machine was not sewing properly. The only tension needed for this chapter is the conscious alteration of dials or the bobbin case.

SAMPLER
Whip Stitch

Whip stitch is made when the top tension is tighter than the bottom tension; the bobbin thread gets pulled up to create tiny dots where the stitch interlocks. Thread tension varies from machine to machine; some machines may need their top thread tension dials moving a tiny bit whilst others need them turned to maximum.

Whip stitch is more effective with contrasting threads and slow hoop movements. Use a strong thread through the needle because tight tension snaps weak threads. Threads that are prone to breakage can be used in the bobbin because the thread is under less tension. Winding weak or cheap threads onto the bobbin for whip stitch is an ideal way to use them up.

YOU WILL NEED

Equipment
- Scanner and printer or photocopier
- Sewing machine with drop feed or darning plate
- Darning or embroidery foot
- Size 90/14 Universal needles
- Empty bobbins
- Spare bobbin case for loose tension embroidery
- Slotted screwdriver
- Two 15cm (6in.) wooden hoops
- Glass-headed pins
- Pencil
- Permanent gel pen
- Pencil sharpener
- Eraser
- Embroidery scissors
- Fabric scissors

Materials
- Plain A4 paper
- Dressmaker's carbon paper
- Two pieces of pre-washed calico approximately 28 × 23cm (11 × 9in.)
- Strong polyester or rayon top threads
- Various threads for the bobbins
- Invisible thread or white Empress Mills HT polyester
- Variegated or shaded thread
- Scrap of calico

Machine used
- Bernina 801
- Feeder teeth down
- Normal tension top thread, depending on machine settings
- Loose bobbin thread tension

① Create a design or copy and enlarge the one shown here. Draw the design so it measures approximately 18 × 14cm (7 × 5½in.). Draw the design with pencil, permanent pen or gel pen. Add the word 'Whip' to remind yourself of the stitch type and tension settings. Include some simple free machine embroidery patterns, an area for experimenting with zigzag or satin stitch and space for using invisible thread through the needle.

② Transfer the design onto a piece of calico using dressmaker's carbon paper. Place the other piece of calico behind and put both in a hoop so the word 'Whip' is central. Embroideries done with whip stitch need extra support because the tight tension pulls at the fabric more than normal stitches.

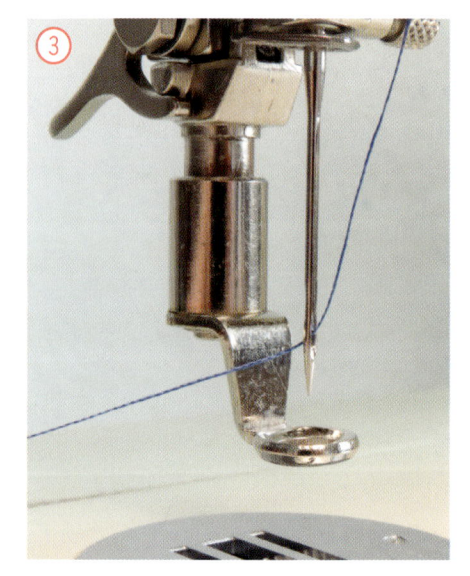

③ Lower the feeder teeth, attach a darning or embroidery foot and set the stitch type to straight. Insert a size 90/14 universal needle and thread the needle with strong plain rayon or polyester thread. Wind a contrasting colour onto the bobbin and insert it into the bobbin case, then load into the machine.

142 Chapter 8 – Experimenting with Stitches and Tension

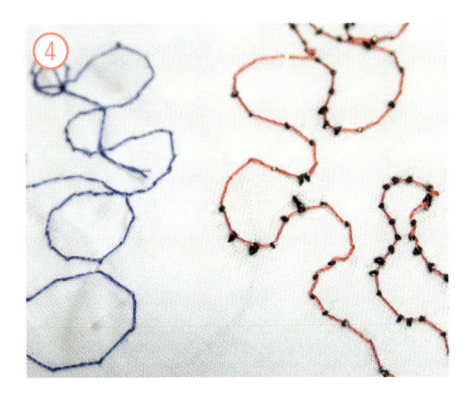

4 Tighten the top tension a bit and stitch a small sample on a hooped scrap of calico. If the bottom thread is not making dots, continue tightening the top thread until it does. If the top thread breaks, the top tension may be too tight or the thread may be too weak for the process, so change the top thread and try again.

5 Every machine is different. Loosen the bobbin case tension screw if the bobbin thread does not come to the top. Swap to a spare bobbin case and loosen the tension screw a tiny amount, thread the bobbin case and try again. If the dots are now too large or loopy, remove the bobbin and tighten the tension screw a fraction. If the balance is still wrong, adjust the top tension dial; it may take some fiddling to get the balance right.

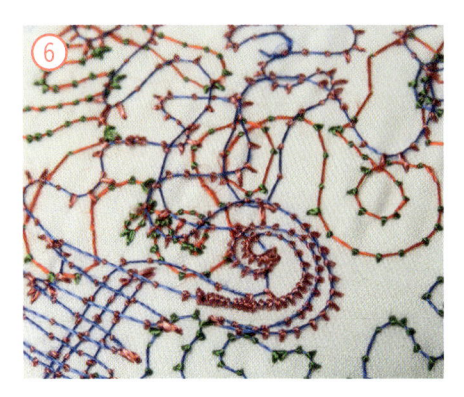

6 Whip stitch sample: the first test had red thread through the needle and green in the loose bobbin case; the second had blue through the needle and pink in the bobbin. Correctly formed whip stitch should have dots or tiny loops of bottom thread covering the top thread. Here, the dots are spaced out more because the hoop was moved quickly.

7 Thread the needle with blue. Wind dark pink into the bobbin, insert it into the loose tension bobbin case and load into the machine. Position the hooped calico under the needle and stitch the word 'Whip' slowly using two rows of straight stitch; this produces blue top thread covered with dots of pink bobbin thread.

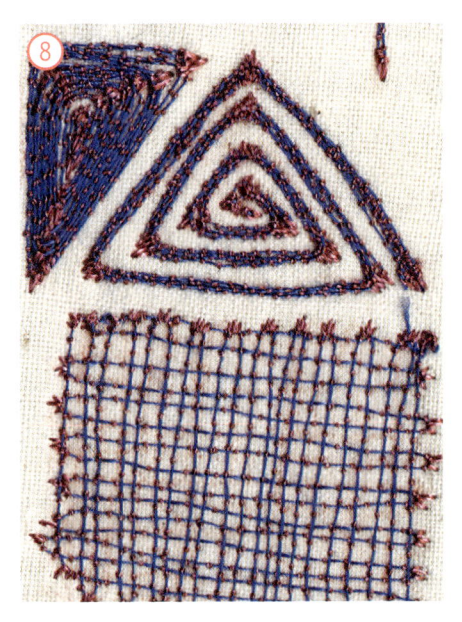

8 Stitch the triangles with concentric rows of straight stitch; embroider the sides fast and the corners slowly. The bottom thread is more prominent at the corners because the hoop is being moved slowly. Stitch the grid with one row of straight stitch; note how the bobbin thread pulls when the hoop changes direction.

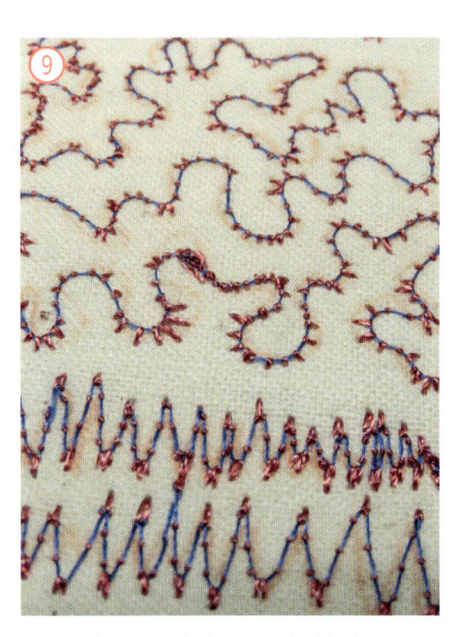

9 Embroider meandering vermicelli; slow hoop movements create a stitch with more pink thread dots. Stitch the zigzag pattern using straight stitch and see how more bobbin thread appears at the edge of the stitch when the hoop slows and changes direction.

Chapter 8 – Experimenting with Stitches and Tension **143**

⑩

Re-position the hoop over the wave patterns. Change the bobbin thread to shaded variegated, and thread the needle with green. Stitch the patterns with straight stitch and move the hoop slowly. Note how the bobbin thread is pulled to the top to create spokes or lines when the hoop changes direction.

⑪

Embroider the zigzag pattern with one row of straight stitch. More spokes of thread are pulled up when the angle of the corner gets tighter. Embroider a few rows of zigzag one on top of another to build up a dense layer of dots and spokes. Stitch close rows of straight stitch to illustrate how variegated thread changes colour.

⑫

Embroider the jagged pattern with straight stitch; the bottom thread comes to the top when the hoop slows or changes direction. Embroider dense vermicelli and a circle pattern; the variegated bobbin thread creates spokes that change colour. Stitch the zigzag patterns, quickly moving the hoop left to right; the green top thread gets covered completely or remains as a small tab in the middle of the stitches.

⑬

Stitch the 'invisible' section. Thread the needle with invisible thread or Empress Mills HT white polyester thread and insert a bobbin wound with green variegated thread. Embroider patterns with straight stitch, including circles, scribble, vermicelli, side-to-side, squares and angular patterns. The combination of tight top tension and invisible thread produces a stitch that's suitable for creating natural textures that are ideal for use in landscape pictures.

⑭

Re-position the hoop over the zigzag section. Thread the needle with red and wind a warm-shaded variegated thread onto an empty bobbin, load it into the bobbin case and insert it into the machine. Embroider the words 'Zig Zag Whip' with two rows of straight stitch, moving the hoop slowly to add more texture.

⑮

Change the stitch type to narrow zigzag and sew a row, the tight tension creating a central line of top thread with spokes or dots of bobbin thread running down either side. Gradually increase the zigzag width for each line and vary the spacing so zigzag becomes satin stitch. The central line of top thread randomly moves to find the best position; it can wobble in the centre or move to one side.

144　Chapter 8 – Experimenting with Stitches and Tension

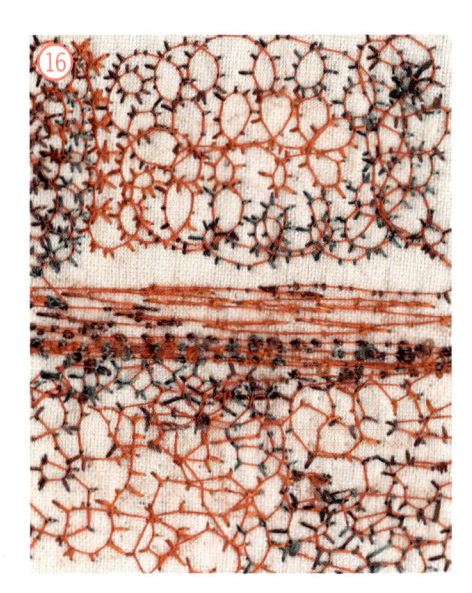

Scribble various patterns with medium-width zigzag. Here, the circular pattern pulled the bottom thread up to produce evenly spaced spokes, side-to-side movement created random dots, whilst angular patterns pulled unpredictable spokes or dots.

The finished sampler reveals how reactive whip stitch is to hoop movement and speed. Some of the patterns can be used decoratively on their own whilst others may benefit from being layered with other embroidery stitches to build up textures.

Chapter 8 – Experimenting with Stitches and Tension

SAMPLER
Moss Stitch

Moss stitch is a variation of whip stitch; it requires slight adjustments to the tension settings. Use whip stitch settings as a starting point, then tighten the top tension and loosen the bobbin tension. The dots of whip stitch become small loops, and when this stitch is sewn densely the loops build up and they look like clumps of moss or lichen.

Moss stitch is more effective when the hoop is moved slowly and the speed of the machine is fast. Moving the hoop slowly allows the bobbin thread to cover the top thread to create a raised wrapped thread. Interesting effects can be achieved by making angular movements and moving the hoop quickly; moving the hoop fast produces similar results to another loose tension stitch called feather stitch.

YOU WILL NEED

Equipment
- Scanner and printer or photocopier for enlarging the design
- Sewing machine with drop feed or darning plate
- Darning foot or embroidery foot
- Size 90/14 universal machine needle
- Two 15cm (6in.) wooden hoops
- Empty bobbins
- Spare bobbin case for loose tension embroidery
- Small slotted screwdriver
- Glass-headed pins
- Pencil
- Permanent pen or gel pen
- Pencil sharpener
- Embroidery scissors
- Fabric scissors

Materials
- A4 white paper
- Strong polyester, viscose or rayon top threads
- Various threads for the bobbins including a shaded one
- Two pieces of pre-washed calico approximately 28 × 23cm (11 × 9in.)
- Scrap of calico
- Dressmaker's carbon paper

Machine used
- Bernina 801
- Feeder teeth down
- Tightened top tension
- Loose bobbin thread tension

1 Create a design measuring approximately 18 × 14cm (7 × 5½in.) or copy and enlarge the one shown here. Make sure the design contains a variety of curved patterns but include some triangular or geometric patterns, as well as space for layering thick stitch patterns and a space for experimenting with zigzag and satin stitch. Include the words 'Moss' and 'Zig Zag Moss' to remind yourself of the stitch type and tension settings.

2 Use dressmaker's carbon to transfer the design onto calico. Stabilize the design with another layer of calico and place them both in the hoop so the word 'Moss' is central. Loose bobbin tension embroideries need extra stabilizing because altered tension distorts the fabric more.

3 Following on from the previous sampler, the tension is currently set up for whip stitch. Tighten the top tension more if the machine will allow you to do so. If you are unable to tighten the top tension remove the bobbin case and use a small screwdriver to loosen the tension screw a fraction. Thread the needle with strong red thread and insert a bobbin wound with a different colour into the bobbin case, then load it into the machine.

④ Place a hooped scrap of calico under the foot and set the stitch to straight. Lower the foot and test the stitch. If the bobbin thread loops are too big, the bobbin tension is too loose or the top tension is too tight; alter one and stitch again. Slow straight stitch produces a line of raised loops; blocks of close stitching create embroidery with a raised pile.

⑤ Wind a bobbin with shaded thread, insert it into the loose tension bobbin case and load into the machine. Position the hooped design under the foot and embroider the word 'Moss' with multiple rows of straight stitch. Outlining the letters with shaded thread creates the illusion of swapping thread colours. Embroider the W-shaped linear pattern; move the hoop very slowly and note how the sharp points become wider and more rounded as the tight thread pulls in.

⑥ Embroider the circles with straight stitch; move the hoop slowly so more thread is pulled to the top. Embroider some circles so they only have one line of outline stitch and fill others working from the centre outwards to create spirals. Embroider small circles on lines of straight stitch to create barnacles of moss stitch.

⑦ Stitch the outside of the first triangle; move the hoop slowly and stitch close concentric lines until the shape is filled. The thread tension rounds off the sharp corners, creating embroidery with the texture of a miniature rug, and the dual-coloured bobbin thread introduces pattern without needing to change the thread.

⑧ Embroider the next triangle more openly; vary the speed of the hoop for each side to change the amount of top thread showing. Slow hoop speed produces closely packed loops whilst fast hoop speed creates spaced-out dots. Embroider the final triangle shapes with one or two rows of slow straight stitch to create a raised effect.

⑨ Stitch two of the wavy lines with straight stitch, moving the hoop slowly so the top thread pulls more of the bottom thread through; this effect is more noticeable on the curved areas. Experiment with stitching layers of wavy lines on top of one another; dual-shaded thread creates the illusion of using two colours through the needle.

Chapter 8 – Experimenting with Stitches and Tension

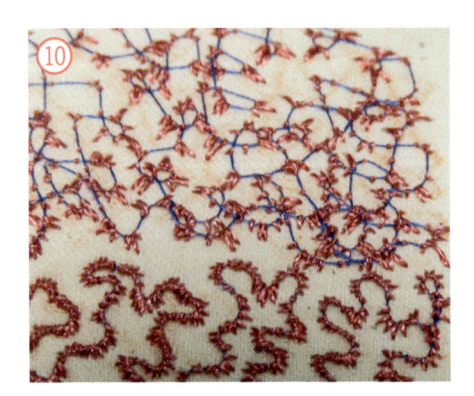

⑩ Thread the needle with blue and insert a bobbin wound with pink. Re-position the hoop over the angular and vermicelli patterns. Move the hoop quickly as you stitch the angular pattern; note how the bobbin thread only comes to the top when the hoop slows down or changes direction. Stitch the vermicelli pattern, moving the hoop slowly and pressing the foot pedal down so the needle is moving fast; this combination creates a continuous line of wrapped stitch.

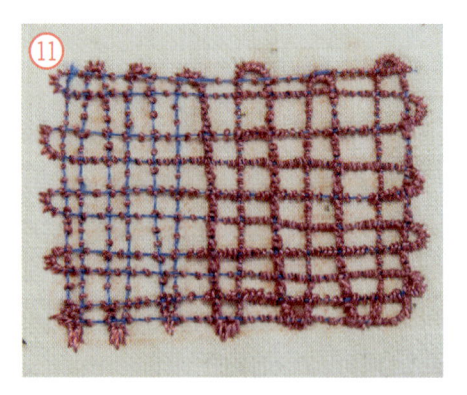

⑪ Stitch the grid pattern with straight stitch, moving the hoop fast on one side of the grid and slowly on the other to get a graduated effect. The fast side has more blue top thread visible whilst the slow side pulls more pink bobbin thread through.

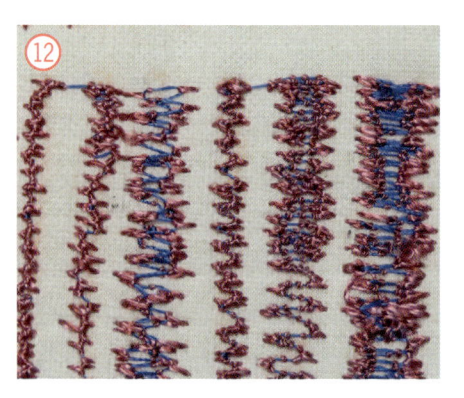

⑫ Stitch the zigzag shapes using straight stitch, varying the width and speed of the zigzag movements. Small movements pull more pink bobbin thread to the top whilst the larger movements produce spaced-out stitches that reveal blue top thread. Zigzag movements pull the bobbin thread to the top when the hoop changes direction; the texture of this stitch can be used in landscape pictures to create furrows in fields.

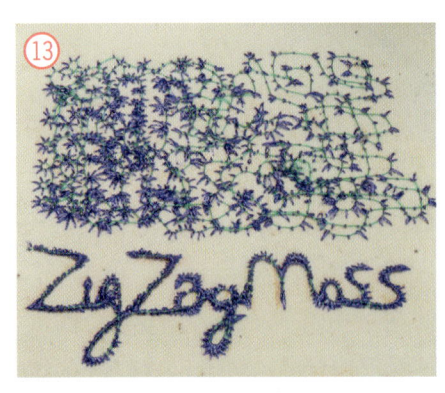

⑬ Thread the needle with green viscose and insert a bobbin wound with violet into the bobbin case and load into the machine. Re-position the hoop over 'Zig Zag Moss' and embroider the words with two rows of straight stitch, moving the hoop slowly to create raised moss stitch. Stitch a block of patterns, embroidering circles, scribbles and squares, and moving the hoop quickly to pull spokes of bobbin thread to the surface.

⑭ Set the stitch type to narrow zigzag. Stitch a row of zigzag, varying the speed of the hoop and machine to create satin stitch. Widen the width of the zigzag and stitch another row of zigzag close to the first. Continue widening the width of the zigzag with each row until the maximum width is reached. Fast hoop speed creates violet dots or spokes where the needle enters the fabric and slow hoop speed creates violet-wrapped top thread.

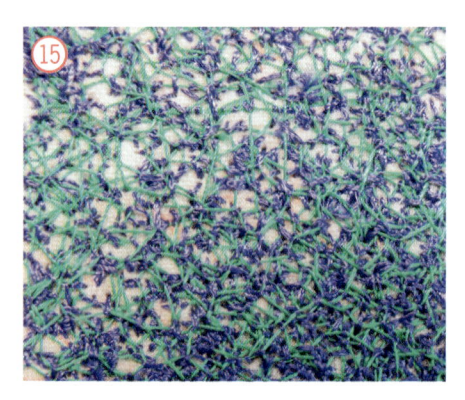

⑮ Set the stitch to medium-width zigzag and scribble randomly, moving the hoop smoothly so the needle does not snag. Build up layers of scribble so the calico is barely visible. Note how the green top thread has pulled to create short tabs whilst the violet bobbin thread comes to the top to create spokes or loops.

⑯ Embroider a few circles with medium-width zigzag, then embroider meandering vermicelli stitch with zigzag. The tight thread pulls the violet bobbin thread to the top to create feathery spokes where the needle enters and leaves the calico. The bobbin thread can form spokes on one side of the thread or both sides; how the spokes form depends on the angle of the stitch and how the hoop is moved.

⑰ The finished sampler reveals that moss stitch can produce dense loops or feathery spokes. The appearance of the stitch is related to the speed of the machine and the speed of the hoop movements.

Chapter 8 – Experimenting with Stitches and Tension   **149**

SAMPLER
FEATHER STITCH

Feather stitch is sewn with the same tension as moss stitch. It appears more delicate than moss stitch because the hoop is moved quickly to create longer distances between the spokes of bobbin thread. Feather stitch is more effective when circular or curved lines are sewn because the spokes are more noticeable where the hoop changes direction.

Feather stitch is even more delicate when invisible thread or near-invisible thread is used through the needle; this technique is very useful for adding foliage to trees or plants or for stippling texture onto a plain background. This delicate stitch can also be bold; layers of stitching build up to produce textured areas of solid embroidery. Try using metallic threads in the bobbin to add dots of sparkle to plain threads.

YOU WILL NEED

Equipment
- Scanner and printer or photocopier to enlarge the design
- Sewing machine with drop feed or darning plate
- Embroidery or darning foot
- Size 90/14 universal machine needle
- Empty bobbins
- Spare bobbin case for loose tension embroidery
- Small slotted screwdriver
- Embroidery scissors
- Fabric scissors
- Two 15cm (6in.) wooden hoops
- Pencil
- Pencil sharpener
- Ballpoint pen or gel pen
- Glass-headed pins

Materials
- White A4 paper
- Two pieces of pre-washed calico approximately 23 × 28cm (9 × 11in.)
- Scrap of calico
- Strong polyester, viscose or rayon top threads
- Various threads for the bobbins including some variegated ones
- Dressmaker's carbon paper

Machine used
- Bernina 801
- Feeder teeth down
- Tightened top tension
- Loose bobbin thread tension

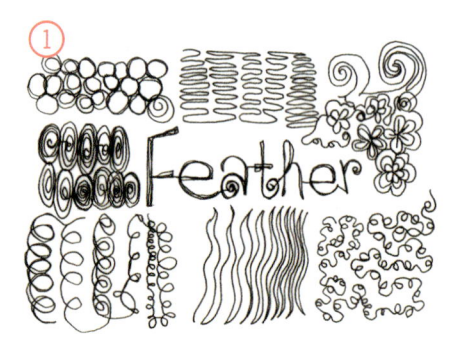

1. Create a design or copy and enlarge the one shown here. The design should measure approximately 18 × 14cm (7 × 5½in.). Include lots of circular patterns, loops and curved lines in the design and add the word 'Feather' to the middle of the design to remind yourself which stitch type was used.

2. Transfer the design to the calico using dressmaker's carbon, pressing hard with a ballpoint pen or pencil to make sure the design transfers properly. Place both layers of calico in the hoop so the circular patterns are central, then pull the fabric drum-tight and fasten the hoop screw.

3. Lower the feeder teeth and attach an embroidery foot. Insert a size 90/14 universal needle and set the stitch type to straight. Feather stitch is sewn with the same tension settings as moss stitch so there is no need to alter the tension unless you are starting from scratch. See the moss stitch sampler for information about how to set the top and bottom tension.

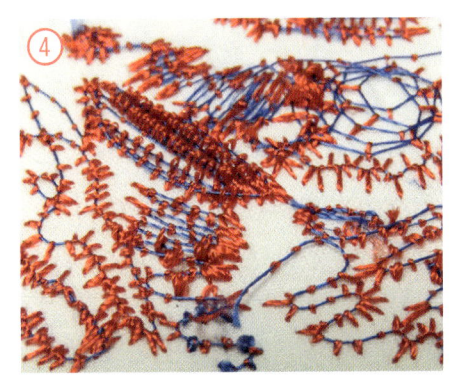

④ Thread the machine with two different thread colours and stitch a sample onto a hooped scrap of calico to check the tension. Fast curvy hoop movements should create a spoke effect to one or both sides of the top thread whilst slow movements create loops of bobbin thread that cover the top thread.

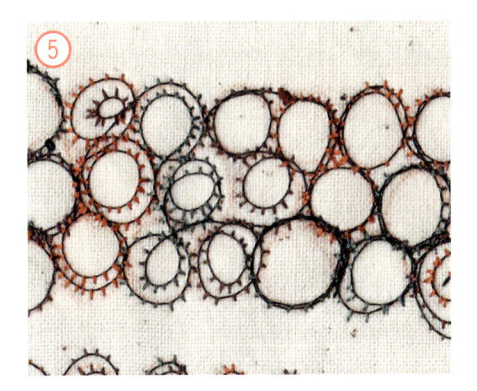

⑤ Thread the needle with black and insert a bobbin wound with variegated thread. Position the hooped fabric under the foot and stitch circles quickly with straight stitch. Embroider them using different methods; you could use single lines of stitch, offset rows of straight stitch or stitch rows on top of one another to create bold circles.

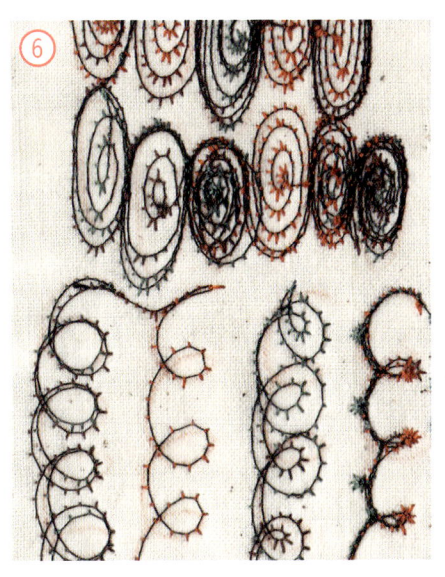

⑥ Embroider the spirals with straight stitch, moving the hoop clockwise and anticlockwise. Embroider some of them slowly to see how the spoked texture builds up. Stitch a series of loops moving the hoop quickly and vary the size of loops to illustrate how the bobbin thread is pulled through to create a star shape.

⑦ Thread the needle with green and insert a bobbin wound with another shade of green. It's useful to see how similar colours influence the appearance of the stitch. Embroider the word 'Feather' using three or four rows of straight stitch, moving the hoop quickly so the thread spokes or dots are spaced out.

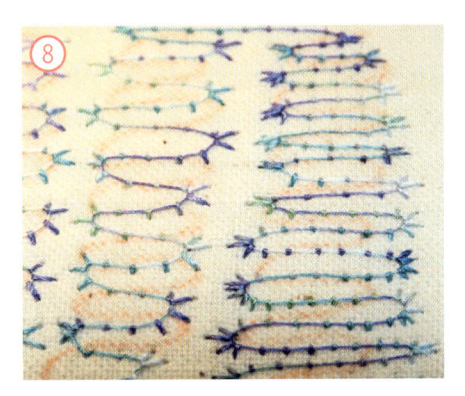

⑧ Re-position the hoop over the meandering line, wind and load a bobbin with variegated blue thread and use the same for the needle. Stitch the meandering line with straight stitch, moving the hoop quickly so the bobbin thread makes dots along the straight sections and spokes on the sharp curves.

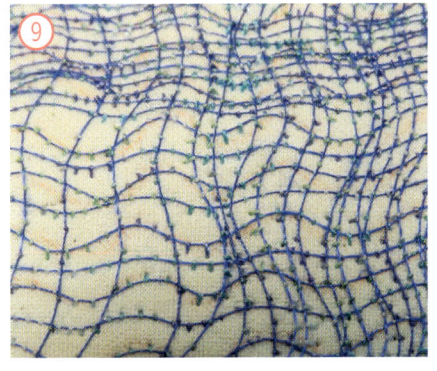

⑨ Re-thread the needle with plain blue thread and stitch a series of wavy lines, overlapping them to create a grid pattern. Swapping threads can change the tension of the stitch; this sample has fewer loops and dots. If you are not happy with the results you can alter the tension and try again.

Chapter 8 – Experimenting with Stitches and Tension

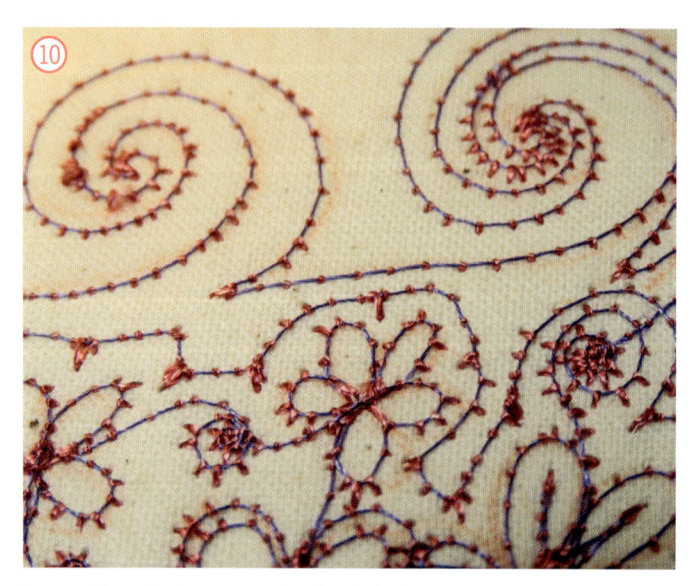

Re-position the hoop over the floral design, swap the top thread for violet and insert a bobbin wound with pink into the loose tension bobbin case. Stitch the curves and floral patterns with straight stitch, moving the hoop quickly to create long spokes.

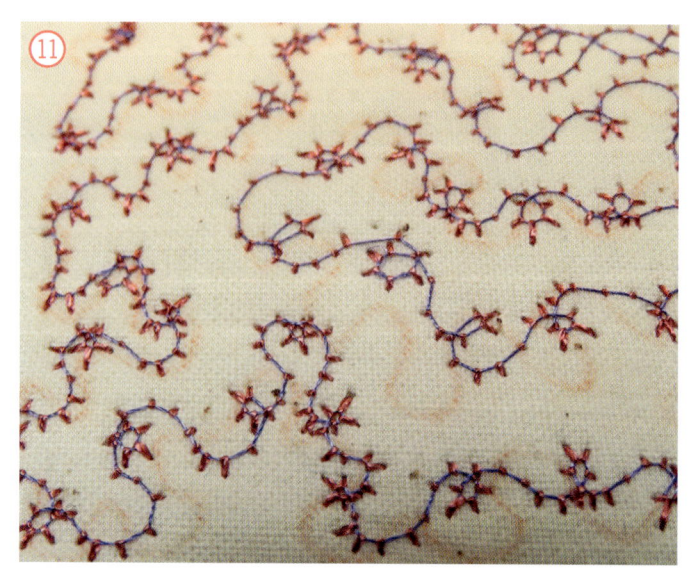

Stitch the vermicelli pattern with one row of straight stitch. The pink bobbin thread pulls to the top to create small spokes or dots on the gentle curves and longer spokes or stars on the tight curves.

The finished sampler does not include areas of dense stitch: you may wish to add them to your sampler. Be more adventurous when choosing threads; try stitching with invisible thread through the needle and experiment with metallic threads on the bobbin.

152   Chapter 8 – Experimenting with Stitches and Tension

SAMPLER
Cable Stitch

Cable stitch is different from other loose tension stitches because the front or right side of the embroidery is turned downwards instead of being on top. This method of embroidery is sometimes called under-thread or bobbin work embroidery because the work is produced upside down. Cable stitch resembles couched thread because the loop of top thread anchors the thick bobbin thread to the fabric.

Yarns or threads that spool smoothly from the loose tension bobbin case can be used. The tension screw will need adjusting for different thread weights or thicknesses: for example, thin four-ply yarn needs a different setting from thick cotton perle. Thick machine threads such as Madeira Lana no. 12, Decora no. 12 and Glamour no. 12 can be used on the bobbin; these threads are ideal for detailed work because they are more flexible than yarns. The only type of thread to avoid are the ones with slubs, loops or fluff because they can get caught in the bobbin case.

YOU WILL NEED

Equipment
- Scanner and printer or photocopier to enlarge the design
- Sewing machine with drop feed or darning plate
- Embroidery or darning foot
- Size 90/14 Universal needle
- Empty bobbins
- Spare bobbin case for loose tension embroidery
- Small slotted screwdriver
- Two 15cm (6in.) wooden hoops
- Embroidery scissors
- Fabric scissors
- Glass-headed pins
- Pencil
- Pencil sharpener
- Ballpoint pen or gel pen

Materials
- A4 plain paper
- Two pieces of pre-washed calico approximately 28 × 23cm (11 × 9in.)
- Scrap of calico
- Suitable yarns to wind on the bobbin: cotton perle, hanks of stranded cotton, four-ply yarn, no. 12 machine thread, chain yarn, thin viscose cord and double knitting yarn
- Strong polyester, viscose or rayon top threads
- Strong metallic top thread
- Dressmaker's carbon paper

Machine used
- Bernina 801
- Feeder teeth down
- Normal top tension
- Loose bobbin thread tension

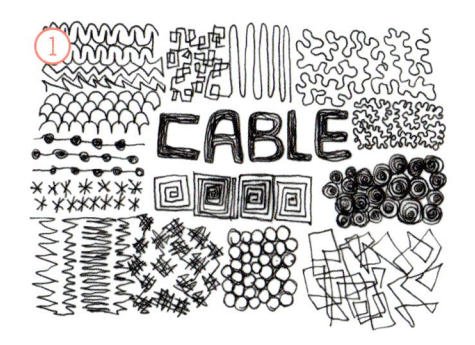

① Create a design or copy the one shown here. The design should measure approximately 18 × 14cm (7 × 5½in.). Make sure the word 'Cable' is large enough to be filled with stitching. Include a variety of patterns: thick threads or yarns work best with bold patterns that have more space around them, intricate patterns are more suitable for extremely thin yarns or no. 12 weight threads.

② Attach an embroidery or darning foot and lower the feeder teeth. Insert a size 90/14 universal needle and thread the needle with strong red top thread. Set the top tension dial to normal and set the stitch type to straight.

③

Wind stranded cotton onto the bobbin; this can be done by hand or by machine, it's best to machine-wind because it produces an even tension. Insert the wound bobbin into the loose bobbin case and pull the thread through the tension spring. The thread should come off the bobbin freely when pulled and the bobbin should drop a bit when dangled from its thread.

④

Place a scrap of calico in a hoop and fasten so it is drum-tight. Position the hooped calico under the embroidery foot and lower it. Turn the hand wheel so the needle goes through the fabric and into the bobbin chamber, then raise the needle and pull the top thread to bring a loop of bobbin thread up through the fabric. The threads are less likely to be sewn into the embroidery because they are visible on top.

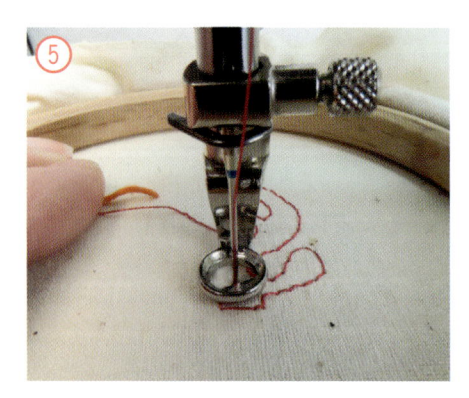

⑤

Hold both thread ends as you begin to stitch; this stops them tangling. Move your fingers back into a safe position and stitch a simple pattern with straight stitch. Raise the needle and foot, then take a peek underneath to see if the stitch is correctly tensioned. The embroidery may look fine on top but it's wise to check what's happening underneath before continuing.

⑥

The sample revealed a loose top thread and tight bobbin thread. I tightened the top tension to reduce the loops of top thread. It's important to retest the stitch after the tension has been altered; this time, the cable stitch formed correctly without altering the bobbin tension.

⑦

Flip or reverse the design to make a mirror image. Transfer the reversed design to calico using dressmaker's carbon paper. The design needs reversing because you are working with the back uppermost; if the design is not reversed the text will be stitched backwards.

⑧

Back the calico with a second piece to stabilize it. Place both layers into a hoop, make sure the calico is pulled drum-tight and that the word 'Cable' is central. Initially I forgot to reverse the design, so to rectify my mistake I wrote 'Cable' backwards using a Stabilo Fineliner. It's important to learn to correct mistakes as you make them because it's too late when the embroidery is stitched.

9 Thread the needle with strong variegated blue thread and wind the bobbin with a thin yarn that's unsuitable for use through the needle. Insert the wound bobbin into the loose tension bobbin case and test the tension by stitching a small sample. Position the needle over the first letter of the word 'Cable', lower the foot and use the hand wheel to bring the bobbin thread to the top.

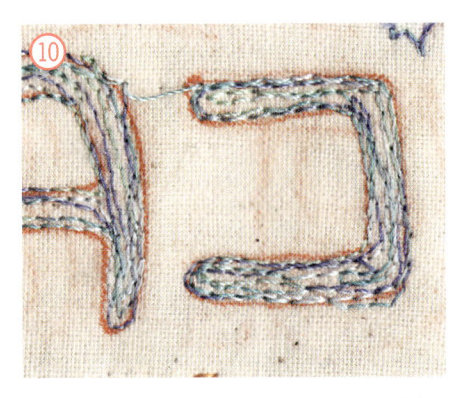

10 Stitch the outside of the letter using straight stitch, moving the hoop so medium-length stitches are made. Once the outside of the first letter is stitched, follow it with another row of stitching; continue working inwards until the letter is filled with concentric rows of stitches.

11 Raise the foot and needle, lift the hoop and look underneath to check the cable stitching. If you are happy with the results, move onto the following letters. Continue embroidering until the whole word is stitched, trim the tabs between the letters and take the thread tails to the back of the work.

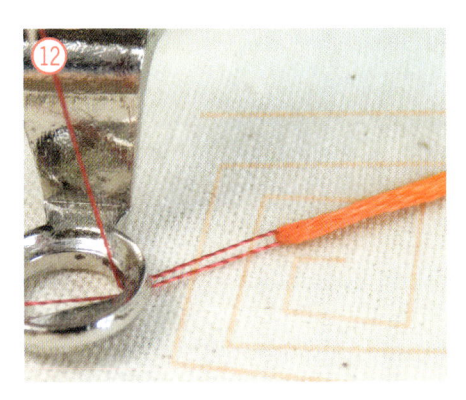

12 Wind shaded cotton perle onto an empty bobbin, insert it into the loose tension bobbin case, check the thread spools off freely and load into the machine. Thread the needle with strong variegated thread. Position the needle over the beginning of the Greek key pattern and bring both threads to the top by turning the hand wheel, then pull a short length of both threads and keep hold of them.

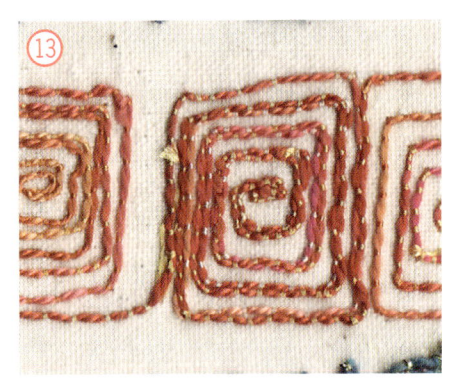

13 Stitch the Greek key pattern with a row of straight stitch. Raise the needle, lift the foot and take a peek underneath. If you are happy with the results, stitch the rest of the pattern, varying the density of the embroidery by stitching a second row almost on top of the first. Take the threads through to the back and tie them off, then trim the ends leaving a small thread tail.

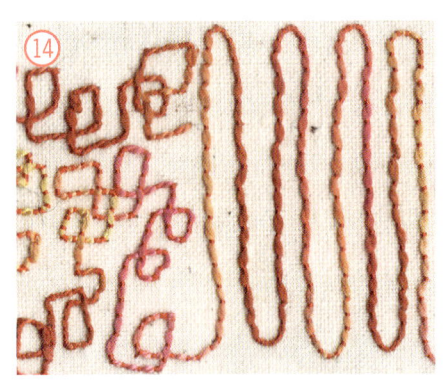

14 Re-position the hoop over the angular pattern. Thread the needle with strong colour-matched thread and turn the hand wheel to bring both threads to the top. Embroider the angular patterns with straight stitch; the simple pattern reveals that cotton perle is quite flexible. Take the threads through to the back, tie them off and trim the ends.

Chapter 8 — Experimenting with Stitches and Tension   **155**

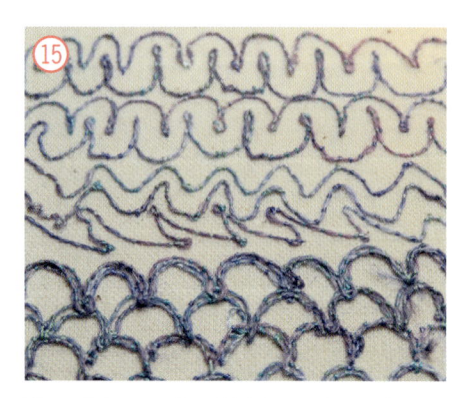

⑮ Thread the needle with blue variegated thread and wind Madeira Lana no. 12 onto an empty bobbin; tighten the bobbin case tension screw if it's too loose. Fine bobbin thread allows you to experiment with intricate patterns. Embroider the scale pattern with straight stitch. Take the threads to the back and tie them off.

⑯ Re-position the hoop over the circle and asterisk patterns. Thread the needle with black and wind the bobbin with thin black glittery yarn, choosing one that is unsuitable for use through the machine needle. Stitch along the line and fill the circles in, stitching the asterisk patterns then sewing back over them to create thicker stitching. Trim the thread ends from the front and back of the embroidery.

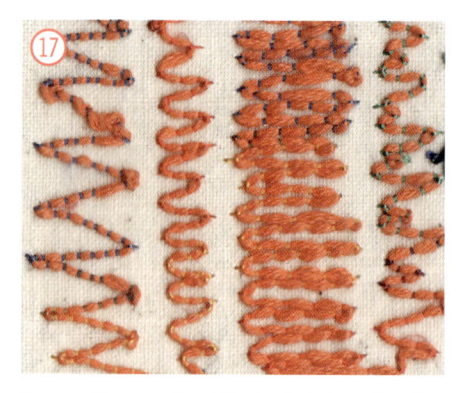

⑰ Thread the needle with shaded thread and wind stranded cotton onto the bobbin. You may need to loosen the bobbin tension screw and stitch a sample to test the tension. Stitch the jagged zigzag pattern with straight stitch and embroider some areas so the zigzag pattern is closed up like satin stitch. Take the threads through to the back and tie them off, cut the ends near to the fabric.

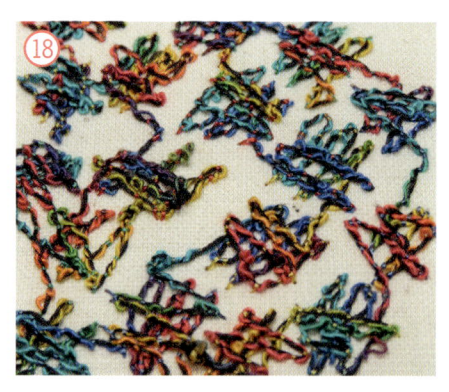

⑱ Wind a bobbin with a fine bouclé yarn and insert it into the bobbin case. Pull a small amount of yarn out to make sure the loops are small enough to pass through the tension spring. Embroider the hashtag scribble pattern using straight stitch, then embroider the open vermicelli pattern using the same combination of threads.

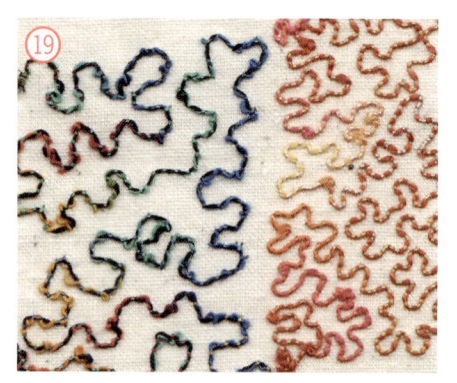

⑲ Wind variegated cotton perle onto an empty bobbin, load it into the bobbin case and insert in the machine. Thread the needle with strong variegated thread and use the hand wheel to bring both threads to the top. Stitch the smaller vermicelli pattern with straight stitch (right); variegated thread adds a touch of luxury to a simple stitch (left).

⑳ Wind thick white viscose thread onto an empty bobbin, place it in the bobbin case, check the tension and load into the machine. Re-position the hoop over the spiral pattern and thread the needle with variegated pastel thread. Turn the hand wheel to bring both threads to the top. Stitch the spirals so the rows of stitches are close to each other. Take the threads to the back, tie them off and trim the ends.

Choose a bobbin that has already been used for this sampler and insert it into the loose tension bobbin case. Thread the needle with strong metallic thread, then test the tension by stitching onto the hooped scrap. Metallic threads can be used to add dots of glitter to plain threads or yarns. Embroider the circle pattern with straight stitch, then take the thread ends to the back and tie them off.

Wind glittery chain yarn onto an empty bobbin, load into the bobbin case and adjust the tension screw to allow the rough yarn to spool from the bobbin case. Thread the needle with pale shaded thread and turn the hand wheel to bring both threads to the top. Embroider the angular pattern with straight stitch; chain yarns can be stiff so you may notice thread spokes where the stitches change direction. Take the threads to the back, tie them off and trim the ends.

This picture shows the side of the calico that's visible whilst embroidering.

Turning the fabric to the right side, it can be seen how the different bobbin threads have added an extra dimension to the embroidered patterns.

Chapter 8 – Experimenting with Stitches and Tension **157**

STEP-BY-STEP PROJECT
Garden Border

YOU WILL NEED

Equipment
- Photocopier or scanner and printer
- Sewing machine with drop feed or darning plate
- Embroidery or darning foot
- Empty bobbins
- Spare bobbin case for loose tension embroidery
- Size 90/14 universal machine needle
- Embroidery scissors
- Fabric scissors
- Paper scissors
- Two 15cm (6in.) wooden hoops
- Hand-sewing needle
- Iron
- Stabilo fineliner pen
- Pencil
- Pencil sharpener
- Eraser
- Sink or bowl of water to wash the embroidery
- Old towel on which to dry the embroidery

Materials
- A4 paper
- Tracing paper
- Sky blue cotton or hand-painted cotton
- Pre-washed calico
- Avalon water-soluble film
- Kingstar no. 40 polyester thread in colours 309 (violet blue), 631 (powder blue)
- Robison-Anton Twister Tweed thread in colour 79030 (sizzling pink)
- Madeira Classic thread no. 40 in colours 1189 (moss green), 1170 (fern green), 1049 (lime green), 1310 (magenta), 1108 (pink carnation), 1039 (brick red)

Design templates
- Garden Border midground
- Garden Border foreground

Machine used
- Bernina 801
- Feeder teeth down
- Normal tension and tightened top tension
- Loose tension bobbin thread

This project shows how to embroider a colourful garden border using variations of whip and moss stitch. Source your own image and sketch an informal design; tall flowers like delphiniums or foxgloves translate well into embroidery. This project is ideal for using up thread remnants or tricky threads that don't work through the needle; wind these threads onto bobbins and use them to stitch the flowers or foliage.

① This project has so many possibilities. Machine embroidery can be mixed with hand embroidery; here, for instance, most of the foliage was embroidered by machine and the poppy flowers sewn by hand. Finished embroideries can be mounted in a hoop, flexi-frame, handbag mirror or pendant.

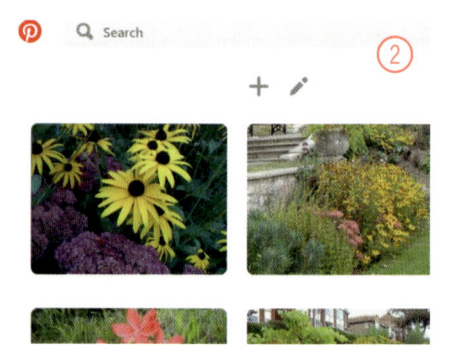

② Find a photo of a garden border, choosing a simple image that does not have too many plant varieties. Gardening books or catalogues are good places to find source material; images can be found on the internet and stored in online scrapbooks such as Pinterest.

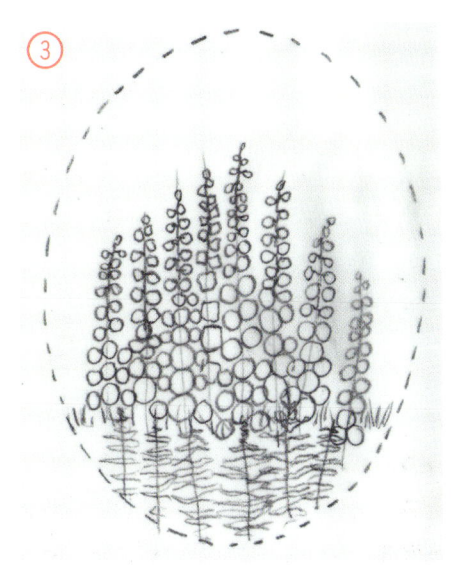

3 Decide the size and shape of the finished embroidery; should the composition be oval, round or square? Draw the design to size and remove flowers that complicate the design: the aim is to produce a design that translates easily to stitch.

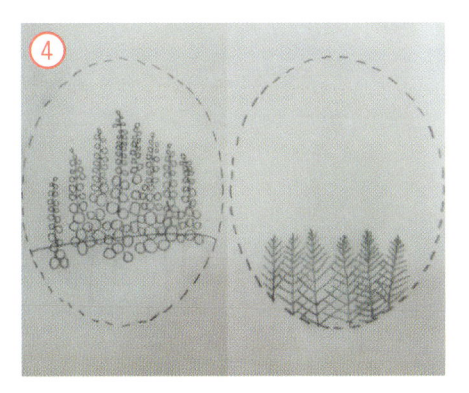

4 Think about how to embroider the flowers and foliage – which parts will be sewn first? Make additional drawings that split the design up into background, middle ground and foreground; it's easier to make these drawings on tracing paper because the originals can be seen below. Look at the garden border templates for guidance and inspiration.

5 Select the threads, considering colour, weight and type. Look at the tension samplers to see which stitches are suitable for replicating the flowers and foliage. Feather, whip and moss stitches are good choices because the raised texture adds more depth to the flowers and foliage.

6 Cut a piece of sky blue cotton for the background or paint some white cotton with watered-down fabric paints. The cotton needs to be large enough for the design and the embroidery hoop. Cut out a piece of pre-washed calico the same size as the cotton and place it behind the cotton to stabilize it.

7 Transfer the background design onto Avalon water-soluble film with a colour-matched Stabilo Fineliner. Pin the traced film onto the cotton, then place the layers in a hoop so the design is central. The hooped fabric needs to be really taut because the altered thread tension pulls the fabric in.

8 Attach an embroidery foot and lower the feeder teeth. Select straight stitch and Insert a size 90/14 universal machine needle. Set the tension up for whip stitch; this stitch needs the top tension to be tighter than the bottom tension so refer to the whip stitch sampler for more information.

Chapter 8 – Experimenting with Stitches and Tension **159**

⑨ Wind an empty bobbin with Madeira Classic 1170 (fern green). Depending on the machine settings, insert the wound bobbin into the loose or normal bobbin case then load both into the machine. Thread the needle with two shades of green thread; I used Madeira Classic 1049 (lime green) and 1170 (fern green).

⑩ Place a scrap of calico in a hoop and test the stitch. Small dots of bobbin thread should come to the top; adjust the tension until you are happy with the stitch. Practise embroidering the grass, stitching up and down with straight stitch, and vary the angle of the stitching slightly to build up layers so the stitching looks more natural.

⑪ Swap back to the hooped design and embroider the grass. As you stitch, the embroidery covers the lower part of the flower spikes but don't worry, you should see enough of the design to stitch the flowers on top.

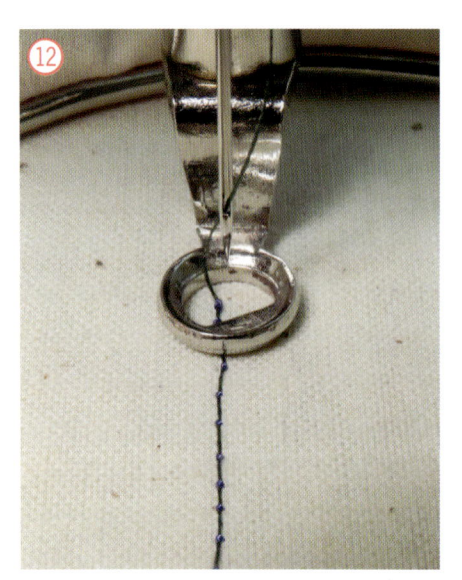

⑫ Thread the needle with Madeira Classic 1189 (moss green) and lower the top tension a little. Insert a bobbin wound with Kingstar 309 (violet blue) into the loose bobbin case. Embroider a sample delphinium flower onto a scrap of hooped calico. Begin by stitching the stalk; start at the base and stitch to the top with one row of straight stitch. Move the hoop quickly so more green thread is visible.

⑬ Stitch the buds at the top of the stalk. Move the hoop slowly and make tiny circular movements; as the buds get bigger move the hoop in a wider circle or make small up-and-down movements. Work left to right down the flower spike, increasing the size of the buds as you work down the stem.

⑭ Adjust the top or bobbin tension ready for moss stitch; refer back to the moss stitch sampler for further instruction. Embroider the opening buds; move the hoop left to right or side to side to create tiny blocks of satin stitch. Slow hoop movements pull more violet blue bobbin thread to the top.

⑮ Delphinium flowers are more open further down the stem. Represent bigger blooms by stitching a small circle in the centre of the stalk, then one either side. The top tension may need tightening to bring more violet blue bobbin thread to the top.

⑯ Stitch circles to create full open blooms; bobbin thread tabs radiate out from the centre like spokes on a wheel. Repeat the circular movement; as the thread builds up it creates a ridge of thread that looks like a flower bell. Continue stitching the large flower heads until the base of the stem is covered.

⑰ Stitch a few more delphinium flowers to get used to changing the tension settings. Experiment with different threads (including variegated) to see how they change the colour of the embroidery. When you have finished practising, swap back to the painted hooped cotton; use the suggested thread colours or choose your own.

⑱ Thread the needle with Madeira 1189 (moss green) and insert a bobbin wound with Kingstar 309 (violet blue). Embroider two delphinium spikes, stitching them in the same way as the practice flowers. Change the bobbin thread to Madeira 1310 (magenta) and stitch two foxglove flower spikes. Embroider these using the same method and trim the thread tabs.

⑲ Thread the needle with Madeira 1170 (fern green) and insert a bobbin wound with Madeira 1108 (pink). Stitch the top part of two foxglove plants, embroidering the closed buds and the half-open ones. Change the top thread to Madeira 1310 (magenta) and stitch the lower half of the flower spike; the magenta thread creates random shading when it mixes with the pale bobbin thread.

⑳ Re-thread the needle with Madeira 1170 (fern green) and swap the bobbin thread to Kingstar 631 (powder blue). Embroider the last two delphinium spikes using the same method.

Chapter 8 — Experimenting with Stitches and Tension **161**

㉑

Peel the soluble film away and trace the foreground foliage design onto a scrap of film with a colour-matched pen. Pin the traced film over the embroidery so it matches up with the stitched design. Place the embroidery in a hoop and pull the fabric taut, then tighten the hoop.

㉒

Set the tension to moss stitch settings; refer to the moss stitch sampler for further guidance. Wind a bobbin with Madeira 1039 (brick red) and insert into the bobbin case. Thread the needle with Robison-Anton Twister Tweed in colour 79030 (sizzling pink); this mottled thread is perfect for plants like valerian or astilbe.

㉓

Practise stitching the astilbe flower heads. Embroider triangular evergreen tree shapes or feather shapes onto a scrap of hooped calico. Use straight stitch and move the hoop slowly so the bobbin thread is pulled to the top. When you have finished practising, swap back to the hooped design.

㉔

Embroider half of the astilbe flowers with this combination of threads. Swap the bobbin thread to Madeira 1108 (pink carnation) and thread the needle with pink Twister Tweed. Stitch the remaining astilbe flowers. If you feel they are too bright you could embroider plain green foliage or leave the embroidery as it is with no foreground.

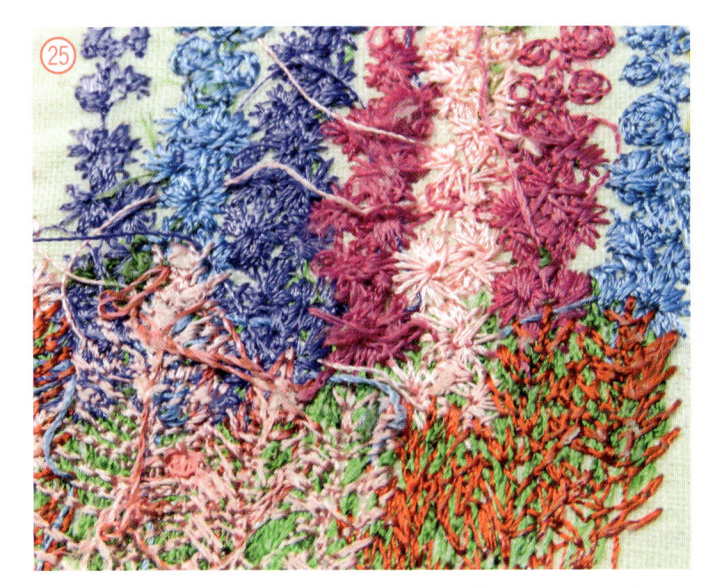

㉕

Remove the embroidery from the hoop and pull away the soluble film. Trim the thread tabs on the front of the embroidery; do not trim the back of the embroidery close to the surface. Soak the embroidery in warm water to dissolve the soluble film, then dry face up on an old towel. If the embroidery has dried hard, soak it again to remove the film residue and leave it to dry.

㉖

Place the embroidery face down onto a clean towel and cover with an ironing cloth; gently press to remove handing marks or creases. Ironing the embroidery on a towel cushions the ironing board and stops the raised stitches being flattened.

㉗

The embroidery is now ready to be displayed in a traditional oval frame or mount. See Chapter 12 for possible methods.

Chapter 8 – Experimenting with Stitches and Tension **163**

STEP-BY-STEP PROJECT
Cable Stitch Needlecase Set

YOU WILL NEED

Equipment
- Photocopier or scanner and printer
- Sewing machine with drop feed or darning plate
- Darning or embroidery foot
- Straight-stitch presser foot
- Size 90/14 machine needle
- Hand-sewing needle
- Chenille or darning needle
- Glass-headed pins
- Spare bobbin case for loose tension embroidery
- Empty bobbins
- Iron
- Baking parchment
- Rotary cutter
- Cutting mat with printed grid
- Set square
- Sharp scissors
- Embroidery scissors
- Metal ruler
- Pencil
- Pencil sharpener
- Eraser
- Colour-matched permanent pen

Materials
- White A4 paper
- Blue or violet embellished quilting fabric approximately 21 × 30cm (8¼ × 11¾in.) (see Chapter 7, velvet cushion project, for more information about embellishing background fabrics)
- Small pieces of pelmet Vilene and mediumweight iron-on interfacing
- Cotton felt colour-matched to the embellished quilting fabric
- Colour-matched ribbon approximately 22cm (8¾in.) long
- Scrap of patterned cotton quilting fabric
- Scrap of calico
- Bondaweb or heat-fusible glue
- Wadding remnants or toy stuffing
- Variegated cotton perle size 8 in colour 1315 or 1375
- Strong top thread to match the colour of the cotton perle
- Strong colour-matched thread for making up
- Black bobbin and top thread

Design templates
- Needlecase
- Pincushion front
- Pincushion back
- Scissor Keeper

Machine used
- Bernina 801
- Feeder teeth up and down
- Normal top tension
- Loose tension bobbin thread and normal tension bobbin thread

---

Throughout history pins and needles have been greatly valued. Before the days of mass production they would have been costly and rare items, and they would be stored safely in containers that reflected their owners' wealth, status and gender: such a container might well have been an elaborate needlecase or an etui sewing box. In our own time, scissor keepers ensure you can always find your scissors under the layers of fabric and paper on your workbench. This project shows you how to make a keepsake set to keep your needles, pins and scissors safe. These little makes are also ideal for craft fairs or fund-raising sales tables. They are inexpensive to make because they use up scraps of fabric and yarn; the only expenditure is time.

① Iron the back of the embellished fabric. Fuse mediumweight interfacing to the back of the fabric, using a layer of baking parchment to help the iron glide.

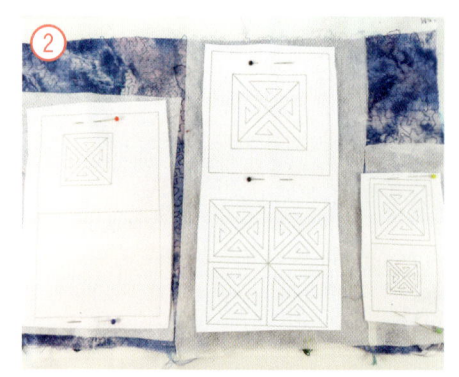

② Find the Needlecase, Pincushion and Scissor Keeper designs in the back of the book and trace or copy them. Make an extra copy of the scissor keeper pattern because it's used to test the stitch. Cut the copies out and pin them to the back of the stabilized embellished fabric.

③ Set the machine up for free embroidery with cable stitch; refer to the cable stitch sampler for more instructions. Set the stitch type to straight. Wind an empty bobbin with variegated cotton perle size 8 in colour 1375, insert it into the loose tension bobbin case and load both into the machine.

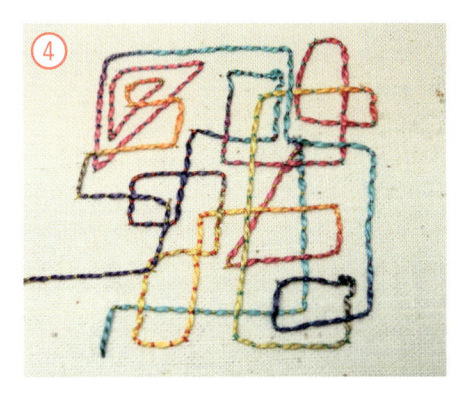

④ Thread the needle with strong colour-matched thread and set the top tension to normal. Place a hooped scrap of calico under the foot, lower the foot and turn the hand wheel to bring both threads to the top. Stitch a small sample of cable stitch to test the tension settings; the cotton perle should be kink-free and there should be no obvious loops in the top thread.

⑤ Place the spare scissor keeper design under the foot so the paper faces upwards. Position the needle over the starting point and lower the embroidery foot. Bring the bobbin thread to the top by turning the hand wheel, then pull both threads behind the needle. Using straight stitch, follow the lines carefully and stitch two or three rows of cable stitch embroidery.

⑥ Turn the fabric over and look at the embroidery. Choose how to stitch the final pieces. Don't be afraid to make changes as you work because it's an important part of the design process. Three rows of stitch dominated the design so I decided to stitch the final pieces with two rows of cable stitch. I used cotton perle no. 8 colour 1315 on the bobbin because it has warm tones to complement the purple background.

⑦ Embroider the designs with two rows of cable stitch. Position the needle over the starting point and turn the hand wheel to pull the bobbin thread to the top, then lower the foot and start stitching. It's important to do this for each motif because it prevents thread tangles.

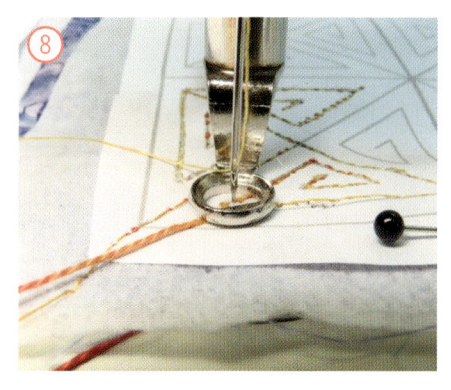

⑧ If the bobbin runs out, bring the end of the cotton perle through to the paper side, wind a bobbin and start again. Position the needle over the spot where the cotton perle ran out and use the hand wheel to bring the cotton perle to the top, then move the thread ends out of the way and start stitching again.

⑨

Decide if you want to embroider a pattern onto the back of the needlecase. I chose to embroider a random angular pattern to complement the Greek key theme. You can leave the back of the case blank to show more of the embellished fabric.

⑩

Check the right side of the embroidery is neat. Tidy up messy clumps of cotton perle by snipping the threads with embroidery scissors. Couch any loose cotton perle into position by hand or use zigzag stitch to secure it. Take the thread ends through to the paper side and tie them off.

⑪

Attach the straight-stitch foot and raise the feeder teeth. Set the top tension dial to normal. Insert a bobbin wound with black into the normal tension bobbin case and load both into the machine. Set the stitch type to long straight or tacking stitch, then thread the needle with black thread.

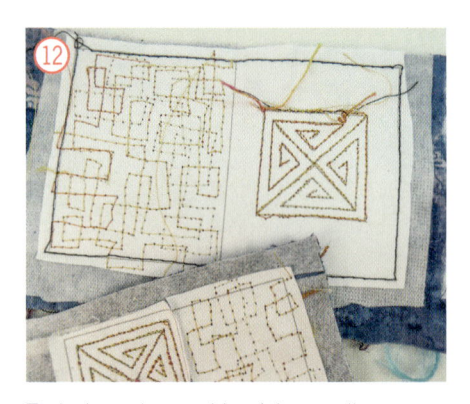

⑫

Tack along the outside of the needlecase, following the printed border on the paper design. Cut the needlecase out, leaving a small seam allowance. Cut the pincushion and scissor keeper pieces out, leaving a larger seam allowance to allow for sewing seams and making up.

⑬

Put the pincushion panels together so the paper is outside. Match the corners, then pin through the paper guidelines. Turn the pinned fabric over to make sure the pins align with the sewn lines on both sides. You may need to re-position the pins and fidget the panels so both sides line up together. Stitch along the outline, leaving a small section open to allow for turning through; reinforce the start, corners and end with backstitch.

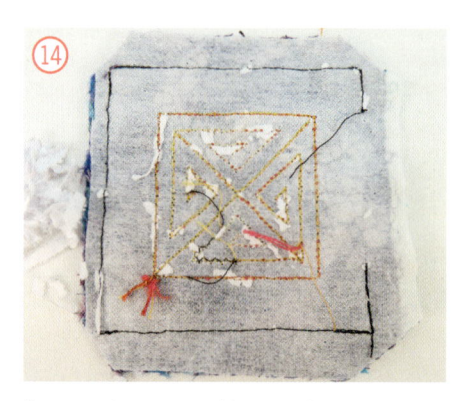

⑭

Remove the paper without pulling the threads. Trim fabric from the side seams to make the edges neat, then cut across the corners so the fabric is trimmed close to the corner stitching. Turn the pincushion through; be careful not to split the seam when you pull the thick fabric through the small opening.

⑮ Use a thick sharp needle to tease out the corners or push them out with blunt scissors (but don't push the scissors through the fabric). Stuff the pincushion with scraps of shredded wadding or toy filling. Push the wadding into the corners then fill the rest of the cushion until it is firm.

⑯ Locate the opening and fold the seam allowance inwards; make sure the edge is straight like the other sides, then pin it closed. Thread a sharp hand-sewing needle with strong colour-matched thread and slip-stitch or lace the opening closed. Fasten off the thread by taking it through to the middle of the pin cushion and trim close to the fabric.

⑰ Position the scissor keeper panel so the right side is upwards. Fold the ribbon in half so it's looped at one end, pin the cut ends to one corner of the scissor keeper. The loop should face towards the centre and the cut ends should overlap the outside seam. Secure the loop by wrapping it around your finger to create a tidy bundle, then pin the bundle from the other side to secure.

⑱ Fold the scissor keeper in half so that the paper is outside and the ribbon inside. Line up the corners and pin them together, using the paper seam lines as a guide. Turn the fabric over to check the pins are going through the seam lines on the back. Sew along two of the seam lines using backstitch at the start, corners and end, then cut the thread tails.

⑲ Peel the paper away and trim the seam allowance and corners. Turn the scissor keeper through. Check the ribbon bundle has not been sewn into the seams and the ribbon is securely attached to the corner. Stuff the scissor keeper with wadding, fold the open side inwards and manipulate so it's straight, pin in place and lace closed with slip stitch. Use the ribbon loop to attach it to your scissors.

⑳ Cut a rectangle of pelmet Vilene slightly larger than the tacking around the needlecase. Cut out two rectangles of paper-backed heat-fusible glue the same size as the pelmet Vilene. Iron one piece of heat-fusible glue to the pelmet Vilene and allow to cool. Peel off the backing paper and place the glue side against the inside of the needlecase. Cover with baking parchment and bond in place.

Chapter 8 – Experimenting with Stitches and Tension **167**

21. Bond the remaining rectangle of fusible glue to the back of the quilting fabric; allow to cool, then cut out around the rectangle shape. Peel the backing off and position the bonded fabric on top of the pelmet Vilene glue side down; no white pelmet Vilene should be visible. Cover with baking parchment and bond in place.

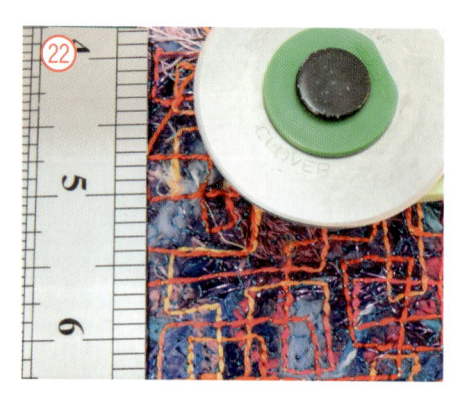

22. Lay the cutting mat on a flat surface and place the needlecase on top, embroidered side upwards. Align the ruler along one of the tacked lines and re-position so the edge is 0.3cm (⅛in.) outside the tacked line that marks the rectangle.

23. Trim the seam allowance, pressing down firmly on the ruler to hold it steady and making sure your fingers are away from the edge. Line the rotary cutter blade up against the edge of the ruler and press down as you push it along the length of the ruler; push down firmly to cut through all the layers.

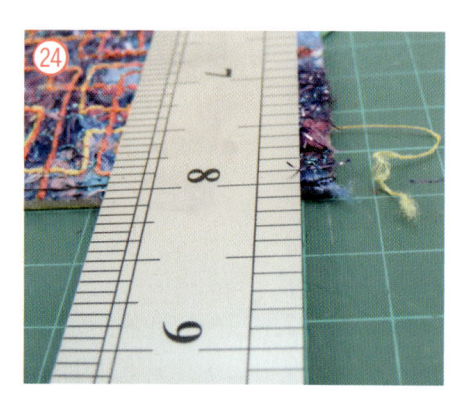

24. Rotate the fabric so the cut edge of the fabric lines up with a vertical line on the cutting mat. Re-position the ruler along the tacked line and make sure the tacked line and cut edge match up with the horizontal and vertical grid on the cutting mat. Check the fabric is square before cutting with the rotary cutter. Trim the remaining sides using the same method.

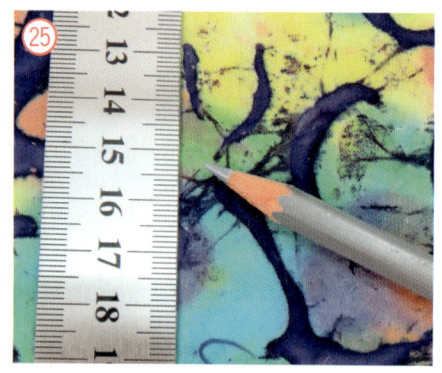

25. Colour the cut edge of the pelmet Vilene with colour-matched permanent marker. Unpick the tacked lines of stitch if they are visible. Turn the case over so the inside faces upwards. Divide the longest length of the rectangle by two and mark the middle in three places with a chalk pencil, line the ruler up with the three marks and draw a line through them. Fold the case along the dawn line to check it folds in half.

26. Change the stitch type to a wide medium-length zigzag. Thread the needle and bobbin with strong colour-matched thread. Test the width and length of the zigzag on a scrap of needlecase fabric. If the stitch has nice balanced spacing, swap to the needlecase and stitch all four sides to stop fraying.

168 Chapter 8 – Experimenting with Stitches and Tension

㉗ Tie off the threads and use a hand-sewing needle to take the threads into the centre of the pelmet Vilene to hide them. Thread a chenille needle with the same cotton perle used for the cable stitch embroidery; I used Anchor no. 8 in colour 1315. Work blanket stitch around the edge of the needlecase, stitching over the zigzag and keeping the stitches the same size.

㉘ Cut two rectangles of felt slightly smaller than the blanket stitch border. Use a ruler, set square, cutting mat and rotary cutter for accuracy or cut them out with pinking shears to create decorative edging. Pin the felt rectangles to the inside of the needlecase, making sure the border around them is equal. Locate the central crease and draw a line on it with chalk pencil and ruler.

㉙ Thread the machine with strong colour-matched thread through the needle and in the bobbin. Set the stitch type to short straight stitch. Line the needle up with the start of the seam and lower the foot. Stitch down the central pencil line to secure the felt pages, turn the fabric and sew back up the line of stitching. Tie off the thread ends and take them through to the middle of the fabric layers.

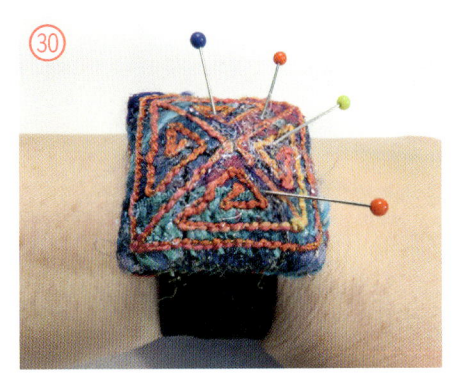

㉚ If you can't get on with a scissor keeper, turn it into a wrist pincushion. Don't attach a ribbon to one corner when sewing the outside seams. Trim and turn through, then stuff more firmly with wadding and sew up the opening. Attach the stuffed pincushion to a cuff of elastic so it's ready to wear.

㉛ None of the embroidery scraps are wasted. I turned the sample embroidery into a fun ethnic-style keyring and I kept the offcuts in a folder to remind me about the process and fabrics used.

㉜ All the sewing keepsakes are double-sided; simply choose your favourite side and use or gift them to a friend.

Chapter 8 – Experimenting with Stitches and Tension   **169**

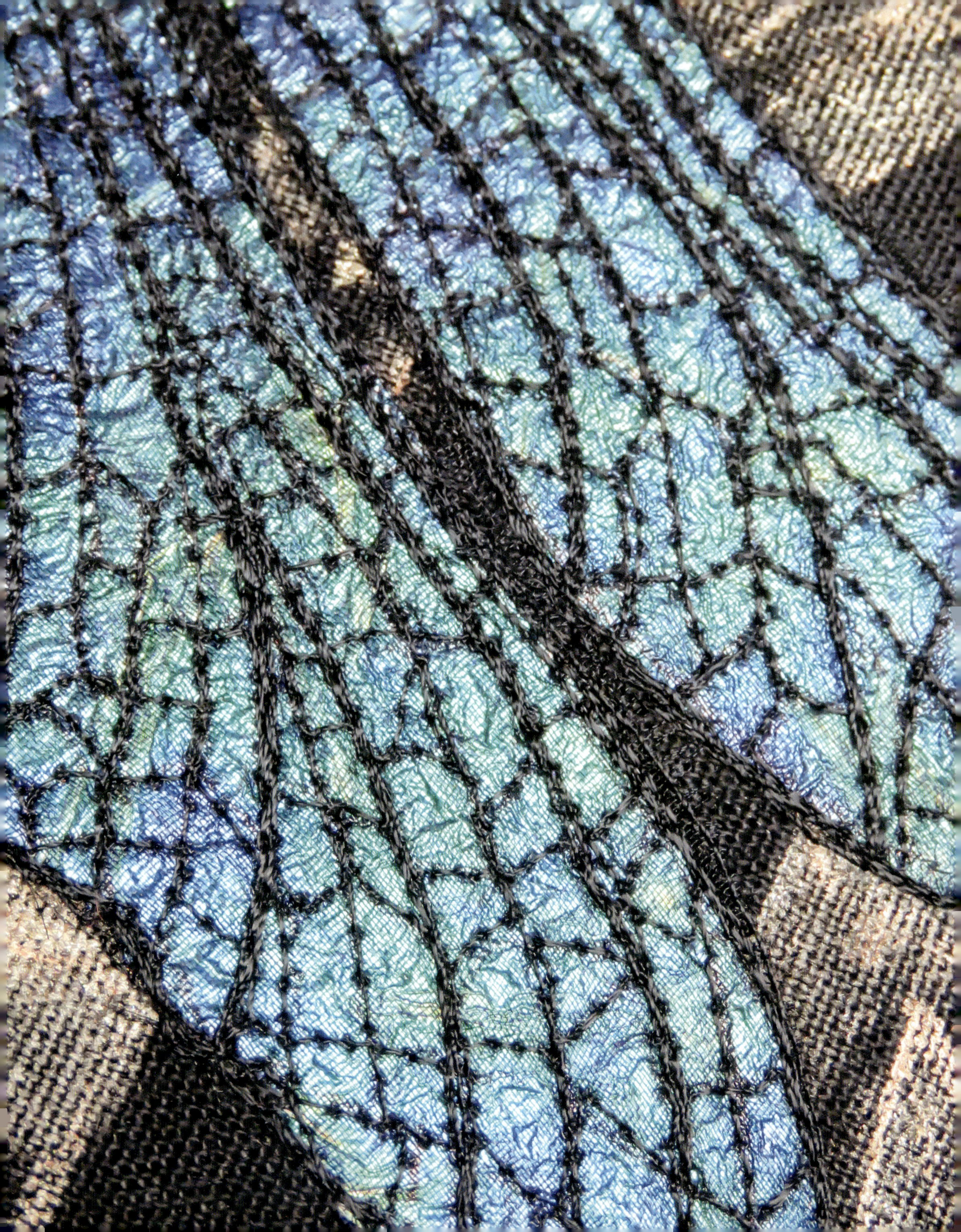

CHAPTER 9

ALL THAT GLITTERS

Goldwork embroideries were historically sewn by hand and the threads and metal purl wires used in them contained real gold. Gold was included in embroideries to represent actual or spiritual wealth and status. Hand embroidery threads such as jap, plate or metal purls still contain precious gold metal. Threads for machine embroidery are very different; the metal in them is likely to be silver or non-tarnishing aluminium. Modern manufacturing techniques mean faux gold threads are available in a range of colours and finishes for all to enjoy a touch of luxury.

This chapter is about finding your inner magpie and learning to tame it. I have a special stash of metallic threads, fabrics, transfer foils, paints, beads and sequins. I save metallics for special projects where sparkly additions suit the subject matter and mood of the embroidery. It's important to learn how to include metallics in your embroideries; the trick is to use them sparingly or go wild and gaudy when appropriate.

Think about how to introduce metallic elements. Should metallic thread be used to outline embroidery motifs? Could the embroidery be stitched with gold threads? Can gold leaf or transfer foil be applied to the fabric and embroidered into? Will beads or sequins be used to decorate the finished embroidery?

How much you use is dependent on your design style and how you want to include the metallic elements. I tend to add metallics as an afterthought; the dragonfly project is an exception to my usual style because I considered how metallics were going to be used right through the embroidery process.

The samplers show how to introduce metallics into projects and demonstrate how to perform each technique. The aim of the samplers is to show that metallics can be used in different ways: for example, the Mistyfuse sampler has metallic textures but they don't overpower the delicate flower design; the butterfly is definitely on the gaudy side but the use of bright metallics really suit the bold style of the embroidery. This chapter is about experimenting and having fun; you can combine what you have already learnt and add some sparkle to your 'oh, wow' moments.

SAMPLER
Embroidering with Metallic Threads

The best way to learn about metallic threads is to use them. There are lots of myths about how temperamental metallic thread can be; the aim of this sampler is to show that metallic threads can be used without too much stress. I recommend using a metallic needle because metallic threads are stiffer than regular embroidery threads. Metallic needles have a large eye so the stiff thread can pass through with less friction; less friction equals less thread breaking, shredding and annoyance.

Begin to build your stash by purchasing small 200m reels. It's more economical to begin building a small collection of threads this way because metallics are a bit more expensive than regular threads. Choose some plain metallics, sparkly glittery threads, flat mono filaments and variegated Astro colours. As you begin to explore using the threads you may find the machine favours a particular brand or colour. Don't worry about the variation; if it doesn't work through the needle it can always be used in the bobbin for under-thread or bobbin embroidery techniques.

YOU WILL NEED:

Equipment
- Sewing machine with drop feed or darning plate
- Darning or embroidery foot
- Straight-stitch presser foot
- Size 90/14 machine needles for metallic thread
- Normal tension bobbin case
- Empty bobbin
- Ruler
- White dressmaker's chalk pencil
- Pencil sharpener
- Iron
- Baking parchment
- Glass-headed pins
- 15cm (6in.) wooden hoop
- Fabric scissors
- Embroidery scissors

Materials
- Black cotton fabric approximately 25.5 × 30.5cm (10 × 12in.)
- Black mediumweight iron-on interfacing 25.5 × 30.5cm (10 × 12in.)
- Tear-away stabilizer slightly larger than embroidery design
- Four shades of metallic gold thread
- Metallic machine threads in various colours and types
- Black Bobbinfil or black thread

Machine used
- Bernina 801
- Feeder teeth up and down
- Normal tension

1. Prepare to draw a grid pattern measuring 20 × 12.5cm (8 × 5in.) onto the front of the black cotton. Use a ruler and dressmaker's chalk pencil to draw the lines. Angle some of the lines to create different shapes, then draw trapezium or rectangle shapes in alternate gaps.

2. Iron black mediumweight interfacing onto the back of the cotton. Use baking parchment to help the iron glide and protect the iron. (Some brands of interfacing can melt onto the iron if too much heat is applied.)

172   Chapter 9 – All That Glitters

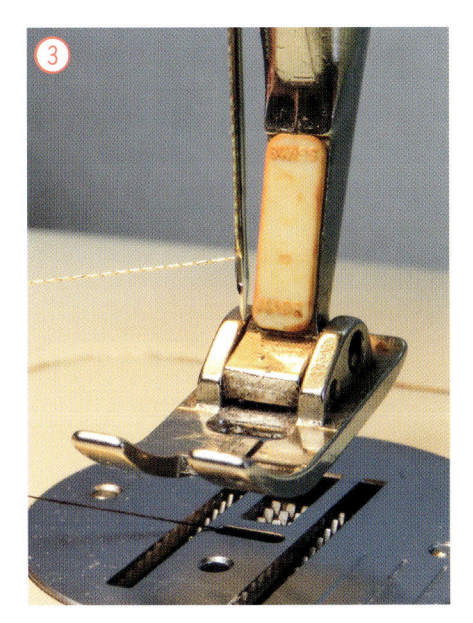

3 Attach the presser foot and raise the feeder teeth. Insert a size 90/14 metallic needle and thread it with metallic gold thread. Insert a bobbin wound with black Bobbinfil into the normal tension bobbin case and load both into the machine.

4 Set the stitch to medium-width zigzag and set the length to satin stitch. Pin two layers of tear-away stabilizer underneath the design. Place the pinned cotton under the foot so the needle lines up with the start of a chalk line, then lower the foot.

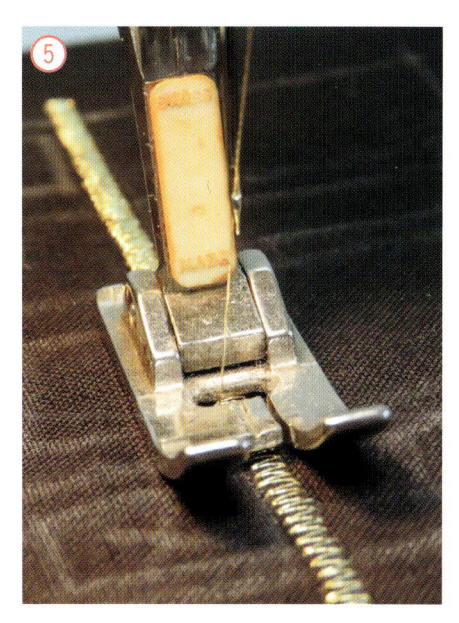

5 Stitch along the length of the chalk line with satin stitch. Metallic threads can look thinner when stitched; rotate the fabric and sew back down the line to build up the stitches. Stitch three or four more grid lines of satin stitch with this thread.

6 Stitch the rest of the grid lines, experimenting with different types of gold thread. I used Madeira metallic no. 40 gold 4, Madeira no. 40 FS gold 2, Madeira Jewel holographic thread colour 525, Madeira Supertwist no. 30 colour 25 and Kingstar MG1 gold.

7 Select reels of brightly coloured metallic threads. Include different manufacturers and fibre contents to get used to sewing with different threads. Good brands to experiment with are Madeira Supertwist no. 30, Madeira FS 2/2 no. 20, Sulky sliver, Anchor metallic and Sulky metallic.

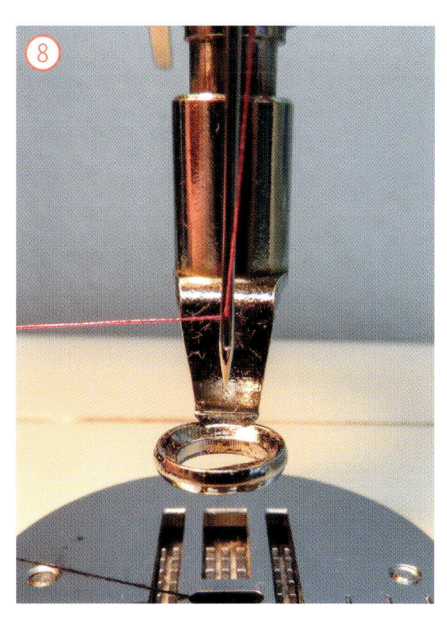

8 Place the embroidered cotton in a hoop and pull it taut. Lower the feeder teeth and attach a darning or embroidery foot. Change the stitch type to straight stitch and thread the needle with a brightly coloured metallic thread.

Chapter 9 – All That Glitters

⑨ Lower the foot and fill a rectangle or trapezium with dense thread-painting. Stitch round the outside of the shape with straight stitch, then fill in the centre of the shape. Trim the thread tails after each colour change.

⑩ Embroider the rest of the shapes, changing the threads so that different colours are next to one another. Note down which threads you prefer and which ones break; doing this will help you choose threads for future projects.

⑪ The finished embroidery is a bold abstract piece. Store it in your sample folder or look in Chapter 12 for information on framing.

SAMPLER
Beaded Gold Star

YOU WILL NEED

Equipment
- Photocopier or scanner and printer
- Sewing machine with drop feed or darning plate
- Darning or embroidery foot
- Normal tension bobbin case
- Empty bobbin
- Size 90/14 needle for metallic thread
- Glass-headed pins
- Bead needle or thin hand-sewing needle
- 15cm (6in.) wooden hoop
- Ballpoint pen
- Hard pencil
- Pencil sharpener

Materials
- A4 plain paper
- Dressmaker's carbon paper
- Scrap of patterned quilting cotton 21.6 × 21.6cm (8½ × 8½in.)
- Stitch 'n' Tear or similar tear-away stabilizer
- Madeira Classic no. 40 thread in colour 1070 (gold tawny tan)
- Madeira Metallic no. 40 thread in colour 6 (gold)
- Metallic gold short glass bugle beads
- Metallic gold and silver lined glass seed beads
- Transparent yellow aurora borealis cup sequins

Design template
- Beaded Gold Star

Machine used
- Bernina 801
- Feeder teeth down
- Normal tension

Beads and sequins add extra sparkle to embroideries. This sampler shows how to include them without overpowering the design. They work best on accessories or items such as bags or boxes or on images that are not going to be framed behind glass.

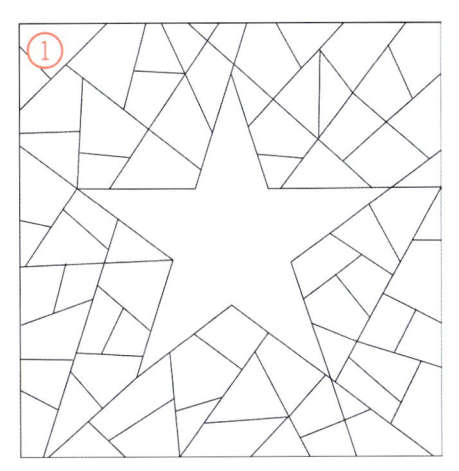

① Find the Beaded Star pattern in the back of the book; trace or photocopy it onto plain A4 paper. Alternatively, design your own. Mine measures approximately 9 × 9cm (3½ × 3½in.). Leave the centre of the star blank; draw patterns around it – these will be embroidered with straight stitch.

② Pin the design to the front of the patterned quilting cotton. Pin along the top of the paper so the pins don't go through the drawn design.

Chapter 9 – All That Glitters

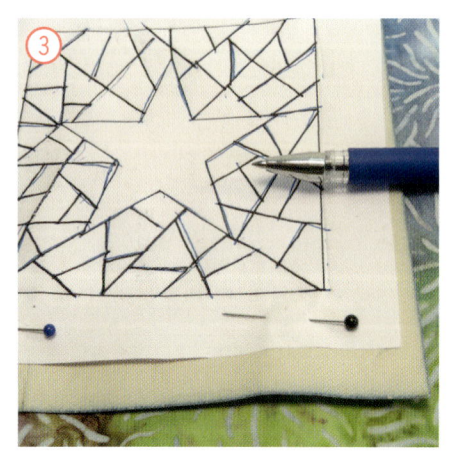

③ Position the dressmaker's carbon under the paper, inky side against the fabric. Pin the paper design at the bottom to stop it moving and place on a hard surface. Trace the design with a ballpoint pen or pencil, pressing hard to transfer the design.

④ Unpin one edge of the paper and lift up the carbon paper to see if the design has transferred properly. Remove the dressmaker's carbon and unpin the paper.

⑤ Place the fabric in a hoop and tighten the screw to make the fabric drum-tight. Pin two layers of tear-away stabilizer underneath the design.

⑥ Lower the feeder teeth and attach an embroidery foot. Wind an empty bobbin with Madeira Classic no. 1070 (gold tawny tan) thread. Insert the wound bobbin into the normal tension bobbin case and load both into the machine.

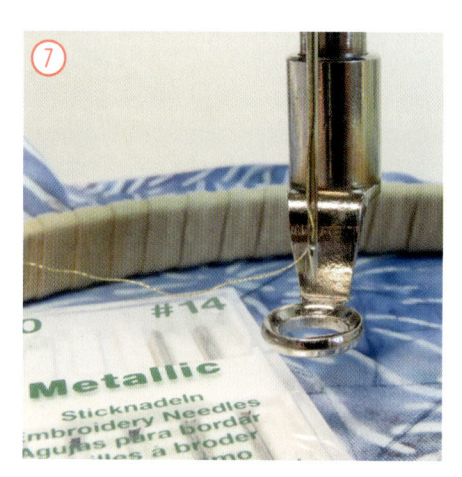

⑦ Insert a size 90/14 metallic needle and thread it with metallic gold thread. Set the stitch type to straight, turn the hand wheel to bring both threads to the top, then pull them to the back of the needle plate.

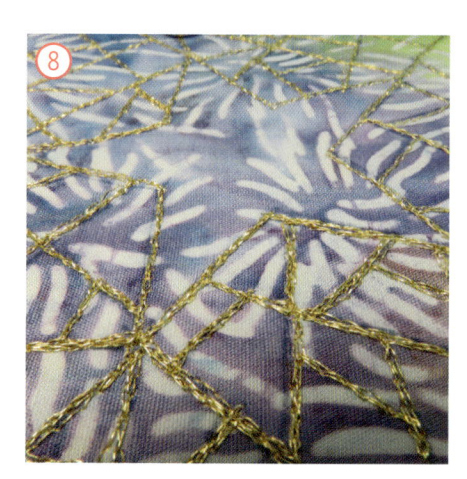

⑧ Position the foot over the design and lower it. Stitch the outline of the design with straight stitch, embroidering two or three rows of straight stitch one on top of another to add more definition.

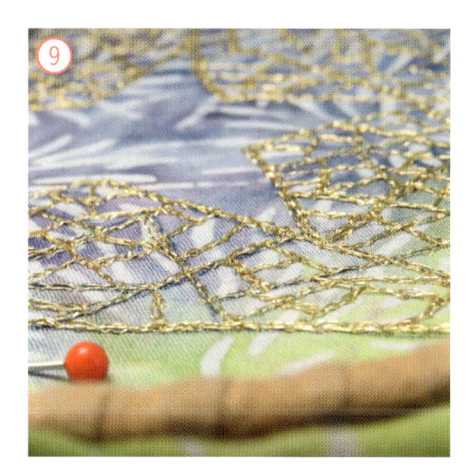

⑨ Stitch more detail into the geometric shapes around the star. Keep the size of the shapes relatively even, building up the stitching so there are two or three rows of straight stitch.

⑩ Trim the threads close to the embroidery and remove the tear-away stabilizer from the middle of the star. Place the embroidery in a hoop set up for hand embroidery. Thread a beading needle with a doubled length of gold-coloured (1070) thread and sew gold bugle beads and seed beads around the star shape.

⑪ Thread a beading needle with a doubled length of gold-coloured (1070) thread. Sew small sequins to the embroidered background, attaching them so the gold-coloured thread blends into the background stitches. Sew small bugles and seed beads around the rectangle shape.

⑫ Remove the embroidery from the hoop and peel off the rest of the stabilizer. Iron the embroidery on the back to remove the creases but avoid ironing the beads and sequins.

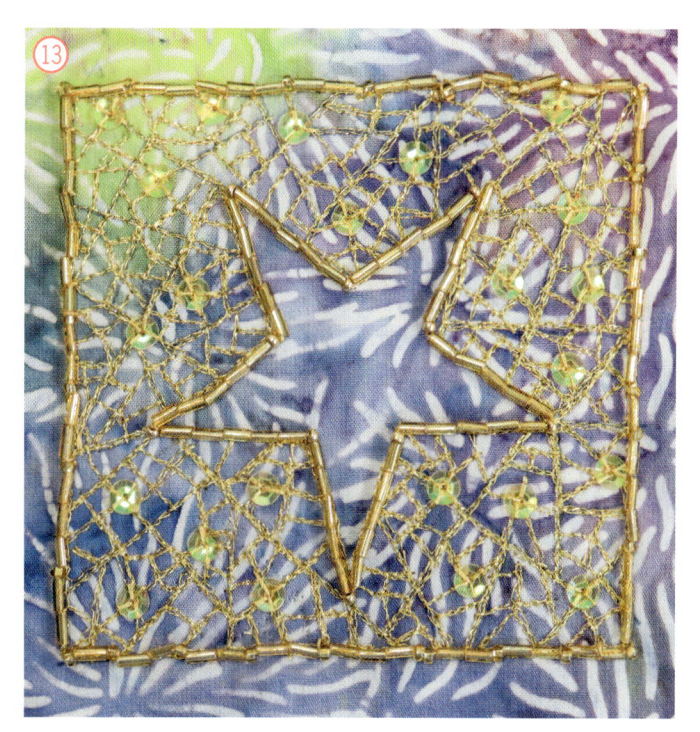

⑬ The finished embroidery can now be mounted in a frame or turned into a greetings card or a decorative box lid.

Chapter 9 – All That Glitters **177**

SAMPLER
Fabric-painted Heat-fusible Glue

YOU WILL NEED

Equipment
- Photocopier or scanner and printer
- Sewing machine with drop feed or darning plate
- Darning or embroidery foot
- Normal tension bobbin case
- Empty bobbin
- Size 90/14 machine needle for metallic thread
- Paintbrush: stiff-bristled flat or stencil
- Paper scissors
- Embroidery scissors
- Fabric scissors
- Iron
- Baking parchment
- Pencil or gel pen
- Pencil sharpener
- Eraser

Materials
- White A4 paper
- Tissue paper (optional)
- Scrap of paper or old newspaper
- Madeira classic no. 40 thread in colour 1070 gold tawny tan
- Madeira Variegated Metallic no. 40 thread in colour Astro 3
- Scrap of cotton velvet large enough for the design
- Stitch 'n' Tear or similar tear-away stabilizer
- Dylon metallic fabric paint, gold and bronze
- Paper-backed fusible glue or webbing (such as Bondaweb)

Design templates
- Leaf outline
- Leaf stitching

Machine used
- Bernina 801
- Feeder teeth down
- Normal tension

This sampler shows how to turn heat-fusible glue into sheets of heat-transferable paint. This technique works best with paper-backed heat-fusible glue because the waxy backing paper supports the wet paint. Metallic paints produce the best effects; designs are more effective when two colours have been used to paint the fusible glue.

The dried transfers are most effective when bonded to cotton velvet as the deep pile of this fabric makes it easier to distress the surface of the paint. Painted transfers come to life when they are embroidered with metallic threads; embroidering into the fused paint is the only way to add accurate detail to the transfers.

① Trace or print a copy of the Leaf outline template found in the back of the book or design your own. Print or trace another copy of the design so it's reversed. This design measures 7.2 × 14.2cm (a generous 2¾ × 5½in.) when printed.

② Pin the heat-fusible glue to the reversed design. Make sure the fusible is large enough to cover the design with some overlap. Trace the Leaf outline onto the backing paper with a gel pen or pencil. Cut the leaf shape out with paper scissors, leaving a wide border.

3. Place the traced heat-fusible onto scrap paper, glue side upwards. Paint the fusible with two colours of metallic fabric paint, using the paint straight out of the jar. Paint with a flat brush or stencil brush; blend the colours together and leave to dry.

4. The dry heat-fusible may curl or wrinkle but this won't affect the paint when it's transferred. Cut out the painted leaf with paper scissors, following the drawn lines for accuracy.

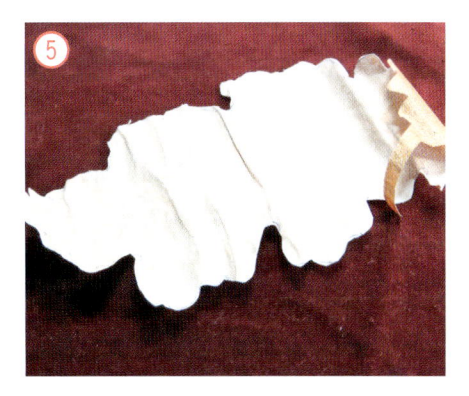

5. Cut out the cotton velvet and make sure the piece is large enough to be mounted or turned into a finished project. Position the heat-fusible leaf in the centre of the velvet, painted side down.

6. Hold the curly leaf in position and cover with baking parchment. Press the leaf with a hot iron until the paint fuses and bonds to the velvet. Allow the fabric to cool, then peel the backing paper away.

7. If the paint lifts away with the backing paper, re-position and iron again. The bonded paint may have creases or smudges; don't worry, as these won't be noticeable when the embroidery is completed.

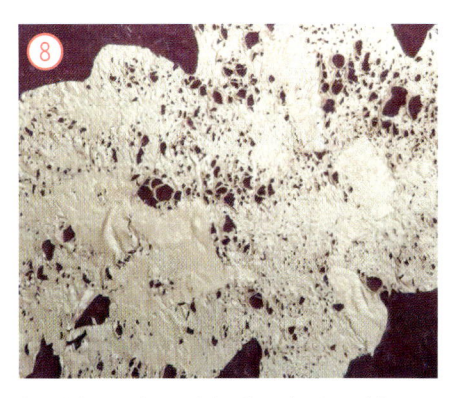

8. Scuff the surface of the fused paint with your fingernails to distress it. Cover the distressed transfer with baking parchment and iron to bond the disturbed paint. Peel the parchment away when the fabric has cooled down.

Trace the Leaf stitching template onto a scrap of baking parchment or tissue paper and pin it over the transferred paint so it lines up with the leaf below. Pin a layer of stitch-and-tear-away stabilizer to the back of the velvet behind the design.

Lower the feeder teeth and attach an embroidery foot. Insert a metallic size 14 needle and thread it with Madeira Metallic no. 40 in colour Astro no. 3. Wind a bobbin with gold-coloured tawny tan thread (1070), insert it into the bobbin case and load both into the machine.

Turn the hand wheel to bring both threads to the top and set the stitch type to straight. Embroider the design with two rows of straight stitch. Take the threads through to the back and tie them off.

Remove the stitched baking parchment or tissue paper and review the embroidery. The leaf needed two more rows of embroidery to make the details stand out from the painted fusible.

Peel away the stabilizer, then take the thread ends to the back and tie them off. Cover the embroidery with baking parchment and press with a cool iron. The embroidery is now ready to be framed, stored in your sample folder or used in another project.

SAMPLER
Bonding Transfer Foils with Vilene Hotspots

Metallic transfer foils are traditionally used in the printing industry: for instance, to add sparkle to greetings cards or to highlight a book title. Transfer foils consist of a heatproof clear carrier sheet backed by metallic or holographic foil. The foil on the back needs something sticky or tacky to cling to for it to be pulled away from the carrier sheet. Heat-fusible glue is the perfect transfer medium for this technique.

This sampler shows how to use small Vilene Hotspots with metallic transfer foil. Bright metallic foils work well on dark backgrounds because the contrast between the background fabric and foil is greater. Using pale foils such as gold, silver or pearl on white fabrics produces a gentle fantasy theme – no unicorn magic needed.

YOU WILL NEED

Equipment
- Photocopier or scanner and printer
- Sewing machine with drop feed or darning plate
- Darning or embroidery foot
- Size 90/14 machine needles for metallic thread
- Empty bobbins
- Loose tension bobbin case
- Paper scissors
- Embroidery scissors
- Fabric scissors
- Glass-headed pins
- Iron
- Baking parchment
- Pencil
- Pencil sharpener.
- Sharp hand sewing needle

Materials
- White A4 paper
- Black cotton fabric
- Mediumweight iron-on interfacing
- Vilene Hotspots, small
- Metallic rainbow transfer foil
- Madeira metallic no. 40 thread in colour 6 (gold)
- Madeira Glamour no. 12 thread in colour 3025 (pure gold)
- Gold-coloured thread for hand sewing

Design templates
- Butterfly outline
- Butterfly stitching

Machine used
- Bernina 801
- Feeder teeth down
- Normal top tension
- Loose tension bobbin thread

1 It's advisable to test small squares of transfer foils with various heat-fusibles to see which ones work best. Some foils won't transfer and excessive heat can dull others so experiment before embarking on a big project.

2 Select a background fabric large enough for the design or project. Stabilize the back of the fabric with mediumweight iron-on interfacing. Use a layer of baking parchment to protect the iron.

3 Find the Butterfly outline template in the back of the book; trace or print a copy of it. Cut round the outline with paper scissors and pin it to the back of the Hotspots. Draw round the butterfly shape with a pencil. It measures 16.5 × 9.3cm (6½ × 3⅝in.) when printed.

Chapter 9 – All That Glitters

4. Cut out the Hotspot butterfly with paper scissors. Position it on the front of the fabric, Hotspot side down against the fabric. Cover with baking parchment and bond with a hot iron.

5. Allow to cool, then peel off the backing paper. Don't worry if some of the dots don't transfer – it adds interest to the design.

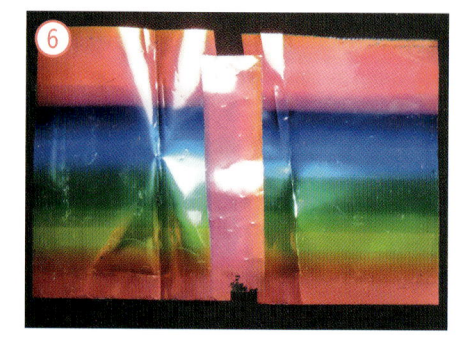

6. Cut the rainbow transfer foil to size and position it over the glue dots. I used different colours for the wings and body. Make sure the side that transfers is face down against the glue dots; the pretty shiny side should be facing upwards.

7. Cover with baking parchment and press with a hot iron. This melts the glue, thus sticking the transfer part of the foil to the Hotspots.

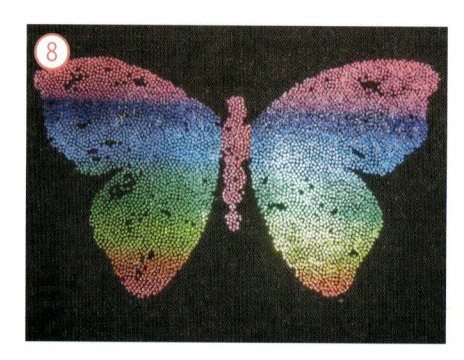

8. Allow to cool. Remove the baking parchment and peel off the transfer foil to reveal the dotty metallic design. Save the dotty transfer foil as it can be used to add metallic texture to another project.

9. Mark the butterfly's position on to the back of the fabric. Hand sew or machine tack around the butterfly with gold-coloured thread. These stitches will be covered by the embroidered outlines.

10. Draw a simple design for the stitch lines onto paper or copy the Butterfly stitching template in the back of this book. Pin the traced design to the back of the butterfly. Use pins to make sure the design outline is lined up with the tacked butterfly outline.

11. Set the machine up for cable stitch and embroider the butterfly with Madeira Glamour no. 12 thread in colour 3025 (pure gold) wound onto the bobbin and metallic gold thread through the needle.

12. This design is really bold so I have added plastic rhinestones for extra kitsch sparkle.

SAMPLER
BONDING TRANSFER FOILS TO MISTYFUSE

YOU WILL NEED

Equipment
- Photocopier or scanner and printer
- Sewing machine with drop feed or darning plate
- Darning or embroidery foot
- Normal tension bobbin case
- Empty bobbin
- Size 90/14 machine needle for metallic thread
- Iron
- Baking parchment
- Glass-headed pins

- Fabric scissors
- Embroidery scissors
- Sink or bowl of water to wash the embroidery
- Old towel on which to dry the embroidery
- Black permanent pen

Materials
- White A4 paper or tracing paper
- Finished scraps and snippets embroidery

- Patterned or plain backing fabric
- Organza fabric
- Madeira Metallic no. 40 thread in colour 481 (peacock)
- Black bobbin thread
- Stitch 'n' Tear or similar tear-away stabilizer
- Avalon water-soluble film
- Mistyfuse
- Transfer foils

Design template
- Flower Pattern

Machine used
- Bernina 801
- Feeder teeth down
- Normal tension

Mistyfuse is slightly different from the other fusible glues in that it does not have a supportive backing paper to aid drawing designs. Its advantage is that it has a lovely lacy texture and it is available in black or white. Mistyfuse is suitable for bonding fabrics together and for bonding metal transfer foils and or gold leaf. It is also ideal for sticking lacy fabrics or embroideries to a fabric background; once bonded the web of glue is almost invisible.

1 Select a finished scraps and snippets embroidery. Choose one that didn't turn out as expected; I chose this one because I didn't like the overpowering texture of the eyelash yarn.

2 Choose a background fabric to match the colour scheme. Cut a rectangle or square larger than the scraps and snippets embroidery. Make sure the fabric is large enough to allow for making up or lacing over card ready to frame.

Chapter 9 – All That Glitters **183**

3. Cut a piece of white or black Mistyfuse slightly larger than the scraps and snippets embroidery.

4. Place the cut Mistyfuse in the middle of the background fabric, position the scraps and snippets embroidery on top of it, and make sure the right side of the embroidery is facing upwards.

5. Cover with baking parchment and iron; the heat of the iron melts the glue to bond the embroidery to the background fabric. Peel away the baking parchment to reveal the fused embroidery.

6. Layer some scraps of transfer foil on top of the fused fabric and cover with baking parchment. Remember to place the transfer foil colourful side upwards.

7. Press with a hot iron to transfer the foil. The transfer foil only sticks to gaps in the embroidery; allow everything to cool, then peel off the transfer foil scraps.

8. Cut some thin strips of Mistyfuse with scissors, then tear these into smaller pieces. Position the Mistyfuse pieces randomly on the surface of the embroidery.

9. Cover the fabric with the used scraps of transfer foil; blank spaces or imprinted patterns add interest to the metallic surface.

10. Cover with baking parchment and iron; allow everything to cool and peel the transfer foil away.

11. Repeat the foiling process to add more distressed texture to the metallic areas.

184   Chapter 9 – All That Glitters

⑫ The foiled fabric is now ready to embroider or you could simply leave it as it is or embellish it with beads.

⑬ Find the Flower Pattern template in the back of the book and copy or trace it. Trace the design onto water-soluble film with a black permanent pen.

⑭ Layer one or two pieces of organza over the foiled fabric, then pin the traced soluble film design on top. Pin two layers of tear-away stabilizer to the back.

⑮ Insert a bobbin wound with black and thread a metallic needle with Madeira Metallic no. 40 thread in colour 481 (peacock). Attach an embroidery foot and lower the feeder teeth. Stitch the design with straight stitch, building up the rows of stitch to create a bold outline.

⑯ Trim the thread tabs and carefully cut the soluble film and organza from the background fabric. Do not cut the foiled embroidery below. Soak the embroidery in warm water to remove the soluble film and leave to dry on an old towel.

⑰ Review the finished embroidery and decide how to use it. This style of embroidery would suit being framed or beaded and turned into a box lid or bag panel.

SAMPLER
Embroidered Angelina Heart

This sampler shows how to fuse and stitch into Angelina fibres to create a simple embroidered heart. Angelina fibres are made from iridescent polyester; the tiny fibres bond to each other when heated but won't fuse to fabric or threads. Sheets of fused fibres look like opalescent webs; the colours of the fibres change and sparkle when light hits them – this effect shows up best against a black background.

Angelina fibres are extremely reactive to heat; a very hot iron will melt them too much and dull the opalescence. The fibres may also stick or melt onto an unprotected iron so always use baking parchment. If you incorporate these fibres into an embroidery remember they can only tolerate silk or low iron settings. They are available in fusible and non-fusible; this project requires fusible or hot-fix fibres.

YOU WILL NEED

Equipment
- Photocopier or scanner and printer
- Sewing machine with drop feed or darning plate
- Darning foot or embroidery foot
- Straight-stitch presser foot
- Size 90/14 universal needles
- Normal tension bobbin case
- Empty bobbin
- Glass-headed pins
- Black permanent pen
- Paper scissors
- Fabric scissors
- Embroidery scissors
- Iron or low-temperature craft iron
- Baking parchment

Materials
- A4 plain paper or tracing paper
- Madeira Classic no. 40 thread in colour 1000 (black)
- Black bobbin thread
- Gütermann Sulky Invisible thread
- Hot-fix Angelina or Crystalina fibres (choose two or three colours from ultra violet, wisteria, peacock, black sparkle, raspberry, gold, iris or forest blaze)
- Black felt or Melton wool fabric

Design template
- Angelina Heart

Machine used
- Bernina 801
- Feeder teeth down and up
- Normal tension

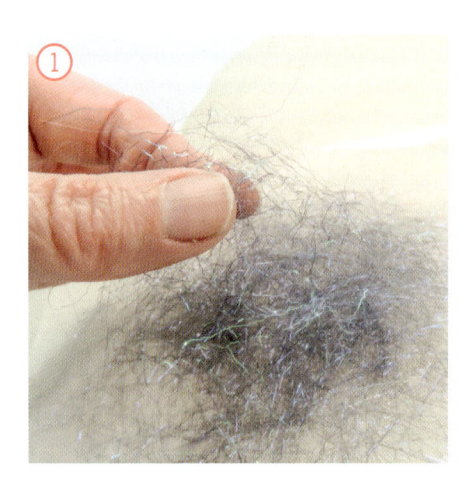

① Turn the iron to a low heat or silk setting. Sprinkle a thin layer of hot-fix Angelina fibres onto baking parchment, mixing two or three colour shades for the best result.

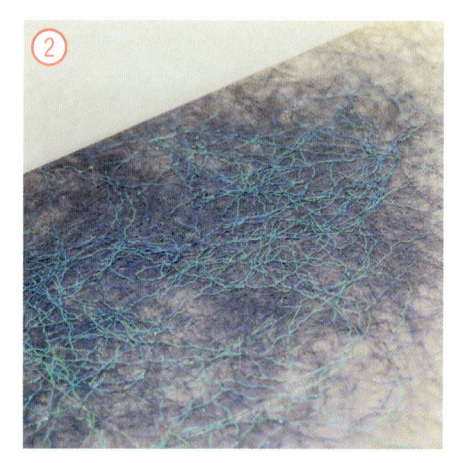

② Cover with another sheet of baking parchment. Set the iron's heat temperature to low and press to fuse the Angelina fibres; don't use steam. Move the iron over the surface to get an even heat distribution; ironing for two to four seconds should be enough time to fuse the fibres together.

③ Allow the baking parchment to cool before peeling the fused Angelina away. Check the fibres are fused properly; those in this picture have fused perfectly. Fibres that have not fused properly appear rough or fluffy; if the iron is too hot they will become dull and lifeless.

4.

Print or trace a copy of the Heart design found in the back of the book or design your own. This design is 7.5 × 7.5cm (3 × 3in); the square bordering it measures (11.4 × 11.4cm (4½ × 4½in.). Cut the design out, leaving a small border of paper around the edge.

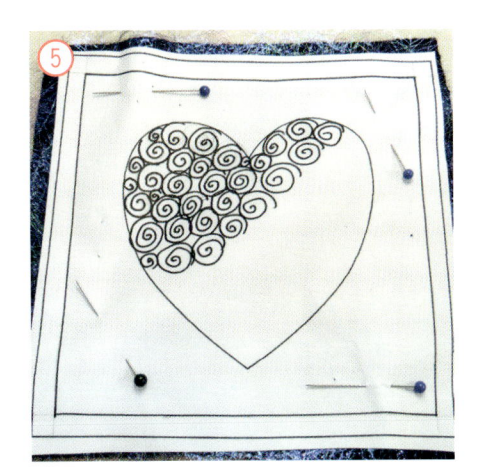

5.

Cut a square of Melton wool or good-quality felt large enough for the design. Place the fused Angelina on top of the wool and pin the paper design on top. My design had a sketch of the stitch pattern I planned to embroider drawn onto it.

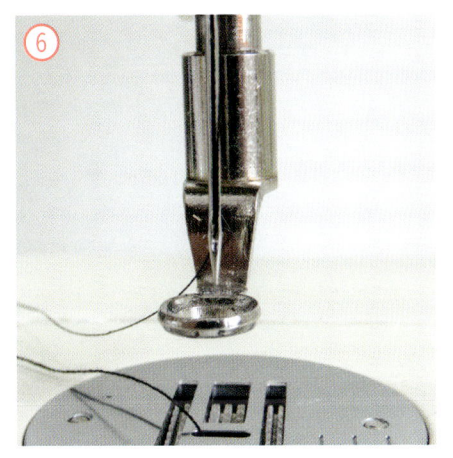

6.

Lower the feeder teeth, attach an embroidery foot and set the stitch type to straight. Insert a size 90/14 universal needle and thread it with black embroidery thread. Wind a bobbin with black bobbin thread, insert it into the normal tension bobbin case, then load both into the machine.

7.

Place the pinned felt under the foot so the needle lines up with the heart outline, then lower the foot. Stitch the heart outline with straight stitch, embroidering two or three rows one on top of another to create a bold outline.

8.

Peel the paper from the middle of the heart to expose the fused Angelina. Embroider the centre of the heart with a spiral pattern or choose your own; curved lines work best with rounded shapes.

9.

Raise the feeder teeth and attach a straight-stitch presser foot. Stitch the inner and outer borders with two or three rows of straight stitch; follow the paper design to keep the stitching straight.

Chapter 9 – All That Glitters 187

Trim the thread tails and tear away the remaining paper. Decide if the background Angelina needs more embroidery to tie it in with the rest of the design.

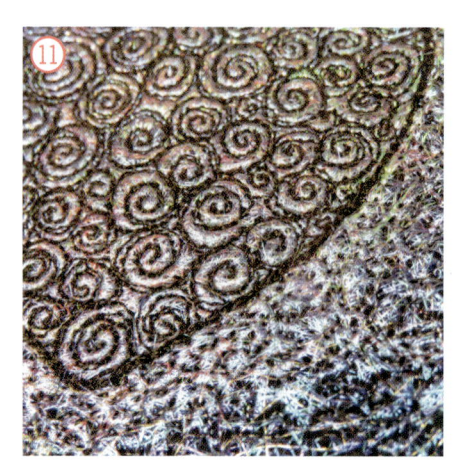

Attach an embroidery foot and lower the feeder teeth. Thread the needle with Gütermann Sulky Invisible thread and stitch the background with meandering vermicelli stitch. Take the threads to the back and tie them off.

Thread the needle with black Madeira Classic no. 40 thread and embroider patterns into the border. Redefine the outline of the heart and border to make them stand out more. Trim the thread tabs close to the embroidery.

Trim the Angelina fibres from the edge of the embroidery. Keep the trimmings because they can be fused again or used in another embroidery project. Colour the remaining spots of white paper with a black permanent pen.

The embroidery is ready to be finished. It would look lovely in a deep box frame or used in another project such as a decorative box lid or a hanging panel made with similar embroideries.

STEP-BY-STEP PROJECT
Dragonfly

YOU WILL NEED

Equipment
- Photocopier or scanner and printer
- Sewing machine with drop feed or darning plate
- Embroidery or darning foot
- Normal tension bobbin case
- Size 90/14 machine needles for metallic thread
- Size 90/14 universal machine needles
- 15cm (6in.) wooden hoop
- Paintbrush: flat or bright brush for small details
- Black permanent pen or Stabilo Fineliner
- Black biro or Ultra-Fine Sharpie
- Hard pencil or ballpoint pen
- Coloured artist's pencils
- Pencil sharpener
- Eraser
- Embroidery scissors
- Fabric scissors
- Paper scissors
- Iron
- Ironing cloth
- Baking parchment
- Glass-headed pins
- Sticky tape or masking tape
- Sink or old bowl to wash the embroidery
- Old towel on which to dry the embroidery

Materials
- Thin white A4 paper
- Plain woven black cotton, canvas or linen approximately 51 × 40.6cm (20 × 16in.)
- Mediumweight black iron-on interfacing approximately 51 × 40.6cm (20 × 16in.)
- Stitch 'n' Tear or similar tear-away stabilizer
- Black organza
- Black bobbin thread
- Metallic thread in turquoise, royal blue, emerald green and gold
- Near-invisible HT polyester thread in black or Madeira Classic thread no. 60 in black
- Madeira Classic no. 40 thread in colour 1000 (black)
- Bronze and gold metallic fabric paint
- Heat-fusible Angelina fantasy film
- Heat-fusible glue or Bondaweb
- Avalon water-soluble film
- White or pale yellow dressmaker's carbon paper

Design templates
- Dragonfly body
- Dragonfly body parts
- Bamboo background

Machine used
- Bernina 801
- Feeder teeth down
- Normal tension

This project uses metallics from beginning to end. Richly coloured metallics are used to describe the dragonfly and its environment. The embroidery design is split into two distinct areas: the matt background and the iridescent metallic dragonfly. The nature of the materials meant I could take a bit of liberty with the embroidery. The dragonfly is based on a photo I found online but by the time I finished designing and choosing materials it was transformed into a cool blue fantasy dragonfly.

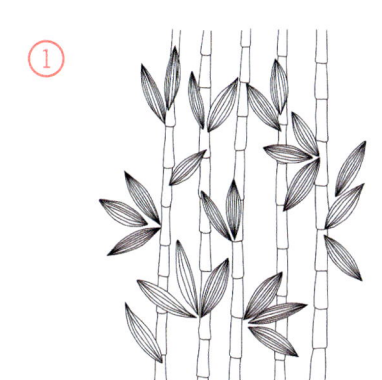

① Enlarge the Bamboo background template from the back of the book by 200 per cent. Print or draw it onto thin paper; the enlarged design should measure approximately 28 × 37cm (11 × 14½in.). If you print the design onto A4 paper the sheets need to be stuck together with sticky tape or masking tape.

② Cut a rectangle of black cotton or canvas measuring 40.6 × 51cm (16 × 20in.), using a ruler and set square for accurate straight lines. Cut a rectangle of mediumweight black interfacing the same size and fuse it to the back of the fabric, covering it with baking parchment to protect the iron.

Chapter 9 – All That Glitters

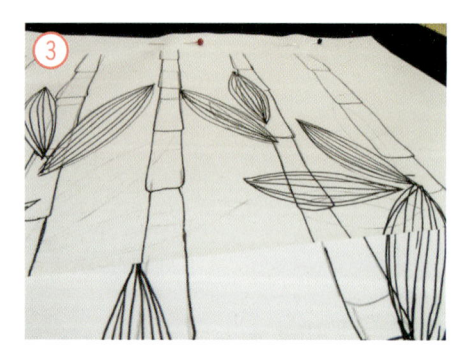

3. Place the fabric on a firm work surface and turn it so the right side is facing upwards. Position the bamboo design in the middle of the fabric, then pin down two sides of the paper to secure it. Slide a sheet of white dressmaker's carbon underneath the paper, inky side down against the fabric.

4. Trace the design's lines, pressing down hard with a pencil or ballpoint pen so the design is transferred to the cotton. Re-position the carbon paper if it's not large enough to trace the entire design.

5. Peel back the paper without removing the pins, check the design has been transferred clearly and retrace any missed or pale areas.

6. Paint the bamboo stalks and leaves with bronze metallic paint straight from the jar. Use a dry flat or bright brush so that more background fabric shows through, and add details and shading with a small detail brush. Leave to dry, then fix with an iron, referring to the instructions on the paint jar for more information.

7. Add more detail with gold paint, thinking about where the highlights are. Use a dry detail or flat or bright brush to blend the colours together or smudge them with your finger. Leave to dry and fix as before.

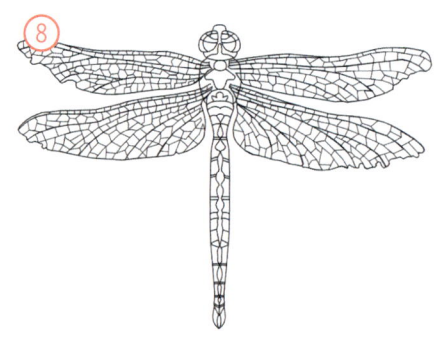

8. Find the Dragonfly body design in the back of the book and trace the design or print two copies of it onto A4 paper. The design measures approximately 16 × 22.5cm (6¼ × 9in.) when printed.

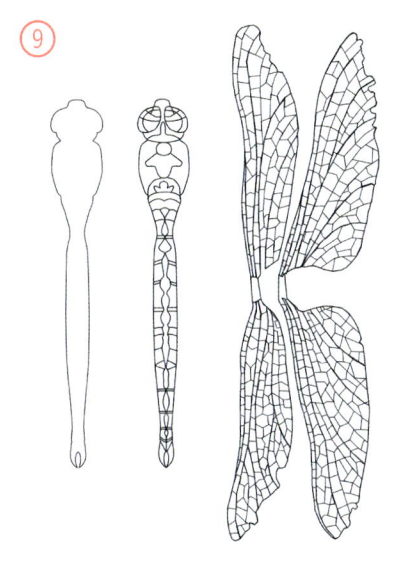

⑨ Print out or trace one copy of the design for the wings and the body parts.

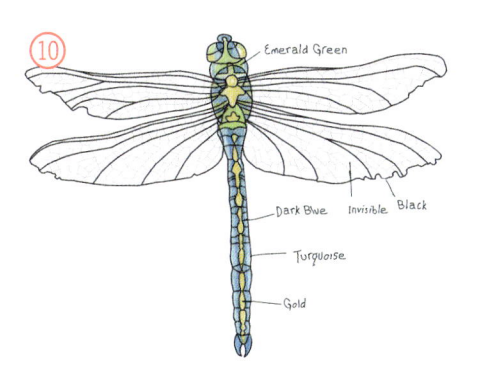

⑩ Look at your metallic thread collection and choose threads with a similar texture and weight. Use my colour scheme or design your own; both cool and warm colour schemes are suitable for the body. Colour in the dragonfly to help you decide where to stitch the selected colours.

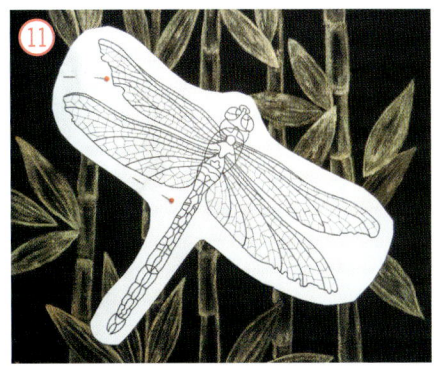

⑪ Roughly cut out the spare printed dragonfly design with paper scissors and place it on the painted background. Move the dragonfly around until you feel happy with the composition, then pin in place.

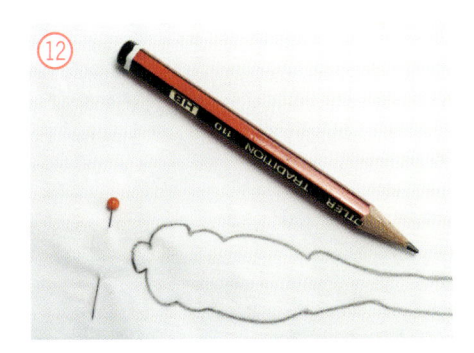

⑫ Trace the outline of the body shape onto the fusible glue's backing paper. Cut it out with paper scissors, leaving a small border of heat-fusible glue around the shape to stop the fabric fraying.

⑬ Select a metallic base fabric for the body to match the main metallic thread colour. Turn the fabric over so the wrong side faces upwards, position the body shape on the fabric glue side down. Align the shape so it follows the fabric grain or warp and weft. Cover with baking parchment and bond with a hot iron.

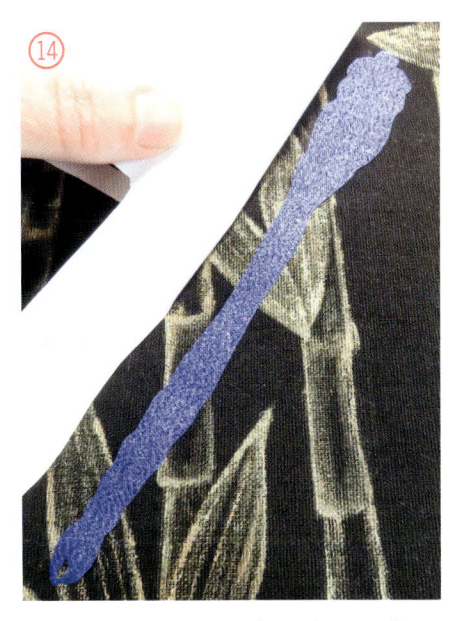

⑭ Cut the body shape out along the pencil lines and peel off the paper backing. Turn the bonded fabric so the glue side is downwards and position it under the pinned dragonfly design. Coax the body into position so it corresponds with the body on the paper design. Cover with baking parchment and iron to bond in position.

Chapter 9 – All That Glitters 191

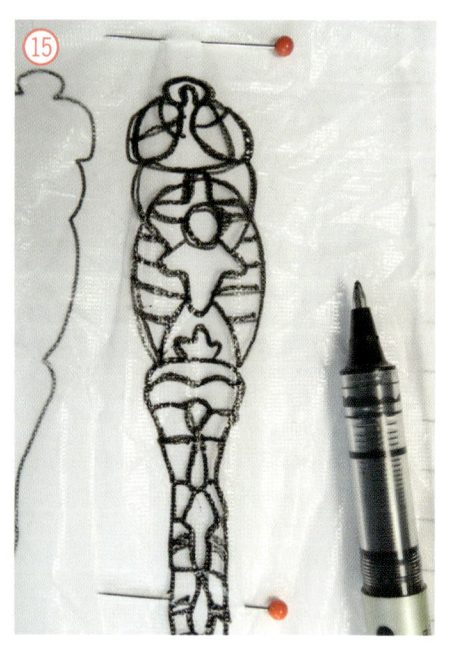

⑮ Pin a layer of Avalon water-soluble film to the body design and trace it onto the film with a black permanent pen or Stabilo Fineliner.

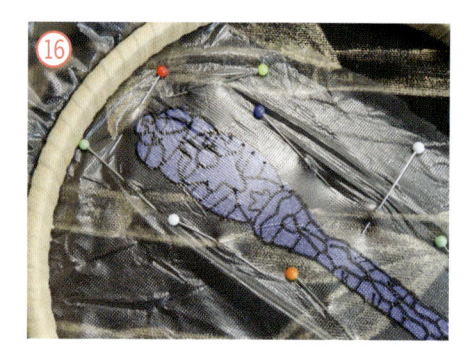

⑯ Unpin the traced Avalon from the design and position it over the bonded fabric body. Manipulate the film as you pin it to the cotton, checking the design lines up with the fabric body. Pin two layers of tear-away stabilizer behind the body and place the cotton in a hoop so the body is central.

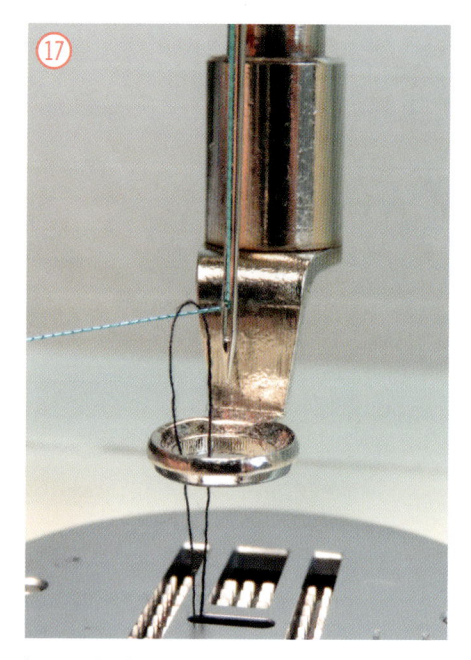

⑰ Lower the feeder teeth, attach an embroidery foot and set the stitch type to straight. Wind an empty bobbin with black bobbin thread, load it into the normal tension bobbin case and insert both into the machine. Insert a size 14 metallic machine needle, thread the needle with turquoise metallic thread and turn the hand wheel to bring both threads to the top.

⑱ Slide the hoop under the foot and lower it. Embroider the turquoise parts of the design with straight stitch. Embroidering along the length of the body is easier than stitching across the width. Re-position the hoop to stitch the rest of the body. Trim the threads close to the fabric.

⑲ Change the thread to royal blue metallic and embroider the dark blue parts of the design. Blend the blue thread into the turquoise stitching, referring to the drawing as you stitch. Trim the threads on the front and back.

⑳ Thread the needle with metallic emerald green and stitch the green parts of the design. My thread broke repeatedly; if this happens, keep re-threading and persevere until the area is stitched, or stop and change the needle or thread if the breaks are too annoying.

21. Thread the needle with metallic gold and stitch the tiny patterns on the body and add highlights to the eyes. Continue embroidering the design with the selected colours, trimming the threads between each colour change.

22. Swap the needle to a size 90/14 universal and thread the needle with black Madeira Classic no. 40 thread. Stitch the details, referring to the body drawing because the traced soluble film is obscured by embroidery.

23. Trim the thread tails and tabs. Peel the soluble film away and remove the tear-away stabilizer from the back of the embroidery. The bonded fabric may have frayed, so carefully trim the raw edges close to the embroidery.

24. Cut two pieces of heat-fusible Angelina fantasy film slightly bigger than the wing template. Blue butterfly flash or peacock suit a cool colour scheme. Screw the film up into a ball to create creases; you can be quite rough but don't rip the film.

25. Place a sheet of baking parchment on the ironing board and smooth out the crumpled fantasy film onto it. The creases add veiny texture to the film when it's fused. Position the crumpled film so one sheet is on top of the other.

26. Turn the iron on and set the temperature to low or medium heat; don't use steam. Cover the fantasy film with another piece of baking parchment. Press to fuse the layered film together, moving the iron around so the film is evenly fused. Ironing time depends on the iron's setting and how dull you want the fantasy film to become.

Chapter 9 – All That Glitters 193

27 Allow to cool and peel back the baking parchment to reveal the fused film. Heating alters the colour intensity and iridescence of the fantasy film. You may wish to continue experimenting or fuse different colours together so that you can choose the best one.

28 Pin the fused fantasy film to the wing design. Trace the wings onto the fantasy film with a black ballpoint pen or an Ultra-Fine Sharpie. The reflective nature of the film may make tracing difficult; if you have problems use a light box or tape the film and design to a sunlit window.

29 Cut out the fantasy film wings with paper scissors. Leave a small bridge of film across the centre because it helps with positioning. Place the wings over the body, re-position until they are in the correct place, then pin to secure.

30 Lay a sheet of black synthetic organza over the wings and pin in place; make sure no pins are trapped beneath the organza. Adding a layer of organza dulls the shine of the fantasy film and traps the film just in case it perforates during stitching.

31 Place the fabric in a hoop so one set of wings is central. Thread the needle with near-invisible black HT polyester or black Madeira Classic no. 60 thread. Embroider the veins and outline with one row of straight stitch, keeping the stitching on top of the drawn lines. Cut the thread tabs and position the hoop over the other set of wings. Stitch this set of wings using the same method.

32 Thread the needle with black Madeira Classic no. 40 thread and stitch the darker veins with straight stitch. Embroider round the wing to make sure the organza is stitched down securely. Trim the thread tabs and position the hoop over the other set of wings; stitch them using the same method.

Take the embroidery out of the hoop, trim the thread tails and tabs at the front and back. Carefully trim away the excess organza and cut the fantasy film tabs between the wings.

Examine the embroidery and decide if anything needs changing. I felt the head needed further work because some of the detail had been lost.

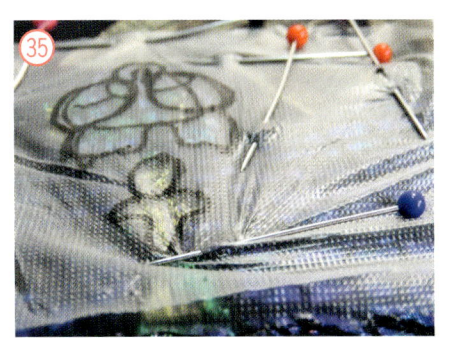

Trace the head section onto a scrap of water-soluble film and pin it over the embroidered head. Stitch the details using straight stitch and the colours used previously. Trim the threads and peel away the soluble film.

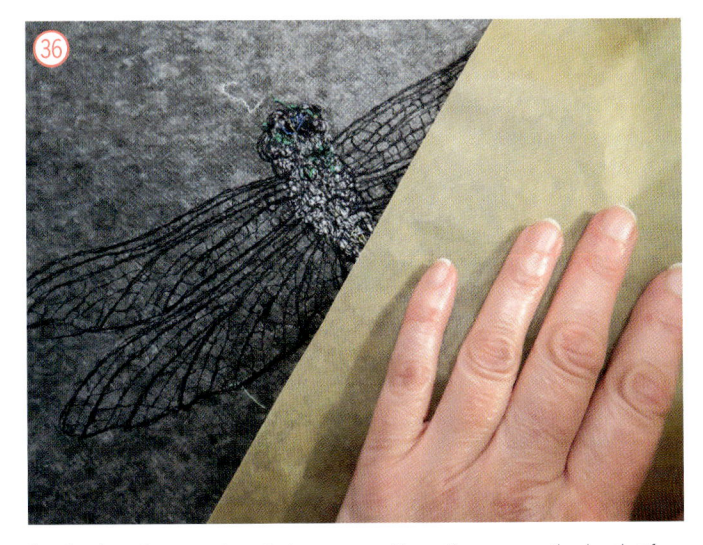

Set the iron temperature to low or medium, then press the back of the embroidery. Cover the embroidery with baking parchment or an ironing cloth and press gently; this should provide enough heat to remove handling marks without discolouring the fantasy film.

The embroidery is now ready to be laced or framed. Look in Chapter 12 for further suggestions.

Chapter 9 – All That Glitters **195**

STEP-BY-STEP PROJECT
Transfer Foiled Book Cover

YOU WILL NEED

Equipment
- Sewing machine with drop feed or darning plate
- Straight-stitch presser foot
- Size 90/14 universal machine needle
- Normal tension bobbin case
- Spare bobbin case for loose tension embroidery
- Empty bobbins
- Fabric scissors
- Paper scissors
- Embroidery scissors
- Iron
- Baking parchment
- Glass-headed pins
- Sharp hand-sewing needle
- Darning needle
- Beading needle
- Dressmaker's chalk pencil or artist's watercolour pencil
- Pencil
- Pencil sharpener
- Metal ruler
- Set square
- Tape measure
- Rotary cutter
- Cutting mat
- Mop brush
- Mixing pots
- Polythene sheet or bin bag

Materials
- Small hard-backed A5 notebook or diary
- Silk fabric paint in yellow, blue, magenta, red and violet
- Colour-matched cotton or polycotton large enough for the cover
- Scrap of cotton
- Lightweight iron-on interfacing
- Pelmet Vilene
- Transfer foils
- Heat-fusible glue or Bondaweb
- Mistyfuse
- Vilene Hotspots, small
- Variety of ribbons in different widths and textures
- Cotton lace, daisy lace trim
- Madeira Polyneon Astro no. 40 thread in colours 1600, 1604, 1608 and 1607
- Metallic gold machine thread
- Colour-matched thread for sewing up
- Thick metallic or glittery yarns for couching or winding onto the bobbin
- Glass seed beads

Machine used
- Janome JF 1018s
- Feeder teeth up
- Normal tension
- Loose tension bobbin thread

This project brings many techniques together to produce a decorated book cover. It's a lengthy process but it does produce something really special. It's the kind of project you can pick up and do a bit at a time and it's good for using up odds and ends of fabric paint, ribbon, metal foils and heat-fusible glue. The stitching is done with the feeder teeth up and a straight-stitch presser foot attached; the embroidery is teamed up with other techniques to create the overall effect.

The project starts with stitching hand-dyed ribbons or lace to a background fabric and embellishing the ribbons with couched yarn or cord. The background is then gilded with metallic transfer foils and decorated with lengths of ribbon. The project has been split up in such a way that you can stop sewing at any time and proceed to the making-up stage.

I like overworking this style of embroidery to transform the mundane into the extraordinary. This project is a great way to make a personalized present for someone special but it does not have to become a book cover – the finished embroidery could be mounted and framed or turned into a hanging.

Measure the closed book carefully; include the front and back cover, the spine and the height from top to bottom. My book measured 31.7 × 21cm (12½ × 8¼in.).

196 Chapter 9 – All That Glitters

②

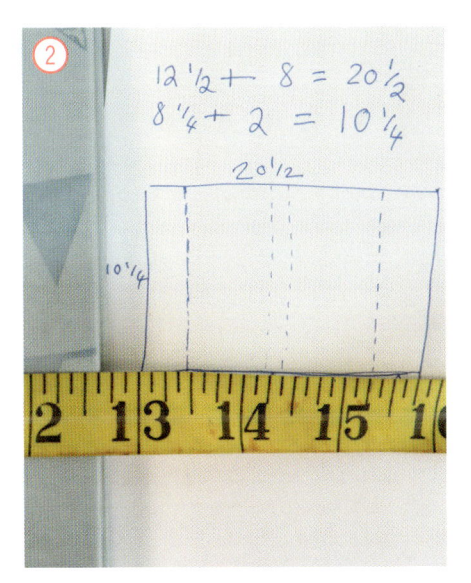

Work out how large the cotton panel for the cover needs to be. Add 20.3cm (8in.) to the horizontal length; the extra fabric will be turned inwards to make flaps. Add 7.5cm (3in.) to the height; this makes the fabric large enough to turn under and seam. My cotton panel needed to measure 52 × 28.6cm (20½ by 11¼in.).

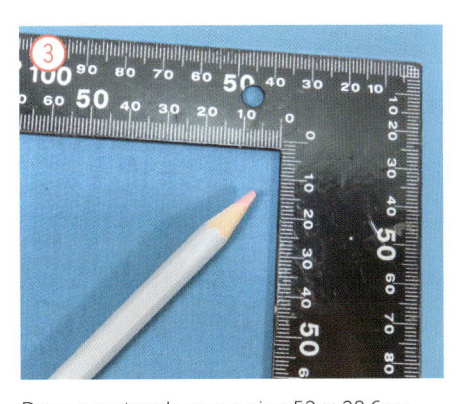

③

Draw a rectangle measuring 52 × 28.6cm (20½ by 11¼in.) onto the backing fabric. Use a ruler and set square for accurate measurements. Cut out the rectangle leaving a small 2.5cm (1in.) seam allowance around it.

④

Cut a rectangle of lightweight iron-on interfacing the same size as the cotton. Position it on the back of the cotton glue side down. Cover with baking parchment and press with a medium iron; the iron should be just hot enough to melt the interfacing glue.

⑤

Cut lengths of ribbon and cotton lace trimmings slightly longer than the rectangle of cotton. Lay them on the rectangle to make sure you have cut enough pieces; it's sensible to cut more than you need. Dunk the ribbons in water to dampen them and lay them best side up on a polythene sheet or bin bag.

⑥

Paint the damp ribbons with neat silk paint using a soft mop brush. Here, I painted yellow first, then added blue, magenta, red and violet. The colours blend together and bleed into the ribbon to create a space-dyed effect. Keep adding colours until you are happy with the result, then leave to dry.

⑦

Iron the ribbons to set the silk paint. I used old hair straighteners set to a low heat; it's easy to pull the ribbon through the heated plates to iron both sides at once. If you don't like the idea of straighteners, use baking parchment and an iron set to low.

Chapter 9 – All That Glitters 197

⑧

Attach the straight-stitch foot and raise the feeder teeth. Insert a size 90/14 universal needle and thread the needle with Astro thread. Wind a colour-matched thread onto a bobbin, insert it into the normal tension bobbin case and load both into the machine.

⑨

Choose some patterned utility stitches and test them on a scrap of cotton. These stitches are used to sew the ribbons to the cotton background fabric. Honeycomb, triple stitch, overlock or overcast stitch are good ones to experiment with.

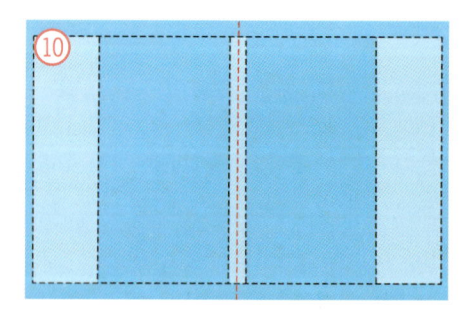

⑩

Position the cotton panel so the right side is upwards. Use a ruler, set square and chalk dressmaker's pencil to mark the middle of the fabric; draw the spine, front and back cover and where the flaps fold over and finish. Refer to your measurements and check the drawing lines against the dimensions of the book.

⑪

Select a wide ribbon, position the edge of the ribbon up against the drawn line that indicates the start of the cover. Lower the foot and sew along the ribbon with a patterned utility stitch, keeping the edge of the ribbon straight as you stitch.

⑫

Lift the foot and rotate the fabric. Position the other side of the ribbon under the foot so it lines up with the needle. Stitch along the ribbon's edge with the same patterned utility stitch.

⑬

Select a different ribbon and position it so it touches the edge of the sewn one. Change the stitch type to another utility stitch and sew down both edges of the ribbon. I used triple stitch; varying the width of the stitch pattern adds more interest to the embroidered ribbons.

⑭

Select more lengths of ribbon and sew them to the cotton panel. Use different utility stitches for each ribbon. Swap the top thread to another Astro colour and attach four more rows of ribbon or lace, changing the utility stitch for each one.

⑮

Lace trimmings need manipulating to ensure the width is even. Align the lace with the edge of a stitched ribbon and pin it. Stitch this side down with zigzag, then measure the width of the lace at its widest point.

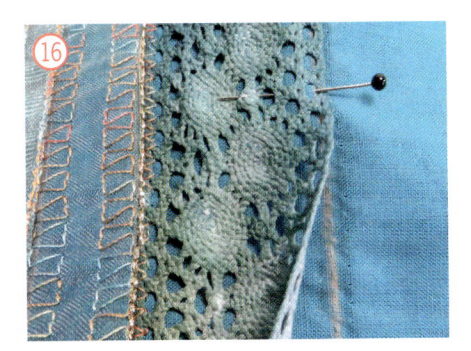

⑯ Mark this measurement on the cotton starting from the sewn side; use three dots, then join them up with a ruler and chalk pencil. Manipulate and pin the unstitched side so it matches the guideline, then secure with a row of zigzag.

⑰ Continue sewing ribbons to the cotton background until it's covered, continuing to vary the stitch pattern and thread colour. Use the spine and flap markings to check the ribbons are straight: the last ribbon should be at the same angle as the end of the cotton panel. Trim the thread tails and ribbon ends and press the back of the cotton panel with a cool iron.

⑱ Insert a size 14 metallic needle and thread it with metallic gold thread. Set the stitch type to a narrow zigzag. Select some glittery threads or yarns that are too thick for the needle and couch these to the background, following the edge of the ribbons to keep the yarn straight. Refer to the section 'Sampler: Couching yarns to a background fabric' for more instructions.

⑲ Another option is to wind the thick thread onto a bobbin and use a loose tension bobbin case. Set the stitch type to straight and turn the fabric so the right side faces down. Locate the fancy stitch securing the ribbon and stitch along the edge of it. Refer to the section 'Sampler: Stitching set patterns with cable stitch' for full instructions.

⑳ Thread a single length of sparkly yarn or thread onto a darning needle and tie a knot in the end. Sew running stitch through the holes in the lace, taking the stitches through the background fabric. Hand-sewing adds more detail and secures the wide lace to the background fabric.

㉑ Work out how large the pelmet Vilene needs to be. Measure the width of the stitched cotton panel. Take the measurement at the top, middle and bottom; the results should be nearly the same. My cover measured 49.5cm (19½in.) from edge to edge so the pelmet Vilene needs to be 49.5cm (19½) wide.

Chapter 9 – All That Glitters   199

㉒ Measure the height of the book and round it off to the nearest 0.3cm (⅛in.); my book measured 21cm (8¼in.). Add 0.8cm (⅜in.) to this measurement, so the pelmet Vilene needs to be 21.8cm (8⅝in.) high.

㉓ Draw a rectangle measuring 49.5 × 21.8cm (19½ × 8⅝in.) onto pelmet Vilene, using a ruler and set square for accuracy. Mark the position of the spine and flaps with a dressmaker's pencil. Cut the pelmet Vilene out with sharp fabric scissors or use a rotary cutter, ruler and cutting mat for accurate straight lines.

㉔ Cut a piece of heat-fusible glue the same size as the pelmet Vilene. Cover the ironing board with baking parchment. Bond the fusible glue to the back of the pelmet Vilene, allow it to cool, then peel the backing paper off.

㉕ Position the pelmet Vilene on the wrong side of the embroidered panel glue side down. Move the pelmet Vilene around until it is in the correct position; make sure the spine and flap markings line up with the direction of the ribbons.

㉖ Cover with baking parchment and bond with a medium-hot iron. You may need to hold the iron in position for longer so that the heat travels through the thick pelmet Vilene, but be careful, as you don't want to melt the ribbons or threads.

㉗ Insert a size 90/14 universal needle and thread it with Astro thread. Insert a bobbin wound with Astro thread into the normal tension bobbin case and load both into the machine. Select an overcasting or overlock stitch.

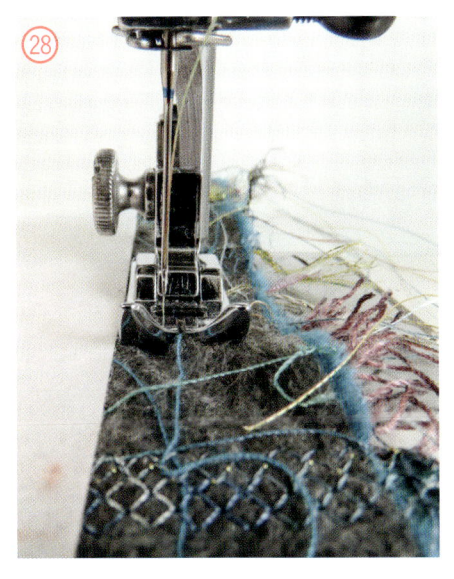

28 Line the edge of the pelmet Vilene up against the edge of the presser foot. Stitch around the rectangle of pelmet Vilene. Tidy the loose threads and ribbons; trim close to the stitching with sharp fabric scissors or use a rotary cutter, cutting mat and ruler.

29 Protect the ironing board with a sheet of baking parchment, then lay the fabric panel on it embroidered side up. Cut a strip of black Mistyfuse the same width as the stitched lace and position it over the lace.

30 Cut a strip of gold transfer foil slightly larger than the Mistyfuse. Place the foil on top of the Mistyfuse gold side up, transfer side down. If the transfer foil is not long enough cut another strip and overlap it; the overlap won't be visible when the foil is transferred.

31 Cover with a sheet of baking parchment and press. Wait for the lace to cool, then peel off the transfer foil; the metallic pigments should be left on the raised areas to create a delicate web of gold.

32 Choose a section of ribbon or lace and cut a strip of Hotspots the same size. Position the Hotspots glue side down onto the chosen area and cover with a layer of baking parchment. Iron to transfer the Hotspots, allow the glue to cool, then peel off the backing paper.

33 Cut a sheet of gold transfer foil large enough to cover the Hotspots and position it on top of the Hotspots transfer side down. Cover with baking parchment and iron to fuse the metallic foil to the glue spots; leave it to cool then peel away the foil carrier sheet to expose the gold spots.

34 Select two more foil colours and continue building up the foiled decoration. Cover previously foiled areas with baking parchment to stop the iron removing the metallic foils.

35 If some areas have been accidentally dulled lay transfer foil over them, cover with baking parchment and press. Leave the cover as it is and proceed to the making-up stage or continue onto the next step to decorate it with ribbons, as shown in the next two pictures.

36 Pin left-over ribbons on top of the embroidery to create a criss-cross pattern. Wind a bobbin with Astro thread, insert it into the normal tension bobbin case and load both into the machine. Thread the needle with the same Astro thread and set the stitch type to straight.

37 Position the needle over the start of a ribbon, lower the foot and stitch down both sides. The ribbons may fidget; use a ruler and dressmaker's chalk or artist's watercolour pencil to draw guidelines. Line the side of the ribbon up with the drawn line and pin it; remove the pins just before the foot reaches them.

38 Fold the two long sides of the embroidered panel over the pelmet Vilene and pin in place. Line the edge of the fabric up with a marker on the foot and stitch a row of straight stitch to secure, removing the pins as you sew.

39 Change the stitch to overcast or overlock. Line the foot up with the row of straight stitch and the raw edge hidden underneath. Stitch along both long sides of the embroidered panel to fasten and neaten the raw edge.

40 Use the same utility stitch to embroider lines across the length of the fabric; this helps the functional stitching blend in with the decorative embroidery. Draw angled lines across the length of the book with a ruler and dressmaker's chalk or artist's watercolour pencil. Line the foot up with the drawn lines and stitch along the length of them.

41 Fold the two short edges over the pelmet Vilene and pin in place. Make sure the corners are neatly folded. Change the stitch type to straight, line the edge of the fabric up with the foot and stitch to secure. Change the stitch back to the patterned utility stitch and sew over the raw edges to neaten. Tie off the threads and take them through to the middle of the fabric.

㊷ Line the spine of the book up with the centre of the cover and fold the flaps over the hard back cover. Manipulate the cover till it fits the book and sits comfortably. Check the flaps are the same size, then use your fingers to press the folded flaps.

㊸ Pin the flaps in position. Thread a sharp hand-sewing needle with a strong doubled colour-matched thread. Slip-stitch the flaps to the long edge of the book cover. Do more stitching to secure the flaps where they join the fabric panel, then take the threads through to the middle of the fabric and trim the ends close to the fabric.

㊹ Bond gold transfer foil to the daisy lace with Mistyfuse, then bond another colour on top to distress the surface of the lace. Pin the lace daisies to the embroidery where the ribbon crosses over. Thread a hand-sewing needle with colour-matched thread and stitch them in place.

㊺ Thread a small sharp hand-sewing or beading needle with colour-matched thread and sew metallic seed beads between the petals. You could also stitch a length of ribbon to the inside of the cover; make sure it's long enough to tie around the book.

㊻ Insert the book into the finished cover. Decide which side is the front and push the front hard back cover into the flap pocket, then do the same with the other side. The book is now ready to be used or gifted to someone special.

Chapter 9 – All That Glitters

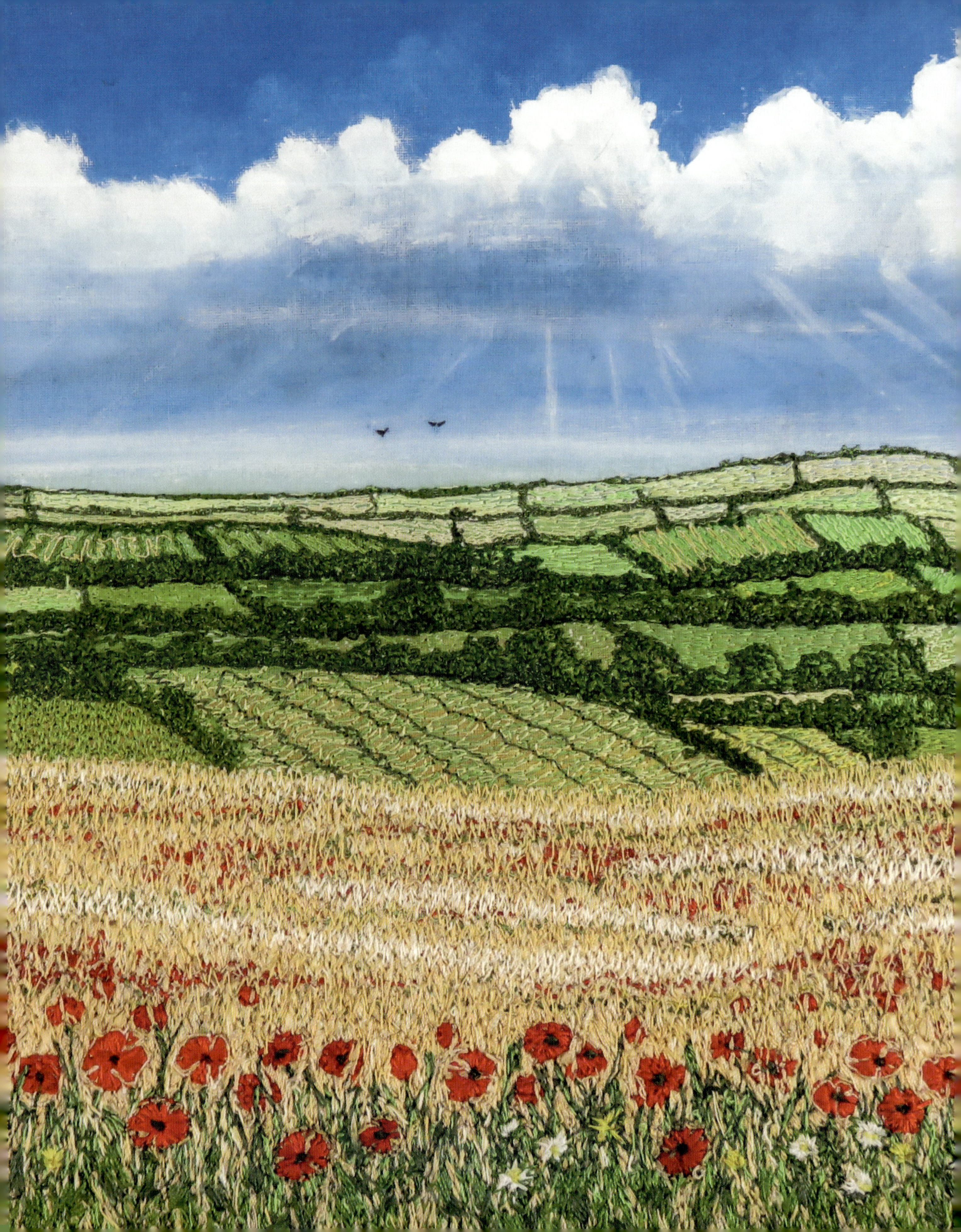

CHAPTER 10

EMBROIDERING THE LANDSCAPE

Embroiderers can stitch realistic landscapes if they follow a few artistic guidelines, most notably:

- using the rule of thirds or elements of the golden section to compose the design
- utilizing perspective to describe what's in the landscape
- applying shade and tonal values to create form
- playing with colour to set the mood or atmosphere.

Textile artists have additional things to consider, for instance:

- how to transfer the design
- which fabrics or threads to use
- how much texture to include
- how to stitch the design
- the order of work
- how to correct mistakes
- how to frame or mount the finished embroidery.

This chapter shows how to break down the rules and processes to make them more manageable, and the projects and examples give an honest account of the methods and materials used.

WHERE TO FIND INSPIRATION

Liking the image or subject matter means you get more enjoyment from designing the composition and embroidering the landscape image. I like stitching woodlands and patchwork fields, so the projects in this chapter reflect that. Another way of finding inspiration is to make drawings of the landscape around you or to draw from memory the places you have visited. Wherever your inspiration comes from, sketch or draw the design on paper; creating the image gives you ownership and the choice to edit the composition.

If you feel uncomfortable drawing from observation, working from a photo is the best way to begin because the subject matter has already been flattened into two dimensions, which makes the image easier to understand and copy. If you are worried about drawing, simply trace the photo onto water-soluble film and pin it to the fabric ready for embroidery. You may need to resize the photo to make it more suitable for machine embroidery, as tiny details are not manageable with machine stitch.

Where to Find Images

Your image can be a photo you have taken or a image found in a magazine or holiday brochure. Images downloaded from the internet work well if the resolution is high. Care must be taken when using other people's images because they may have copyright restrictions placed on them. I prefer to work with colour images because it makes choosing fabric and thread colours easier – the atmosphere of the image has already been set by the photographer.

Planning the Design

You don't have to keep something just because it's in the photo; you can move elements around and decide which parts to keep and which to remove. Doing some simple drawings will help you to plan which parts to sew first and decide what size or shape the embroidery should be.

I prefer to use pencil or black pen when designing and I like loose paper in case I make a mistake. I copy the finished design onto tracing paper because it enables me to move elements of the landscape about. I use a printer scanner to copy the drawings so the originals don't become tatty. A computer and scanner are handy for resizing drawings as they save lots of time; scaling up or down by hand can be tricky and time-consuming.

We are all different and there are no rules when it comes to designing; you may enjoy working in a sketch book or beginning with a specific colour, or you could start by choosing fabrics and threads, meditating or listening to music. How you start is up to you. You will begin to develop your own style of design; this can be influenced by how you were taught in school, the way you learn or artists or craftspeople whom you admire.

Landscape compositions need careful design; this one is dull because the tree is in the middle of the composition.

Moving the tree to the left and extending the sky improves the composition and makes it more interesting.

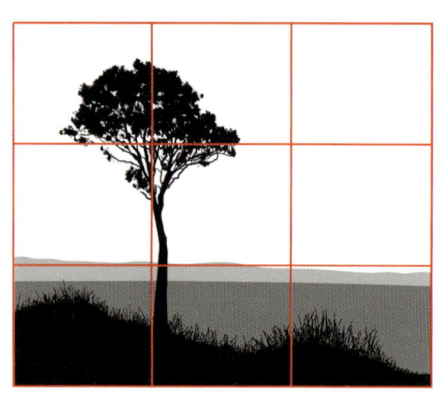

The rule of thirds divides the picture into nine sections. Areas of interest should ideally be placed so they correspond with the grid lines or the sections. The middle of the tree crown is at a point where the lines cross and the horizon line matches the lower grid line.

Painters traditionally use the golden section. The spaces between the grid lines are not equal as in the rule of thirds. Note that the composition still works because the tree lines up with the first part of the grid and the horizon fits into the bottom section.

Composing the Design

Composition is about how you position elements of the design, such as a tree, a building, a gate or a lake. The elements of the composition are confined within a frame, which is the edge of the paper or the fabric. Frame size and shape is important. Rectangular format is the most common and it can be landscape or portrait depending on the orientation of the paper or fabric. Just because you are designing a landscape it does not have to be in landscape format. You can choose any shape for the frame, such as oval, round or square; remember the choice will influence how the design is cropped.

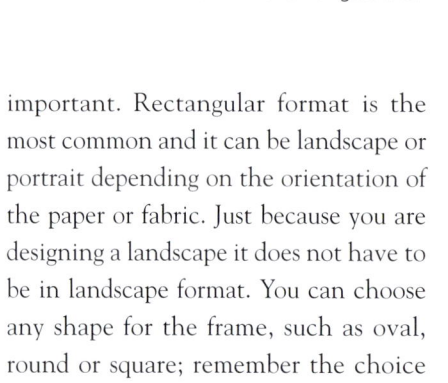

The design should have a background, middle ground and foreground; each should have elements of interest to lead the eye around the landscape. Most of the detail should be in the foreground because it's closest to the observer. The design should be pleasing and have balance.

Photographers use the rule of thirds to assist them with composition. The image is divided into nine sections and key elements of the composition are near the guidelines or in the sections. Traditional artists use the golden section to help compose their paintings; this concept is very similar to that of the rule of thirds.

For the rule of thirds or the golden section to work, the horizon line must never be halfway up a composition; position it two thirds or one third up and areas of interest must be positioned near the grid lines or where they intersect. These composition rules are quite mathematical, although when I'm designing maths is the last thing on my mind; I work instinctively and find that I've followed the rules without realizing.

Using Perspective

Most landscapes contain some elements of perspective. The simplest kind is one-point perspective, which has one vanishing point and a horizon line. Imagine a single path towards the horizon line; it gets smaller as it reaches the horizon. Where buildings are concerned perspective may include two or three vanishing points. If you want your images to be realistic it is important to learn the basics of perspective. Beginners' art books are a good place to learn about drawing in one-, two- and three-point perspective. Simple one-point perspective can be used to depict distance in a landscape or the bends in a river; I use it to add curves to furrows in fields or make a path through woodland areas. Do you want your landscape to be naive or realistic? A naive landscape can really push the boundaries as you can introduce perspective that does not make sense or add colours that are not realistic.

One-point perspective can be used to draw simple landscapes like this tree-lined avenue. The guidelines converge at the vanishing point which is situated on the horizon line. Move the horizon line and vanishing point to suit the composition. The vanishing point could be further up or set to one side.

The furrows were drawn with one-point perspective. The vanishing point is placed slightly above the horizon line. The guidelines helped me to create curved furrows and dips in the land.

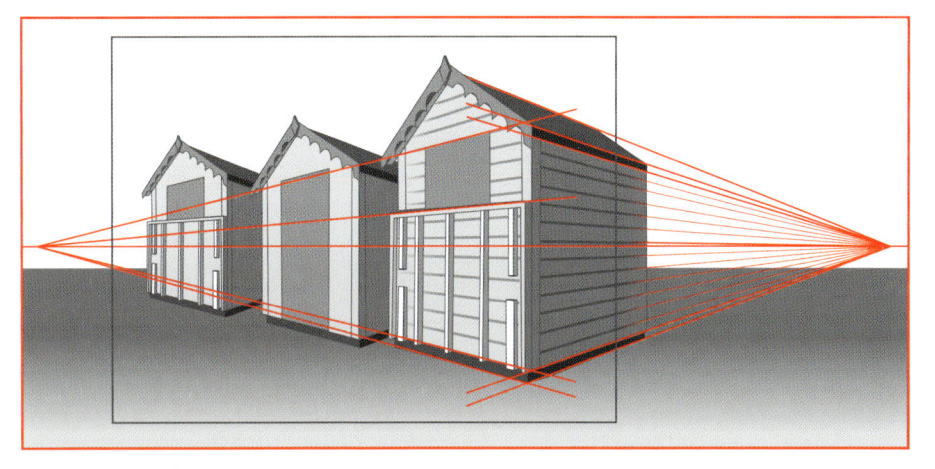

Two-point perspective has two vanishing points on the same horizon line. Two-point perspective can be used to draw buildings accurately; it would be very difficult to draw the slats on these wooden beach huts without using perspective.

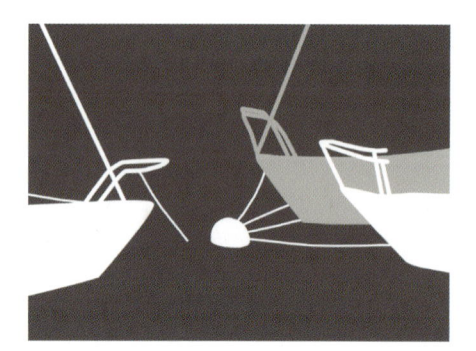

In this picture some of the boats were removed to create the composition. With cropping, the buoy becomes the focal point of the design. The shapes of the boats create positive and negative space within the frame of the composition.

The tonal values set the dramatic mood of this seascape. The sunlit sea provides a stark contrast to the dark sky. Thick bobbin thread work and hand-sewn sea foam add to the drama. I would not want to be caught in the coming storm.

The still atmosphere of this embroidery was created by using a limited colour palette. It was completed in a mixture of brown, black and green threads; the texture of the ploughed field was enhanced with black and green Chromacolour paint.

Negative Space

This is the area around the positive objects within a composition. If you are struggling to draw something complicated look for the space around the objects. Some artists use a viewfinder when drawing from life because it helps them to put a boundary around the things they are drawing so that it's easier to transfer the image onto paper. If working from a photograph you can simply trace the edges of the objects to find the negative space. Once you have found the negative spaces you can use them to add drama to the landscape.

Tonal Values (Light and Dark)

Tonal values are an important part of the composition, as shadows or areas of light and dark can be used to create a dramatic atmosphere. Look at the design or landscape outside – where is the sun? Is it a bright sunny day with distinct shadows or a misty twilight with little contrast between light and dark?

Light and shade also describe the shape of objects and create depth within the landscape. If I am unable to graduate shade with thread, I use paint to add darkness. It is not so easy to add light as white pigments are chalky and can look painted on, so it's important to choose threads that have light, medium and dark shades; it is good to have a lot of in-between thread shades as well.

Colour in Landscapes

The colour of the fabrics and threads chosen will set the season of the embroidery. Colours are often described as being warm or cold: bright greens and sky blue lean towards summer or spring, whilst brown, olive and rust are more autumnal; monochrome greys and browns indicate winter months. The colours I choose are dictated by how natural I want the landscape to be or the atmosphere I want to create. It's useful to work with a limited colour palette because this can depict the season; this approach works well for winter scenes.

Choice of Materials

The fabrics you choose must be strong enough to support dense stitching, able to accept paint and withstand heat and immersion into water. The ideal background material is white cotton because it can be dyed with fabric paints or acrylics.

The texture of the embroidery should be considered because it influences how the eye moves across the composition. Texture can be applied to unify the composition so it appears flat or it can separate it into foreground and background. Texture can be used to describe distance: use fine fabrics in the background and thick ones for the foreground. Thin fabrics work best for cutting snips and layering while thick fabrics add bulk to the embroidery and can make it difficult to sew.

Texture and thread thickness were used to create depth in this seascape. The breaking waves are embroidered with cable stitch using thick viscose thread and hand-sewn with bouclé yarn and straight stitch. The beach pebbles are seed-stitched by hand with cotton perle, silk and sparkly thread.

This embroidery uses a combination of perspective, colour and texture to capture the spirit of Bonfire Night. The painted linen background has free machine embroidery trees, cable-stitched fields and hand-stitched fireworks.

Fine threads are used in the background because distant objects appear smaller; thick threads are used in the foreground because the thickness helps to bring the foreground forward. Hand stitching worked into the foreground adds detail and creates a sense of closeness. Another way to add texture is to work upside down and do some cable-stitched bobbin embroidery; the raised couched yarn will make the foreground more prominent when compared to the flat background.

Planning the Process of Landscape Embroidery

A landscape embroidery needs careful planning. The embroidery process needs to be split into stages and put in work order: for example, paint the background fabric, embroider the background, embroider the middle ground and embroider the foreground. Completing the stages in the correct order is the difference between a failed embroidery and a successful one.

Which part of the landscape should be embroidered first? Start at the back and work forward, or start at the top and work downwards. Begin with the sky because it's the most distant part of the landscape. Keep the sky simple so that it doesn't overpower the rest of the embroidery. The sky can be plain fabric, painted cotton or made from snips of fabric secured with stitch. The sky is important because it sets the tone for the whole composition: a fair-weather sky with white fluffy clouds is uplifting whilst a dark stormy sky can be oppressive and foreboding. Dark grey clouds work well when juxtaposed next to bright landscapes; think of a stormy sky against an autumnal tree or a field of yellow oilseed rape.

Start stitching the distant background first, using smaller stitches and pale cool colours; this combination tricks the eye into making distant objects recede more. As you work through the middle ground use warm colours and begin to add more detail and texture. Use thicker threads when you work on the foreground because they help to create the illusion of closeness. Use two threads through the needle; this doubles the thread weight, enabling you to build the embroidery up quickly whilst adding more texture.

As you work on the foreground the embroidery may become quite thick and the needle may make a noise as it enters and exits the fabric – this is completely normal. It is important to keep looking at the image you have chosen and your embroidery, as this will help you to be more accurate and keep the atmosphere or mood you are aiming for. Solid blocks of colour can be harsh; threads must be changed frequently and layered to obtain the illusion of realism.

EXAMPLE

Planning and Embroidering a Landscape from a Photograph

This example shows how I turned the photo into a design for machine embroidery and broke the project down into a series of steps. It gives an honest account of how I made decisions and rectified mistakes.

1 The photo was taken in Paignton looking towards the beach at Redhill. On close inspection, there are some elements that would be difficult to replicate in stitch but it's acceptable to use artistic licence to change a design.

2 The composition was created over the scanned photo with a graphics programme. Some elements were removed or changed: for instance, the pier is too small to stitch, part of the harbour wall is visible and the bush is in the way. Other changes included increasing the depth occupied by the sea and extending the sky at the top.

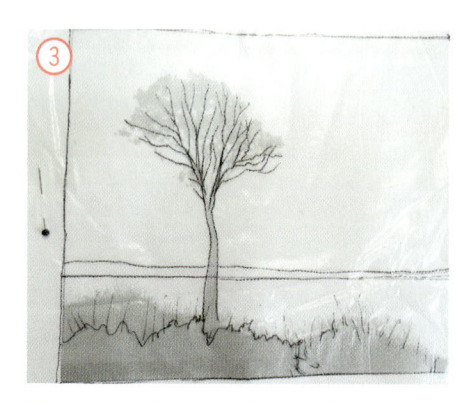

3 The composition is printed out the same size as the intended embroidery and traced onto water-soluble film with a black permanent pen. I didn't trace all the details: it's okay to change the design as you work.

4 I choose cotton-backed pale blue synthetic lining for the sky, silver lamé tissue for the sea and green cotton quilting fabric for the foliage. Using coloured fabric beneath the embroidery saves time as there's no need to stitch densely. I pinned the soluble film drawing on top of the layered fabrics and secured it with pins.

5 I stitched the distant background with straight stitch, then the sea, leaving gaps between the stitching so that the silver lamé could shine through. I used a metal hoop for quick re-positioning but the fabric pulled in quite badly; I should have used a wooden hoop because it would have gripped the fabric better.

6 I embroidered the tree's branches and trunk using straight stitch and dark chocolate brown thread. The needle pulled the warp and weft of the lining material used for the sky. I was not going to stitch into the sky area but the pulled fabric was very visible. I decided to hand-sew the sky with tiny running stitches after finishing the tree.

⑦ I embroidered the tree foliage with moss stitch, winding a bobbin with two threads and inserting it into the loose tension bobbin case. This combination creates a thick marled stitch that's ideal for leaves. I felt the foreground was a bit bland and dark so I drew an outline of an herbaceous border on water-soluble film and pinned it to the fabric.

⑧ I stitched the plants at the back with normal tension straight stitch. As I moved forward I used two threads through the needle and began adding flowers with loose bobbin tension feather stitch. I worked from memory and images found on the internet so perhaps the plants are more fantasy than real. I washed the film away and left the embroidery to dry overnight. I placed the embroidery in a hoop and hand-embroidered the sky with running stitch.

⑨ I examined the embroidery to see if anything needed changing. I decided the herbaceous border needed stronger colours and bigger blooms and the foliage needed more detail. I stitched more detail with loose tension bobbin embroidery.

⑩ I reviewed the embroidery again and decided the border looked a bit flat. I used watered-down acrylic paint to change the colour of some of the flowers and darken the shading of the tree. I pressed the embroidery on the back to set the paint and remove the hoop marks. The embroidery was now ready to be framed or mounted.

STEP-BY-STEP PROJECT
Sunlit Wood

YOU WILL NEED

Equipment
- Photocopier or printer and scanner
- Photo of a wood
- Design drawn from the photo
- Sewing machine with drop feed or darning plate
- Darning or embroidery foot
- Straight stitch presser foot
- Spare bobbin case for loose tension embroidery
- Empty bobbins
- Size 90/14 universal machine needle
- Glass-headed pins
- 15cm (6in.) wooden hoop
- Medium-sized sharp fabric scissors
- Embroidery scissors
- Iron
- Ironing cloth
- Baking parchment
- Ruler
- Set square
- Pencil
- Pencil sharpener
- Eraser
- Green Stabilo Fineliner point 88
- Sink or bowl of water to wash the embroidery
- Old towel on which to dry the embroidery

Materials
- A4 paper
- Tracing paper
- White cotton backing fabric approximately 25.5 × 28cm (10 × 11in.)
- Scrap of calico
- Stiff iron-on interfacing approximately 15 × 20cm (6 × 8in.)
- Temporary spray glue
- Avalon soluble film, two pieces approximately 18 × 23cm (7 × 9in.)
- Scraps of white lining, white poly cotton organza and mirror organza, lime green poly cotton organza, dark green mirror organza, green lining, patterned or plain green quilting fabric in various shades of green
- White and brown bobbin thread
- Empress Mills 2/74 HT Polyester white or invisible thread
- Madeira Classic no. 40 thread in colours 1003 (white), 1150 (lime green), 1102 (pale green), 1248 (acid green), 1169 (leaf green), 1170 (mid dark green), 1189 (dark green), 1329 (warm brown), 1336 (brown), 1144 (mid brown), 1136 (pale brown), 1128 (beige brown), 1129 (dark brown) (please note these are not the official names for the thread colours; I named them thus to make your thread selection easier during the project)

Design template
- Sunlit Wood

Machine used
- Janome JF 1018s
- Feeder teeth covered with darning plate
- Normal tension
- Loose tension bobbin thread

This project demonstrates how to work an embroidery in stages. It combines embroidery on soluble film, embroidery with the presser foot and loose tension embroidery with whip, moss and feather stitch. It is embroidered with a variety of threads and stitches. The machine stitches are very basic; the combination of layering thread colours and stitching over snips draws you in to create the illusion of reality – I'd love to take a walk in a wood like this one.

1 Copy the Sunlit Wood template and enlarge it so it measures 15 × 10cm (6 × 4in.) or find your own reference photo or drawing and enlarge it to a similar size.

2 Cut the fabric scraps into small square pieces. These should measure no more than 0.6cm (¼in.), and small pieces work best. A quick way to cut snips is to fold or roll the fabric into a tube and cut a strip off the end, then cut the square snips from the rolled strip; this method prevents thumb strain. I store the cut snips in zip-lock bags because it stops them getting spilled or mixed up.

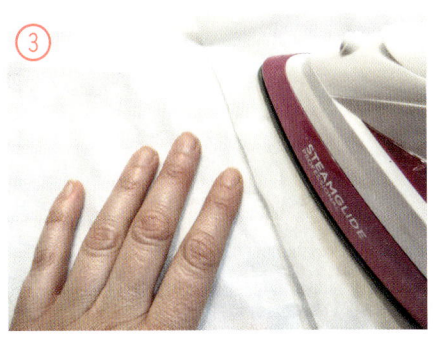

3 Iron the white cotton backing, then place the interfacing on the back so it's centrally positioned. Cover with baking parchment and press (baking parchment helps the iron slide over the interfacing as it fuses). Turn the cotton so it's in portrait orientation with the interfacing underneath. Use a pencil, ruler and set square to draw a rectangle measuring 15 × 10cm (6 × 4in.) in the centre of the cotton.

4 Look at the photo to see where the sunlight is coming through the trees. Sprinkle snips of white lining and white organza to represent the sky, then scatter lime green snips on top to create sunlit leaves. Soften the strength of the light by layering more white organza over the lime green, positioning the fabric snips one at a time so the bottom layer is not disturbed. Sprinkle a layer of lime green organza over the bottom to create the forest floor.

5 Look at the photo and find the light and dark areas. Squint to see the tonal values (squinting eliminates the mid-tones, making the light and dark areas easier to see). When you have located the light areas, start sprinkling pale green quilting and lining scraps to create leaves. Move on to the medium green tones and add some medium green snips to the forest floor. Cut the dark snips slightly smaller and place them to create areas of shadow. Use the lime green organza to blend the dark areas so they are not too harsh.

6 Spray one piece of Avalon soluble film with temporary glue: work in a ventilated area away from sources of ignition. Carefully lay the film sticky side down over the snips. If you misjudge the placement don't be tempted to move the film; just spray another piece and position it on top. Gently smooth your hand over the film to flatten the creases and secure the snips. If you are worried about the snips falling out, pin the edge of the film to the cotton backing fabric.

Chapter 10 – Embroidering the Landscape

⑦ Lower the feeder teeth or clip on a darning plate. Insert a size 90/14 universal needle and attach the embroidery foot. Set the stitch type to straight and thread the needle with Madeira Classic thread in colour 1003 (white). Wind a bobbin with white bobbin thread, insert it into the normal tension bobbin case and load both into the machine. Put the film-topped fabric in a hoop and place under the foot.

⑧ Stitch the white parts of the sky with tiny meandering vermicelli stitch. Swap the top thread to Madeira Classic 1150 (lime green) and vermicelli-stitch the remaining snips. Stitch beyond the edge of the rectangle; most embroideries shrink during stitching and it is easier to mount the finished embroidery if there is more leeway for the frame or mount. When the snips are sewn remove the hoop and cut the thread tabs front and back.

⑨ Pin the second piece of soluble film to the design and trace it with a green Stabilo Fineliner; I used green because it blended into the washed embroidery. Write 'this way' on the bottom of the film drawing to prevent flipping the design the wrong way round. Pin the soluble film drawing to the embroidery so the drawing matches the background. Place the embroidery back in the hoop; you may need to re-position the pins to stop them being bent by the hoop.

⑩ Wind Madeira Classic no. 1170 (mid green) into the bobbin and insert it into the normal tension bobbin case. Thread the needle with 1189 (dark green) thread and stitch some up-and-down lines with straight stitch to represent the distant foliage. Thread the needle with 1170 (mid dark green) and add more rows of straight stitch to the shading.

214   Chapter 10 – Embroidering the Landscape

Change the bobbin to brown and thread the needle with 1329 (warm brown). Re-position the hoop so that the distant trees are central. Use straight stitch to embroider the distant trees, going up and down the trunk and branches, then filling the trunks with straight stitch. Complete three distant trees using this colour. Thread the needle with 1336 (brown) and stitch three more distant trees. Don't add much detail – a few rows of straight stitch should be enough. If the stitching has a wobble, unpick from the back with sharp embroidery scissors or a quick unpick. Cut the thread tabs from the front and back.

The next tree is stitched with two threads through the needle. Change the top thread to 1144 (mid brown) and 1136 (pale brown). Make sure both threads are engaged in the tension disk to prevent looping. Stitch the middle-ground tree with straight stitch; you may need to loosen the top tension for two threads. When the tree is stitched, remove both threads from the needle and reset the tension (if you altered it). Thread the needle with 1128 (beige brown) and add highlights to one side of the trunk and branches. Thread the needle with 1336 (brown) and add shade to the opposite side of the branches and trunk.

Remove the darning plate or raise the feeder teeth. Attach a straight-stitch presser foot and check the needle is still using 1336 (brown). Set the stitch type to zigzag, shorten the length to satin stitch and adjust the width to approximately 0.3cm (1/8in.). Test the stitch on a scrap of calico; this sample shows a variety of zigzag widths and lengths. The tension is not quite right because the bobbin thread has been pulled to the top. Don't be afraid to adjust the tension.

Chapter 10 – Embroidering the Landscape

Remove the embroidery from the hoop and position it under the foot so the needle lines up with the edge of the drawn trunk. Turn the hand wheel to check the needle is in the correct position; it should pierce the drawn line and be just inside the tree trunk. Stitch the edge of the trunk with a row of satin stitch. When you reach the end, raise the foot and turn the embroidery. Align the needle with the edge of the sewn satin stitch and follow the previous row back up the trunk.

When the trunk is filled with stitches, change the top thread to 1129 (dark brown) and lengthen the satin stitch so it becomes more open like zigzag. You may also need to reduce the stitch width. Stitch the shaded side of the tree to give it more form, then swap to 1136 (pale brown) and stitch some highlights. My machine was not sewing properly at this point but changing the needle solved the problem because the needle was blunt.

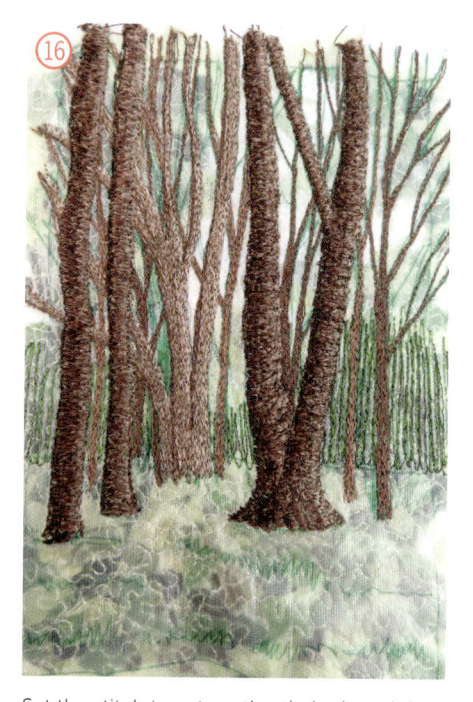

Set the stitch type to satin stitch, thread the needle with 1336 (brown) and embroider the two remaining tree trunks with satin stitch. Thread the needle with 1129 (dark brown) and stitch shade on one side of the tree trunk; alter the width and length of the zigzag until you get the desired effect. Thread the needle with 1136 (pale brown) and stitch highlights on the other side of the trunk.

⑰ Reset the stitch to straight and attach a darning or embroidery foot. Lower the feeder teeth or use a darning plate. Put the embroidery in a hoop so the foreground trees are central. The embroidery is starting to get thick, which makes is more difficult to hoop. You can work without a hoop because the fabric is thick enough but it will place more strain on your hands and be more difficult to manoeuvre.

⑱ Add more detail to the foreground tree trunks. Thread the needle with 1136 (pale brown) and embroider into the sunlit side of the trunk using straight stitch, thus giving more definition. Thread the needle with 1129 (dark brown) and work into the shaded side using the same method. Continue working on the tree trunks until you are happy with the details.

⑲ Put the grassy area of the fabric in a hoop. Wind 1170 (mid dark green) onto a bobbin, insert it into a normal tension bobbin case and load both into the machine. Thread the needle with 1102 (pale green) and set the stitch type to straight. Use an up-and-down movement to embroider the sunlit areas of the forest floor; don't overstitch because more stitching will be layered on top. Sew over the base of the tree trunks to create tufts of grass. Swap the top thread to 1169 (leaf green) and sew the rest of the forest floor, keeping the stitching open so that the background shows through.

Tear the soluble film from the embroidery and pin the scraps over the trees. If you are worried about catching the foot on the scraps cut a fresh piece of film; I'm just being frugal. Use a green Stabilo Fineliner to mark where the leaves are. Don't draw every leaf – an oval or rounded shape is sufficient. Add cross-hatching to the shapes so they are easier to see.

Set the machine up so it's ready to sew feather stitch (refer to the feather stitch sampler for more guidance). Wind a bobbin with 1169 (leaf green), insert it into the loose tension bobbin case and load both into the machine. Thread the needle with invisible or polyester HT thread and set the stitch type to straight. Place a scrap of calico in a hoop and test the stitch. Embroidering vermicelli or tiny scribbles pulls loops of bobbin thread to create a leafy effect; alter the tension until you get the desired result.

Stitch the patches of leaves. Look at the photo to see where the sun shines through and think about how the leaves grow from the branches. Stitch some texture into the grass to represent mid-shaded areas of the forest floor; use straight stitch and move the hoop with the direction of growth. Cut the tabs on the top of the embroidery but leave the bottom tabs intact because it stops the loose-tension embroidery unravelling.

Wind 1150 (lime green) onto a bobbin, insert it into the loose tension bobbin case and load both into the machine. Stitch the sunlit leaves and light patches of grass on the forest floor. Wind 1189 (dark green) onto the bobbin, insert it into the loose tension bobbin case and load both into the machine. Embroider the shaded areas of tree foliage and forest floor. Wind 1248 (acid green) onto the bobbin, insert it into the loose tension bobbin case and load both into the machine. Stitch into the trees to create the sunlit leaves. Continue swapping bobbins until you are happy with the leaves on the trees, then cut the thread tabs on the front of the embroidery.

Thread the needle with 1102 (pale green) and swap the loose tension bobbin case back to a normal one; insert a 1336 (brown) bobbin and load both into the machine. Adjust the top tension to create whip stitch (refer to the whip stitch sampler for more instructions). Stitch a sample; small dots of brown bobbin thread should come to the top to create the illusion of soil or fallen leaves. Stitch into the sunlit areas of the forest floor and into the loose bobbin tension to create a grassy texture. Thread 1169 (leaf green) through the needle and continue stitching the forest floor to catch any loose tension embroidery that's too loopy. Thread the needle with 1248 (acid green) and add more sunlit clumps of grass to the forest floor.

Cut the tabs on the front of the embroidery; do not cut any on the back, just trim the thread tails. Peel off the soluble film and examine the embroidery to decide if it needs further work. Use any combination of greens and browns already used; for example, I added more grass near the base of the trees and worked more texture into the grass.

Fill a bowl with warm water and soak the finished embroidery face upwards. The soluble film will begin to lift and dissolve. Gently rub the surface of the embroidery with your fingertips to disperse the dissolving film; leave the embroidery to soak for about an hour. Change the water and leave to soak upside down for another hour. Soaking for this long ensures the film has gone; film residue stiffens the embroidery and darkens the thread colours. Take the embroidery out of the water. Do not wring it, just smooth it out and leave it to dry facing upwards on an old towel.

Inspect the dry embroidery and trim any remaining tabs or frayed fabric from the top. Place the embroidery face down onto a colour-fast towel and cover with a damp ironing cloth. Press the embroidery with a medium-hot iron, smoothing out the creases, handling marks or undulations caused by the dense stitching. Don't iron the front of the embroidery because pressing flattens the raised stitches. The embroidery is now ready to be mounted and framed so take a look at Chapter 12 for suggestions.

28

29

This version of the wood has a carpet of bluebells. The flowers are embroidered with loose tension feather stitch. After finishing the embroidery I decided it needed more contrast between light and shade. I therefore diluted some black Chromacolour acrylic paint with water and painted shadows onto the forest floor and darkened one side of the tree trunks. I added light by painting the sunlit side of the trees with green; the paint caught on the stitches to give the tree trunks a mossy appearance.

Rusty browns and oranges create an autumnal theme for this embroidery of silver birches. Less machine embroidery was used to stitch this embroidery. The satin-stitched tree trunks have been worked into with simple hand stitch and space-dyed cotton perle seed stitch added further detail to the leaves. The grey satin background wrinkled; this was disguised by fine seed stitching with grey cotton thread.

STEP-BY-STEP PROJECT
Summer Cornfield with Painted Sky

YOU WILL NEED

Equipment
- Photocopier or printer and scanner
- Sewing machine with drop feed or darning plate
- Darning or embroidery foot
- Spare bobbin case for loose tension embroidery
- Empty bobbins
- Size 90/14 universal machine needle
- Iron
- Ironing cloth
- Baking parchment
- Fabric scissors
- Embroidery scissors
- Glass-headed pins
- Pencil
- Pencil sharpener
- Green Stabilo Fineliner pen
- Ruler
- Set square
- Paintbrushes: large flat or bright and stencil
- Kitchen paper
- White palette or plate
- Scrap paper or plastic sheeting
- Sink or bowl of water to wash the embroidery
- Old towel on which to dry the embroidery

Materials
- White A4 paper or tracing paper
- Pre-washed and ironed white cotton approximately 35.5 × 30.5cm (14 × 12in.)
- Dylon fabric paint in white, royal blue, red, yellow
- Gütermann Sulky Ultra-Stable thick iron-on interfacing 30.5 × 23cm (12 × 9in.)
- Lightweight Avalon water-soluble film
- Scrap of cotton or calico
- Corn- or straw-coloured acrylic double knitting wool
- White Bobbinfil or poly cotton thread for the bobbin
- Madeira Classic no. 40 thread in colours (for pale greens) 1150 (lime green), 1102 (pale green), 1248 (acid green), 1260 (canvas green); (for mid greens) 1049 (mid lime green), 1048 (mid aloe green), 1169 (leaf green); (for dark greens) 1170 (mid dark green), 1189 (dark green), 1396 (dark sage green), 1303 (dark evening green). Also 2033 (ombre green), 1064 (yellow), 1147 (red); (for the corn) 1070 (tawny tan), 1128 (beige brown), 1149 (beige tusk); (optional) 1003 (cream white)

Design template
- Summer Cornfield

Machine used
- Bernina 801
- Feeder teeth down
- Normal tension
- Loose tension bobbin thread

This project shows how to plan and stitch an embroidery of a cornfield with a background of patchwork fields and a painted sky. The design combines painting and stitching; you will learn how to blend thread colours together like paint and use two threads through the needle. This project uses stitching to create texture; the cornfield is worked over a layer of wool and soluble film. The poppies are embroidered with a combination of normal tension and loose tension stitches. The embroidery is stitched without a hoop because the stiff interfacing should be thick enough to support the embroidery.

Landscapes are very organic things and they can end up very different from how you imagined or intended them to be. You can draw your own patchwork fields or copy a photograph and use these instructions as just a guide. The threads I have used are only a suggestion: you can choose your own brand and colours or use a smaller palette of colours.

Draw a rectangle measuring 23 × 18cm (9 × 7in.) in the centre of the white cotton, using a pencil, ruler and set square for accuracy. Draw a line across the rectangle slightly above the middle to mark the horizon. This drawing is a rough guide for painting the background; it will be covered by paint and stitching.

② Protect the work surface with scrap paper or plastic sheeting; make sure there are no wrinkles in the plastic because they can transfer to the painted fabric. Give the pots of fabric paint a good shake before opening them; the pigments and binder need a good mix. Prepare the palette, brushes and mixing water. It's a good idea to have paper towels close by; they are great for testing colours or mopping up accidental spills.

③ Mix three parts royal blue to one part white fabric paint. Add a small amount of water, then use a flat brush to mix until the colours are blended. Paint the sky with the flat brush, starting at the top and brushing horizontally across the cotton. Take the paint over the pencil marks. As you work downwards begin adding more white and water to the mixed paint; this creates a paler tint as you reach the horizon line.

④ Mix blue, yellow and white to make a pale green. Add a drop of water and mix well, then paint the distant fields. Mix yellow, red and white with the leftover green paint to make brown and paint the bottom of the cotton. The painted fields do not have to be neat because they will be covered with stitching. Leave the paint to dry and fix with a hot iron (refer to the instructions on the pot). Iron the back first, then the front. Work in a ventilated area because fabric paints can create fumes during fixing.

⑤ Decant some white fabric paint onto a clean dry palette and use a dry stencil or hard-bristled brush to paint the clouds. Stippling and blending with a dry brush moves the paint around to create soft cloud-like shapes. Fair-weather clouds are rarely pure white because sunlight creates shadows within their mass. Mix a small amount of red and blue to create a stormy purple, mix a dot of this into white and begin painting shadows beneath the clouds. Continue working on the sky; you may need to paint a few layers to get the right effect. When you are happy with the results leave the fabric to dry and fix as directed.

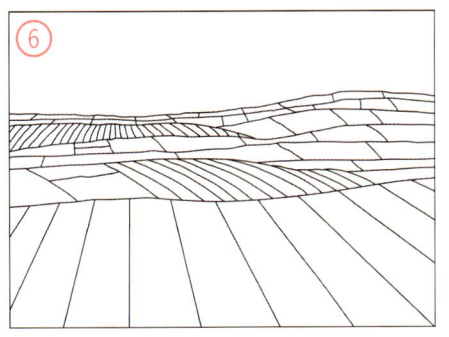

⑥ Find the Summer Cornfield design in the back of the book and trace or copy it onto plain A4 paper; the design should measure approximately 16.5 × 23cm (6½ × 9in.). The rows on the field give you the option of sewing ploughed furrows or corn. Pin a piece of Avalon water-soluble film to the design and trace it with a green Stabilo Fineliner.

⑦ Iron the stiff interfacing onto the back of the painted fabric. Make sure the glue side of the interfacing is against the cotton and use baking parchment to protect the iron. This embroidery can be stitched without a hoop; if you feel the fabric is still too flexible apply another layer of interfacing to the back.

Chapter 10 – Embroidering the Landscape   223

⑧ Lay the traced water-soluble film over the painted cotton and re-position until the traced design matches the painted background. Pin the soluble film to the painted cotton; use lots of pins because the soluble film is very thin but avoid pinning the painted sky because the pins leave visible holes in the thick paint.

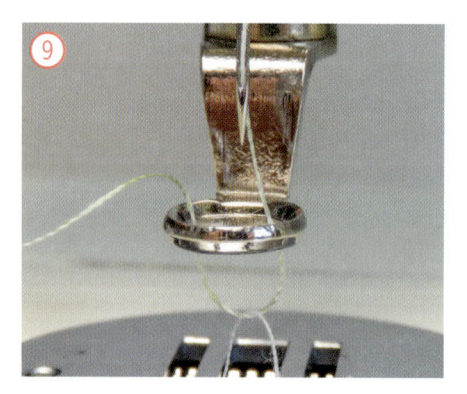

⑨ Drop the feeder teeth and attach an embroidery foot or darning foot. Wind a bobbin with white Bobbinfil or white poly cotton thread, insert into the normal tension bobbin case and load both into the machine. Insert a size 90/14 universal needle and set the stitch type to straight. Thread the needle with 1260 (canvas green) thread and turn the hand wheel to bring both threads to the top.

⑩ Position the fabric so the needle is over one of the furthest distant fields and lower the foot. Stitch the field with horizontal straight stitch, keeping the stitch length short and allowing the green background show through. Swap pale green threads, using different shades for adjacent fields. I used 1102 (pale green), 1248 (acid green), 1260 (canvas green) and 1150 (lime green). You could use 1064 (yellow) to add an oilseed rape field. Cut the tabs between the fields because the thread can get caught on the embroidery foot. Stitch beyond the guidelines on the edge to allow for shrinkage when framing.

⑪ Once the two back rows of fields have been stitched, think about adding stitch direction to the next three rows. Imagine how the crops grow and the lines made by farm machinery. Use medium green colours to bring the middle ground forward. I used 1049 (mid lime green), 1169 (leaf green) and 1048 (mid aloe green). Sew each field with a different colour, texture or stitch direction.

⑫ Wind a bobbin with 1170 (mid dark green), insert it into the bobbin case and load both into the machine. Get the tension ready for whip stitch; tighten the top tension until it brings the bobbin thread to the top. Stitch a sample onto a scrap of calico before working on the landscape. Continue stitching into the middle-ground fields; reworking the embroidery adds more texture to the crops.

⑬ Keep the top tension set to whip and begin working on the nearer fields. Swap thread colour for each field and vary the stitch direction to add variety to the farmland. When the first layer of stitch is complete reset the top tension to normal; leave the green bobbin in or change it back to white. Think about the growing crops, use stitch direction to describe them and add more character to the fields. Variegated green is a good option for adding more texture because it has light, medium and dark on the same reel; I used 2033 (ombre green) to unify parts of the landscape and found that the colour changes can be predicted with practice.

⑭ Thread the needle with 1396 (dark sage green) and begin stitching the hedges and trees near the horizon line. Use straight stitch to depict the hedges; make tiny controlled circular or overlapping vermicelli movements with the hoop. Don't complete the horizon line; leave some gaps in it. Complete the two back rows of hedging and cut the thread close to the embroidery.

⑮ Thread 1189 (dark green) and 1396 (dark sage green) through the needle; make sure both threads are engaged in the tension disc to prevent big loops forming. Sewing with two threads through the needle adds more texture and builds the embroidery up quickly. As you stitch the nearer hedges, begin to add more detail and make the trees and bushes a bit bigger.

⑯ Tighten the top tension ready for whip stitch, insert a bobbin wound with 1170 (mid dark green) into the bobbin case and load both into the machine. Start stitching the trees and hedgerows in the middle ground, using a close overlapping meandering vermicelli stitch. Using two threads through the needle and whip stitch creates the illusion of foliage. When you have finished stitching the hedges reset the tension to normal.

⑰ Review the embroidery and decide if anything needs changing: for example, some of the fields needed more definition. I used 1170 (mid dark green) to stitch rows between the furrows of the closest field and to fill in the horizon line. I used 1303 (dark evening green) to add shade to the base of the closer hedgerows and added highlights to some of the trees and hedging with 1170 (mid dark green). Trim the tabs from the front and back of the embroidery. The stitching will have begun to pull the fabric in and make it wrinkle; these distortions disappear when the embroidery is soaked, ironed and mounted.

⑱ Wind straw-coloured double knitting wool around your fingers and cut it into strands measuring about (1.5–2cm (⅝–¾in.). Fold the soluble film back to expose the brown-painted field and position the yarn snips on top so they look like stalks of corn. Begin just below the fold and work from the top downwards, overlapping the yarn and re-positioning it so it's mostly pointing towards the horizon line. Fold the film back over the yarn and secure with pins. Pin around the edge as well as the middle to stop the wool fidgeting or falling out.

⑲ Insert a white bobbin into the normal tension bobbin case and load both into the machine. Thread the needle with 1149 (beige tusk) and 1070 (tawny tan) make sure both threads are engaged in the tension disc. Tack the wool with straight stitch, making up-and-down zigzag marks to help the stitches blend in with the wool snips. Follow the direction of growth – imagine upright stalks of corn. Avoid the pins as these can be removed when the wool is secure.

Chapter 10 – Embroidering the Landscape **225**

⑳ Begin stitching the corn in the background with short upright stitches. Stagger and overlap the stitches so they imitate growing corn. Don't fill the whole field; leave some patches bare for another layer of colour. If the white bobbin thread comes to the top, loosen the top tension or swap the bobbin to a matching colour. Thread the needle with 1128 (beige brown) and 1070 (tawny tan) and stitch the bare patches of cornfield using the same style of stitch. Random patches of colour look more natural than one colour across the whole area.

㉑ Tear the soluble film away from the sky and pin it over the cornfield. If the leftover film is not big enough cut a new piece and pin this in place. Draw a few poppies in the foreground using a green pen. Group them together in patches and mark a few circles a bit further away to represent flowers growing in the field. Look online and in gardening or flower design books for good reference images to help you draw the leaves and petals.

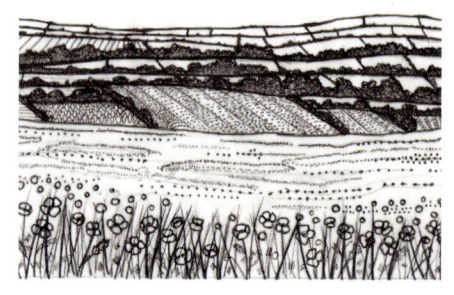

㉒ This sketch shows the placement of the poppies. If you don't like working freehand, enlarge the sketch so it is the same width as the summer cornfield design (23cm or 9in) then trace the position of the poppies onto soluble film and pin over the embroidered cornfield. Trace or draw some poppies onto a hooped scrap of calico ready to practise stitching them.

㉓ Wind 1147 (red) onto a bobbin, insert it into the normal tension bobbin case and load into the machine. Thread the needle with 1147 (red). Practise embroidering the poppies. Stitch the outside of the petals with straight stitch, and then fill them in with long machine stitches. Radiate the stitches out from the centre of the flower for each petal. Slow the speed of the machine down if you can; my machine does not have this facility, so I use light foot control to stitch slowly. The best way to make long stitches is to time when the needle is going upwards and use that moment to move the hoop a bit further than normal. This method requires practice; if you get the timing wrong you risk bending or breaking the needle. Swap to the real embroidery and stitch the poppy flowers. Cut the thread tabs between the flowers on the top of the embroidery.

㉔ Swap to the hooped calico and thread the needle with 1396 (dark sage green) and insert a bobbin wound with 1170 (mid dark green). Stitch a small dot in the centre of the larger poppies and practise stitching the stalks and leaves.

㉕ When you are happy with the results swap back to the real embroidery. Alternatively, stitch the poppies by hand, threading a chenille needle with four strands of 1147 (red) and using long stitches to fill in the petals. Use four strands of 1396 (dark sage green) to make a French knot in the middle of the poppy.

226 Chapter 10 – Embroidering the Landscape

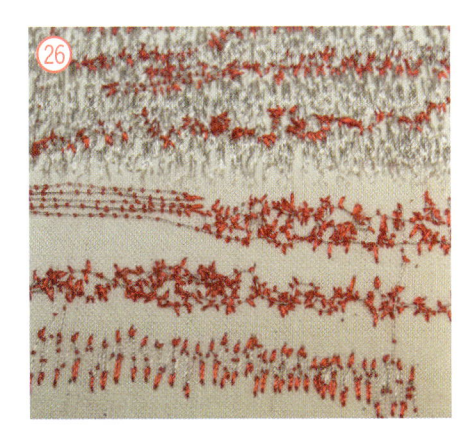

Wind a bobbin with 1147 (red), insert it into the loose tension bobbin case and load into the machine. Thread the needle with 1128 (beige brown) and tighten the tension so the machine is ready for moss stitch (refer to the moss stitch sampler for more instructions). Test the stitch on a scrap of calico. Make up-and-down zig zag movements, and look at the stitched patterns on the moss and feather stitch samplers for inspiration. The red bobbin thread should get pulled to the top to create red dots; adjust the tension until you get the right effect. Test the stitch on an embroidered patch of corn; you will notice the beige top thread blends into the background stitching.

Swap back to the embroidery and stitch patches of distant poppies, making zigzag movements so the top thread blends into the stitched corn. The red bobbin thread should get pulled to the top to create red dots; adjust the tension until you get the right effect. You can also use 1064 (yellow) or 2033 (ombre green) on the bobbin to make patches of dandelions or weeds.
Set the top tension to normal and thread the needle with 1149 (beige tusk). Insert a bobbin wound with white into the normal tension bobbin case and load both into the machine. Embroider into the corn to create some lighter bleached patches of it.

Insert a bobbin wound with 1170 (mid dark green) and thread the needle with 1396 (dark sage green) and 1048 (mid aloe green). Embroider the poppy foliage, imagining stalks, buds and leaves, then remove the paler green and stitch more detail within the foliage. Thread the needle with 1149 (beige tusk) and 1070 (tawny tan) and stitch around the poppies to tidy up the petals. Add a few straggly ears of corn by embroidering over some of the poppies. The needle might make a noise as it enters and leaves the fabric; this will be because the cotton is embroidered so densely.

㉙ Review the embroidery and make sure it's finished. Trim the thread tabs from the front and back. Immerse the embroidery in warm water, right side facing down. This helps the soluble film to dissolve from behind the dense stitching. Leave the embroidery to soak for thirty minutes to an hour, then change the water and soak again. It's best to rinse properly because film residue makes the embroidery dull. Do not wring the embroidery because wringing could damage or crack the paint. Place the embroidery right side up on an old clean towel and leave to dry.

㉚ Examine the embroidery to see if you want to make any improvements. It is important to examine the embroidery before it's mounted because it is very difficult to make changes once it's framed. The embroidery may have pulled in and warped the fabric sky but don't worry – these lumps and bumps flatten out when the embroidery is ironed. Damp press the back of the embroidery to smooth out the creases or undulations.

My embroidery needed a few alterations. I made the mistake of pinning the design to the sky, and it made holes that didn't close up with damp pressing so I disguised the holes with hand-sewn flying birds. Some of the pale patches of corn were too light so I darkened them with more stitching. I added more detail to the distant fields and added an area of yellow oilseed rape. The dipped field needed a hedge to divide it and the horizontal hedgerows needed more definition, so I threaded the needle with two threads and stitched into them.

I extended the greenery in the foreground because I felt there should be different plants growing alongside the poppies. I threaded the needle with two shades of green and embroidered around the poppies to build up the greenery. I swapped the green threads to add more variety to the foliage. I also added daisies, dandelions and stray stalks of corn.

Cut the thread tails and tabs from the front and back of the embroidery and damp press it to remove the handling marks. The finished embroidery is now ready to be mounted and framed. It could be laced over card or matted with a mount board backing, so look in Chapter 12 for further ideas and instructions.

This version of the embroidery was done following the same instructions; it has a cirrus sky and slight differences to the fields and hedgerows.

Chapter 10 – Embroidering the Landscape **229**

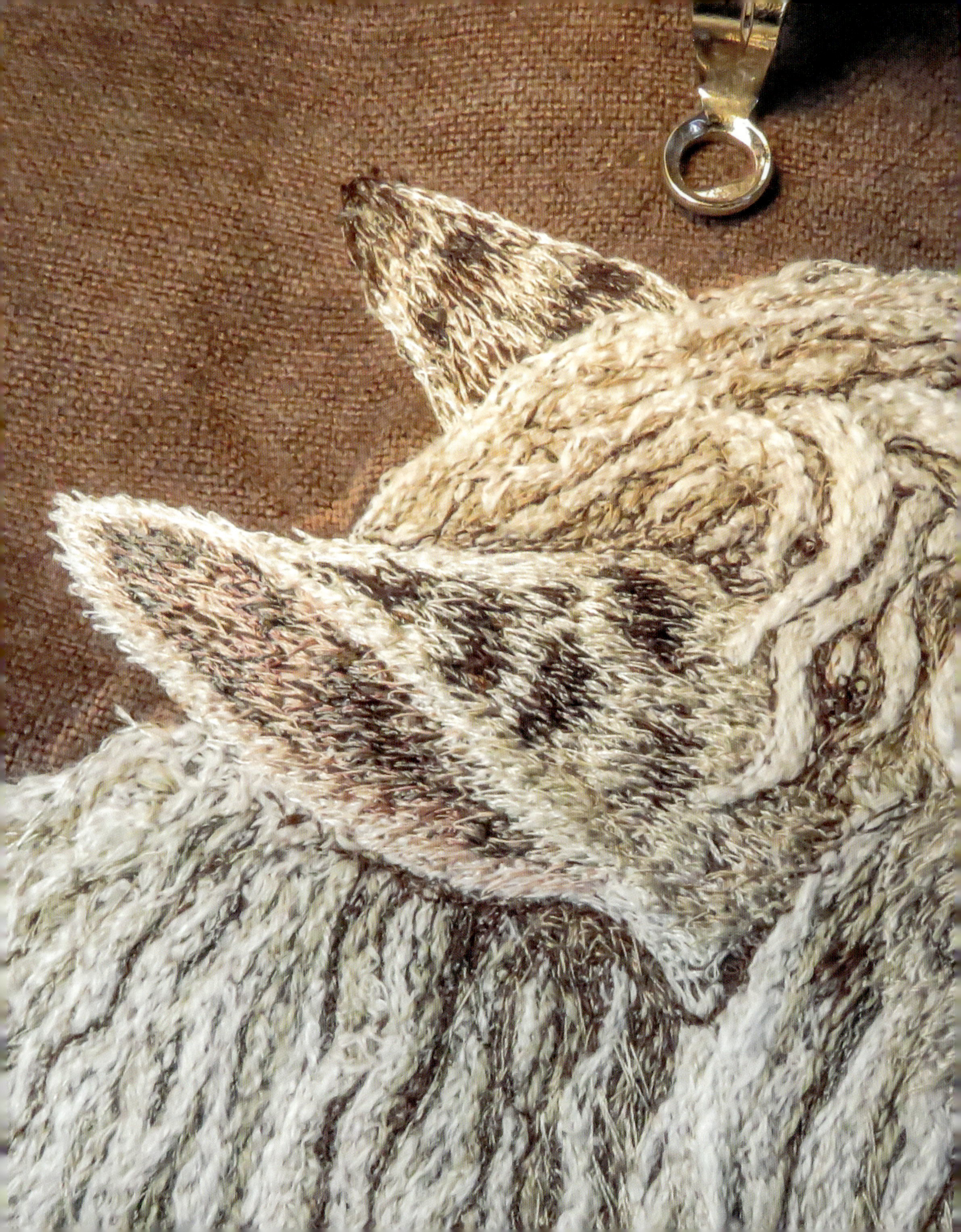

CHAPTER 11

Animals and Birds

Animals will always be close to my heart. They are among my favourite subjects to embroider, robins and foxes being much-loved muses. This chapter guides you through the process of drawing, planning and embroidering a realistic creature with straight stitch. Bring your creation to life by combining the skills and techniques you have learnt so far. How you choose to represent the animal with embroidery is down to personal choice. Embroideries of animals or birds don't have to be completely realistic; you can have fun with your subject matter and add a bit of character.

Choosing an Image

I usually start with a photo or illustration. The main advantage of using a photo is that the image is already flattened into two dimensions and it is still. Drawing a moving creature can be very frustrating, unless you like the immediacy of a quick sketch. I prefer to capture as much detail as I can because it saves time and guesswork.

Capturing personality or character is important. This was one of my first attempts to produce an animal portrait, and my dog had a dark brindle coat which made stitching her a challenge.

It's easier to translate images into embroidery that are simple. Choose a photo that is clear, and avoid images with distracting backgrounds or objects obstructing the view of the animal. Select a photo that has a strong contrast between the animal and background as

Embroidered creatures don't have to be serious. This cheeky fox was embroidered onto soluble film and organza, then appliquéd onto recycled fabric to make a fun shoulder bag.

this will help you see the negative spaces around the animal, making it easier to translate into a drawing. If the animal is too far away or blurred it won't give you a good starting point and the result will be a poorly executed embroidery. Care must be taken when using another artist's illustrations because the image may have copyright restrictions; this can cause problems if you plan to sell your finished embroideries later.

If you have not embroidered animals before, start with a simple portrait. Concentrating on the face means the features are large enough to be manageable with stitch and you don't have to worry about getting the other parts right. Choose a view that does not have much perspective; side views or front-facing heads are much easier to draw than three-quarter views.

Make sure the features such as nose, eyes and ears are clearly visible. If you are tracing a reference photo directly for embroidery it needs to be large enough to embroider. When the details are too small the hoop can become stationary, causing a lump of stitching to form underneath; such lumps are very difficult to unpick and they can cause problems when trying to move the hoop freely or stitch close to them.

How to Depict Form

Study the photo to see if you can spot the shapes that make up the form of the animal. What shape are the eyes, nose and mouth? How are they positioned on the head? Look beneath the fur; there are bones and muscles hidden under it. Look at the way the light falls on the fur or feathers and use that to help you describe the form. Avoid dark or black animals because the fur absorbs the light, making it very difficult to see the details. However, if the animal has a glossy coat you may see enough information to make an embroidery.

I made a detailed pencil study of the photo using the grid method to help me produce an accurate likeness of the robin.

Another way to depict form is to use stitch direction; look at the fur and see in which direction it is growing. Copy the direction of growth with embroidery. Is the fur coarse or smooth, short or long? Try to depict the length and texture of the fur with stitch. Does it have a pattern? Break the pattern down into separate areas of colour. What are the main colours and are they easy to replicate in thread? Can you select enough threads to match the photo? Simple questions like these help you plan the embroidery in your mind before you have begun to stitch.

Making a Drawing or Tracing

When you have selected the photo, the next stage is to make a drawing of it. How you draw is down to personal choice. You may like to use descriptive lines or cross-hatching rather than pencil shading. Use a medium that you are familiar with: you may prefer to use pen and ink, coloured pencils or marker pens. Drawing is beneficial because it helps you to understand the structure and anatomy of the animal and plan stages ready for embroidery. Proper

The colour changes on this working drawing look like a painting-by-numbers instruction sheet. Taking time to plan colour changes saves time when embroidering because you have already decided the shape and size of each patch of colour.

Look at the direction of the fur or feathers; this will be the stitch direction too. Make a new tracing of the photo, draw round each area to show where the direction of growth changes and draw arrows to indicate the direction. Use the tracing as a reminder to alter stitch direction when embroidering.

looking and observation is the key to creating a good-quality drawing.

If drawing is not your thing simply enlarge the photo to the size of the embroidery and trace it – to be honest, tracing saves a lot of time. Tracing is not cheating because it still helps you see the structure of the animal. Begin by tracing the features and details; once you have those you will start to see how the fur grows and where it changes direction. Tracing paper also mutes the photo, making it easier to see

If you like drawing outlines and working in black and white you may prefer to stitch a simple outline. Plain threads and fabrics suit this method. The design was traced onto soluble film and pinned to calico. The outline is embroidered with straight stitch and the thickness of the lines altered by embroidering them twice. The design is sewn with Madeira Cotona no. 50 in colour 791 (chocolate).

This appliqué is an extension of the previous line embroidery. Blocks of colour are added with patterned quilting fabrics. Once in position the carefully cut pieces are bonded to the background with heat-fusible glue. The design is traced onto water-soluble film and pinned over the appliqué. Details are embroidered with straight stitch, using Madeira Cotona no. 50 in colour 500 (black).

This solid embroidery is built up with layers of straight stitch. This type of embroidery is called thread-painting because areas of colour are filled in with thread. Thread colours can be mixed and blended with careful layering. Thread-paintings require thoughtful planning to get the colour changes in the right order.

colour changes and areas of light and dark. You may need to make more than one tracing if the reference photo or drawing is complex.

Planning the Embroidery

You need to decide what the finished animal embroidery will become, as the end use determines the method and choice of materials used. Will the embroidery be an image or turned into something functional like a bag, cushion or box lid? Making this decision early helps you choose the correct fabric, thread and stabilizers for the project.

The style or method of embroidery influences the type of fabric, soluble film, interfacing or threads used. Are you going to produce a simple outline, solid thread-painting, appliqué or quilted embroidery? Fabrics with less stitching do not need much support compared to those that are heavily embroidered. The stitched robin shows the same subject matter stitched using different techniques and materials.

The finished embroidery can be enhanced with acrylic paint, fabric paint or ink. Cotton, viscose or rayon threads accept watered-down fabric paint or dye very well. The fence and robin have been painted to add shading and detail.

This is my first embroidery of a robin. He is padded to make him stand out, as are the tiny pebbles. The padding was done after the embroidery was finished; this technique is called trapunto quilting.

Chapter 11 – Animals and Birds   233

Choosing a pale background for a sheep with a light fleece means the embroidery blends in more and the overall effect is gentle and calming.

Changing the background to a dark brown makes the sheep stand out more and become more dramatic and imposing.

Choosing Fabric for Animal Embroideries

Thread-paintings work best stitched onto a plain background; keep away from printed fabrics, slubs or woven patterns because the pattern can be seen through the embroidery. Look at the original photo to help you choose a suitable background colour. You need a strong contrast between the background and the embroidery to make it visible.

Natural fibres and plain weaves work best for dense embroideries. Woven cotton, linen or fine canvas are a good choice because they handle dense stitching and being put into a hoop. Firm cotton or calico needs the support of tear-away interfacing if the embroidery is going to be heavily stitched.

Think about fibre content in relation to the subject and the methods used; heavy stitching on satin weaves can pull the woven threads causing unsightly lines so these fabrics are best avoided for heavy embroidery. Fabrics with pile such as velvet can distort detailed embroidery, and bulges or tucks are difficult to remove because damp pressing flattens the pile of the fabric.

Choosing Thread

Select a good-quality brand with a large range of natural colours. Look for a good choice of brown, rust, beige, tan, grey, black, cream and white, as not having the right shade or tone can spoil the finished embroidery. Realistic embroideries need a wide range of colours to replicate the ones in the reference photo: for instance, the little robin project has sixteen thread colours.

Studying the texture of the fur will help you choose the right thread for the embroidery. Fibre content is very important because it changes the appearance of the embroidery. Do you need the sheen of rayon or viscose, the subtlety of matt cotton or the fluffy texture of wool? Shiny viscose, rayon or polyester work best for animals with glossy fur, feathers or scales. Matt threads like cotton may be more suitable for creatures with rough coats such as sheep or big cats.

The next important thing to consider is thread weight. Thread weight or thickness is indicated on the reel or cop, indicated by 'Nr' or 'No'. The thread weight or thickness must be taken into consideration when choosing threads for animal portraits because the weight of the thread changes the appearance of the fur. The most popular thread weight for machine embroidery is no. 40, which was used for the little robin project. As you become more experienced you can begin introducing different thread weights.

Animals with fine fur embroider more effectively when stitched with medium- or lightweight threads such as nos. 40, 50, 60 or 80. Fine threads are very useful for adding detail and layering colours without adding bulk. Medium- or fine-weight threads can be threaded through the needle two or three at a time: using multiple threads fills in areas of stitch quickly, imitates thicker thread and blends colours to create a marled effect, very useful for animals with brindle or ticked fur.

Animals with thick fur can be stitched with medium- or heavyweight threads such as nos. 40, 30 or 12. Thick threads are great for filling in areas of dense stitch quickly but it's harder to add fine detail and blend colours with them. No. 12 is one of the thickest threads available for machine embroidery, Madeira produce Lana, a no. 12 weight thread that has a wool content; this thread is very effective when used with other threads for animal portraits and is used in the rustic sheep project.

Machine embroidery requires a size 90/14 universal needle. I have had no problems running no. 30, 40, 50 and 60

This sheep is embroidered with Madeira Lana; the thick thread has a wool content that suits the subject matter. The embroidery is stitched with seven shades of Lana thread. The eyes are stitched with a single shade of Madeira Cotona; these are backed with metallic tissue and organza so less stitching is needed to add the details.

Madeira Lana can be brushed with a special brush or the rough side of Velcro to tease out the fibres to create a fluffy pile. This method works better with long stitches because more fibres are be caught when brushing.

threads through a size 14 universal needle. Thick or specialist machine threads need a thicker needle, otherwise they will break or shred. Lana needs a special size 110/18 sharp Madeira wool needle for it to run smoothly. You will also find that the machine needs to be cleaned more often when using Lana because fluff collects under the feeder teeth; unwanted fluff can cause noise or missed stitches.

Stitch Types

I embroider my animals and birds with straight stitch, using stitch length and direction to describe the texture of the fur or feathers. Long stitches are really good at replicating feathers or sleek fur but they are harder to make because the hoop needs to travel further to create them. Moving the hoop quickly creates longer stitches; it's important to get your timing right because moving the hoop at the wrong moment can bend or break the needle. Short stitches are easier to make so it's easy to get stuck in short stitch mode. Short stitches are useful for depicting short coats or rough fur. When I started embroidering animals I didn't like mixing stitch length or thread type; this gave my early work a flat appearance but with experience I have learnt to experiment and be brave with my choices.

STEP-BY-STEP PROJECT
Little Robin

YOU WILL NEED

Equipment
- Photo of a robin
- Photocopier or computer with scanner and printer
- Sewing machine with drop feed or darning plate
- Darning or embroidery foot
- Empty bobbins
- 15cm (6in.) wooden hoop
- Small slotted screwdriver
- Size 90/14 universal machine needle
- Sharp hand-sewing needle
- Glass-headed pins
- Embroidery scissors
- Fabric scissors
- Iron
- Ironing cloth
- Graphite pencils in various grades
- Brown water-soluble watercolour pencil
- Pencil sharpener
- Eraser
- Ruler
- Set square
- Sink or bowl of water to wash the embroidery
- Old towel on which to dry the embroidery

Materials
- A4 white paper
- Drawing paper
- Tracing paper
- Pre-washed calico approximately 35.5 × 30.5cm (14 × 12in.)
- Vilene Solufleece or similar non-woven water-soluble fabric
- Stitch 'n' Tear or similar tear-away stabilizer
- Madeira Bobbinfil no. 70 in colour 1001 (white)
- Madeira Cotona thread no. 50 in colours 612 (dark ecru), 791 (chocolate), 500 (black)
- Gütermann Sulky rayon no. 40 thread in colours 1327 (dark whisper grey), 1059 (dark tawny brown), 1313 (bittersweet), 1179 (dark taupe), 1071 (off white), 1002 (soft white), 1021 (maple), 1055 (tawny tan), 1180 (medium taupe).
- Madeira Classic no. 40 thread in colours 1128 (taupe), 1060 (pussy willow), 1240 (stone), 1259 (cocoa)
- Fine silk or cotton perle

Design template
- Little Robin

Machine used
- Bernina 801
- Feeder teeth down
- Normal tension

Robins and sparrows are my favourite garden birds; I love the cheeky chatter of the sparrows and the flash of colour from the robin. One robin is very friendly and follows me around when I'm gardening; it's not so courageous when it sees a camera, and it disappears or perches on the highest bough. The best photo was when it decided to settle on the ugliest thing in the garden, a wheelie bin wheel. The best way to resolve the ugly perch was to draw the robin and edit the bin wheel from the drawing. Drawing the image helped me understand the shape and form of the body so that I could redraw the feet on a more suitable surface.

This project demonstrates how to use the grid method to copy a photograph and turn it into a realistic drawing. The drawing is edited and turned into a working drawing, which helps decide the method of embroidery, the threads and colours used and which parts to sew first. Non-woven soluble fabric is used to stabilize the fabric and transfer the design. The robin is embroidered with straight stitch and layered threads to create a detailed thread-painting. The background is kept simple and decorated with hand-sewn running stitch and French knots because the robin needs to be the star of the embroidery.

Print out a colour copy of the robin, using my photo or sourcing your own. You may need to enlarge the photo to make it easier to see. My photo measured approximately 16 × 12.5cm (6¼ × 5in.) when printed. Look at the photo and decide which parts to remove; this composes the design ready for embroidery.

Use a ruler and HB pencil to draw a grid onto the printed copy. The size of the grid squares depends on the complexity of the image. I divided my grid into 12 vertical × 16 horizontal squares, each one measuring 1 × 1cm (3/8 × 3/8 in.). I chose this size because the print was small and had lots of detail.

Draw a grid on the plain paper, using a ruler, set square and HB pencil. Make sure the number of squares in each row and column are the same as the print. To keep the drawing the same size make the grid squares 1 × 1cm (3/8 × 3/8 in.). Alter the size of the destination grid squares to increase or reduce the size of the drawing. For example, drawing a grid with 1.5cm (5/8in.) squares increases the size of the image by about 50 per cent. The grid method is handy if you don't have access to a photocopier.

Copy the image one square at a time; this stops you looking at the whole thing and panicking about drawing the difficult bits. Be prepared to rub out parts of the drawing and redraw to get things right. I sometimes turn my photo and paper upside down because it helps me to see the negative space in the squares. When most of the information is transferred to the grid drawing, rub away the grid lines and work into the drawing, adding shade and detail.

You may prefer to use another medium to finish the design; you can add watercolour pencil, pastels or paint freely. Scan and print or photocopy the finished drawing; making a copy prevents accidental damage to the original artwork.

Trace the details of the copy onto tracing paper with a sharp pencil. Pay particular attention to the wing feather divisions and describe colour changes and the direction of feather growth. Make sure the beak, eye and feet are accurately portrayed as errors can be greatly exaggerated in stitch. The Little Robin template can be found in the back of this book.

Cut out two pieces of Vilene Solufleece water-soluble fabric large enough to cover the design. Pin one piece of soluble fabric to the traced design and trace it with a brown water-soluble pencil. Coloured pencils work better on soluble fabric because they don't get caught in the fibres. Pin two layers of soluble fabric to the middle of the calico, traced design on top. Two layers of water-soluble add more stability to the fabric.

Chapter 11 – Animals and Birds 237

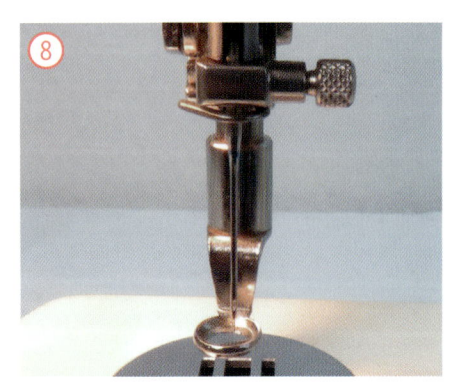

⑧ Lower the feeder teeth or clip on a darning plate. Attach a darning foot or embroidery foot and insert a size 90/14 universal needle. Wind Madeira Bobbinfil onto an empty bobbin, load into a normal tension bobbin case and insert both into the machine. Thread the needle with Cotona in colour 612 (dark ecru) and turn the balance wheel to bring both threads to the top, then set the stitch type to straight.

⑨ Pin two layers of tear-away stabilizer to the back of the design. Put the calico in a hoop so the pinned robin design is central; pull the calico taut and tighten the hoop with a screwdriver.

⑩ Straight-stitch the outline and dark areas of the feet. Stitch the details; do not fill the foot with embroidery because this makes the bird look heavy. Thread the needle with Madeira Classic 1259 (cocoa) and add some more detail to the legs; embroider over the areas to darken them but do not overwork the legs. Thread the needle with Cotona 500 in black and stitch the eye and beak division. Trim the thread tabs with small embroidery scissors.

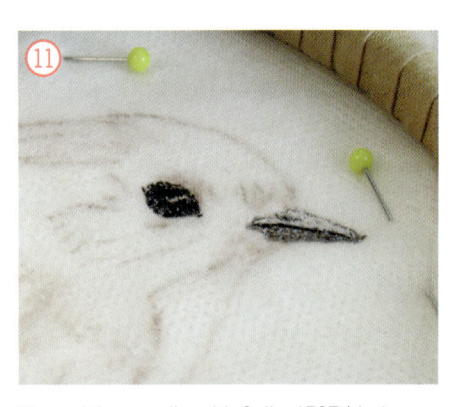

⑪ Thread the needle with Sulky 1327 (dark whisper grey) and embroider the pale upper beak. Ensure the straight stitches are horizontal along the length of the beak. Thread the needle with Madeira Classic 1240 (stone) and stitch the dark part of the beak and nostril. Trim the loose ends and thread tabs.

⑫ Thread the needle with Sulky 1313 (bittersweet) and embroider the pale part of the red breast. Follow the direction of the feathers and make the stitches a bit longer by slowing down the speed of the foot pedal or moving the hoop more quickly. Long machine stitches have more of a sheen so they look like feathers. Thread the needle with Sulky 1021 (maple) and embroider the dark parts of the red breast, allowing the stitches to mix with the paler ones. Trim the thread tabs with embroidery scissors.

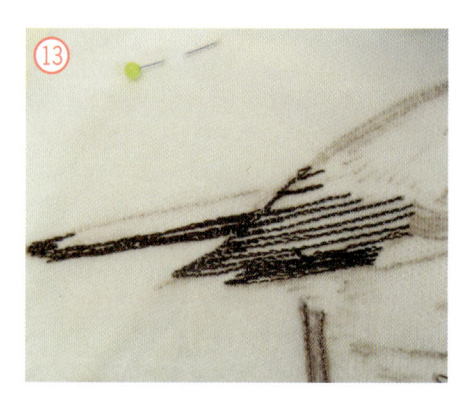

⑬ Re-position the hoop so the tail and wings are central. Thread the needle with Sulky 1059 (dark tawny brown) and embroider the wing divisions. Sew two rows of neat straight stitch on the drawn lines; sew down the line then sew back up it. Try to control the hoop so the later stitches are on top of the first without any wobbles. Cut the thread tabs between the stitches and unpick the wobbles.

14 Thread the machine with Sulky 1180 (medium taupe) and stitch the darker parts of the wing, tail and back. Thread the machine with Madeira Classic 1128 (taupe) and embroider the paler parts of the wing, tail, back and belly near the base of the tail. Trim the thread tabs to avoid catching the machine foot on them.

15 Re-position the hoop so the body is central. Embroider the pale part of the head and back with Madeira Classic 1128 (taupe). Thread the needle with Madeira 1060 (pussy willow) and stitch highlights on the back, head and wings. Use the same colour to embroider the mid-tones on the belly, then cut the thread tabs and tails.

16 Thread the needle with Sulky 1071 (off white) and embroider the pale part of the belly. Stitch the eye highlight with 1071 too, stitching by hand if it is too difficult to stitch by machine.

17 Thread the needle with Cotona 791 (chocolate) and stitch the wing divisions, then stitch a small amount of brown into the eye. Thread the needle with Sulky 1179 (dark taupe) and embroider more shading on the body, tail and wings. Cut the thread tabs close to the embroidery.

18 Thread the needle with Sulky 1002 (soft white) and add some brightness to the pale feathers near the breast, but do not add too many white stitches. Thread the needle with Sulky 1055 (tawny tan) and embroider some highlights on the breast and areas around the beak. Use any combination of colours already used to finish the embroidery and add more detail if needed. Remember to cut the thread tabs when changing threads.

19 Take the embroidery out of the hoop and remove the tear-away stabilizer. Put the embroidery back in the hoop so it's ready for hand-sewing. Thread a sharp hand-sewing needle with three threads: Sulky 1179 (dark taupe), 1180 (medium taupe) and Madeira Classic 1259 (cocoa). The three threads blend together when stitched and create the illusion of thicker thread.

Chapter 11 – Animals and Birds   **239**

20 Use simple running stitch to embroider the ground. Vary the stitch length and re-sew some areas to add thickness to random stitches. Thread a needle with brown variegated silk or fine cotton perle and add some French knots and straight stitches to the ground. Thread the needle with Sulky 1179 (dark taupe) and 1180 (medium taupe) and use these two threads to embroider some small running stitches in the gaps. Thread the needle with just Sulky 1180 (medium taupe) and embroider some tiny running stitches on the ends of the lines.

21 Wash the soluble fabric away and leave the embroidery to soak in warm water for thirty minutes to an hour. Rinse the embroidery in clean water and leave to dry face up on an old towel. Soluble can be trapped behind the stitches and leave a residue; the calico will become stiff and the threads transparent and dark. Repeat the washing process if this happens.

22 Press the embroidery on the back, using a cloth to protect the stitches. If the creases won't come out use a damp cloth and press the back again. Look at the embroidery to decide if anything needs changing. I felt the ground was too sparse and needed some more hand stitching so I drew the design directly onto the calico with a brown watercolour pencil.

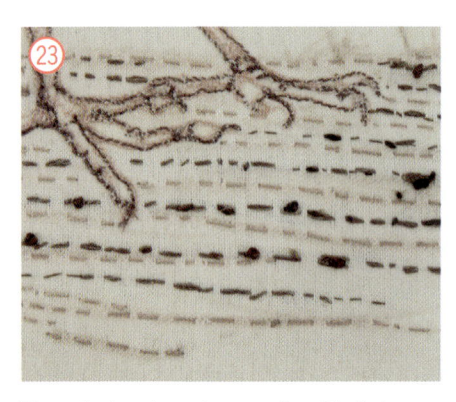

23 Thread a hand-sewing needle with Cotona 612 (dark ecru) and Madeira Classic 1128 (taupe) and embroider over the brown pencil lines with running stitch. I decided the robin needed some roughing up – he was too neat and tidy – so I added some ruffled feathers with a few simple hand stitches.

24 I noticed the newly embroidered thread had more sheen and colour; this meant dissolved soluble fabric was still trapped in the stitches. I soaked the embroidery in water to remove the remaining soluble and brown watercolour pencil. The embroidery was damp pressed on the back to remove the creases. The eye had some white dots from the bobbin so I darkened them with a black Staedtler pigment liner.

25 The robin is now ready to be framed in an embroidery hoop; see Chapter 12 for suggestions.

STEP-BY-STEP PROJECT
Rustic Sheep

YOU WILL NEED

Equipment
- Colour photo or image of a sheep
- Photocopier or computer with scanner and printer
- Sewing machine with drop feed or darning plate
- Embroidery or darning foot
- Empty bobbins
- Size 90/14 universal machine needles
- Madeira Lana size 110/18 needle
- Embroidery scissors
- Fabric scissors
- Glass-headed pins
- 15cm (6in.) wooden hoop
- Paintbrush
- Sponge brush
- Palette
- Iron
- Damp ironing cloth
- Seam ripper or quick unpick
- Brown Stabilo Fineliner or permanent black pen
- HB pencil
- Pencil sharpener
- Eraser
- Sink or bowl of water to wash the embroidery
- Old towel on which to dry the embroidery

Materials
- White A4 paper
- Tracing paper
- Linen canvas
- Romeo water-soluble film
- Waterproof sepia ink
- Brown acrylic paint
- Madeira Bobbinfil no. 70 thread in black and white
- Madeira Cotona no 50 thread on colours 660 (light brown), 678 (coffee brown), 500 (black), 792 (dark charcoal), 503 (antique white), 791 (chocolate), 688 (grey), 504 (ecru), 735 (tawny tan), 700 (greige), 612 (dark ecru), 670 (peach)
- Madeira Classic no. 40 thread in colours 1240 (stone), 1141 (mauve)
- Madeira Lana no. 12 thread in colours 3890 (off white), 3845 (coffee), 3841 (light tan), 3601 (white)

Design template
- Rustic Sheep

Machine used
- Bernina 801
- Feeder teeth down
- Normal tension

This project shows how to embroider a realistic sheep directly from a photograph. It gives an honest account of the embroidery process and teaches you that it's okay to make mistakes by showing you how to correct them. You begin by tracing the photo to capture the details and describe the tonal changes, then transfer the design to painted linen by tracing it onto Romeo soluble film.

You will discover how versatile straight stitch can be and see how stitch length and direction are used to create the embroidery. You will use different thread types to add character and depth and learn the importance of using the correct needle for each thread type. As the embroidery builds up you will begin to blend different colours and fibres together to create gentle shading. You will review the embroidery and make important decisions about its progress.

Choose a photo of a sheep; it's easier to translate a profile or front view into embroidery. Use a computer with a scanner or a photocopier to enlarge the photo to the exact size of the finished embroidery. Print off a colour copy; the print must be the same size as the embroidery because the design is traced directly from this copy.

The metal gate is distracting because it hides part of the face. Tracing the photo helps you to fill in the blanks and understand the structure of the sheep's head: for instance, how the ears join the head or the shape of the nose. Tracing paper mutes the tonal values, making the detailed areas easier to copy. Different colours are represented with dotted outlines, and the tracing becomes a working drawing, instructing you where to sew the details and make thread changes.

Chapter 11 – Animals and Birds   241

3 You may prefer to trace the Rustic Sheep template at the back of this book. Whatever, the source, cut a piece of Romeo soluble film large enough to cover the tracing. Pin the Romeo to the tracing paper and trace the design with a brown Stabilo Fineliner or permanent black pen. Take care when removing the pins because the drawing might not be dry and it could smudge.

4 Choose a background fabric and decide what size it needs to be. I picked linen canvas because it suited the rustic nature of the sheep. However, the linen was too pale, so it was soaked to remove the size and prepare it for painting. If you do this, pin the damp linen to a silk painting frame and paint both sides with a mixture of waterproof sepia ink and brown acrylic paint.

5 Leave it to dry then rinse in warm water to make sure the paint is colour-fast; you don't want the paint to dye the embroidery threads. Some of the paint may wash out, giving the linen a worn effect; this adds to the rustic nature of the subject. Iron the damp linen to set the colour and remove the creases.

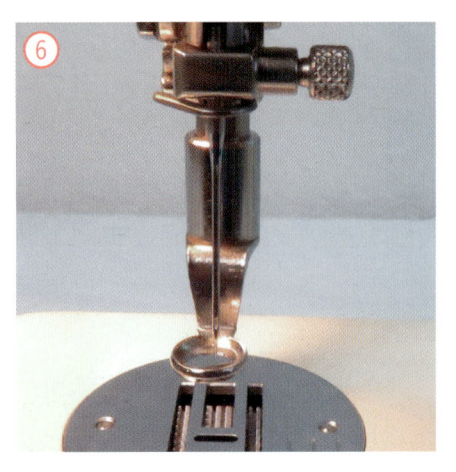

6 Drop the feeder teeth or attach a darning plate and attach an embroidery or darning foot. Insert a size 90/14 universal needle and set the stitch type to straight. Wind an empty bobbin with Madeira black Bobbinfil, insert it into the normal tension bobbin case and load both into the machine.

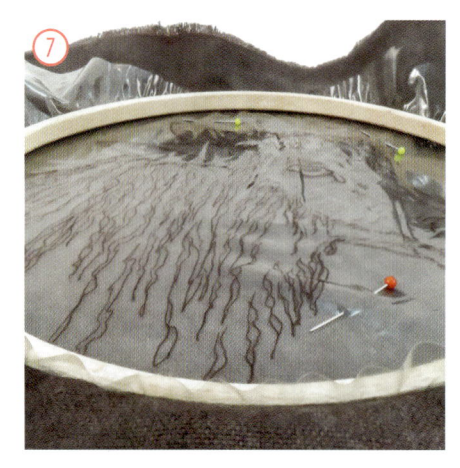

7 Position the film so it's in the middle of the fabric or wherever you want the embroidery to be placed; pin to secure. Place the pinned linen in an embroidery hoop, taking care not to catch yourself on the pins. Note that thick fabric can be troublesome to hoop but it needs to be hooped because the sheep will be embroidered with dense stitch.

8 Thread the needle with Cotona 660 (light brown) and stitch the eye's iris. Thread the needle with Cotona 678 (coffee brown) and blend some of this colour into the embroidered iris. Thread the needle with Cotona 500 (black) and stitch the pupil. Note that a sheep's pupil is much more like a rectangle with rounded corners than you might expect. Thread the needle with Cotona 792 (dark charcoal) and embroider the lower lid and corner tear drop. Change the bobbin to Madeira Bobbinfil in white and thread the needle with Cotona 503 (antique white). Stitch the fur around the eye, following the direction of growth, then stitch the eyelashes.

Thread the needle with Cotona 500 (black) and stitch the darkest part of the nostril and lip. Thread the needle with Cotona 792 (dark charcoal) and add more detail to the dark nose and mouth. Thread the needle with Cotona 791 (chocolate) and stitch some of the fur around the nostril and muzzle; some of this stitching acts as an undercoat for the pale fleece. Thread the needle with Madeira Classic 1240 (stone) and sew the pale parts of the muzzle where the fur starts to grow around the nose and mouth.

Thread the needle with Cotona 688 (grey) and blend stitches into the pale areas of the muzzle. Follow the direction of the fur; this stitching acts as a base for the pale fur and fleece.

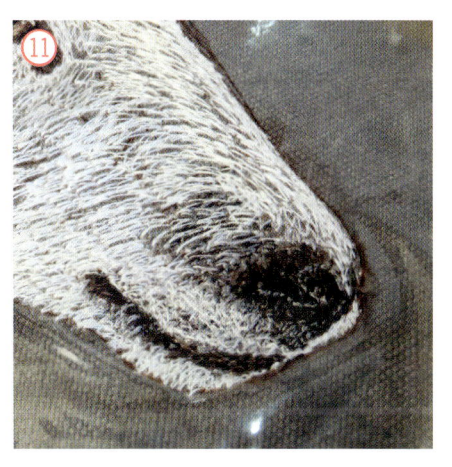

Change the bobbin to Madeira Bobbinfil in white and thread the needle with Cotona 503 (antique white). Stitch the palest parts of the face, allowing some of the linen to show through and following the direction of fur growth. Thread the needle with Cotona 504 (ecru) and embroider the medium tones of the face. Blend the stitches together; don't stitch densely.

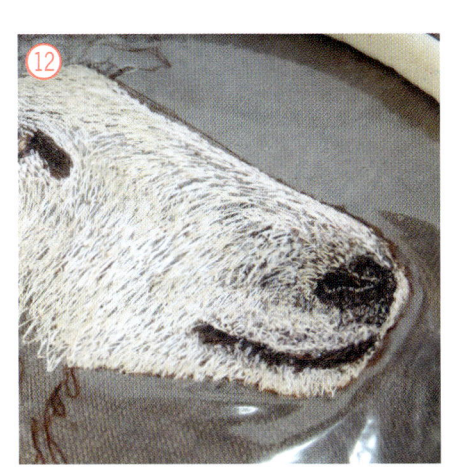

Thread the needle with Cotona 735 (tawny tan) and begin to stitch into the dark areas of the face, blending some of the stitching into the previous embroidery. Thread the needle with Cotona 700 (greige) and add areas of shade to the face and muzzle.

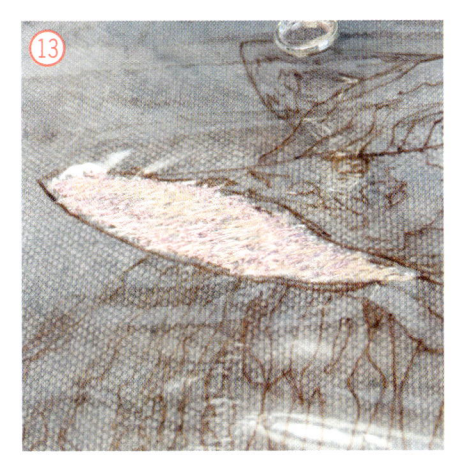

Re-position the hoop so the ear is central and thread the needle with Cotona 612 (dark ecru). Stitch the pinkest parts of the ear; follow the direction of the fur and don't stitch densely. Thread the needle with Cotona 660 (light brown) and embroider the darker parts of the inner ear. Thread the needle with Madeira Classic 1141 (mauve) and work some deeper pink shading into the inner ear.

Thread the needle with Madeira Classic 1240 (stone). Embroider the dark grey spots of the inner ear, allowing some of the pink thread to show through. Thread the needle with Cotona 503 (antique white) and stitch the pale outer edge of the ear and the highlighted parts on the top of the ear. Thread the needle with Cotona 670 (peach) and stitch the darker parts of the outer ear, working the stitches so they blend in with the paler parts of the ear.

Chapter 11 – Animals and Birds   **243**

15 Thread the needle with Cotona 504 (ecru) and layer more stitching on the outside of the ear. Thread the needle with Cotona 791 (chocolate) and stitch the centre of the dark ear spots to allow previous stitches to show through. Thread the needle with Cotona 792 (dark charcoal) and work into the dark ear spots. Thread the needle with Cotona 500 (black) and stitch the centre of the ear dots. Continue using a combination of threads already used to complete the ears.

16 Re-position the hoop so the top of the head is central. Change the needle to a Madeira Lana size 110/18 needle. Thread the needle with Lana 3890 (off white); the wool and acrylic content means it's the ideal thread to stitch the fleece. The top tension may need reducing to allow for the thickness of the thread. Embroider the palest parts of the fleece around the head, following the direction of growth.

17 Thread the needle with Lana 3845 (coffee) and start stitching mid-tones into the fleece. Thread the needle with Lana 3841 (light tan) and blend some of this darker shade into the mid-tones and shadows. Thread the needle with Lana 3601 (white) and add highlights to the tips of the fleece.

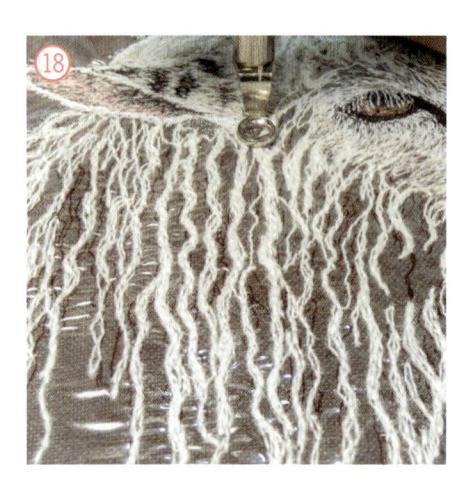

18 Re-position the hoop to stitch the lower part of the fleece. Thread the needle with Lana 3890 (off white) and embroider the lightest tones. Follow the direction of growth and try to capture some of the characteristics of the fleece. The hoop may need to be re-positioned several times to stitch all of the fleece.

19 Thread the needle with Lana 3845 (coffee) and embroider some mid-tones into the fleece. Thread the needle with Lana 3841 (light tan) and use this to add dark details to the fleece. Thread the needle with Lana 3601 (white) and embroider some highlights but don't stitch too many white areas because fleece is not pure white. Change the machine needle back to a size 90/14 universal. Thread the needle with Cotona 791 (chocolate) and add definition to some areas of the fleece. Pay particular attention to areas around the ear and where the fur turns to fleece.

20 Continue blending thinner threads into the embroidery; layering colours breaks up the harshness of Cotona 791 (chocolate). Define the fleece and face with a combination of threads: Cotona 735 (tawny tan), Cotona 670 (peach), Cotona 660 (light brown) and Madeira Classic 1240 (stone).

㉑ Study the embroidery to decide if it needs further work: for example, the nose had lost its shape and the nostrils were not clear enough. If a complicated area needs refining, trace the corresponding part of the design on a scrap of soluble film and pin in place. Machine embroidery distorts the fabric so the soluble patch may not line up with the embroidery below.

㉒ When the stitching is done, peel away the excess film from the patch and look to see if anything else needs further work or correction. The fabric is starting to pull because of the dense stitching in the nose area. The last stages of an embroidery should be approached with caution: you need to be aware of your mistakes and correct them but you must be able to stop so you don't overwork the embroidery.

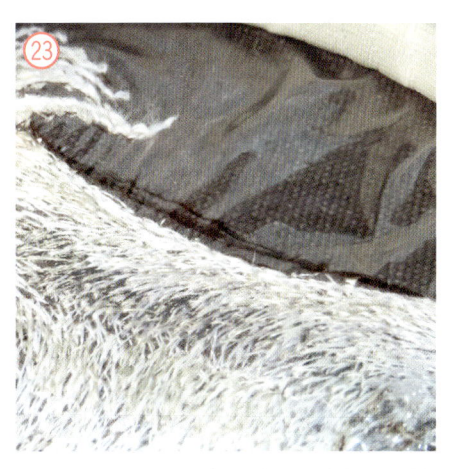

㉓ The fabric distortion had changed the profile of the face, which now curved and made the sheep look more like a Shetland pony. I redrew the outline onto the film and filled in the gap, blending the stitches so there was no visible join. I could then remove the embroidery from the hoop and cut away the remnants of soluble film.

㉔ Have another look at your embroidery to see if anything needs changing. I was not happy with the shading on the face; it needed darker tones. I cut a piece of scrap film and pinned it to the embroidery, then drew outlines directly onto the film with a brown Stabilo Fineliner pen so I could see exactly where I needed to sew. I embroidered shadows onto the face to create more form and used Cotona 700 (greige) to add more definition to the curls in the fleece.

㉕ Soluble film will be trapped beneath the embroidery stitches. Dissolve the film away in warm water then leave the embroidery to soak. Residue from the paint or pen may colour the water, so rinse the embroidery and leave to dry face up on a towel. Do not wring out the embroidery because this could break threads or mark the linen. When the embroidery is nearly dry, damp press it on the back to remove the creases and undulations. Use a damp cloth to protect the embroidery and don't press the front of the work.

㉖ You may find areas that need further tweaking. In my case, the eyelashes were too long so I carefully unpicked some of the length with embroidery scissors and a seam ripper. The unpicking was done on the back of the embroidery; the stitch length is small enough to stop the embroidery fraying. Check for loose ends or tabs on the front of the embroidery and cut them off. The embroidery may need pressing again to remove marks caused by handling. Iron the back using a cloth to protect the surface of the embroidery.

㉗ The embroidery is now ready to be framed. My sheep looked cheeky and bold so I felt he would benefit being mounted away from the wall. See Chapter 12 for more ideas about framing.

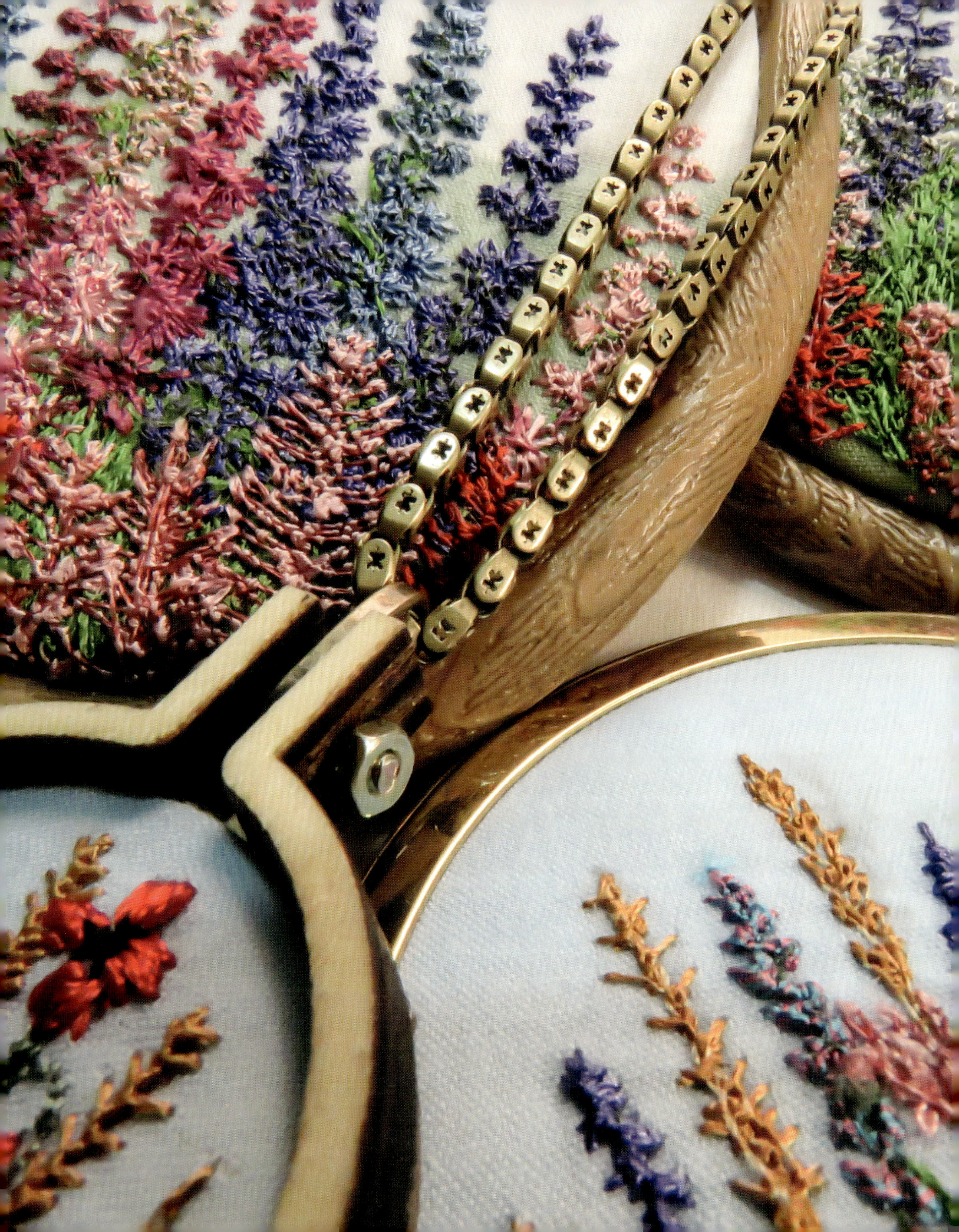

CHAPTER 12

Finishing Your Work

Finishing your work is the final stage of the creative process, and beautiful embroideries deserve to be used, displayed and enjoyed. I certainly have my fair share of semi-finished projects languishing in boxes and portfolios. There are many reasons for leaving work unfinished: it could be that the work no longer matches the decor, you didn't know how to finish it or you simply ran out of time or energy.

The first step is choosing a finished embroidery, so think about how it's going to be mounted, presented or used. To help you decide, think about the subject matter, materials used and size of the work. An embroidery doesn't have to be turned into a framed image or hanging; it can become a useful or wearable item such as clothing, jewellery, a brooch, a hair accessory, or a scarf, bag or box.

Displaying a Finished Embroidery

There are many ways to display and mount finished embroideries; suitable methods include:

- lacing over a board without a frame
- framing in a wooden embroidery hoop or plastic flexi-hoop
- framing without glass
- framing with glass and mount board
- turning the embroidery into a hanging.

The method chosen depends on how the embroidery was made and the subject matter. For instance, traditional embroideries benefit from being mounted in a conventional manner using a frame mount and glass whilst modern abstract pieces might suit being laced over a backing board for display without a frame. The depth of the embroidery determines how it is going to be mounted or framed; raised surfaces need to be separated from the glass to prevent the embroidery being squashed or distorted.

Professional Framing

Using an experienced framer has many advantages. They can advise you how to prepare the embroidery so it is ready for framing, and they may even lace or stretch the embroidery for you. A good framer will tell you if a mount board and spacer are needed and help you choose a frame style and mount colour suitable for the embroidery. If the embroidery has been specifically commissioned I would recommend having it framed because it adds value to the work; also the frame should last longer and look more professional. Having the image framed removes a lot of stress and saves time. The drawbacks are you may have to travel to find a reputable framer and it costs a lot more than doing it yourself.

DIY Framing

A DIY-framed embroidery can look just as good as one framed by a professional. The advantage of DIY framing is that it gives you total control over the whole creative process. Framing an embroidery can be time-consuming but it is worth the effort to get the finish and style that you want. Before you begin framing you need to ask yourself a few questions about the embroidery.

Should the Embroidery be Protected from Dust?

If this is the case the embroidery should be framed behind glass. The problem with this method is that it flattens the embroidery, both physically and visually. There are many types of glass available for framing: the glass can have a matt finish to prevent glare, it can have UV protection to prevent fading or it can be ultra-clear. If you buy a readymade frame off the shelf the glass might not have these special properties.

What Type of Frame is Needed?

The frame needs to be the right size, shape, colour and style for the embroidery. Consider the shape of the frame – will the embroidery suit a square, rectangular, round or oval frame? Modern works suit simple plain frames whilst traditional embroideries could be framed with a more ornate style of frame. The colour of the frame should be in harmony with the embroidery and it should not detract from or steal attention from the embroidery. A frame that is too small cramps the design and a frame that is too big makes the embroidery look like an island in an ocean of fabric.

I have made plenty of mistakes by buying the perfect frame only to find it's not quite the right colour or style when I get home. Be watchful of quality as there is no point in framing a beautiful embroidery in a cheap badly made frame; the motto is choose carefully and double-check your measurements. You may find that shop-bought frames are not deep enough to accommodate the glass, mount board and embroidery. Laced embroideries need a lot of depth; they are best suited to deep box frames which ensure there is room for the glass, mount board, spacer, embroidery, backing board and MDF back panel.

Does the Embroidery Need to be Laced?

This depends on how the embroidery was made, how dense the stitching is and how the fabric reacted to being embroidered. If the embroidery is lying nice and flat when the final press is done it can be framed without lacing; mounting over an acid-free backing board could provide enough support for a stiff embroidery.

Lacing over a board retains the tension of the stitches and stops the fabric from sagging or splitting, thus preserving it for future generations. If the embroidery has pulled or distorted it will need a good damp press before being laced over a backing board. The backing board is usually cut from acid-free mount board or foam board, and can be used with or without padding.

Using Only a Simple Mat Board

A mat board is simply a backing board that is placed behind a work of art to stabilize and protect it. Mat boards are made from acid-free card such as mount board or foam board. Mat boards are traditionally used when framing prints; the work is affixed to the mat board by a hinge of acid-free masking tape at the top. The print is usually covered with a window of mount board to separate it from the glass. The mat board method is best suited to lightweight embroideries stitched on stabilized fabric that has no distortions.

Framing Without Glass or Mount Board

The simplest way to frame an embroidery is in a frame without glass or mount board. Framing without glass is easy but it does have problems, as textured embroidery has the potential for being a dust trap or a feast for hungry moths. The depth of the frame needs to be deep enough to accommodate the embroidery, backing board and MDF back panel. A box frame may be more suitable for laced embroideries because the folded fabric makes the embroidery thicker.

Framing an Embroidery with a Mount Board and Glass

Mount boards are functional and visual. The colour of the board can be used to highlight key colours within the embroidery whilst the board acts as a spacer to separate the embroidery from the glass. Mount boards can be used to crop the embroidery or hide messy raw edges.

Such boards can be tricky to cut if you don't have strong wrists or specialist equipment; they are traditionally cut with a 45-degree bevel to expose their own central white core. The board can also be cut at 90 degrees; this method does not expose as much of the white core so may better suit modern or abstract embroideries.

If you decide to cut your own mount boards ask yourself the question: do I have the expertise, strength and time to do this? Measure the size of the frame properly, check what size the aperture or window needs to be; it's good practice to check these measurements twice because mount board is expensive and simple mistakes can be costly.

Always use a cutting mat and metal ruler. If possible use a deep-edged ruler with a non-slip base for extra safety; craft knifes can easily slip over thin rulers, causing unexpected cuts or injuries. Make sure the blade is sharp, since blunt blades scuff or tear the mount board, creating a messy edge. I use a freestyle hand-held cutter for 45-degree bevels because my wrists are not strong enough to hold the knife at that angle. Hand-held cutters have slots that hold the blade at the desired angle, which means it's easier to achieve a more consistent accurate cut.

Framing in a Hoop

Some embroideries can be framed in the wooden hoop they were stitched in. This method of framing is more suitable for traditional embroideries such as flowers or birds. Simple motifs can be displayed more effectively in a round or oval frame rather than a square one. Flexi-hoops have been designed for framing embroideries; these have a rigid plastic inner part with an indent to hold the flexible outer frame, and then have a metal attachment at the top for hanging. Flexi-hoops are more suitable for small embroideries because it's easier to tension the fabric and fit the hoop.

Craft knives are economical; blunt blades are simply snapped off to create a new sharp edge. Freestyle hand-held cutters are easier to hold; the model I use has been discontinued but similar tools are available from framing suppliers. Positioning the blade in the right spot takes practice; always test-cut a scrap of mount board before cutting the real thing.

FRAMING WITHOUT GLASS
Fusing the Embroidery to Pelmet Vilene

This example demonstrates how to frame the beach hut from Chapter 6. The size of the framed embroidery had already been decided so a simple white 12.5 × 18cm (5 × 7in.) frame was purchased. The white frame was too harsh for the subject, so it was distressed with various grades of sandpaper to reveal the brown MDF below, then polished using a beeswax block and soft cloth. The worn effect is in keeping with the colours used and the beach theme.

The embroidery is bonded onto pelmet Vilene and framed without a mount. Bonding the embroidery in this way stiffens the embroidery so it can be mounted without lacing over card. The advantage of using pelmet Vilene is that the edges can be bound with zigzag to stop further fraying.

YOU WILL NEED

Equipment
- Sewing machine
- Straight-stitch presser foot
- Normal tension bobbin case
- Empty bobbin
- Size 90/14 universal machine needle
- Iron
- Baking parchment
- Paper scissors
- Fabric scissors or rotary cutter
- Pencil
- Pencil sharpener
- Metal ruler
- Craft knife
- Cutting mat
- Screwdriver or teaspoon
- Sandpaper for distressing the frame
- Lint-free cloth

Materials
- Finished beach hut embroidery
- White image frame measuring 12.5 × 18cm (5 × 7in.)
- Paper-backed heat-fusible glue
- Foam board
- Pelmet Vilene
- White thread
- Madeira classic no. 40, 1296 deep ocean blue

Machine used
- Bernina 801
- Feeder teeth up
- Normal tension

1 Cut a rectangle of pelmet Vilene measuring approximately 20 × 15cm (8 × 6in.), then use paper scissors to cut a piece of paper-backed heat-fusible glue the same size. Iron the heat-fusible glue to the pelmet Vilene, using a sheet of baking parchment to protect the iron.

2 Peel the backing paper away and position the pelmet Vilene on the back of the embroidery glue side down, cover with backing parchment and press. You might need to keep the iron in the same position for the heat to transmit through the thick layers but don't scorch the fabric. Turn the embroidery over and use a clean iron to press the front. Concentrate on the background fabric to create a firm bond; do not iron the embroidery.

3 Remove the glass and MDF backing board from the frame. Sand the frame to distress it, then use a lint-free cloth to remove the dust. Lay the glass on top of the embroidery and move it until you are happy with its position over the embroidery. Draw round the glass with a pencil; take care not to cut yourself or the embroidery. Using the glass to crop the embroidery saves time.

250   Chapter 12 – Finishing Your Work

④ Cut the embroidery out along the pencil lines using sharp fabric scissors or a rotary cutter, ruler and cutting mat. Put the embroidery into the frame to see how it looks; it should fit perfectly because the glass was used as a template.

⑤ Attach the straight-stitch foot and raise the feeder teeth. Thread the needle with white cotton and insert a bobbin wound with white into the normal tension bobbin case. Set the stitch to a medium-width zigzag. Sew around the edge of the bonded embroidery to stop it fraying, tie the thread ends and cut them off.

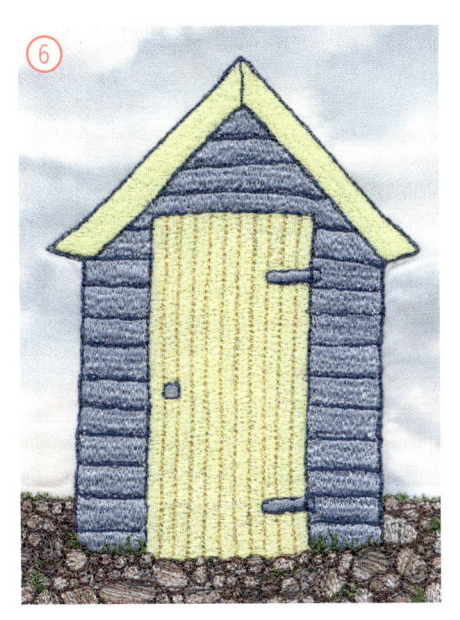

⑥ Place the embroidery in the frame to check the row of zigzag is hidden behind the frame lip. Remove the embroidery from the frame, and thread the machine with Madeira Classic 1296 (deep ocean blue) and set the stitch type to straight, then sew around the beach hut with straight stitch to secure the embroidery to the pelmet Vilene.

⑦ Cut a piece of foam board or acid-free mount board the same size as the glass, using a metal ruler and cutting mat for accuracy and safety.

⑧ Place the embroidery in the frame and back it with the foam board. Position the glass behind the foam board, then add the paper insert that came with the frame. Press the MDF backing into place, making sure the backing board is the right way up. Use a screwdriver or teaspoon to fold down the picture pins to hold everything in place. I decided not to use the glass; placing it behind the foam board means it was stored safely.

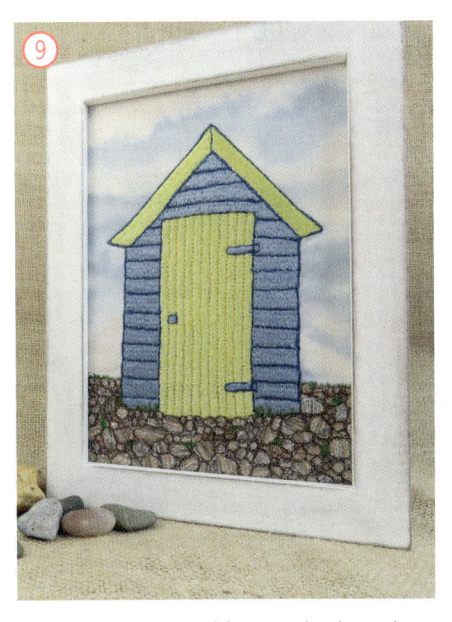

⑨ The simple distressed frame suits the style and theme of the embroidery.

Chapter 12 – Finishing Your Work   **251**

FRAMING BEHIND GLASS AND MOUNT BOARD

Mounting an Embroidery onto a Backing Board

Using a backing board saves time but this method only works if the embroidery is lightweight and free from wrinkles. The embroidered cornfield from Chapter 10 is the ideal candidate for this framing method because it is supported by stiff iron-on interfacing.

The embroidery does not need to be overpowered by an ornate frame. I have chosen a simple natural wood frame and cream mount board to complement the bright summer colours. The mount board and spacer are essential additions because they stop the embroidery touching the glass.

YOU WILL NEED

Equipment
- Glass cleaner or washing-up liquid and water
- Cutting mat
- Craft knife or freehand mount board cutter
- Pencil
- Pencil sharpener
- Eraser
- Metal ruler
- Set square
- Tape measure

Materials
- Finished summer cornfield embroidery
- Box frame
- Pre-cut mount board
- Foam board
- Mount board
- Kitchen paper
- Masking tape or gummed artist's tape

1. Look at the embroidery and decide how to crop it. The size of the cropped area becomes the window or aperture of the mount board. I decided to break from convention and choose a square format. I ordered a wooden frame measuring 40 × 40cm (15¾ × 15¾in.) and matching mount board with a 22 × 22cm (8¾ × 8¾in.) window.

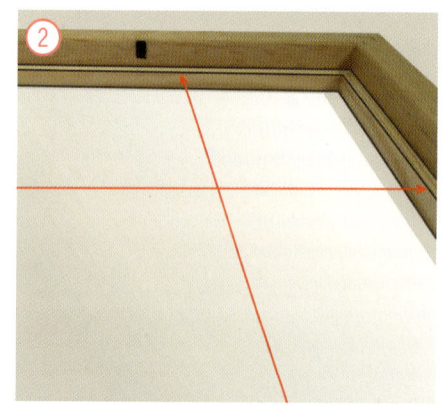

2. Remove the glass, clean and dry it, then put it to one side. Turn the frame so the back faces upwards and measure the inside of the frame width and height. If the frame has a loose box frame insert take the measurement inside it.

3. Cut two pieces of foam board the same size as your measurements. Use a ruler, set square and pencil for accurate measurements. Cut the foam board using a cutting mat, metal ruler and craft knife. Take care when cutting; this ruler has a deep scratch caused by a knife slipping. Place the foam board into the frame or loose box frame insert to check it fits properly.

④ Place one piece of foam board on the cutting mat and lay the pre-cut mount board on top, coloured side down. Make sure both pieces are aligned and use a pencil to mark the perimeter of the window that's been cut into the mount board; don't mark the mount board bevel with pencil.

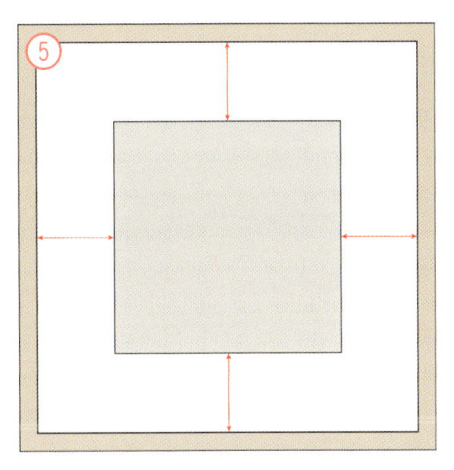

⑤ If the mount and foam board are different sizes because of the box frame insert, you will need to mark the window aperture onto foam board by measuring the mount board window aperture then transfer the measurements to the foam board. In the diagram the buff layer is larger mount board; white layer is the foam board; and the grey area is the window aperture to measure and draw.

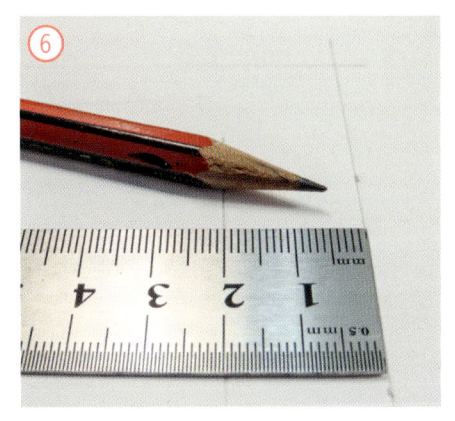

⑥ Remove the mount board and draw another box 2cm (¾in.) larger all the way around, using a pencil, ruler and set square to mark the foam board accurately. Cut this out using a craft knife, cutting mat and metal ruler. Creating this larger window ensures the ugly foam core is not seen beneath the mount board.

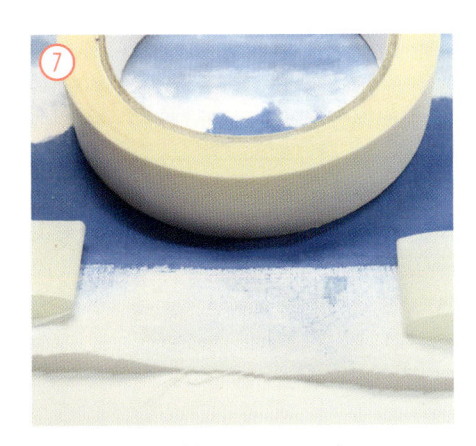

⑦ Wind some masking tape around your fingers so the sticky side is outside and it makes a circle. Stick this to the left top side of the embroidery where it will be hidden by the mount board. Do the same near the top on the right side. I turned the embroidery round so the top was nearest to me; it was much easier to position the circles of tape.

⑧ Place the embroidery face up on a clean flat surface. Hover the mount board above it until it's in the right position, then lower the mount board on top. Gently turn the board over whilst keeping hold of the embroidery so it doesn't fidget. Check the embroidery is in the correct position. It does not matter if the masking tape is visible as it will be removed during the next stage.

⑨ Turn the embroidery and mount board over so the back of the embroidery is facing upwards. Wind some more masking tape around your fingers to make two sticky bundles and position these on the back of the embroidery near the edge. Lay the solid piece of cut foam board on top so the edges match the edges of the mount board and press down near the tape. If the foam board is smaller, make sure the distance around it is equal.

Chapter 12 – Finishing Your Work   253

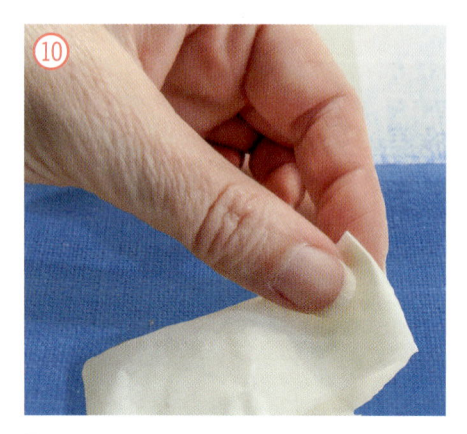

10 Turn the embroidery back over, carefully remove the mount board with the window cut-out and peel off the bundled masking tape from the front of the embroidery. Don't disturb the position of the embroidery whilst removing the tape.

11 Tape the embroidery to the backing board along the edge where the bundles of tape were, then lift the embroidery up and peel off the circles of tape. Lay the mount board over the embroidery to check it hasn't moved, then fasten the three remaining sides to the backing board with masking tape.

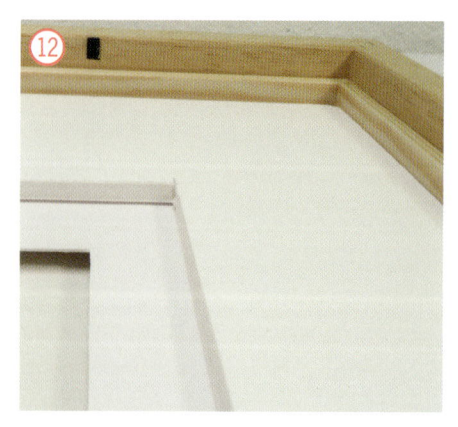

12 Check the glass is clean, place the mount board in the frame, then replace the decorative box frame insert. Push the foam board spacer into position so the cut area matches the window cut into the mount board, place the backing board with the embroidery into the frame and check the positioning.

13 Cover the back with the MDF panel, making sure the fixtures for hanging are at the top. Fold the metal tacks down with a screwdriver or teaspoon; don't press them down with your fingers because the metal may have sharp edges.

14 Seal the backing board to the frame with some masking tape or artist's gummed tape. Try to keep the tape level with the frame and trim the ends neatly. Taping the gap prevents insects or dust getting in to spoil the view.

15 The finished frame is minimal and suits the style and colour of the embroidery.

FRAMING BEHIND GLASS AND MOUNT BOARD
Lacing an Embroidery Over Card

YOU WILL NEED

Equipment
- Metal ruler
- Set square
- Tape measure
- Dressmaker's chalk pencil
- Pencil
- Pencil sharpener
- Eraser
- Fabric scissors
- Embroidery scissors
- Old pins
- Cutting mat
- Craft knife
- Clothes pegs
- Screwdriver or old teaspoon
- Bradawl

Materials
- Finished vintage flower embroidery
- Picture frame
- Mount board
- Foam board
- 2oz wadding (thin)
- Block of beeswax
- Washing-up liquid or glass cleaner
- Kitchen paper
- Colour-matched strong thread
- Strong thick thread for lacing
- Acid-free double-sided tape
- Masking tape or artist's gummed paper tape
- Picture wire or firm cord
- Mirror plates or picture frame D-rings and screws

This example demonstrates how to lace the vintage flower embroidery from Chapter 6. Note that some embroideries show signs of pulling or warping after they have been pressed. Also, dense embroidery stitches can pull the warp and the weft out of line; this can be more troublesome around embroideries that have no stitching in the background. Distortions are more visible on pale plain fabrics that have a close weave.

Lacing the embroidery helps to preserve the tension of the fabric and to correct issues caused by heavy stitching. The fabric would have been pulled taut in the hoop; lacing replicates this. Embroideries can be laced over acid-free board, a padded board or one that's been covered with cotton fabric. Firm board can be a bit unforgiving when teamed with a traditional embroidery; the optional padding counteracts the firmness of the board and helps to soften the fabric and disguise the remaining wrinkles.

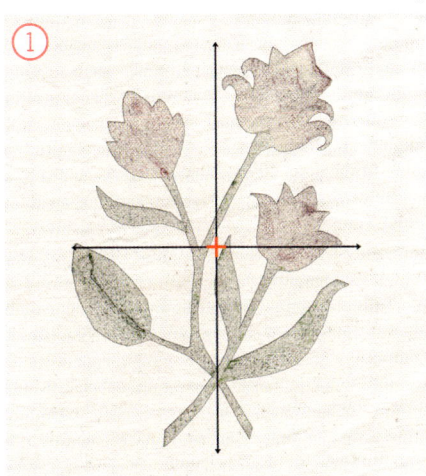

1 Turn the embroidery over so the wrong side is facing upwards. Find the central point. To do this, measure the width of the embroidery at its widest part and divide by two, then mark the middle point with a pin or dressmaker's chalk pencil. Do the same for the height. The central point can be found where the pins or chalk lines cross.

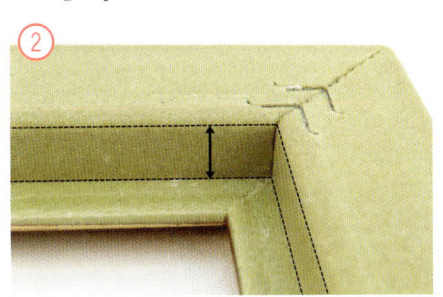

2 Decide how large the laced embroidery will be; this governs the size of the backing board and frame. I chose a 28 × 35.5cm (11 × 14in.) frame. It's cheaper to make the finished embroidery the same size as an off-the-shelf frame. The problem with using a shop-bought frame is that the depth of the inner recess might not be deep enough to accommodate the MDF frame backing plus embroidery, foam board spacing, mount and glass.

3 Remove the backing board and measure the width and length of the recessed frame aperture. It should be the same size as the measurements given on the packaging. The recess of my frame did indeed measure 28 × 35.5cm (11 × 14in.). The mount board backing needs to be slightly smaller than the frame aperture to ensure it fits once the embroidery is laced. Cut a piece of mount board measuring 27.5 × 35cm (10¾ × 13¾in.). Use a cutting mat, craft knife and metal ruler for accuracy.

Chapter 12 – Finishing Your Work   **255**

4

Stick acid-free double-sided tape near to the edge of the board on the white side and peel off the backing. Cut a piece of wadding the same size as the mount board, stick it to the double-sided tape and trim away the excess.

5

The fabric needs to be marked with a rectangle the same size as the mount board to provide guidelines for pinning and lacing. It's important to have an equal amount of fabric on all sides round the embroidery so it remains central when framed. The cut mount board measured 27.5 × 35cm (10¾ × 13¾in.); divide these measurements by two to find the middle of the board.

6

The central point of the board is approximately 13.7cm (5⅞in.) in from the longer sides and 17.5cm (6⅞in.) from the shorter sides. Put the embroidery on a flat surface wrong side up and in portrait orientation. Place the start of the tape measure on the central point of the embroidery and measure outwards 13.7cm (5⅝in.). Use a chalk pencil to mark the measurement; do the same the other side of the middle mark. The space between the marks should add up to approximately 27.5cm (10¾in.).

7

Rotate the tape measure so it's vertical and line the start up with the middle of the embroidery. Mark 17.5cm (6⅞in.) up from the middle point, then mark 17.5cm (6⅞in.) down from the middle point. The gap between the marks should measure approximately 35cm (13¾in.). The marker points are used to draw a rectangle which becomes the guidelines for folding and lacing over the mount board.

8

Use a ruler and dressmaker's chalk pencil to draw the rectangle's base. Make sure the ruler is level with the embroidery and fabric grain before drawing the line. Line the bottom of the set square up with the drawn base line so it crosses through the mark on the right-hand side and draw the right-hand guideline.

9

Measure 27.5cm (10¾in.) across from the right-hand guideline and mark; repeat the measurement at least three times and mark the positions. Use a ruler and chalk pencil to join the marks up; the drawn line should pass through all the marked points.

256   Chapter 12 – Finishing Your Work

⑩ Measure 35cm (13¾in.) up from the base line and mark; repeat this at least three times and use a ruler and chalk pencil to join the markers up. Check the accuracy of the rectangle: if the width is measured near the top, middle and bottom it should be the same; likewise, if the height is measured near the left, middle and right the measurement should be the same.

⑪ If the rectangle has been drawn correctly the embroidery should be in the middle. This can be checked by measuring the top, bottom and side gaps between the embroidery and the border of the rectangle. Mark an equal seam allowance around the border and trim.

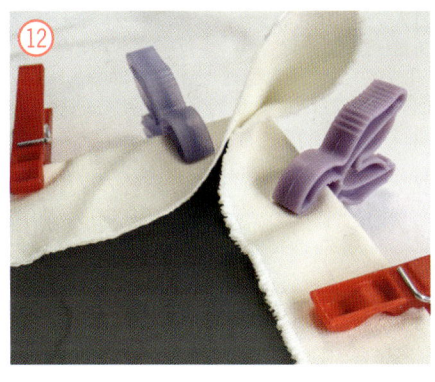

⑫ Position the embroidery drawn rectangle facing upwards. Place the padded side of the mount board against the embroidered fabric and position the board so it's in line with the drawn rectangle. Fold the fabric flaps over to the back and pin or peg in place. Turn the board over and check the position of the embroidery; it should still be in the middle.

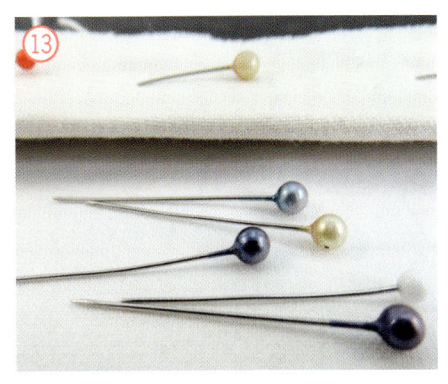

⑬ The fabric needs to be tensioned for lacing. Pin the long edge of the mount board; the first pins should be central and opposite each other. Pull the fabric to stretch it over the board as you pin. Pin the short edges of the mount board the same way. Work out from the central pins, pulling and manipulating as you pin and working on each side in turn so that the fabric is stretched evenly.

⑭ Thread a sharp hand-sewing needle with a long length of doubled strong thread. Long lengths of thread are more likely to knot or tangle; this problem can be reduced by pulling the thread through a block of beeswax.

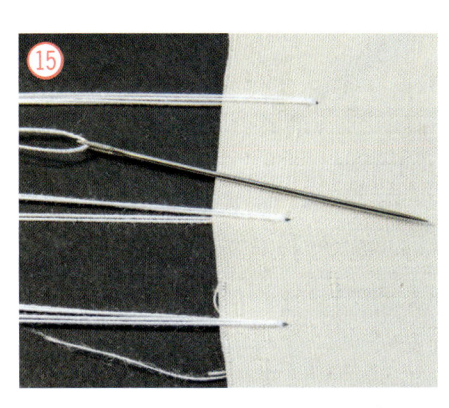

⑮ Push the needle through the middle of a long pinned flap and secure the thread with a knot. Push the needle through the long flap directly opposite and pull the thread tight, then take the needle back to the opposite flap, push through and pull tight. Continue lacing the middle section; when the thread runs out knot another in and trim the thread tails when finished.

Chapter 12 – Finishing Your Work   **257**

⑯ Rotate the embroidery and start lacing the short flaps. It may save time to have two needles on the go, one for lacing the short sides and one for the long sides. Stop about 4cm (1½in.) short of the corners to allow for folding the fabric under. Continue rotating the backing board to lace both sides evenly. The fabric and board should be flat with no bows or buckles.

⑰ Tuck the corners under and pin in place; they should lie nice and flat without any bulges. When lacing the corners catch both layers of folded fabric. Hand-stitch the corners in place with slip stitch and a strong colour-matched thread. To finish, take the thread tails through to the middle of the fabric and cut them off. Trim the lacing thread tails close to the knots on the backing board.

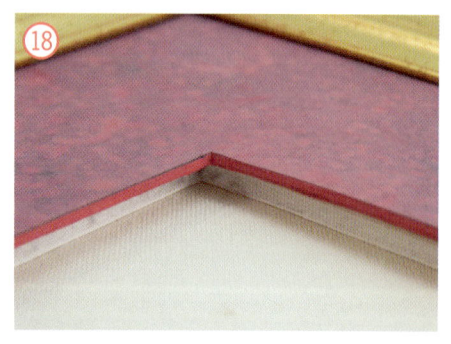

⑱ Remove the glass from the frame and carefully wash it in soapy water, then dry it with kitchen paper. Put the cleaned glass back into the frame, then the mount board. Cut a piece of foam board so the window aperture is slightly larger than the mount board one. Place the foam board in the frame followed by the laced embroidery. Hold all the layers together whilst turning the frame over to check the position of the embroidery.

⑲ If the embroidery is in the correct position and the glass free of smears, turn the assembled frame over to expose the back. Insert the backing paper and MDF backing board; make sure the fittings are in the correct position towards the top of the frame. Fold the metal points down to secure the backing board, using an old metal teaspoon or screwdriver to protect your fingers. Use masking tape or artist's gummed paper to seal the back of the frame, pressing the tape down firmly to get a good seal.

⑳ The best place to put the hanging eyes or mirror plates is a third of the way down the frame. To hang a picture like this in portrait orientation, measure the longest side and divide by three. This frame measures 39.3cm (15½in.) so the hanging D-rings need to be affixed about 12.5cm (5in.) from the top of the frame. Mark the position with pencil and make a hole with a bradawl; this makes it easier to screw the fixings in place. Make sure the screws are shorter than the depth of the frame. Use picture wire or cord to hang the finished embroidery, ideally something that will not stretch.

㉑ The bold colour of the hand-painted mount board brings the traditional embroidery to life.

258 Chapter 12 – Finishing Your Work

HANGING AN EMBROIDERY WITHOUT A FRAME
Using Lacing and Attaching Velcro

YOU WILL NEED

Equipment
- Sewing machine
- Empty bobbin
- Normal tension bobbin case
- Straight-stitch presser foot
- Size 90/14 universal machine needles
- Glass-headed pins and old pins
- Sharp hand-sewing needle
- Small curved needle
- Dressmaker's chalk pencil
- Pencil
- Pencil sharpener
- Disappearing fabric pen
- Metal ruler
- Set square
- Craft knife
- Cutting mat
- Paintbrush
- Palette
- Water

Materials
- Finished sheep embroidery
- Box frame
- Waterproof sepia ink
- Brown acrylic paint
- Quick-dry acrylic varnish
- Mount board
- 3mm white foam board
- Unwashed calico
- Sew-in Velcro or other sew-in hook-and-loop tape
- Thick strong thread for lacing
- Strong colour-matched thread for hand-sewing
- Strong colour-matched thread to sew on the Velcro
- Acid-free double-sided tape
- Araldite glue or two-part epoxy glue

Machine used
- Bernina 801
- Feeder teeth up
- Normal tension

This example demonstrates how to finish the rustic sheep project from Chapter 11. Hook-and-loop tape (such as Velcro) is used to attach the laced embroidery to another surface. The main advantage of using Velcro for displaying embroideries is that the work can sit flush to the wall without any visible means of hanging. The embroidery can be easily re-positioned onto another surface. If the embroidery is mounted on top of a box frame it will appear as if it is floating away from the wall; to carry off this illusion the mounted embroidery should be larger than the box frame.

① The sheep is going to be laced so there are two options to hang the embroidery: flush against the wall or floating away from the wall over a box frame. The recycled box frame that I had to hand could not be used as it was, so the old picture was removed and the wooden edges painted with sepia ink and varnished.

② The laced embroidery needs to match the shape of the box frame and be larger than it. The box frame measures 20 x 20cm (8 x 8in.) and there is enough fabric to make the embroidery 25.5 x 25.5cm (10 x 10in.). Turn the embroidery over so the back is facing upwards. Use a dressmaker's chalk pencil, ruler and set square to mark out the square. Follow the grain of the linen. Mistakes can be marked with a cross.

Chapter 12 – Finishing Your Work 259

③

Check the boundary is in the right place by folding the seams over and checking the position of the embroidery on the front. If the edge seams are in the correct place, press them firmly with a finger or iron them down to crease. Use the width of the ruler to draw a seam allowance and cut away the excess fabric. Seams that have equal length are easier to fold into a neat mitred corner.

④

Cut the mount and foam boards 0.3cm (⅛in.) smaller than the size of the folded embroidery, 24.7 x 24.7cm (9⅞ x 9⅞in.). Use a pencil, ruler and set square to draw accurate squares. Protect the work surface with a cutting mat and cut the mount board. Position the metal ruler along the drawn line and use the sharp craft knife to cut out the mount board square. When cutting the foam board keep the knife at 90 degrees because you don't want a bevelled edge on the thicker foam board.

⑤

When cut, put the two pieces together; they should be exactly the same size. Use acid-free double-sided tape to stick the two pieces together; the two layers of card provide a stable base for lacing heavy canvas. Place the layered card on the back of the embroidery so the mount board side is against the embroidery. Line the edges of the card up with the boundary lines. Pin the linen in place with old pins along the edge of the board so they go into the foam core. (Use old pins because linen is tough and they may bend.)

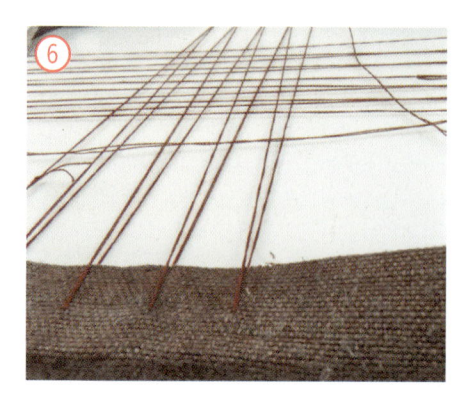

⑥

Thread a sharp hand-sewing needle with a long length of strong thread and pull the thread through the needle to double it. Starting roughly from the centre of one side, push the needle through the linen flap and tie the thread so it's secured firmly. Take the needle to the opposite side, push it through the flap and pull the thread tight. Continue working from the centre outwards until the middle section is pulled taut. Start at the centre again and work in the other direction. Lace the other sides in the same way, working from the middle outwards. Continue lacing both sides until you almost reach the corners, then fasten off the thick thread.

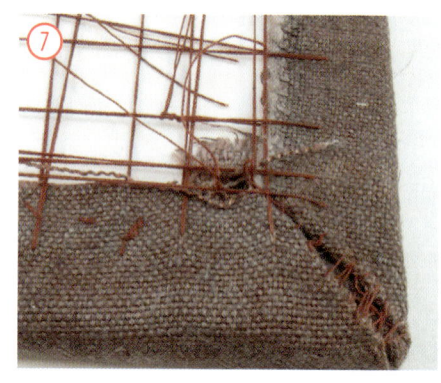

⑦

Fold the corners so they are neatly mitred and pin in place. Stitch the mitred seam together with a strong matching thread. It may be difficult to get a neat finish because of the thickness of the linen. Starting with a shorter piece of lacing thread, continue lacing until you reach the seam allowance near the corner, then fasten off the thread and trim the long ends.

⑧

My laced embroidery measured 24.7 x 24.7cm (9⅞ x 9⅞in.). The backing fabric needs to be smaller than the embroidery, so in this case it would need to be 24 x 24cm (9½ x 9½in.) when folded. Add a 3cm (1¼in.) seam allowance on each side for folding, so the backing calico needs to measure 30 x 30cm (12 x 12in.). Use a pencil, ruler and set square to draw this square onto the calico accurately. Cut the square out with sharp fabric scissors. Mark the 3cm (1¼in.) seam allowance on all four sides using a pencil and ruler. Fold the calico on the drawn lines and check it fits the back of the embroidery.

9. Iron the folded seams to make firm creases; this should create a small square in each corner when the seams are folded back. Fold the pressed seams over the square to create the mitre. Iron the mitred corners and pin in place.

10. Turn the mitred calico so the unfolded side faces upwards. Draw a line corner to corner with vanishing pen. Align the box frame so the corners match the crossed lines. Draw around the box frame with the disappearing pen. Decide which edge of the calico backing is going to be the top and write 'top' with vanishing pen.

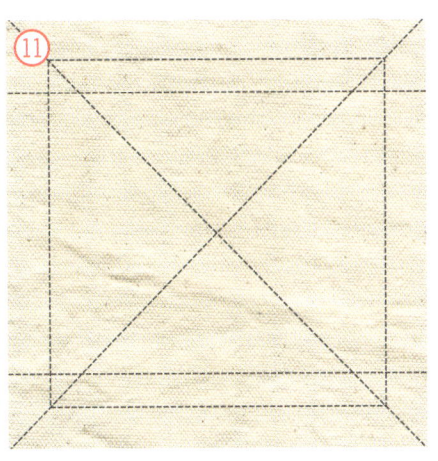

11. Measure 2cm (¾in.) down from the box frame guideline, mark in three places and join the dots with a ruler. Rotate the calico and do the same on the opposite side. The back of the calico should look like the diagram.

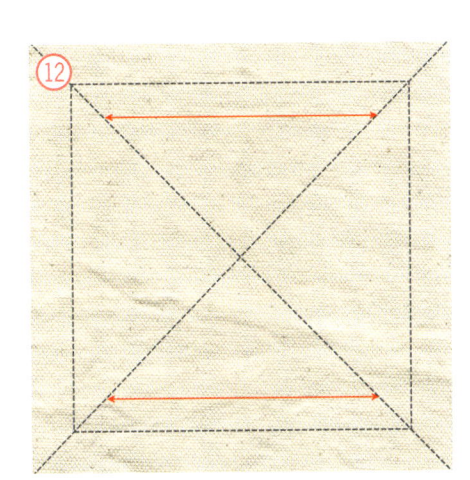

12. Work out how much Velcro is needed; the length of the Velcro is from cross mark to cross mark. My gap between the crossed lines measured 17cm (6¾in.) so I cut two pieces of sew-in Velcro to this length. Using Velcro means the embroidery can be fixed to the box frame or directly to a wall.

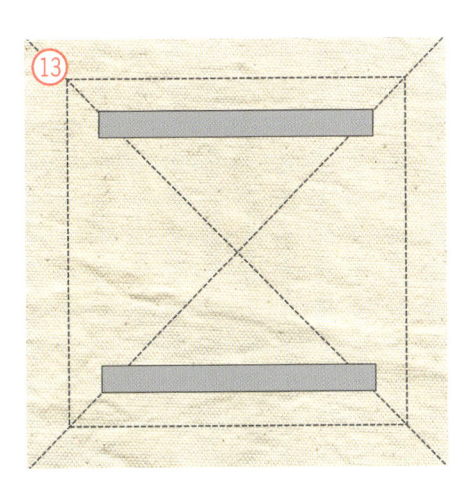

13. Position the soft part of the Velcro so it lines up inside the drawn guideline. The Velcro should be placed 2cm (¾in.) in from the edge of the box frame guideline so that both ends touch the crossed lines. Pin the Velcro in place; take care as it is tough to pin.

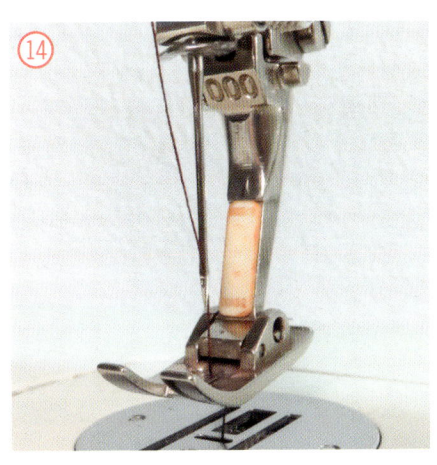

14. Set the machine up for normal sewing, raise the feeder teeth, attach a straight-stitch foot and set the stitch length to normal. Wind a bobbin with strong colour-matched thread, insert it into the normal tension bobbin case and load both into the machine. Thread the needle with the same colour-matched thread.

Chapter 12 – Finishing Your Work   **261**

⑮ Sew the Velcro to the calico backing, positioning the foot so the needle enters just before the loops of Velcro begin. Sew close to the edge on all four sides. To strengthen the start and finish, press reverse to backstitch for a few stitches. Take the thread tails to the back, tie them off and cut them.

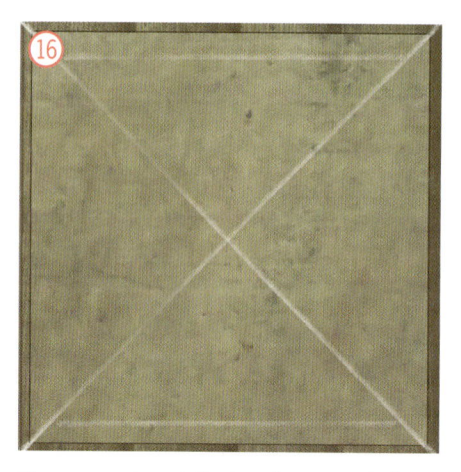

⑯ Measure and mark the box frame ready for gluing the Velcro in position. Turn the box so the solid top is facing upwards. Draw a diagonal line from corner to corner using dressmaker's chalk pencil and a ruler. Measure down 2cm (¾in.) from the top and mark this between the diagonal line. Rotate the box frame 180 degrees and repeat.

⑰ Mix the Araldite glue according to the instructions on the tube. Spread the glue on the back of the rough Velcro and press into place. It should be positioned 2cm (¾in.) down from the edge of the box. Do the same for the strip on the bottom. Wipe away any excess glue with kitchen paper, lay a sheet of baking parchment on top of the box frame and use a heavy book or similar flat object to hold the Velcro in place; leave to cure for the instructed time.

⑱ Pin the calico panel to the back of the embroidery, making sure the top of the embroidery matches the top of the calico, otherwise the Velcro won't match the Velcro on the box frame. Use old pins because the linen is tough and it may bend them.

⑲ Thread a curved needle with a strong colour-matched thread. Slip-stitch the calico backing to the linen. Stitch all the way around the edges to make sure the calico is securely fixed. Stitching through thick linen is difficult; try to keep the stitches small. Remove all pins.

⑳ Attach the sheep embroidery to the box frame. Make sure the top of the embroidery is at the top of the box frame and hang the finished picture from a nail or picture hook.

262 Chapter 12 – Finishing Your Work

Framing an Embroidery in a Wooden Hoop

This example shows how to frame the little robin from Chapter 11 in a wooden embroidery hoop. Traditional designs such as portraits or nature studies suit a round or oval frame. The finished robin will come to life when displayed in a simple wooden 20cm (8in.) embroidery hoop. Please bear in mind that the embroidery won't be protected from dust or grime and the hoop may need to be sanded with fine sandpaper before it is used to display the embroidery.

YOU WILL NEED

Equipment
- Sharp needle
- Fabric scissors
- Embroidery scissors
- Paper scissors
- Pencil
- Pencil sharpener
- Glass-headed pins
- Glue gun and clear glue sticks
- Iron
- Screwdriver or pliers

Materials
- Finished little robin embroidery
- 20cm (8in.) wooden embroidery hoop
- Ironed thick white cotton large enough to back the embroidery
- Backing fabric, pre-washed calico or colour-matched cotton
- White buttonhole thread for gathering and securing
- Thin white card

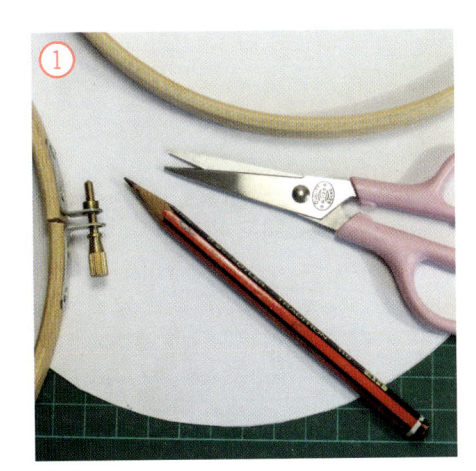

1 Put the inner part of the hoop onto the thin white card and draw round the outside with pencil. Cut out the card circle with paper scissors. Lay the inner part of the hoop on top of the backing fabric and draw a faint line around the outside of the hoop with a pencil.

2 The backing fabric needs a seam allowance to allow for folding over and gathering. An easy way to add this is to use the width of a pencil sharpener. Line the pencil sharpener up with the outside of the drawn circle and make a mark, then move the sharpener along and make another mark. Continue marking until the seam allowance is drawn, then cut away the excess fabric with fabric scissors.

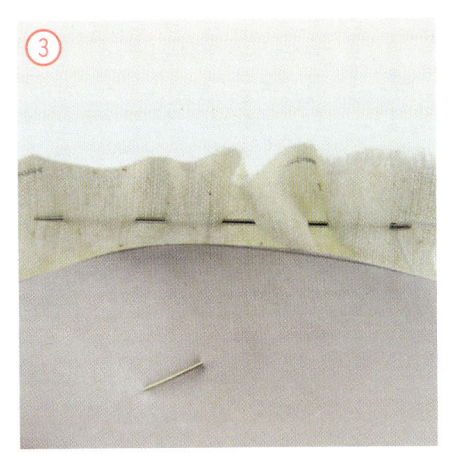

3 Pin the card to the calico so it lines up with the drawn circle. Thread a needle with buttonhole thread and tack round the circumference with running stitch. Pull both ends of the thread to draw the seam allowance over the card circle so it forms neat gathers. When the tension of the calico and card is even tie the thread ends together and cut away the excess thread.

Chapter 12 – Finishing Your Work

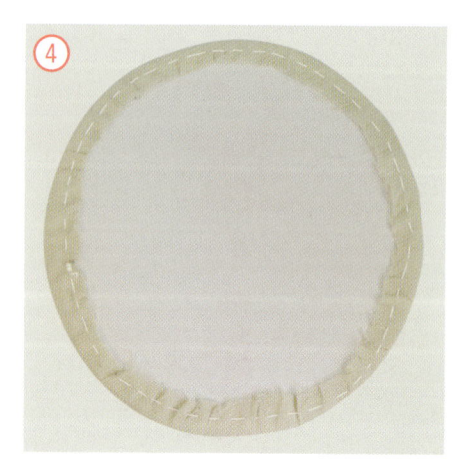

4 Remove the pins and iron the backing fabric to flatten the gathered pleats. If the card buckles with the heat, replace it with a new piece cut to the same size. It's important to iron the fabric with the card inset because the card stops the fabric stretching on the bias.

5 Calico can be transparent and you don't want the gathered fabric to be visible beneath the embroidery. Cut a thick piece of white cotton the same size as the embroidered calico and lay it behind the embroidered calico. Position the layers so the robin is standing upright. Place the outer part of the hoop on the fabric so the robin is central and make sure the screw fastening is in the twelve o'clock position above his back.

6 Slide the inner part of the hoop under both layers of fabric without disturbing the position of the outer hoop ring. Press the outer hoop down so it engages with the inner hoop to grip the fabric. Re-position the embroidery if necessary and pull both layers of fabric tight; when flicked the fabric should sound like a drum. When the robin is in position, use a screwdriver or pliers to tighten the screw so that the hoops hold the fabric securely.

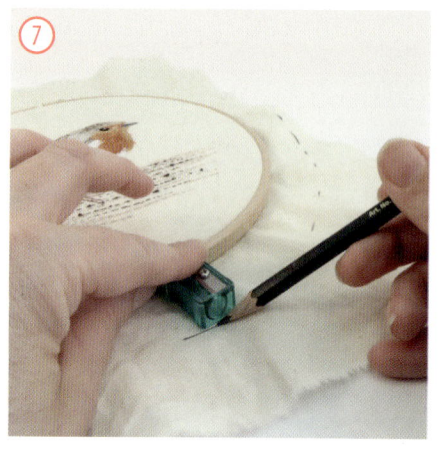

7 The excess fabric needs to be cut away to make gathering easier. Draw the cutting line an consistent distance away from the hoop. An easy way to do this is to use the length of a pencil sharpener. Place the pencil sharpener against the hoop so it rests on the gathered fabric and mark the position of the end. Move the sharpener a bit and make another mark. Continue marking until the circumference of the seam allowance is drawn, then trim off the excess fabric.

8 Thread a sharp needle with buttonhole thread and tack round the circumference of the seam allowance. Don't fasten the thread at the start and keep the length of the running stitches even. Make sure the tacking stitches catch both layers of fabric because it makes neater gathers when the threads are drawn.

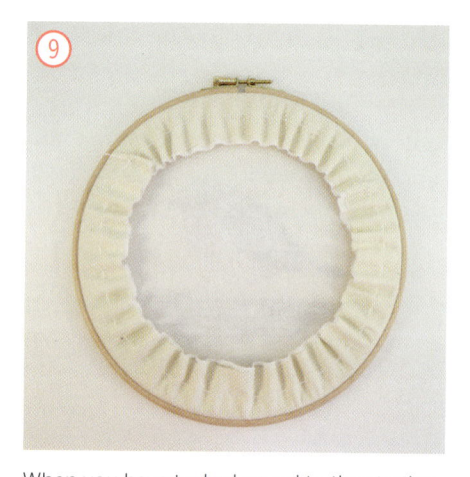

9 When you have tacked round to the starting point, pull both ends of the thread to gather up the loose fabric. Manipulate the ruffles of fabric so that they are even and tie the two threads together to secure.

⑩

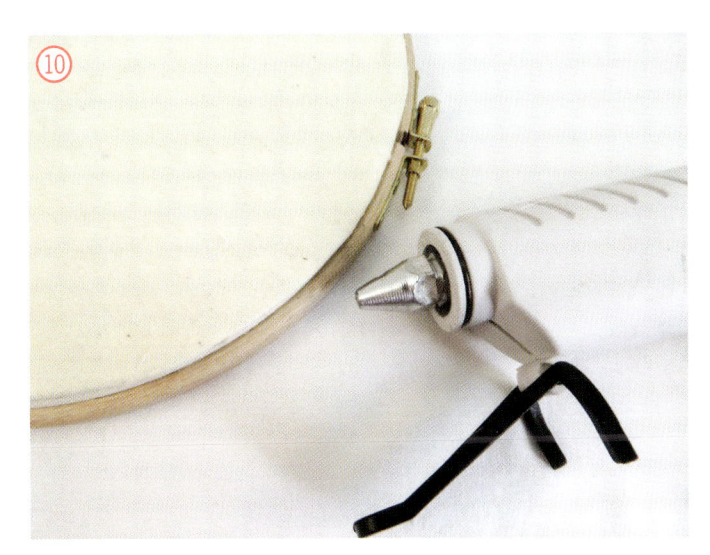

Pin the fabric-covered circle to the back of the embroidery hoop. Heat the glue gun up and protect your work surface because hot glue continues to ooze out of the nozzle after the trigger is released. Peel back a small portion of the fabric-covered circle, apply a small amount of glue to the underside of the backing and press in place. Continue gluing one small section at a time until the backing fabric is securely glued in place.

⑪

The embroidery is now ready to hang. Thread a small loop of ribbon through the metal screw or hang directly from a picture nail.

Chapter 12 – Finishing Your Work **265**

Framing an Embroidery in an Oval Flexi-hoop

This example shows how to mount the garden border stitched in Chapter 8. The process is very similar to mounting an embroidery in a round hoop. This type of frame is suitable for small embroideries that have a traditional theme. The advantage of using a flexi-hoop is that it can be done inexpensively at home without using any special tools.

YOU WILL NEED

Equipment
- Fabric scissors
- Embroidery scissors
- Paper scissors
- Pencil
- Pencil sharpener
- Glass-headed pins

Materials
- Finished garden border embroidery
- Flexi-hoop
- Thin white card or paper
- White felt large enough to back the embroidery
- White buttonhole thread for gathering and securing

1 Place the rigid inner part of the flexi-hoop on the back of the embroidery and position it so the embroidery is framed pleasingly – not too much space at the top and no gaps at the side or bottom. Add a small seam allowance; the width of a pencil sharpener is ideal. Position the pencil sharpener against the outside of the hoop, make a mark then move the pencil sharpener along and repeat. Join the marks up with pencil.

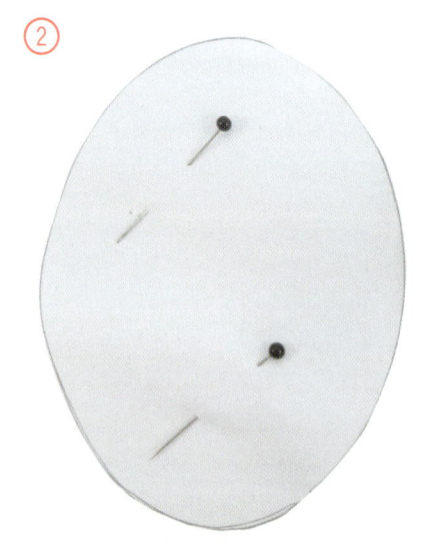

2 Place the rigid part of the hoop onto some paper and trace round the outside. Pin the paper to a piece of felt and cut the oval shape out. Discard the paper template and put the cut felt to one side; this is used to back the embroidery later.

3 Cut the embroidery out along the drawn seam allowance. Thread a sharp hand-sewing needle with a doubled length of strong buttonhole thread. Tack around the oval shape with running stitch until the stitches meet. Leave both ends of the threads long; don't gather the fabric yet.

266 Chapter 12 – Finishing Your Work

④

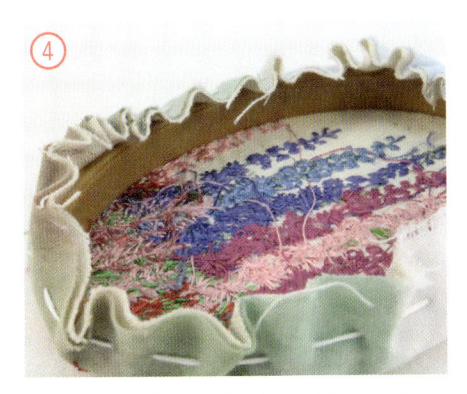

Place the rigid inner ring in position on the back of the embroidery. The plastic inner ring may have mould registration marks; transfer such marks to the fabric because it's easier to line the top of the embroidery up with the top of the frame. Pull both of the running stitch thread ends to slightly gather the fabric but do not tie.

⑤

Align the hanging ring of the flexible hoop with the top of the rigid hoop and press in place so the rounded part sits in the groove. Press the rest of the flexible hoop into position. Because the outer ring of the hoop is flexible it's quite difficult to get the embroidery in the right position; you may need to attempt this stage a few times to get the embroidery in the correct place. The drawn mark should match the metal hanging hook.

⑥

When the embroidery is in position, gently pull the fabric taut, taking care not to pull the embroidery out of the flexi-hoop. When the fabric is taut, pull both ends of the tacking thread and secure with a few knots. If you feel it needs it, you could now lace the back to flatten the gathered fabric.

⑦

Pin the felt to the back of the embroidery and stitch in place using strong colour-matched cotton. On finishing, fasten off the thread and take the ends through the fabric to the middle of the embroidery.

⑧

The finished embroidery can now be hung from the decorative metal hanging loop with ribbon.

Chapter 12 – Finishing Your Work   **267**

Templates

All templates are full size unless stated otherwise.

Straight-Stitch Tulip

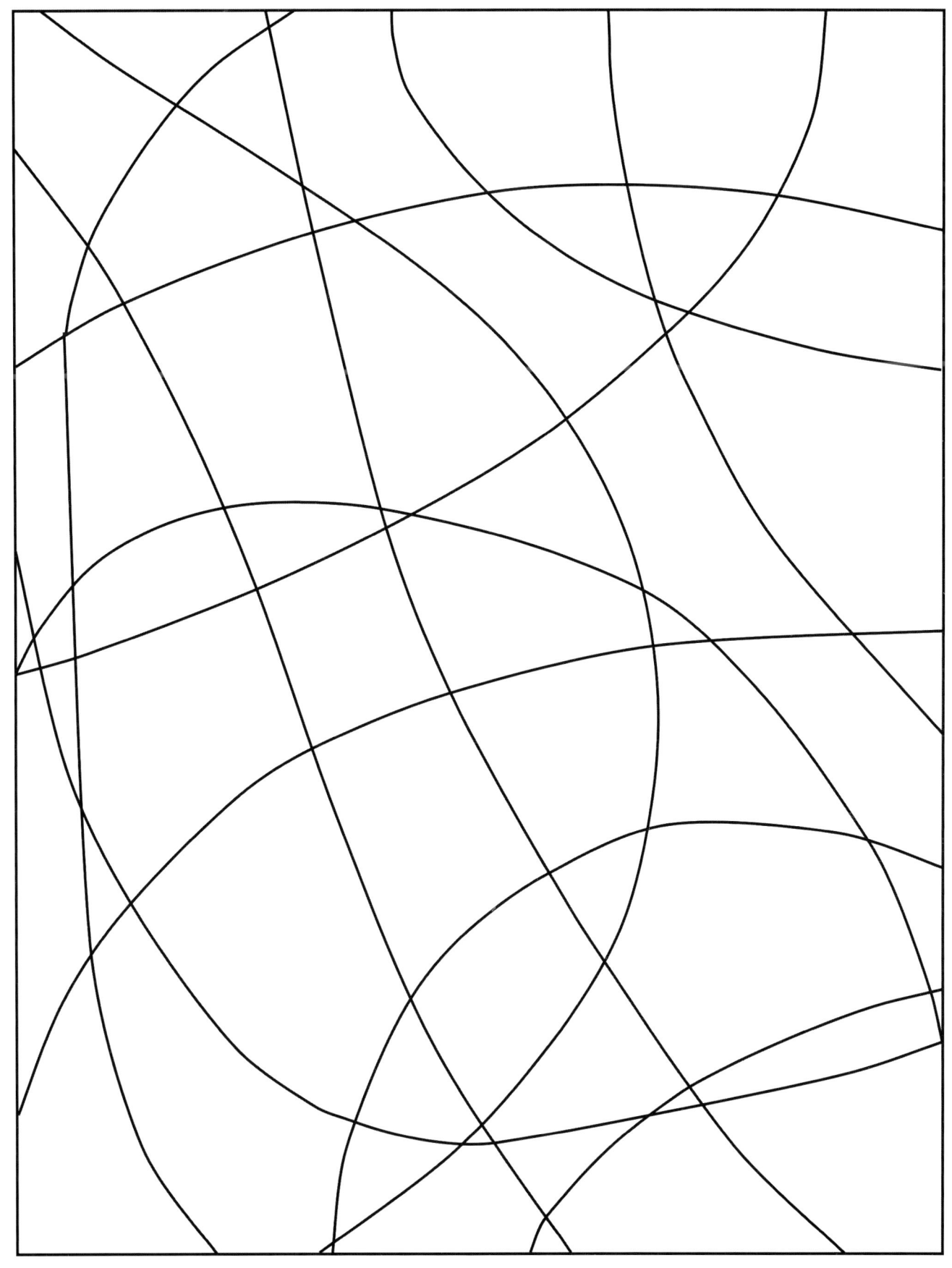

Swirl Pattern

Whimsical Beach Hut

270 Templates

Paisley Motif

Paisley Flowers

Vintage Flower

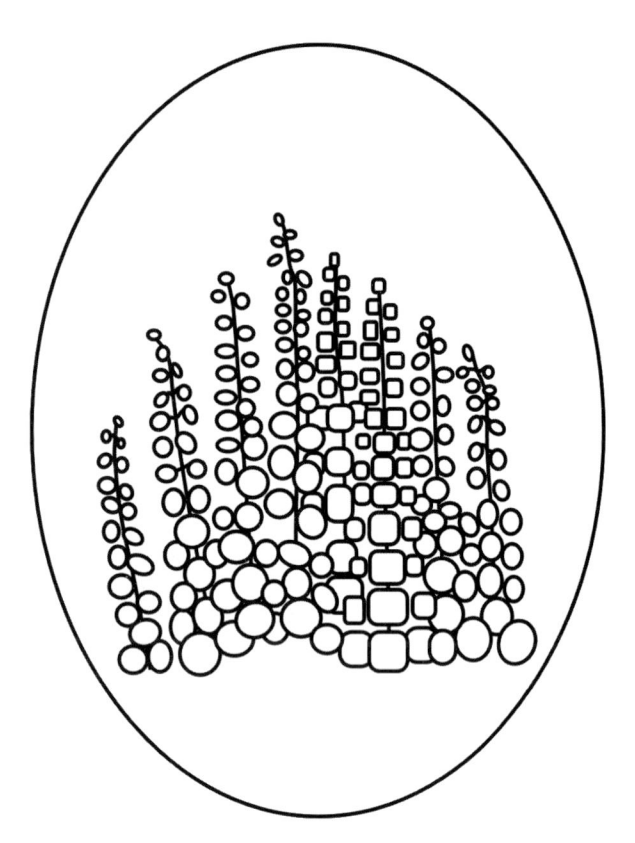

Garden Border midground

Garden Border foreground

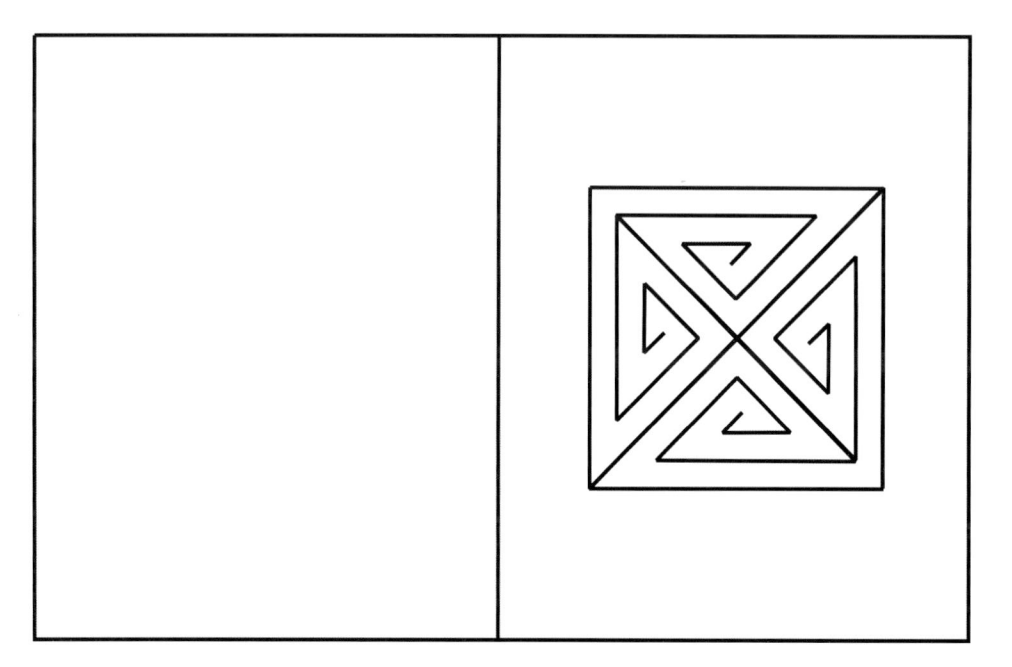

Needlecase

274 Templates

Pincushion front

Pincushion back

Scissor Keeper

Beaded Gold Star

Templates **275**

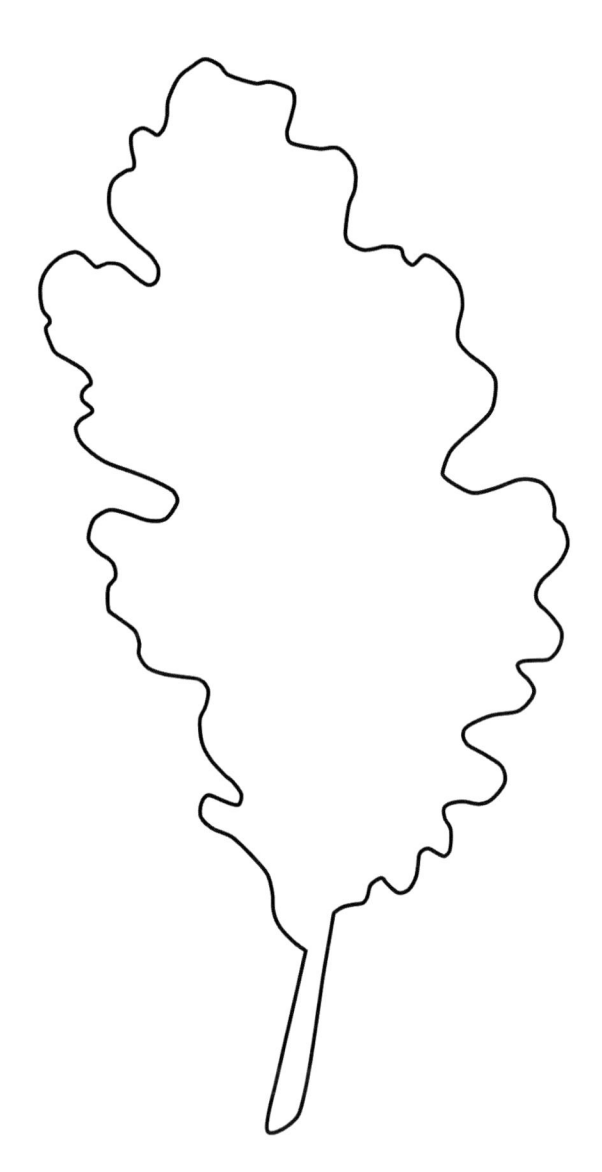

Leaf outline

Leaf stitching

276 Templates

Butterfly outline

Butterfly design

Templates 277

Flower Pattern

Angelina Heart

278 Templates

Dragonfly body

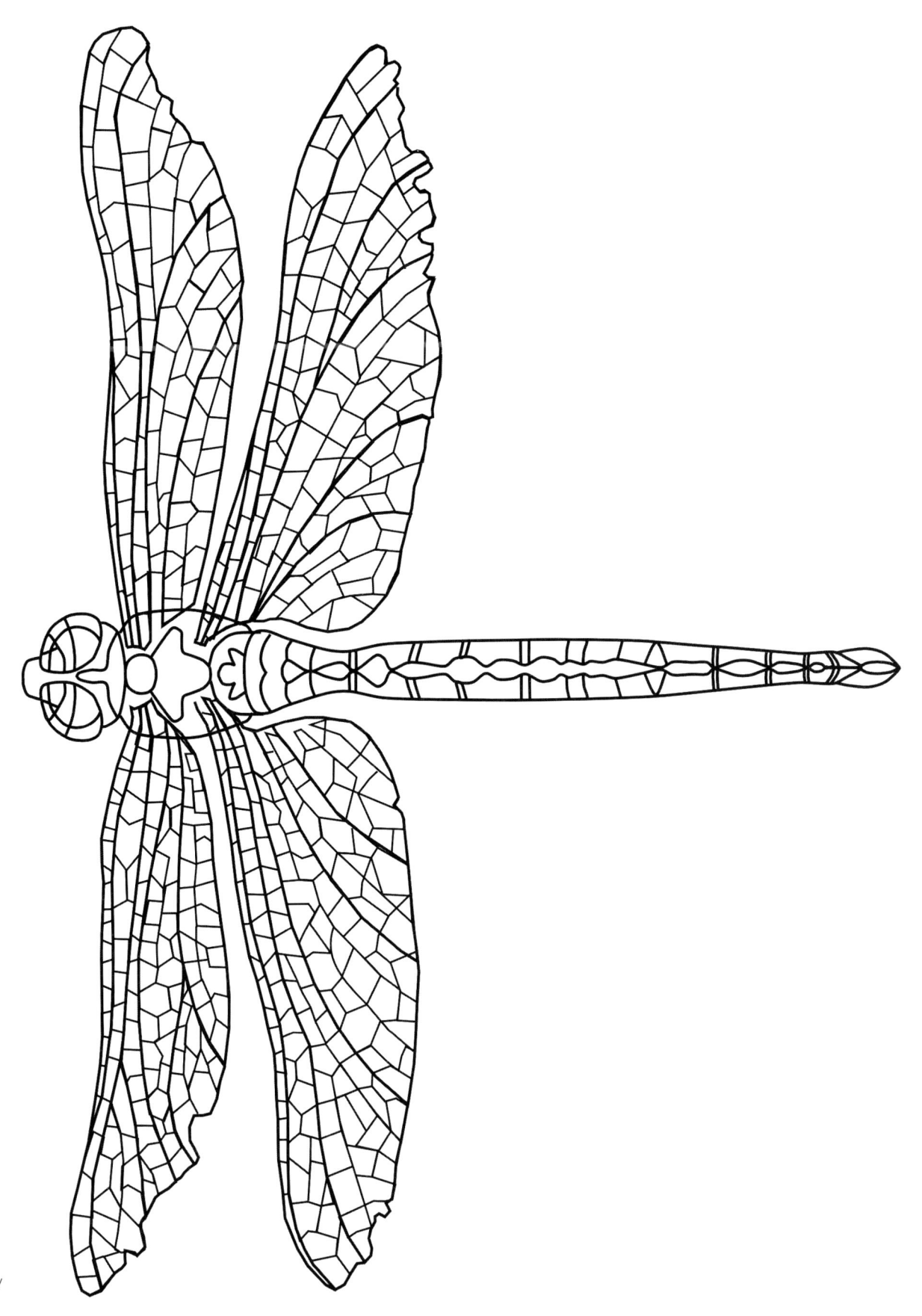

Templates 279

Dragonfly body parts

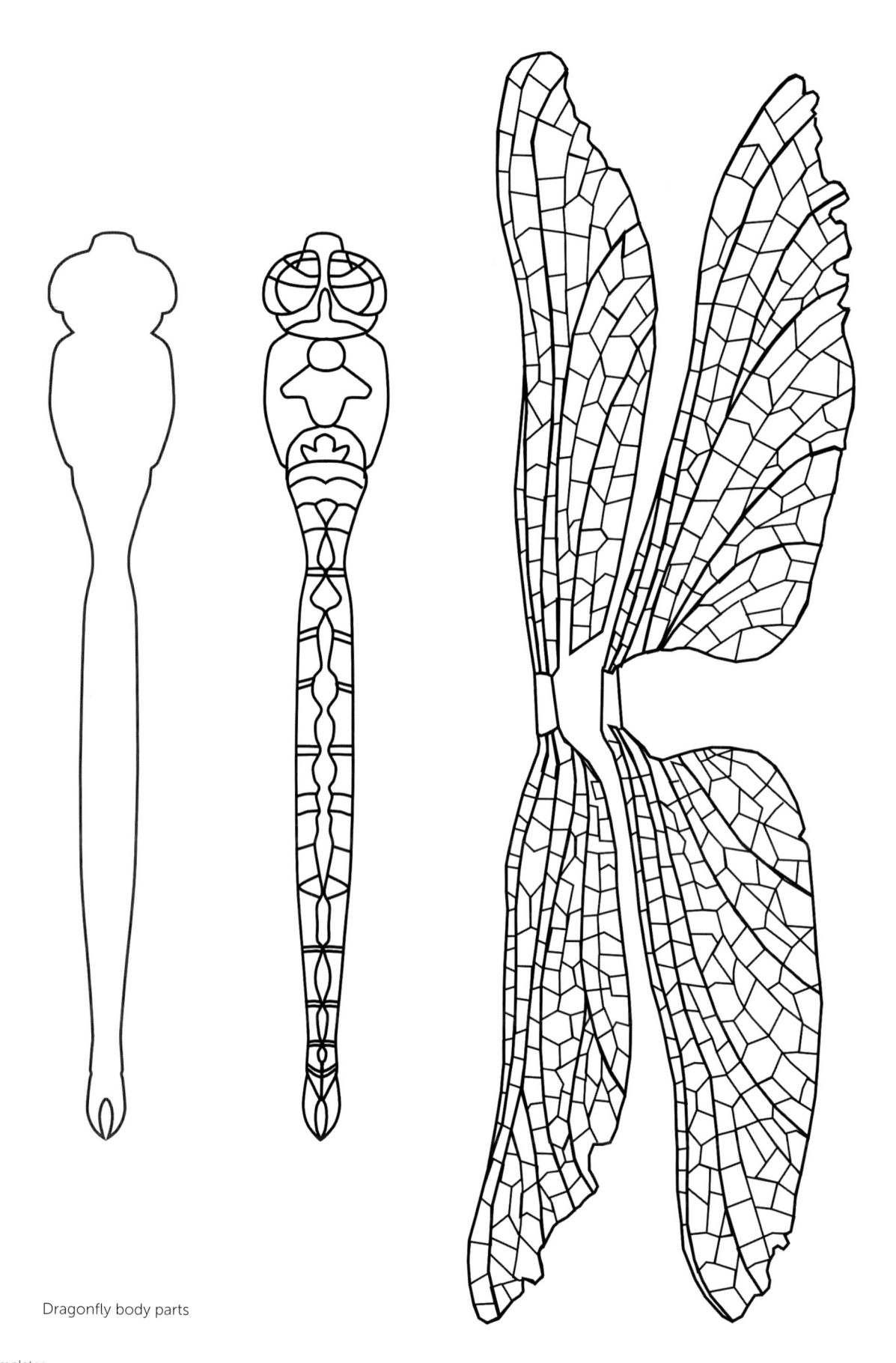

280   Templates

Bamboo background – enlarge to twice the size

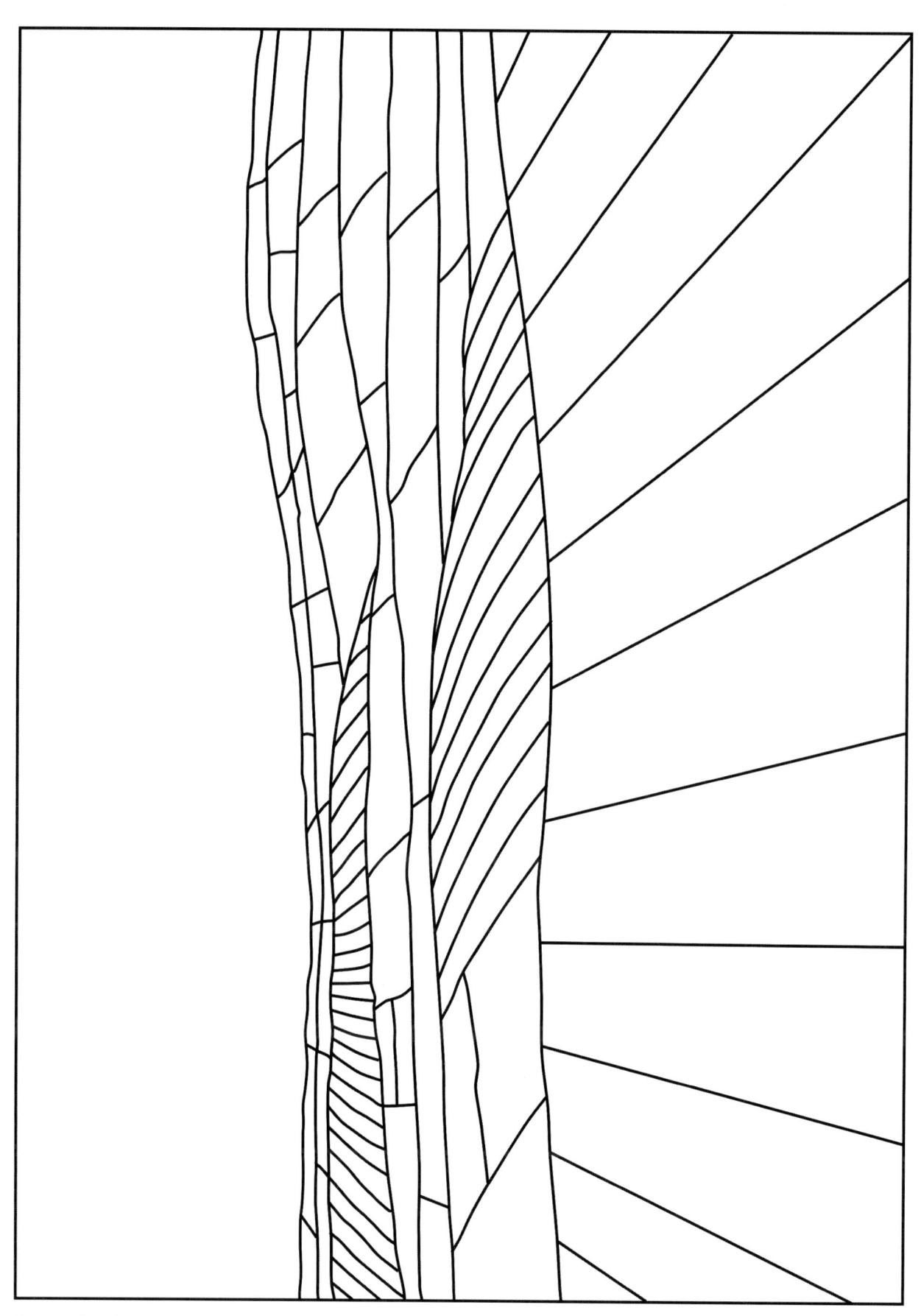

Summer Cornfield

Sunlit Wood

Little Robin

Rustic Sheep (enlarge 200%)

SUPPLIERS

Airedale Yarns
Keighley, UK
www.airedaleyarns.co.uk
Yarns for chopping, couching and winding onto the bobbin

Art Van Go
Knebworth, UK
www.vycombe-arts.co.uk
Soluble film, Angelina fibres, Angelina fantasy film, transfer foils, fabric paints and lots of useful items for mixed media work

Barnyarns
Ripon, UK
www.barnyarns.co.uk
Madeira thread, machine needles, soluble film, Mistyfuse, Hotspots, square hoops, bobbin saver rings – lots to peruse on the website

Beads Unlimited
West Sussex, UK
www.beadsunlimited.co.uk
Beads, stringing and findings

Colourcraft
Sheffield, UK
www.colourcraftltd.com
Transfer foils, Angelina fibres, fabric paints and artist's materials

Cotton Patch
Birmingham, UK
www.cottonpatch.co.uk
Quilting fabrics, mini-irons, rotary cutters, sewing machine feet and lots more

Empress Mills
Colne, UK
www.empressmills.co.uk
Threads, HT polyester (near-invisible blind hemming thread), pelmet Vilene, soluble film and other useful items

Fabric Land
Bristol, UK (and other branches)
www.fabricland.co.uk
Fabric, ribbons and haberdashery

Graphics Direct
www.graphicsdirect.co.uk
Mount board, foam board and cutters

Great Art
www.greatart.co.uk
Mount board, foam board, frames and other artist's materials

Gur Sewing Machines
Birmingham, UK
www.gursewingmachines.com
Sewing machines, accessories, parts and haberdashery

Jaycotts
Chester, UK
www.jaycotts.co.uk
Sewing machines, parts, accessories and haberdashery

Linton Tweeds
Carlisle, UK
www.lintondirect.co.uk
Yarn and woven tweed manufacturer, novelty yarns and tweed fabric

Minerva Crafts
Darwen, UK
www.minervacrafts.com
Fabric, ribbons, needles and haberdashery

Oliver Twists
Durham, UK
www.olivertwists.co.uk
Hand-dyed machine threads and special thread packs

Somac Threads
Chester, UK
www.somac-shop.co.uk
Kingstar threads, metallic threads, machine needles, spray glue, interfacing and other sundries

Sulky Shop
Nottingham, UK
www.sulky-shop.co.uk
Sulky threads, Sulky stabilizers, water-soluble film and machine needles

Totally Beads
Clacton, UK
www.totallybeads.co.uk
Beads, stringing and findings

The Wool Warehouse
Warwickshire, UK
www.woolwarehouse.co.uk
Wool and fabric

Contact details are correct at the time of printing. Some of these businesses operate from premises that are not open to the public so please check before planning a visit.

BIBLIOGRAPHY

- Barton, Julia, *The Art of Embroidery*, Merehurst Press 1989
- Campbell-Harding, Valerie, and Watts, Pamela, *Machine Embroidery: Stitch Techniques*, Batsford 2000
- Dolan, Wendy, *Layer, Paint and Stitch: Create Textile Art Using Freehand Machine Embroidery and Hand Stitching (The Textile Artist)*, Search Press 2015
- Edwards, Betty, *Drawing on the Right Side of the Brain*, HarperCollins 1993
- Holt, Alison, *Beginner's Guide to Machine Embroidered Landscapes*, Search Press 2001
- Holt, Alison, *Machine Embroidered Landscapes*, Batsford 1990
- Hubbard, Liz, *Thread Painting*, David & Charles 1988
- Itten, Johannes, *The Elements of Colour*, John Wiley & Sons 1970
- Jones, Owen, *The Grammar of Ornament*, Studio Editions 1986
- Mein, Annemieke, *The Art of Annemieke Mein: Wildlife Artist in Textiles*, Search Press 2019
- Messent, Jan, *Embroidery and Nature*, Batsford 1983
- Meyer, Franz, *Handbook of Ornament*, Dover Pictorial Archive 2000
- Midgelow-Marsden, Alysn, *Between the Sheets with Angelina: A Workbook for Fusible Fibres*, Word4word 2003
- Parks, Carol, *Making Handbags and Purses*, Lark Books 2000
- Terry, Terence, *Handmade Bags*, A & C Black 2003

Some of these books are out of print but can still be found online. Look out for out-of-print vintage books by Jan Messent, Jean Littlejohn and Jan Beaney.

Index

adjusting the tension settings 34–35
all that glitters 171
Angelina and fusible film 23–24
    Angelina fantasy film 23, 24, 189, 193
    Angelina fibres 23–24, 186, 188
    Crystalina 23–24, 186
    embroidered Angelina heart 186–188, 278
animals and birds 231
attaching the presser foot 31
appliqué 11, 21, 23, 43, 119, 123–124, 231, 233

backstitching, reverse 78, 109, 110, 136, 138, 262
baking parchment 15, 23, 23
beach hut 43, 49, 101–105, 250–251, 270
beaded gold star 175–177, 275
beads 24, 171, 175, 177, 203
Bernina 801 9, 10, 29, 36, 86, 89, 91, 101, 106, 112, 126, 133, 142, 146, 150, 153, 158, 164, 172, 175, 178, 181, 183, 186, 189, 222, 236, 241
bias binding 17, 25
bobbin 10, 11, 13, 19–20, 29, 30, 36–39
    bobbin, checking the bobbin 34–35
    bobbin, winding a 35
bobbin case 10, 11, 29, 30, 34–37, 58–59
bobbin case, spare loose tension 10, 58–61, 71–72, 76, 141–157, 158–162, 164–166, 199, 211, 218–219, 227
bobbin case, testing tension 59
bonding transfer foils to Mistyfuse 183–185
    flower pattern 278
bonding transfer foils with Vilene hotspots 181–182
    butterfly design 277
    butterfly outline 277
book cover 196–203
buttons 25

cable stitch needlecase set 164–169, 274, 275
choice of materials 208, 233
    choosing fabric for, animal embroideries 234
    landscape 208–209
    thread-painting 99
choosing an image, animals and birds 231
choosing what to make 41–42
cleaning the machine 36–37
colour theory 46–49
    colour in landscapes 208
    colour wheel 48
    primary 48–49
    secondary 48–49
    using colour 46–49
cut work 123
cording 11, 19, 63–65, 66–68
couching 11, 19, 63–65

darning plate 9–10
darning foot 83–95, 101, 106, 112, 126, 133, 142, 146, 150, 153, 158, 164, 172, 175, 178, 181, 183, 186, 189, 212, 222, 236, 241
designing for machine embroidery 41
    choosing thread 50, 100, 234
    composing the design 206–207
    composition and negative space 43
    designing a paisley pattern 44–45
    finishing the embroidery 51
    golden section, rule of thirds 205–206
    how to depict form 232
    images, where to find, choosing 205, 231
    inspiration 41, 42, 205
    line, form and stitch type 42–43
    negative space 43, 93, 208, 231, 237
    planning the work 50–51
    rule of thirds 205–206
    sourcing materials 48–49
    tonal values 43, 208, 213, 241
    using perspective 207
displaying a finished embroidery 247
dragonfly 189–195, 279, 280
    bamboo background 281
drawing or tracing 44–45, 232
drawing supplies and related items 15–16
    brushes 17
    dressmaker's chalk pencil 16
    eraser and pencil sharpener 16
    foam board 15, 248, 250–251, 252–254, 255–258, 259–260
    geometry set 16
    grey board 128–129
    mat board 248
    mount board 13, 15, 128, 247–249, 252–254, 255–258, 259–260
    paint and dye 16
    paper and card 15–16
    pencils and crayons 16
    pens and markers 15, 16, 44–45
    ruler, set square, tape measure 15–16
dropping the feeder teeth for free machine embroidery 9

embroidered greetings card 131–132
embroidering set patterns with a twin needle 56–57
embroidering the landscape 205
embroidering with metallic threads 172–174
equipment tools and materials 9
example, 44–45, 210–211
exercise 29–32, 36–37, 86–88, 89–90
experimenting with stitches and tension 141

fabric paint 15–17, 20, 24–25, 159, 178–179, 189–190, 196–197, 222–223, 233
fabrics 20–22
    calico 20, 29, 33, 54, 56, 58, 63, 74, 91, 142, 146, 150, 153, 158, 164, 212, 222, 236, 259, 263
    canvas and cotton duck 20–21, 112, 189, 241
    cotton 20, 21, 29, 54, 56, 58, 63, 69, 74, 86, 89, 91, 101, 106, 112, 158, 164, 172, 175, 181, 189, 196, 212, 222, 263
    dance 21, 22
    devoré 22
    fat quarters, quilting fabric 21, 164, 212
    felt 22, 119, 120, 164, 169, 186–187, 266–267
    linen 21, 69, 189, 241
    nets and tulle 22, 74
    organza and chiffon 21–22, 119–121, 123, 124, 126–127, 183, 185, 189, 194–195, 212–213
    paper lame 22
    poly cotton 21, 196, 212
    synthetic lining 21, 101, 126, 212
    tricot lame 22
    velvet and velour 21, 74, 119, 121–122, 133–139, 178–180
fabric-painted heat fusible glue 178–180
    leaf outline 276
    leaf stitching 276
fancy stitch 7, 53–62, 65, 69–73, 75–77, 198–199, 202
fastenings and findings 25
feeder teeth, dropping, 9, 83
feeder teeth, feed dogs 7, 9–11, 29, 34, 36, 53, 83–86
finishing the embroidery 51
finishing your work 247
foot pedal 10, 28, 29–30, 33, 53, 83–84, 87–90, 101, 148, 238
framing 247–249
    behind glass and mount board 249, 252–254, 255–258
    DIY framing 248
    framing an embroidery, oval flexi hoop 249, 266–267
    framing an embroidery, wooden hoop 249, 263–265
    framing without glass or mount board 249, 250
    fusing the embroidery to pelmet Vilene 250–251
    hanging an embroidery without a frame 259–262
    lacing an embroidery over card 248, 255–258
    mounting onto a backing board 252–254
    professional framing 247
    using lacing and attaching Velcro 259–262
free machine embroidery 7, 9, 10, 82–195, 210–245
free machine embroidery basic stitch types 84–85
free machine embroidery sampler 91–95
free machine embroidery with a spring needle 89–90
free machine embroidery with an embroidery foot 86–88

garden border 158–163, 274

hand sewing needles 14–15
    beading 14, 15, 175, 177, 196, 203
    chenille 14, 15, 164, 169, 226
    curved 14, 15, 259, 262
    darning 14, 15, 164, 196, 199
    embroidery 15
    sharps 14, 15, 69, 74, 79, 80, 106, 110, 128, 129, 167, 181, 196, 203, 236, 239, 258, 259, 260, 263, 264, 266, 267
hand sewing stitch, blanket 169
    slip 79, 110, 167, 203, 258, 262, running, straight 199, 210–211, 236, 240, 263, 264, 267
    tacking 129, 264
    French knots 226, 236, 240
hand wheel 29, 30, 32, 54, 56–57, 59, 75, 103, 154–157, 165
heat-bondable glue, heat-fusible glue 22–23, 101–102, 128–129, 167–168, 178–180, 181–182, 183–185, 191, 196, 200, 250
hook race, shuttle cover 29, 36–37
hook race, shuttle hook 34, 36–37
hoops 17
hotspots 23, 181–182, 201

inserting the needle 31
interfacing and backings 22
    felt 22
    fusible iron on 22
    non-woven 22
    pelmet Vilene 22
    stabilizer 22, 48
    Stitch 'n' Tear 22
    tear-away 22
iron, clover mini 15, 112, 115
ironing cloth 15
irons 15

Janome JF 1018s 9–10, 53, 54, 56, 58, 66, 69, 74, 133, 196, 212

lacing 247–248, 255–258, 259–260
lighting 27, 28
little robin 236–240, 263, 284
lowering the teeth 9, 83–85

machine embroidery with the feeder teeth down 7, 9, 82–195, 210–245
machine embroidery with the feeder teeth up 7, 53–81, 172–173, 196–202
metallic transfer foil 23, 171, 181–182, 183–184, 196, 201, 203
Mistyfuse 23, 183–184, 201, 203
monochrome bag 74–81

other useful items 23–24

padding 22, 233, 248, 255
painting a background 16–17, 159, 189–190, 208–209, 222–233, 242
painting embroidered threads 16–17, 47, 211, 221, 233
Paisley pennant 106–111, 271–272
pelmet Vilene 22, 128–129, 167–168, 199–202, 250–251

287

planning 41–42
planning and embroidering a landscape from a photograph 210–211
planning the design 206
planning the work 50–51
planning, the embroidery, animals and birds 231–233
planning, the process landscape embroidery 209
press studs 25, 74, 79–81
presser or straight stitch foot 11, 29, 31–33, 53–54, 56, 58–60, 63–64, 66–67, 69–73, 74–78, 106, 109–111, 133–138, 164, 166–169, 172–173, 186, 187, 196, 198–202, 212, 215–216, 250, 251, 259, 261–262
printing and copying 16

raising the teeth 53
ribbon 24, 63–65, 164, 167, 196–203
robin 232–234, 236– 240, 263–265, 284
rustic sheep 241–245, 259–262, 284

sewing machine 9–10, 29
sewing machine bobbin case 10, 11, 29, 30, 34–37, 58–59
sewing machine bobbin 10, 11, 29, 30, 32–39
sewing machine diagram 29
   bobbin winder stopper 30
   bobbin winding spindle 29
   buttonhole dial 29
   free arm 9
   hand wheel 29
   hand wheel release 29
   hook race, shuttle cover 29
   needle holder clamp 29, 31
   needle plate 9, 11, 29, 32–34, 36–39, 53–54, 56
   needle position dial 29
   pre-tensioning winder 29, 30
   reel holder pin 30, 32, 38
   shuttle hook, race cover 29, 36–37
   spool pin 30
   stitch length dial 29, 53, 54, 55, 57
   stitch type selector 29, 53
   stitch width dial 29, 60, 85
   thread guide 29, 32–33, 38
   thread reel holder 29
   thread regulator 29, 32
   thread take-up lever 29, 32–33
   thread tension disc 29, 32–33, 108, 225
   thread tension selector 29
   thread tension slot 29, 32
sewing machine feet 10–11
   applique foot 11
   buttonhole foot 11
   cording foot 11
   embroidery, darning foot 7, 9, 10–11, 83–95, 101, 106, 112, 126, 133, 142, 146, 150, 153, 158, 164, 172, 175, 178, 181, 183, 186, 189, 212, 222, 236, 241
   utility feet 11
   zip foot 11, 133, 136
sewing machine maintenance, basic cleaning 36–37
sewing machine manual 10, 29–32, 36–38
sewing machine needles 11–12
   embroidery needle 12
   jeans needle 12
   metallic needle 12, 38, 126–127, 172–173, 175–177, 178, 180, 181, 182, 183, 185, 189, 192–193

quilting needle 12
specialist thread 12
spring needle 11, 12, 83, 89–90
top stitch needle 12
twin needle 12, 56–57, 74–76
universal 90/14 9, 11, 12, 29, 31, 54, 58, 63, 66, 69, 74, 86, 91, 101, 106, 112, 133, 142, 146, 150, 153, 158, 164, 186, 189, 196, 212, 222, 234, 236, 241, 250, 259
sewing machine oil 13, 36, 37
sewing machine stitches
   cable stitch 7, 10, 43, 58–62, 71–72, 76–77, 122, 141, 153–157, 164–166, 182, 199, 209
   feather stitch 141, 146, 150–152, 159, 211–212, 218, 221, 227
   honeycomb 61, 70, 198
   moss stitch 141, 146–149, 150, 158–162, 211–212, 227
   overlock, overcast 70, 198, 200, 202
   satin 11, 43, 54–55, 66–68, 85, 88, 93–94, 101–105, 123, 144, 148, 156, 160, 173, 215–216, 221
   set pattern, fancy, utility 7, 53–62, 65, 69–73, 75–77, 198–199, 202
   straight 7, 33, 42–43, 46–47, 53– 55, 56–57, 69–73, 76–78, 84, 86–88, 90, 92–95, 97–98, 100, 103–105, 106–111, 112–114, 118–125, 126–127, 134–138, 143–144, 147–148, 151–152, 154–157, 159–162, 165–167, 169, 174, 176–177, 180, 185, 187, 192–195, 198–199, 202, 210–211, 214–215, 217–218, 224–226, 231, 233, 238–239, 242–245, 251, 261–262
   tricot 54, 55, 61, 64, 70
   triple 57, 198
   triple zigzag 55, 61, 76
   vermicelli 46, 93–94, 121–122, 126–127, 135, 143–144, 148–149, 152, 156, 188, 214, 218, 225
   whip stitch 141–145, 158–159, 212, 219, 224–225
   zigzag 7, 11, 19, 34–35, 54–55, 56–57, 60–62, 63–64, 66–68, 79, 85, 88, 93–95, 103–104, 142–145, 146, 148–149, 168, 198–199, 215–216, 250–251
sampler 54–55, 56–57, 58–62, 63–65, 66–68, 91–95, 142–145, 146–149, 150–152, 153–157, 172–174, 175–177, 178–180, 181–182, 183–185, 186–188
scissor keeper 164–169, 275
scissors 13–14
   dressmaking shears 13
   embroidery 13
   large fabric 13
   medium–size fabric 14
   paper scissors 14
   pinking shears 14
scraps and snippets 126–127, 128–130, 131–132, 183–185
sequins 24, 171, 175, 177
setting up the machine 29–32
setting up the workspace 27
sheep 234–235, 241–245, 259–262, 284
should the embroidery be protected from dust? 248
solving machine problems 33–39
   adjust the tension settings 34
   change the needle 33
   change the top thread 35
   check the bobbin and under the feeder teeth 34

check the foot 34
check the manual 38
fabric-eating problems 39
re-thread everything and try again 33, 34
unexpected noises 33, 39
solving thread problems 38–39
spring needle 11, 12, 83, 89–90
stain removal 15
step-by-step project 69–73, 74–81, 91–95, 101–105, 106–111, 112–115, 126–127, 128–130, 131–132, 133–139, 158–163, 164–169, 189–195, 196–203, 212–221, 222–229, 236–240, 241–245
stitch type 42–43, 46, 50, 51, 53–55, 84, 100, 235
stitching set patterns 54–55
stitching set patterns with cable stitch 58–62
straight stitch tulip 69–73, 268
summer cornfield with painted sky 222–229, 282
sunlit wood 212–221, 283

tape and adhesive 25
   Araldite glue 25, 259, 262
   Impex Very Sticky Glue 25, 74, 80, 128–130
   masking tape 25, 81, 111, 112, 189, 252–254, 258
templates 268–284
tension screw 34–35, 58, 60, 141, 143, 146, 153, 156, 157
tension settings, adjust 34–35
tension spring 10, 19, 30, 34, 58, 154, 156
testing the stitch 33
thread colour 46–48, 100
thread problems 38–39
thread weight 18, 234
thread painting 97
   adapting a design 99
   choosing fabric 99
   choosing thread 100
   stitch type 100
threading the needle 32
threads 18–19
   bobbin 19
   buttonhole 19
   cotton 18
   cotton perle 19
   floss 19
   hand embroidery threads 19
   invisible 19
   metallic 18
   Mylar 18
   polyester 18
   sew-all 19
   silk 18
   stranded cotton 19
   strong thread 19
   thick threads for couching and use on the bobbin 19–20
   top threads 18–19
   Viscose and Rayon 18
   wool 18
tools 12–13
   craft knife 13
   cutting mat 13
   machine oil 13
   magnet 13
   metal ruler 13, 249
   pins 14
   pliers 13
   rotary cutter 13, 14, 78, 131–132, 164, 168–169, 196, 200–201, 250–251

screwdriver 13, 29, 31, 36, 58, 69, 74, 86–87, 91, 142, 146, 150, 153, 250–251, 254, 255, 258, 263–264
seam ripper, quick unpick 14, 104, 215, 245
soft brush 13, 36–37
tweezers 13
transfer foiled book cover 196–203
transferring the design 97–99
   dressmaker's carbon 23, 98, 101–102, 142, 146, 150, 153, 175, 176, 189–190
   paper or tissue 70–72, 98, 106–108, 164–167, 186–187
   tracing the design onto fabric 97–99, 112, 194
   transfer pencil 98
   water-soluble fabric or film 98–99
trimmings 24–25, 197–198
twin needle 12, 56–57, 74–76

using water-soluble film 117–119

Velcro 18, 25, 235, 259, 261–262
velvet cushion 133–139
Vilene bondaweb 22, 23, 101–102, 164, 167288168, 178–179, 189, 191, 196, 200, 250
Vilene hotspots 23, 181–182, 196, 201
vintage flower 99, 112–115, 255–258, 273

wadding, Dacron 22, 74, 77, 128–129, 133, 164, 167, 169, 255–256
water-soluble film and fabric 23, 117–139
   avalon 23, 98, 117, 126, 127, 158, 183, 189, 212, 222
   clear water-soluble film 117
   creating fabric with two layers of film 120, 121, 126–127
   creating motifs for applique 123–124, 125
   cut work 123
   machine lace 124, 125
   non-woven water-soluble fabric 23, 118, 236–240
   opaque water-soluble fabric 118
   opaque woven soluble fabric 118
   stabilizing fine fabrics with water-soluble 119
   sticky water-soluble fabric 118, 133–135
   three-dimensional embroidery 124, 125
   transferring a design 119, 122, 185, 192, 210, 214, 223, 226, 242, 245
   using water-soluble film to transform a base fabric 120–122, 134–135
   water-soluble film topper 118–119
   water-soluble film extra tips and hints 124
   water-soluble film weights 117–119
   water-soluble paper 23, 118–119, 123
what is machine embroidery? 7
what type of frame is needed? 248
whimsical beach hut 101–105, 270
wooden trinket box 128–130
wrapping threads 66–68, 79
yarns for chopping 20

zip 25, 133, 135–137